COMPLETE INDEX TO TALENT AND SERVICES

(11) 11
TAB | PAGE

SUBJECTS

LISTED BY TAB NUMBER

N.Y.GOLD

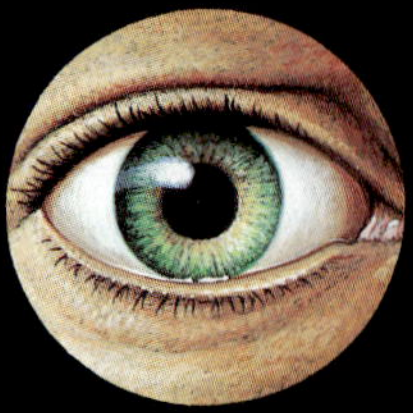

2

A
SELECTIVE
RESOURCE
OF
NEW YORK
TALENT

President
Arie Kopelman

Chairman of the Board
Ira Shapiro

Associate Publishers
Jane Flanagan
Julia Morris

Production Consultant
Fiona L'Estrange

Production Associate
Amie Cooper

Production Assistant
Victoria Winn

Sales Representatives
Robyn Selman
David Tabler

List Management
Robyn Selman

Cover & Book Design
M&Co. New York

Typesetting
Microcomputer
Publishing Center
Trufont Typographers, Inc.

Color Separation,
Printing & Binding
Dai Nippon Printing Co. Ltd.,
Tokyo, Japan

In acknowledgment and
thanks to those who
helped make
N.Y. Gold a reality

Scott Holden
Wendl Kornfeld
Ann Middlebrook
Liz Siroka
Stephanie Whitney

U.S. Book Trade Distribution
Watson-Guptill Publications
1515 Broadway,
New York, N.Y. 10036
(212) 764-7300

For Sales Outside U.S.
Rotovision S.A.
Route Suisse 9
1295 Mies
Switzerland
Telephone: (22) 553055
Telex: 419246 ROVI CH

Published by
New York Gold, Inc.
150 Fifth Avenue,
New York, N.Y. 10011
Telephone: (212) 645-8022

N.Y. Gold
ISBN: 0-9618685-1-1
ISSN: 0893-3170
ISBN: (Watson-Guptill)
8230-3181-0

Cover Illustration
Mark Hess

INDEX TO TAB

1

ILLUSTRATION

ILLUSTRATORS & *Representatives*

LETTERING AND DESIGN

LETTERERS/DESIGNERS

& *Representatives*

ILLUSTRATION DESIGN LETTERING

ILLUSTRATION

LETTERING

DESIGN

INDEX TO TAB

1

ILLUSTRATION

LETTERING AND DESIGN

ILLUSTRATION

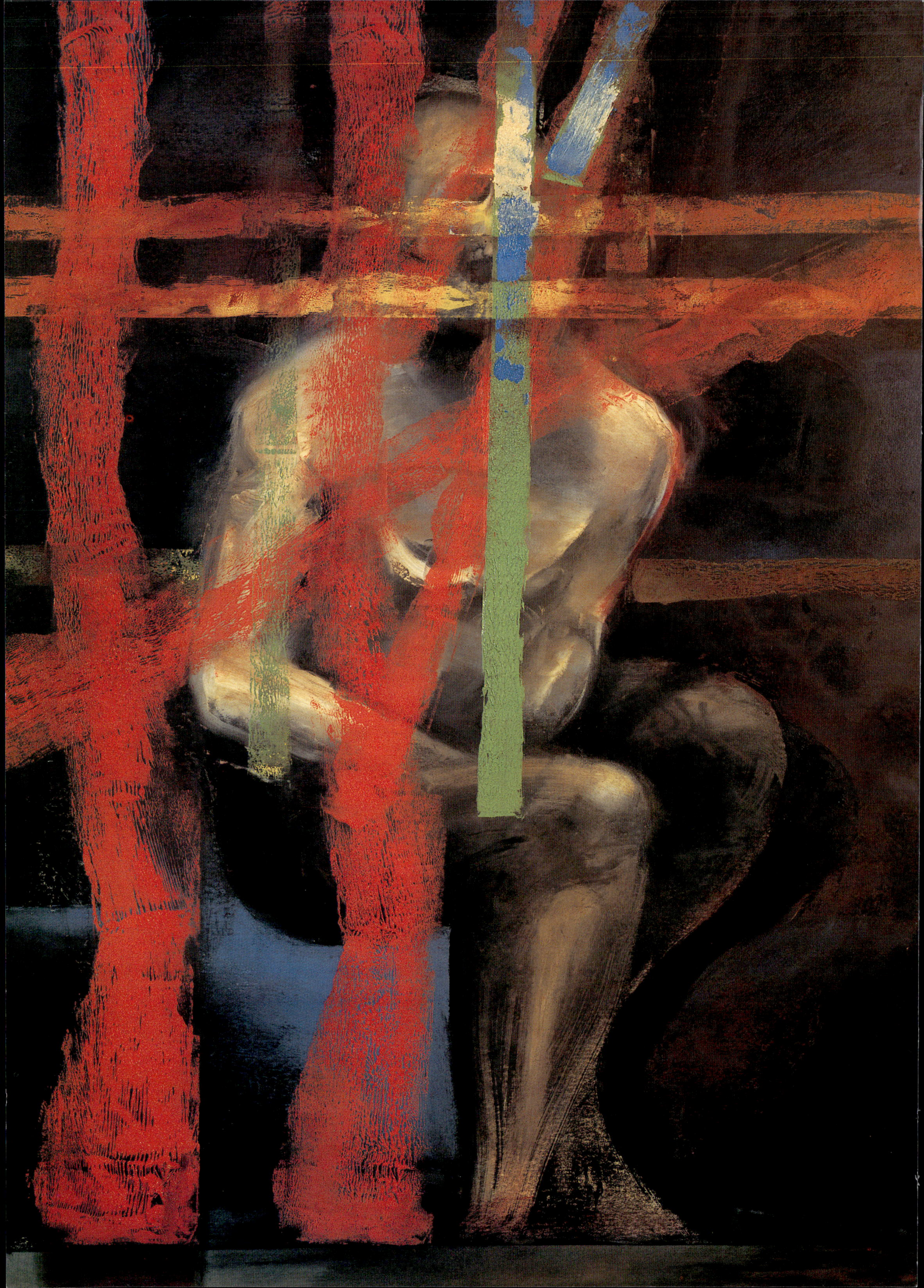

Marshall Arisman
314 West 100th Street
New York, New York 10025
(212) 662-2289

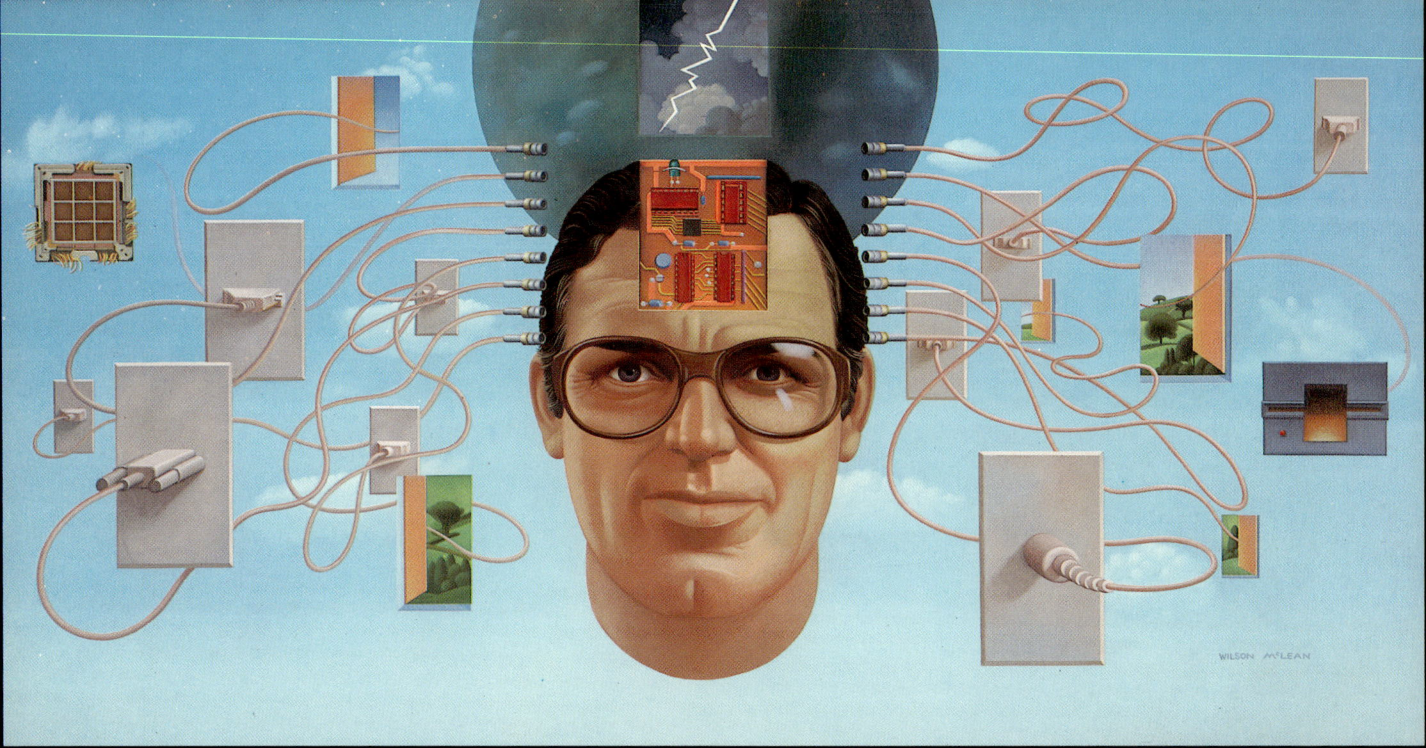

Chase Manhattan Bank • ***Scali, McCabe, Sloves Inc.***

'Oasis'

·Wilson McLean·

902 Broadway • Suite 1603
New York, NY 10010
212 • 473 • 5554

'The Spirit of Innovation' • BASF • *Geer Dubois Advertising*

Canon • Communication Works

Spy Magazine

Graphis called him "the natural."

ALAN E. COBER

Croton Dam Road,
Ossining, New York 10562
914-941-8696

CLIENT: APPLE COMPUTER (NEW YORK MAGAZINE, ONLINE ACCESS)

He has produced sketchbooks of the presidential campaign for TIME, the space shuttle for NASA, the Pope's visit to the USA for Rolling Stone in 1987, and has worked for every major magazine and most of the Fortune 500 companies including IBM, CBS, TWA, AT&T, Ciba-Geigy and Mobil.

CA magazine said, "he draws the way he speaks."

CORPORATE COBER

Croton Dam Road
Ossining, New York 10562
914-941-8696

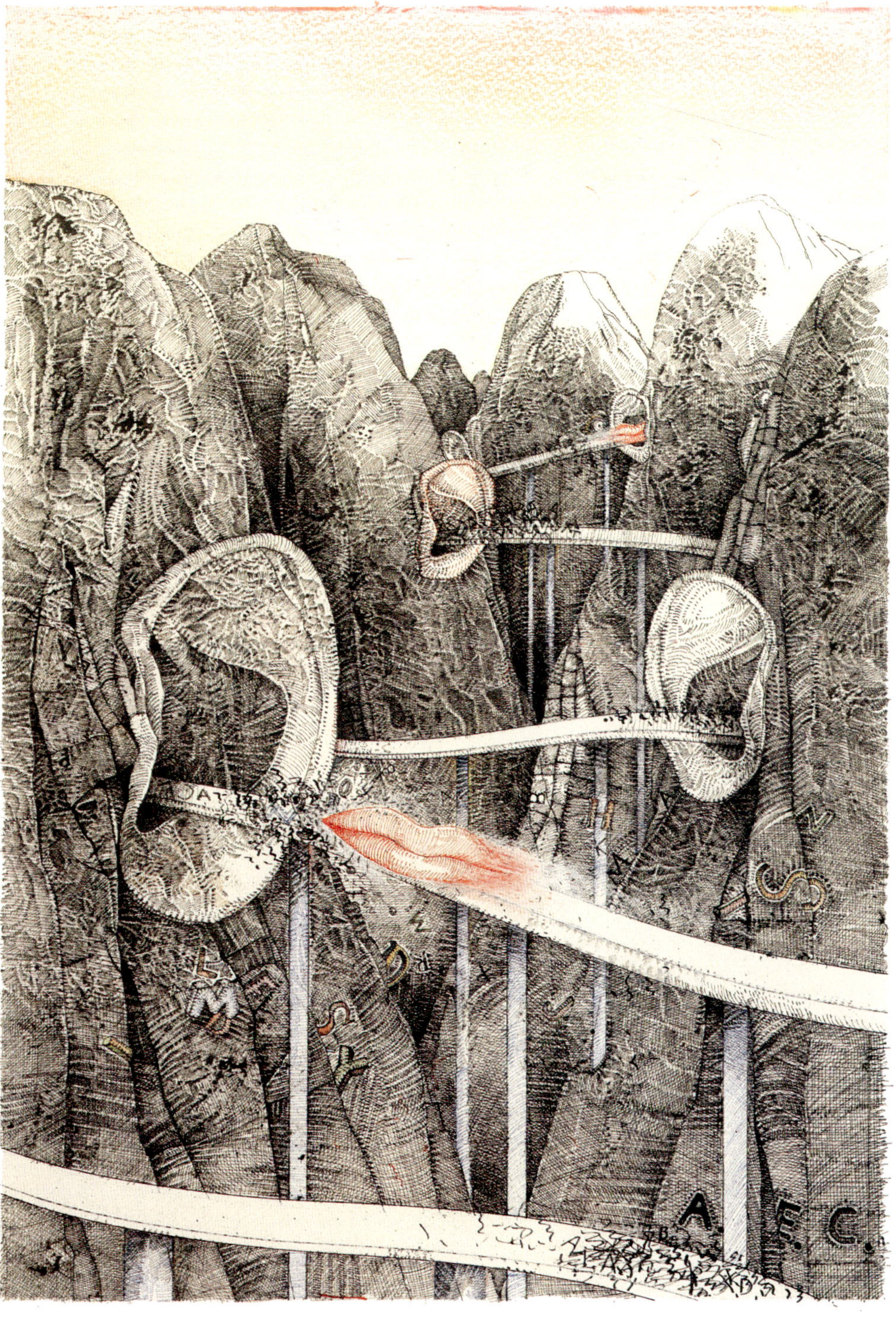

CLIENT: KIMBERLY-CLARK COMPANY (NEENAH PAPER)

Included in over 300 awards are Artist of the Year,
11 medals from the Society of Illustrators, and 6 gold medals from NYADC.

Call him! He'll Listen.

119 WYKEHAM ROAD
WASHINGTON, CONNECTICUT 06793
(203) 868-7577

Represented By:
MILTON NEWBORN ASSOCIATES
135 EAST 54TH STREET
NEW YORK, NEW YORK 10022
(212) 421-0050

ROLLING STONE

BUDWEISER

TEXAS MONTHLY

119 WYKEHAM ROAD
WASHINGTON, CONNECTICUT 06793
(203) 868-7577

Represented By:
MILTON NEWBORN ASSOCIATES
135 EAST 54TH STREET
NEW YORK, NEW YORK 10022
(212) 421-0050

M A R K H E S S

88 QUICKS LANE
KATONAH, NEW YORK 10536
(914) 232-5870

Represented By:
MILTON NEWBORN ASSOCIATES
135 EAST 54TH STREET
NEW YORK, NEW YORK 10022
(212) 421-0050

TIME MAGAZINE

PENNSYLVANIA TOURIST BOARD

3M CORPORATION

M A R K H E S S

88 QUICKS LANE
KATONAH, NEW YORK 10536
(914) 232-5870

Represented By:
MILTON NEWBORN ASSOCIATES
135 EAST 54TH STREET
NEW YORK, NEW YORK 10022
(212) 421-0050

PRINCE SPAGHETTI

GORDON'S MAGAZINE

FIRST MINNEAPOLIS BANK

ROBERT GIUSTI

340 LONG MOUNTAIN ROAD
NEW MILFORD, CONNECTICUT 06776
(203) 354-6539

Represented By:
MILTON NEWBORN ASSOCIATES
135 EAST 54TH STREET
NEW YORK, NEW YORK 10022
(212) 421-0050

FRENCH TRANSIT LTD.

PLAYBOY

THAI AIRWAYS INT'L.

R O B E R T   G I U S T I

340 LONG MOUNTAIN ROAD
NEW MILFORD, CONNECTICUT 06776
(203) 354-6539

Represented By:
MILTON NEWBORN ASSOCIATES
135 EAST 54TH STREET
NEW YORK, NEW YORK 10022
(212) 421-0050

FRENCH TRANSIT LTD.

D A V I D   W I L C O X

5955 SAWMILL ROAD
DOYLESTOWN, PENNSYLVANIA 18901
(215) 297-0849

Represented By:
MILTON NEWBORN ASSOCIATES
135 EAST 54TH STREET
NEW YORK, NEW YORK 10022
(212) 421-0050

SQUIBB

LOMAS & NETTLETON

WEEKEND MAGAZINE

AT&T

V I C T O R   J U H A S Z

576 WESTMINSTER AVENUE
ELIZABETH, NEW JERSEY 07208
(201) 351-4227

Represented By:
MILTON NEWBORN ASSOCIATES
135 EAST 54TH STREET
NEW YORK, NEW YORK 10022
(212) 421-0050

NIXDORF COMPUTER

BUSINESS WEEK

SPORTS ILLUSTRATED

THE NEW YORK TIMES

WENDELL MINOR

277 WEST 4TH STREET
NEW YORK CITY 10014
PH 212 • 691 • 6925

15 OLD NORTH ROAD
WASHINGTON, CT. 06793
PH 203 • 868 • 9101

Annual Report, 1983

TIME MAGAZINE, January, 1986

NEW YORK MAGAZINE, September, 1987

BURTON SILVERMAN
324 West 71 Street, New York, NY 10023 • (212) 799-3399

JACQUELINE DEDELL, INC.

58 West 15th Street
New York, New York 10011
(212) 741-2539

Representing:
Teresa Fasolino

HARCOURT, BRACE, JOVANOVICH

WORKMAN PUBLISHING

SIMPSON PAPER COMPANY

MASTER CARD

PRENTICE HALL

JACQUELINE DEDELL, INC.
58 West 15th Street
New York, New York 10011
(212) 741-2539

Representing:
Ivan Chermayeff

CHIEF EXECUTIVE MAGAZINE

NEWSDAY

TIME INC.

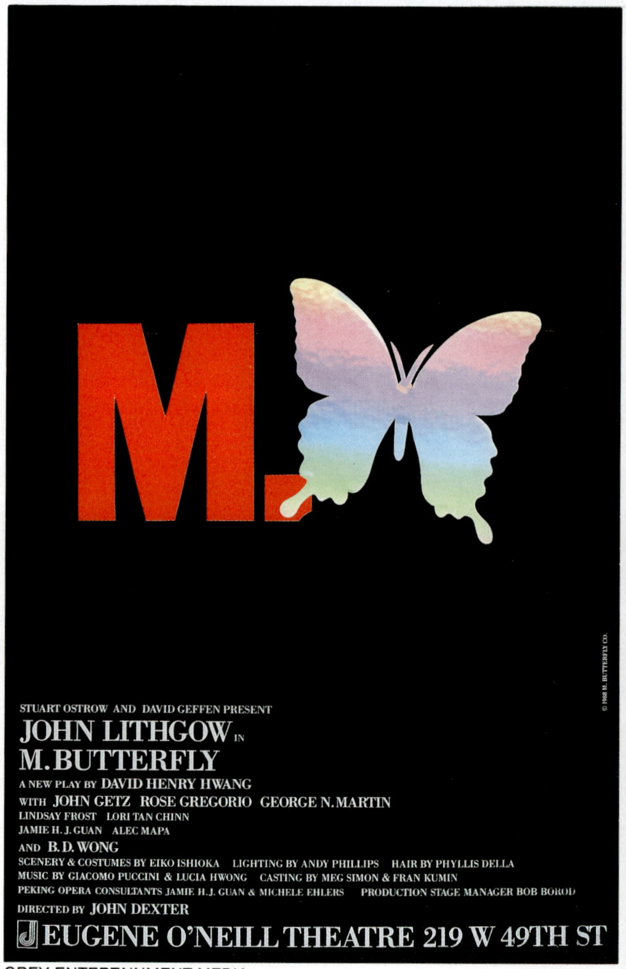

GREY ENTERTAINMENT MEDIA

JACQUELINE DEDELL, INC.

HECHINGER COMPANY

JACQUELINE DEDELL, INC.

58 West 15th Street
New York, New York 10011
(212) 741-2539

Representing:

Isadore Seltzer

CHIEF EXECUTIVE MAGAZINE

NEWSWEEK

PRUDENTIAL

MACMILLAN BOOKS

CBS

NEW YORK TIMES

Lou Brooks Illustration, Design, Lettering, and Animatio

415 W. 55th St., New York, NY 10019 Tel: (212)245-3632 Fax: (212)489-6360

© 1987 **Bruce Wolfe.** Limited Edition Poster, San Francisco Chamber Orchestra at Lake Tahoe.

B R U C E W O L F E

"I have been in love with painting
ever since I became conscious of it
at the age of six.
I drew some pictures
I thought fairly good when I was fifty,
but really nothing I did
before the age of seventy

was of any value at all.
At seventy-three I have at last caught
every aspect of nature—
birds, fish, animals, insects,
trees, grasses, all.
When I am eighty,
I will have developed still further,
and I will really master the secrets
of art at ninety.
When I reach a hundred
my work will be truly sublime,
and my final goal will be attained
around the age of one hundred and ten,
when every line and dot I draw
will be imbued with life."

194 THIRD AVENUE NEW YORK NY 10003
VICKI MORGAN ASSOCIATES
(212) 475·0440

NANCY STAHL

194 THIRD AVENUE NEW YORK NY 10003
VICKI MORGAN ASSOCIATES
(212) 475-0440

WARD SCHUMAKER

194 THIRD AVENUE NEW YORK NY 10003
VICKI MORGAN ASSOCIATES
(212) 475·0440

PATTY DRYDEN

VICKI MORGAN ASSOCIATES
194 THIRD AVENUE NEW YORK NY 10003
(212) 475·0440

VIVIENNE FLESHER

VICKI MORGAN ASSOCIATES
194 THIRD AVENUE NEW YORK NY 10003
(212) 475-0440

RICH GROTE

609-586-5896

21 TYNDALE ROAD, HAMILTON SQUARE, NJ 08690

THE NEW YORK PORTFOLIO DEPOT, 41 UNION SQUARE, NEW YORK, NY 10003
212-989-8588

Renard Represents

MICHAEL SCHWAB

Renard Represents Inc. 501 Fifth Avenue New York N.Y. 10017 Tel: 212 490-2450 Fax: 212 697-6828

Renard Represents

JOHN MARTIN

"Executive Stress"

BASF

"What sort of beast is tenure?"

Renard Represents Inc. 501 Fifth Avenue New York N.Y. 10017 Tel: 212 490-2450 Fax: 212 697-6828

Renard Represents

BART FORBES

© PHILIP MORRIS INC. 1988

© AGRICULTURE COUNCIL OF AMERICA 1988

© BART FORBES 1988

PRIVATE COMMISSION

Renard Represents Inc. 501 Fifth Avenue New York N.Y. 10017 Tel: 212 490-2450 Fax: 212 697-6828

Björkman

Renard Represents

JOHN COLLIER

ALLIANCE CAPITAL MANAGEMENT CORP.

OSCAR DE LA RENTA

© 1988 JOHN COLLIER

David Lesh
5693 N. Meridian Street
Indianapolis, IN 46208
1•317•253•3141

Represented by:
Joanne Palulian
18 McKinley Street
Rowayton, CT 06853
1•203•866•3734
1•212•581•8338

Julian Allen

Represented by:

DARWIN BAHM

6 Jane Street
New York, N.Y. 10014
(212) 989-7074

Bob Bahm
(216) 398-1338

CELEBRATION IN VENEZUELA
HEINZ COMPANY/ CORPORATE GRAPHICS

"THE PROFUMO AFFAIR"
FATAL MOMENTS

UNDER THE BOARDWALK
ROLLING STONE MAGAZINE/SPOT DESIGN

PERON
RANDOM HOUSE/LOUISE FILI

MILLER BREWING CO.

VLSI SYSTEMS DESIGN

MOTHER EARTH NEWS

Joan Landis

Represented by:

DARWIN
BAHM

6 Jane Street
New York, N.Y. 10014
(212) 989-7074

Bob Bahm
(216) 398-1338

POSTER FOR LINCOLN CENTER

NATIONAL LAMPOON ED DEMANDS A RAISE

POSTER FOR
ABIE'S BABY OFFICE FURNITURE

SEAGRAM'S
"NOW THAT'S A GRAND CANYON"

Rick Meyerowit

Represented by:

DARWIN
BAHM

6 Jane Street
New York, N.Y. 100
(212) 989-7074

Bob Bahm
(216) 398-1338

ohn Thompson

epresented by:

DARWIN
BAHM

Jane Street
ew York, N.Y. 10014
'12) 989-7074

ob Bahm
16) 398-1338

ALLENDALE INSURANCE

COORS

MOBIL OIL CORPORATION

FIELD & STREAM

Jacqui Morgan

692 Greenwich Street • New York, NY 10014 • 212•463•8488

Clients include: AICPA, Architectural Digest, AT&T, Avon, American Home Products, Booz-Allen & Hamilton, Burlington Mills, Busch Gardens, Champion Papers, Citibank, Colgate Palmolive, Communications Week, Diversion Magazine, E.P. Dutton, General Electric, General Foods, Hilton International, Holland American, IBM, ITC, Irving Trust, Johnson Wax, Lear's Magazine, NBC, New Woman Magazine, New York Magazine, New York Times, Pfizer, Playboy, Proctor & Gamble, RCA, Scott Paper Company, TransAtlantik Magazine.

Jacqui Morgan

692 Greenwich Street • New York, NY 10014 • 212•463•8488

Clients include: AICPA, Architectural Digest, AT&T, Avon, American Home Products, Booz-Allen & Hamilton, Burlington Mills, Busch Gardens, Champion Papers, Citibank, Colgate Palmolive, Communications Week, Diversion Magazine, E.P. Dutton, General Electric, General Foods, Hilton International, Holland American, IBM, ITC, Irving Trust, Johnson Wax, Lear's Magazine, NBC, New Woman Magazine, New York Magazine, New York Times, Pfizer, Playboy, Proctor & Gamble, RCA, Scott Paper Company, TransAtlantik Magazine.

Alex Tiani • Bright ideas captured on video and paper
Fax: 203 869-5823 • Represented in New York and France by
Daniele Collignon 212 243-4209 • Clients include
American Express, AT&T, Bantam Books, Black Book, CBS Records, Chemical Bank, CitiBank, Comdial, IBM, Illinois Bell, Kemper, Long Island Savings Bank, Mass Mutual, Mobil Oil, New York Life, Pitney Bowes, SAS, Scott Paper, Sony, Western Union

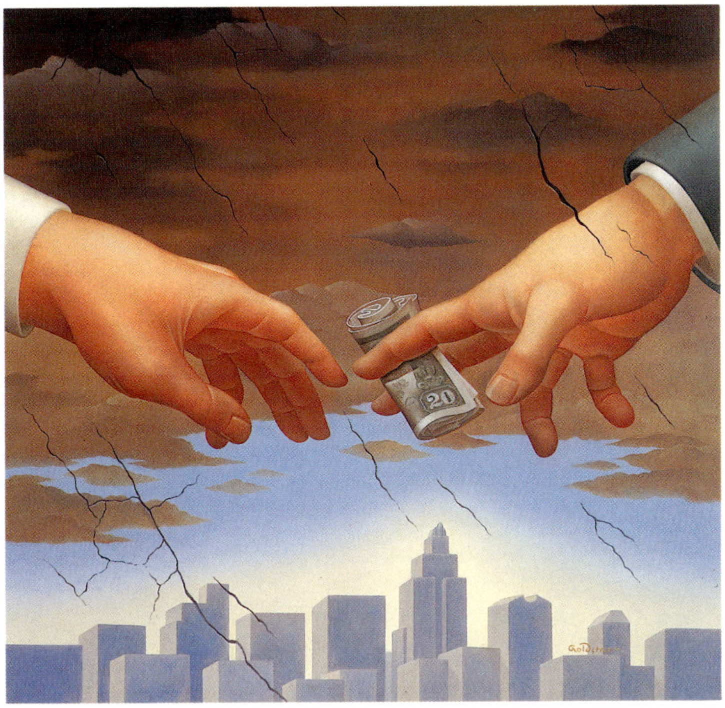

New York Magazine

Avon Books

Chicago Reader

Robert Goldstrom

471 Fifth St.
Brooklyn, NY
11215
718 768-7367

represented by

Joan Sigman
336 E. 54th St.
New York, NY
10022
212 421-0050
212 832-7980

J · U · D · Y
PEDERSEN

96 *Greene Street*
New York, N.Y. 10012
(212) 226-3675

Marvin Mattelson Paintings and Concepts
Represented by Judy Mattelson (212) 684-2974

ROBERT NEUBECKER

345 broadway
N. Y. C.
212-219-8435

RAGLAND

GREG RAGLAND
ILLUSTRATION
258 BROADWAY, LOFT 4E
NEW YORK, NY 10007
212·513·7218

ANITA
KUNZ
(416) 364-3846

Represented by
LISA NEWMAN
(212) 787-1340

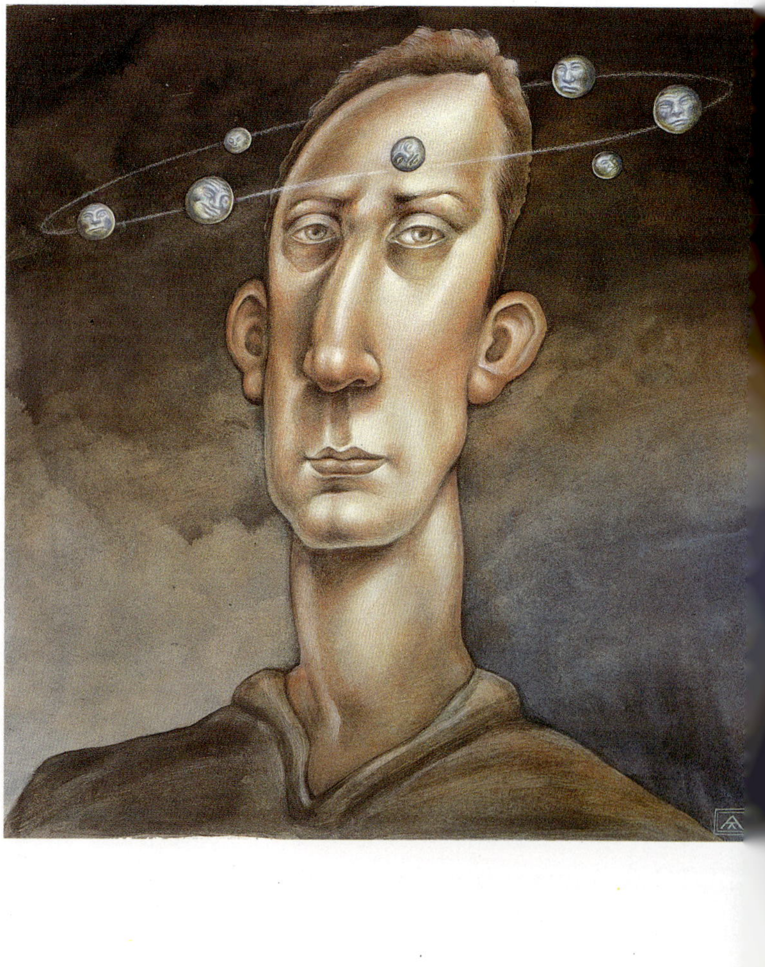

GLENN HARRINGTON

REPRESENTED BY BARBARA GORDON ASSOC. LTD. 165 EAST 32 ST. N.Y., N.Y. 10016 212·686·3514

Pushpin Associates

215 Park Avenue South
New York, New York 10003
(212) 674-8080

Contact: James Burris,
Phyllis Rich Flood, Ilse Lebrecht

Robert Crawford

FORTUNE MAGAZINE

VOLKSWAGON AG

BRITISH PETROLEUM

NORTHWESTERN LIFE

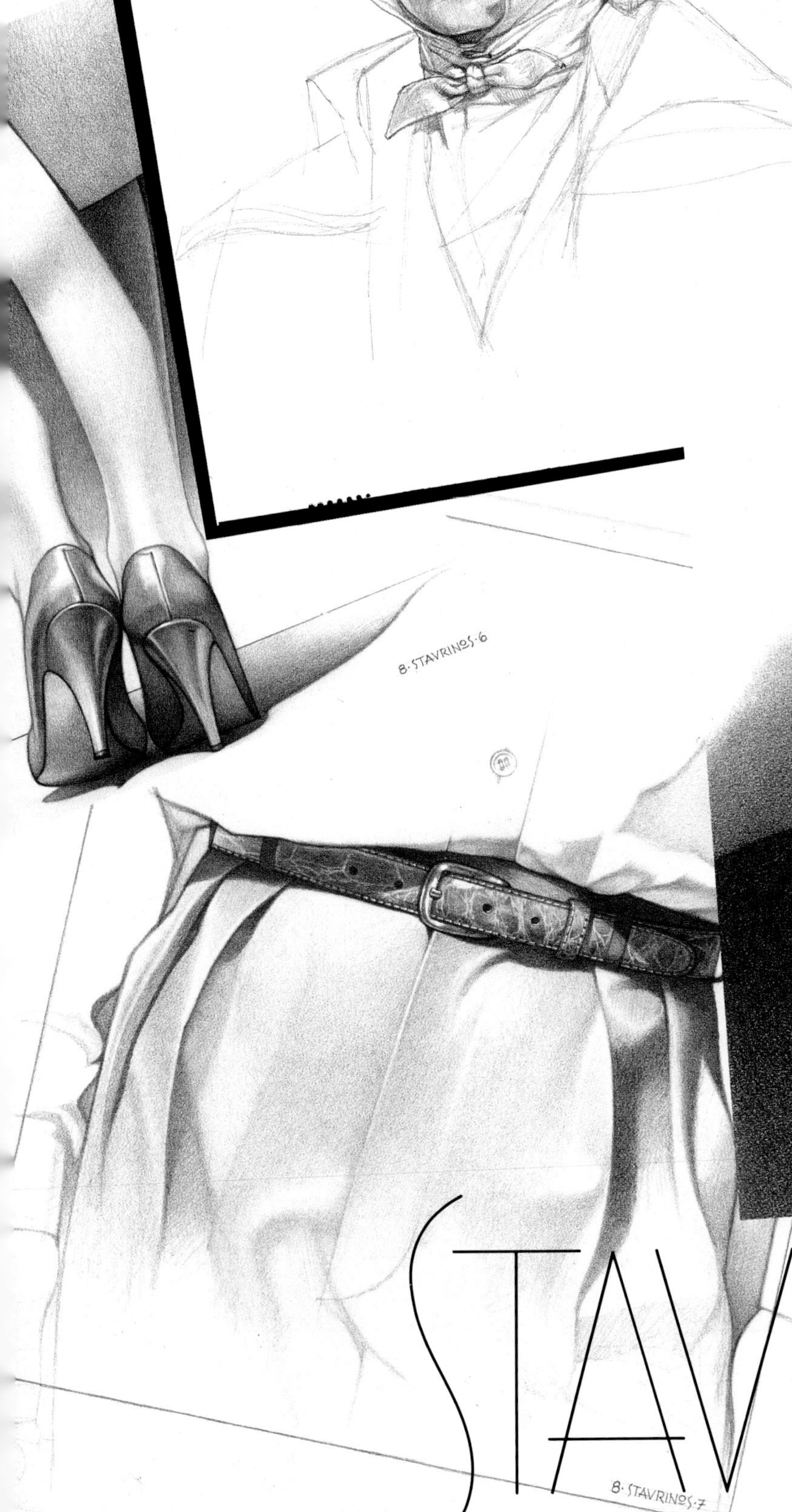

STAVRINOS

George Stavrinos 212 724 1557

JEAN-FRANCOIS PODEVIN

2 1 2 / 9 6 4 - 4 2 4 4

THINGS I LIKE TO DRAW
BY ELWOOD H. SMITH
1
CACTUS
HATS:
2
3
I OFTEN DRAW MYSELF
4
THESE THINGS!
5
THE BUSH
SHORT, FAT, BALD OLD MEN
GRRR!
HARES
6
SHORT, FAT, BALD OLD DOGS
7
8
9
ICE CREAM
ICE CREAM
I LOVE THIS HERE DOG!
10
11
HEALTH FOOD IS GOOD!
CATS AND COWS!
12
HEY!! WANNA SEE MORE? DIAL 914~876·2358 AND ASK FOR MAGGIE PICKARD, REP!
13
MICE
14
PORTFOLIO
BUGS
© EHSmith '88
2 LOCUST GROVE ROAD ★ RHINEBECK, NEW YORK 12572

A BABE IN THE WOODS
COWBOY
BODY BUILDER
RUTH
3
HEAVY SMOKER
SHORT ORDER COOK
PAUL YALOWITZ
212 532-0859
215 EAST 26 St. #7 NEW YORK, N.Y. 10010

M A R K   E N G L I S H

■ **MARK ENGLISH** REPRESENTED BY ■ BILL ERLACHER, ARTISTS ASSOCIATES ■ 211 E. 51 STREET, N.Y., N.Y. 10022 ■ (212) 755-1365/6 ■

LIEPKE

■ **SKIP LIEPKE** REPRESENTED BY ■ BILL ERLACHER, ARTISTS ASSOCIATES ■ 211 E. 51 STREET, N.Y., N.Y. 10022 ■ (212) 755-1365/6 ■

C. MICHAEL DUDASH

Represented By: Bill Erlacher, Artists Associates
211 E. 51 Street, New York, New York 10022, (212) 755-1365/6

A
12
K
Stanley Morison
·1889–1967·

S T E V E ▫ K A R C H I N

V I S U A L   I N T E R P R E T A T I O N S

REPRESENTED BY BILL ERLACHER ▫ ARTISTS ASSOCIATES ▫ 211 EAST 51 STREET, NEW YORK, NEW YORK 10022 ▫ (212) 755-1365/6

Chuck Wilkinson

epresented by:

DARWIN
BAHM

Jane Street
ew York, N.Y. 10014
12) 989-7074

ob Bahm
16) 398-1338

JIM CHERRY

I L L U S T R A T I O N · D E S I G N

REPRESENTED BY MAUREEN HYMERS

(212) 807-6914

LETTERING & DESIGN

ICK JAGGER
ET'S WORK
IN THE SPOTLIGHT
HONG KONG AND TAIWAN
'88
Macy Kids
Pretty in Pink
Into the night
Whitney
Milan
VON
Customer Club
Artistic
RBAN
Smooch
Smooch
Freedom
Simply smashing stuff
BERNARD MAISNER
Calligraphy and Handlettering
exture
The gift of fiery diamonds
vital signs
Alive and Screamin'
Spring Break
Tidal Raves
Expressions
ORIENT EXPRESS
Bernard Maisner
Calligraphy and Handlettering
Represented by
GAYLENE FRASER
(212) 475-5911

Paul Perlow Design
212•758•4358
Fine Typography & Lettering
Graphic Images & Trademarks
Represented in Paris, France:
Hugo Weinberg Associés
1-4 266 6200

Partial Client List:
CBS Records International
Prentice Hall/JC Penney
NY Times/Reader's Digest
Polygram Records/SSC&B
Saatchi, Saatchi, & Compton
Business Week, Family Circle

Logo, Family Circle Magazine

Software Packaging, Henry Holt

Bookcover, Prentice Hall

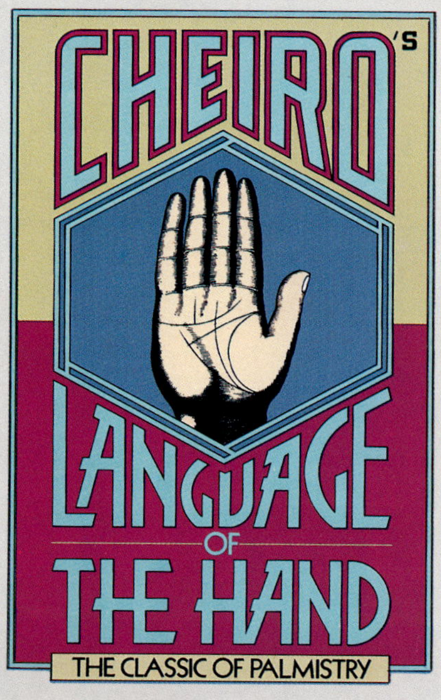

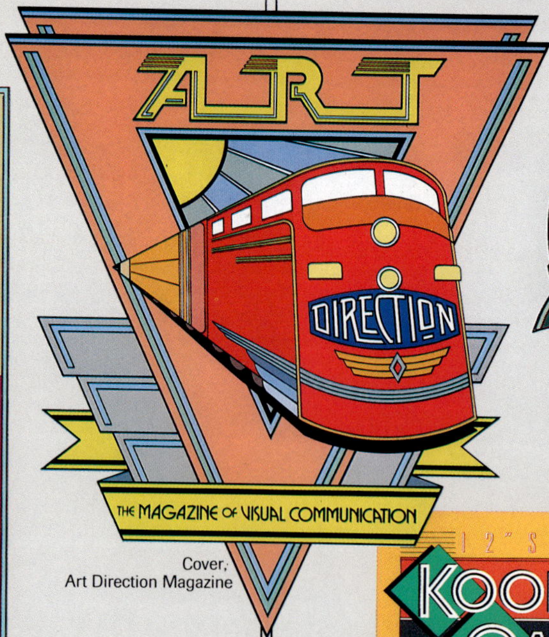

Cover,
Art Direction Magazine

Logo, Greenwich Symphony Guild

Album Design & Lettering, Polygram Records

Lettering, Business Week Magazine

PAUL PERLOW DESIGN • 123 EAST 54TH ST. • NEW YORK, NY 10022 • 212 • 758 • 4358

BINIASZ
GRAPHIC DESIGN
ILLUSTRATION

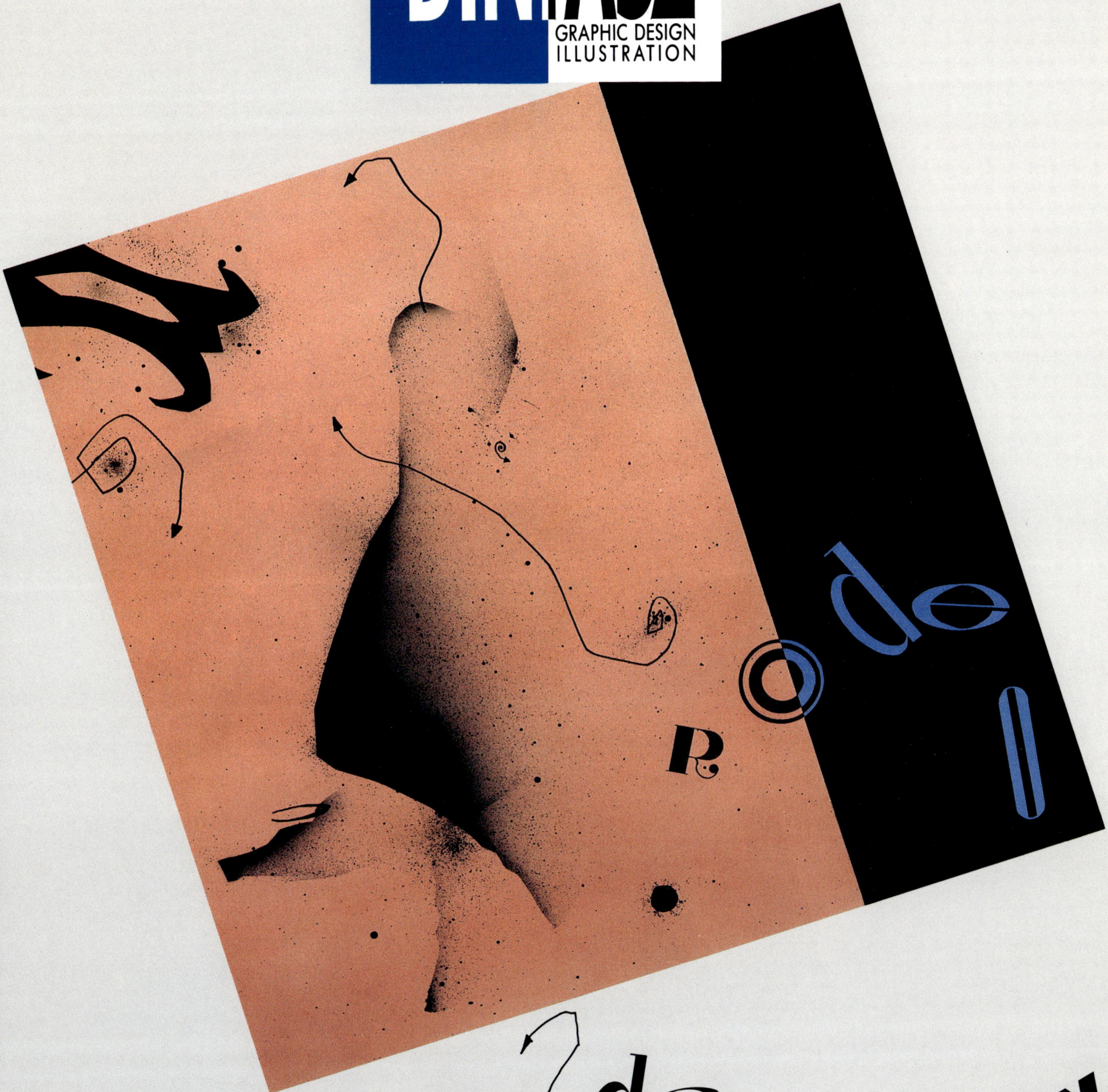

BINIASZ GRAPHIC DESIGN•ILLUSTRATION
FOR LOGOS•BROCHURES•POSTERS•PACKAGING
CORPORATE IDENTITY AND ILLUSTRATION

CALL PAUL BINIASZ IN N.Y.C. 212•979•0025

Woodbury Common

THE UNCOMMON SHOPPING EXPERIENCE

Dirty Looks

HBO Showcase

Signatures

The Old Atlantean Press

Splendid Plumage

Bird Illustrations 1550-1900

from The New York Public Library

It's a Dog's Life

Smirnoff Style!

Wells Ruddle Jennings Miller

1st Quarter 1988 Promotion

Cinderella

Marilyn Martin

Glemby International

ABC Records

Art & Design Alumni Association

Fitzner Caps (a Lettergraphics International typeface)

McGraw Hill (plaster letter construction)

YVONNE FITZNER

GRAPHIC AND TYPOGRAPHIC DESIGN, LOGOS, CORPORATE IDENTITY
231 EAST 76TH STREET, NEW YORK, NY 10021
(212) 988-4039

Member, Type Directors Club and Graphic Artists Guild.

M GIRVIN DESIGN, INC.
1 Western Avenue
uite 408
eattle, WA 98104
06.623.7808
AX 206.340.1837

Tim Girvin Design offers an innovative and diverse range of lettering treatments, identity, illustration, packaging, promotional campaign and retail graphic design.

Current clients include Bloomingdale's, Hoffmann-La-Roche, Inc., Levi Strauss, Milton Bradley, Nordstrom, Paramount Studios, Universal Studios and United Airlines.

Represented in New York by Renard Represents, Inc. 212.490.2450

CHAPS RALPH LAUREN

THE BEST OF TIMES

CHRISTMAS
Glorious
CHRISTMAS

WOODBRIDGE
CENTER

JON
CISLER
DESIGN
INC.

JON CISLER DESIGN, INC.
148 W. 4TH STREET/4TH FLOOR • NEW YORK, NY 10012-1051
(212) 995-8933

CORPORATE IDENTITY • LETTERING • DESIGN • LOGOTYPES • PACKAGING • P.O.P. • SIGNAGE

JOHN SPOSATO·Design & Illustration 43 E. 22 St., NYC, 10010·(212)477-3909

Paul Shaw / Letter Design 110 Morningside Drive · New York City 10027 · 212 / 666·3738

Clients include:
Clarion Books
Design Ensemble
Doubleday
Dun + Bradstreet
Gips + Balkind
Kordet Graphics
Metropolitan Museum of Art
Muir Cornelius Moore
NBC
Page, Arbitrio and Resen
Port Authority of NY and NJ
Vignelli Associates

Member:
AIGA
ATypI
Type Directors Club

ILLUSTRATION

a

ABRAHAM, DANIEL E *(718) 499-4006* **Box** 2528/Rockefeller Sta NY, NY 10185

ABRAMS, KATHIE *(212) 741-1333* 41 Union Square W NY, NY 10003

ACCARDO, ANTHONY *(212) 838-0050* 19 E 48th St NY, NY 10017

ACCORNERO, FRANCO *(212) 674-0068* 620 Broadway NY, NY 10012

ACUNA, ED *(212) 489-8777* 24 W 57th St NY, NY 10019

ADAMS, ANGELA *(212) 644-2020* 866 UN Plaza NY, NY 10017

ADAMS, JEANETTE *(212) 732-3878* 261 Broadway NY, NY 10007

ADAMS, JEFFREY *(212) 807-0840* **95** Horatio St NY, NY 10014

AIESE, BOB *(718) 596-2240* 60 Pineapple St Brooklyn, NY 11201

AJHAR, BRIAN *(212) 254-0694* 321 E 12th St NY, NY 10003

ALBAHAE, ANDREA *(718) 934-7004* 2364 Brigham St Brooklyn, NY 11229

ALBANESE, ERNEST *(212) 243-1333* 156 Fifth Ave NY, NY 10010

ALCORN, JOHN *(212) 475-0440* 194 Third Ave NY, NY 10003

ALCORN, STEPHEN *(212) 475-0440* 194 Third Ave NY, NY 10002

ALLAUX, JEAN FRANCOIS *(212) 799-0399* 21 W 86th St NY, NY 10024

ALLEN, JULIAN *(212) 989-7074* 6 Jane St NY, NY 10014

PAGE 40

ALLEN, TERRY *(718) 727-0723* 164 Daniel Low Terr Staten Island, NY 10301

ALLERT, KATHY *(212) 532-0928* 201 E 28th St NY, NY 10016

ALOISIO, RICHARD *(212) 473-5635* 145 E 16th St NY, NY 10003

ALPERT, ALAN *(212) 741-1631* 405 E 54th St NY, NY 10022

ALPERT, OLIVE *(718) 833-3092* 9511 Shore Rd Brooklyn, NY 11209

ALTER, JUDY *(718) 667-5643* 539 Naughton Ave Staten Island, NY 10305

AMICOSANTE, VINCENT *(212) 775-1810* 280 Madison Ave NY, NY 10016

ANDERSON, MARK *(212) 674-3831* 166 Second Ave NY, NY 10003

ANGELAKIS, MANOS *(212) 243-4412* 48 W 21st St NY, NY 10010

ANGELINI, GEORGE *(212) 489-8777* 24 W 57th St NY, NY 10019

ANGELO, PETER *(212) 246-1243* 328 W 46th St NY, NY 10036

ANGERAME, DIANE *(718) 428-7794* 57-30 254th St Little Neck, NY 11362

ANTONIOS, TONY *(212) 682-1490* 60 E 42nd St NY, NY 10165

ARCELLE, JOAN *(212) 924-1865* 430 W 24th St NY, NY 10011

ARISMAN, MARSHALL *(212) 662-2289* 314 W 100th St NY, NY 10025

PAGE 2-3

ARISTOVULOS, NICK *(212) 725-2454* 16 E 30th St NY, NY 10016

ARNOLD, ROBERT *(212) 989-7049* 149 W 14th St NY, NY 10011

ARNOLDI, PER *(212) 682-1490* 60 E 42nd St NY, NY 10165

ASBAGHI, ZITA *(718) 275-1995* 104-40 Queens Blvd Forest Hills, NY 11375

ASSEL, STEVEN *(718) 789-1725* 472 Myrtle Ave Brooklyn, NY 11205

ASTRAHAN, IRENE *(212) 532-0928* 201 E 28th St NY, NY 10016

AZZOPARDI, FRANK *(718) 273-4343* 1039 Victory Blvd Staten Island, NY 10301

b

BACALL, AARON *(718) 494-0711* 204 Arlene St Staten Island, NY 10314

BAILEY, PAT/AIRSTREAM *(212) 682-1490* 60 E 42nd St NY, NY 10165

BAKER, GARIN *(212) 865-1975* 35 W 92nd St NY, NY 10025

BALDUS, FRED *(212) 620-0423* 29 Jones St NY, NY 10014

BALDWIN, READ *(212) 481-7311* 230 Fifth Ave NY, NY 10001

BANFIELD, ELLIOT *(212) 925-3053* 81 Greene St NY, NY 10012

BARANCIK, CATHY *(212) 472-2202* 140 Grand St NY, NY 10013

BARBER, KAREN *(212) 619-6790* 51 Warren St NY, NY 10007

BARBERIS, JUAN C *(212) 687-4185* 60 E 42nd St NY, NY 10165

BARNER, BOB *(212) 644-2020* 866 UN Plaza NY, NY 10017

BARNES, MICHELE *(212) 219-9269* 111 Sullivan St NY, NY 10012

BARNES-MURPHY, ROWAN *(212) 532-0928* 201 E 28th St NY, NY 10016

BARON, ESTHER *(212) 644-2020* 866 UN Plaza NY, NY 10017

BARR, KEN *(212) 697-8525* 420 Lexingron Ave NY, NY 10170

BARRERA, ALBERTO *(212) 645-2544* 463 West St NY, NY 10014

BARRETT, RON *(212) 874-1370* 2112 Broadway NY, NY 10023

BARRITT, RANDI *(212) 255-5333* 240 W 15th St NY, NY 10011

BARRY, RON *(212) 686-3514* 165 E 32nd St NY, NY 10016

BARTALOS, MICHAEL *(212) 254-5858* 81 Second Ave NY, NY 10003

BARTHOLOMEW, CATHY

(718) 596-8863 217 Dean St Brooklyn, NY 11217

BARTOLONI, GARY *(212) 749-4498* 203 W 98th St NY, NY 10025

BASCOVE *(212) 888-0038* 319 E 50th St NY, NY 10022

BASEMAN, GARY *(718) 398-2313* 628 President St Brooklyn, NY 11215

BAUER, CARLA STUDIO *(212) 807-8305* 156 Fifth Ave NY, NY 10010

BAUMAN, JILL *(718) 631-3160* PO Box 152 Jamaica, NY 11415

BAUMANN, KAREN *(212) 688-1080* 43 E 19th St NY, NY 10014

BEACH, LOU *(212) 674-8080* 215 Park Ave So NY, NY 10003

BECKER, RON *(212) 535-8052* 265 E 78th St NY, NY 10021

BEECHAM, TOM *(212) 697-8525* 420 Lexington Ave NY, NY 10170

BEGO, DOLORES *(212) 697-6170* 155 E 38th St NY, NY 10016

BELLAIR & INOUE VISUAL COMM

(212) 473-8330 323 Park Ave So NY, NY 10010

BEN-AMI, DORON *(718) 230-3348* 808 Union St Brooklyn, NY 11215

BENDELL, NORM *(212) 807-6627* 41 Union Sq W NY, NY 10003

BENSON, LINDA *(212) 686-3514* 165 E 32nd St NY, NY 10016

BERGER, STEPHEN *(212) 254-4996* 43 E 19th St NY, NY 10003

BERKEY, JOHN *(212) 355-0910* 50 E 50th St NY, NY 10022

BERRAN, ROBERT *(212) 986-5680* 420 Lexington Ave NY, NY 10170

BERRY, FANNY MELLET *(212) 697-6170* 155 E 38th St NY, NY 10016

BEYLON, CATHY *(212) 532-0928* 201 E 28th St NY, NY 10016

BIANCO, GERALDO *(718) 836-8637* 1040 82nd St Brooklyn, NY 11228

BILLOUT, GARY *(212) 490-2450* 501 Fifth Ave NY, NY 10017

BITTMAN, MONIKA *(718) 622-2061* 709 Carroll St Brooklyn, NY 11215

BJORKMAN, STEVE *(212) 490-2450* 501 Fifth Ave NY, NY 10017

PAGE 36

BLACKWELL, GARIE *(212) 682-1490* 60 E 42nd St NY, NY 10165

BLAKE, MARTY *(212) 929-4440* 24 Jane St NY, NY 10014

BLAKE, QUENTIN *(212) 925-3053* 81 Greene St NY, NY 10012

BLAKEY, PAUL *(212) 242-6367* 470 W 23rd St NY, NY 10011

BLAS, BOB *(212) 254-4996* 43 E 19th St NY, NY 10003

BLASUTTA, MARY LYNN *(212) 675-0287* 1 Union Sq W NY, NY 10003

BLECHMAN, R O *(212) 869-1630* 2 W 47th St NY, NY 10036

BLECK, CATHIE *(212) 288-3708* 303 E 71st St NY, NY 10021

BLEVINS, STEVE *(718) 768-6702* 475 18th St Brooklyn, NY 11215

BLOCH, ALEX *(212) 838-0050* 19 E 48th St NY, NY 10017

BLOOM, TOM *(212) 628-6861* 235 E 84th St NY, NY 10028

BLOUNT, LESTER *(718) 768-0059* 302 5th St Brooklyn, NY 11215

BLUBAUGH, SUSAN *(718) 858-4360* 191 Amity St Brooklyn, NY 11201

BLUM, ZEVI *(212) 925-3053* 81 Greene St NY, NY 10012

BLUME, GEORGE *(212) 502-3976* 350 E 89th St NY, NY 10128

BLUMRICH, CHRISTOPH *(212) 674-8080* 215 Park Ave So NY, NY 10003

BOCHNER, NURIT *(718) 596-3476* 28 Tompkins Pl Brooklyn, NY 11231

BOGUSLAV, RAPHAEL *(212) 570-9069* 200 E 78th St NY, NY 10021

BOLOGNESE, DON *(212) 838-0050* 19 E 48th St NY, NY 10017

BONFORTE, LISA *(212) 532-0928* 201 E 28th St NY, NY 10016

BONHOMME, BERNARD *(212) 925-0491* 111 Wooster St NY, NY 10012

BONO, MARY *(212) 475-6266* PO Box 1502 NY, NY 10009

BOOTH, GEORGE *(203) 227-7806* 158 Hills Point Rd Westport, CT 06880

BORDELON, MELINDA *(212) 682-1490* 60 E 42nd St NY, NY 10165

BOREA, PHYLLIS *(212) 663-4463* 245 W 104th St NY, NY 10025

BOSTIC, ALEX *(212) 677-9100* 853 Broadway NY, NY 10003

BOTAS, JUAN *(212) 420-5984* 207 E 32nd St NY, NY 10016

BOYD, HARVEY *(212) 475-5235* 24 Fifth Ave NY, NY 10011

BOYD, KRIS *(718) 648-7138* 318 E 89th St NY, NY 10128

BOZZO, FRANK *(212) 535-9182* 400 E 85th St NY, NY 10028

BRACKEN, CAROLYN *(212) 532-0928* 201 E 28th St NY, NY 10016

BRALDS, BRALDT *(212) 421-0050* 135 E 54th St NY, NY 10022

PAGE 8-9

BRAMHALL, WILLIAM *(212) 925-3053* 81 Greene St NY, NY 10012

BRANDT, JOAN *(212) 473-7874* 15 Gramercy Park So NY, NY 10003

BREAKEY, JOHN *(718) 507-6467* 42-52 Layton Queens, NY 11373

BREINBERG, AARON *(212) 243-4929* 1123 Broadway NY, NY 10010

BRICHER, SCOTT *(212) 714-0147* 330 W 42nd St NY, NY 10036

BRICKNER, ALICE *(212) 549-5909* 4720 Grosvenor Ave Bronx, NY 10471

BRILLHART, RALPH *(212) 867-8092* 60 E 42nd St NY, NY 10165

BRINDAK, HERMINE *(212) 620-0604* 29 W 15th St NY, NY 10011

BRODERSON, CHARLES *(212) 925-9392* 873 Broadway NY, NY 10003

BRODNER, STEVE *(212) 586-1267* 446 W 58th St NY, NY 10019

BROFSKY, MIRIAM *(212) 595-8094* 186 Riverside Dr NY, NY 10024

BROOKS, ANDREA *(212) 645-0644* 41 Union Sq W NY, NY 10003

BROOKS, CLARE VANACORE

(212) 245-3632 415 W 55th St NY, NY 10019

BROOKS, HAL *(212) 595-5980* 20 W 87th St NY, NY 10024

BROOKS, LOU *(212) 245-3632* 415 W 55th St NY, NY 10019

PAGE 24-25

BROTHERS, BARRY *(718) 336-7540* 1922 E 18th St Brooklyn, NY 11229

BROWN, BRADFORD *(212) 231-8223* 4103 Lowerre Pl Bronx, NY 10466

BROWN, COLIN *(212) 473-8747* 145 E 22nd St NY, NY 10022

BROWN, DAN *(212) 489-8777* 24 W 57th St NY, NY 10019

BROWN, DONALD *(212) 532-1705* 129 E 29th St NY, NY 10016

BROWN, JUDITH GWYN *(212) 288-1599* 522 E 85th St NY, NY 10028

BROWN, KIRK *(718) 342-4565* 1092 Blake Ave Brooklyn, NY 11208

BROWN, MICHAEL DAVID *(212) 889-3337* 108 E 35th St NY, NY 10016

BROWN, PETER D *(212) 684-7080* 235 E 22nd St NY, NY 10010

BROWN, RS *(212) 398-9540* 62 W 45th St NY, NY 10036

BRUNDAGE, CHERYL

(718) 789-6392 314 Washington Ave Brooklyn, NY 11205

BRUSCA, JACK *(212) 254-4996* 43 E 19th St NY, NY 10003

BRYAN, DIANA *(212) 475-7927* 200 E 16th St NY, NY 10003

BRYAN, MIKE *(212) 697-8525* 420 Lexington Ave NY, NY 10170

BRYANT, RICK J *(212) 594-6718* 18 W 37th St NY, NY 10018

BUCHANAN, YVONNE *(718) 965-3021* 411 14th St Brooklyn, NY 11215

BUEHLER, MARK *(718) 797-3689* 418 Atlantic Ave Brooklyn, NY 11217

BURGER, ROBERT *(212) 925-0491* 111 Wooster St NY, NY 10012

BURGOYNE, JOHN *(212) 570-9069* 200 E 78th St NY, NY 10021

BUSCHMAN, LYNNE *(212) 925-4701* 186 Franklin St NY, NY 10013

BUSH, GEORGE *(212) 867-8092* 60 E 42nd St NY, NY 10165

Byskiniewicz, Maryika *(718) 261-5883* 75-23 113th St Forest Hills, NY 11375

C

Caggiano, Tom *(718) 651-8993* 83-25 Dongan Ave Elmhurst, NY 11373

Cain, David *(212) 633-0258* 200 W 20th St NY, NY 10011

Caldwell, Kirk *(212) 242-6367* 470 W 23rd St NY, NY 10011

Campbell, Jim *(212) 986-5680* 420 Lexington Ave NY, NY 10170

Cantarella, Virginia Hoyt

(718) 622-2061 107 Sterling Pl Brooklyn, NY 11217

Carbone, Kye *(718) 802-9143* 241 Union St Brooklyn, NY 11231

Carr, Noell *(212) 675-1015* 30 E 14th St NY, NY 10003

Carter, Abby *(718) 729-6822* 2109 45th Ave Long Island City, NY 11101

Carter, Bunny *(212) 570-9069* 200 E 78th St NY, NY 10021

Carter, Penny *(212) 772-3715* 430 E 66th St NY, NY 10032

Carver, Steve *(212) 473-8747* 145 E 22nd St NY, NY 10010

Casale, Paul *(718) 871-6848* 5304 11th Ave Brooklyn, NY 11219

Cassler, Carl *(212) 986-5680* 420 Lexington Ave NY, NY 10170

Castelluccio, Frederico *(212) 867-8092* 60 E 42nd St NY, NY 10165

Cavaliere, Jamie *(212) 867-8092* 60 E 42nd St NY, NY 10165

Celsi, David *(212) 475-1325* 91 E 3rd St NY, NY 10003

Ceribello, Jim

(718) 317-5972 11 W Cedar View Ave Staten Island, NY 10306

Cesc *(212) 925-3053* 81 Greene St NY, NY 10012

Cetlin, Marshall *(212) 243-7869* 62 LeRoy St NY, NY 10014

Chabrian, Deborah *(212) 986-5680* 420 Lexington Ave NY, NY 10170

Chambless-Rigie, Jane *(212) 532-0928* 201 E 28th St NY, NY 10016

Chang, Alain *(212) 489-8777* 24 W 57th St NY, NY 10019

Charmatz, Bill *(212) 595-3907* 25 W 68th St NY, NY 10023

Cheng, Judith *(718) 465-5598* 88-57 195th St Hollis, NY 11423

Chermayeff, Ivan *(212) 741-2539* 58 W 15th St NY, NY 10011

PAGE 20-21

Chernishov, Anatoly

(201) 951-0039 4 Willow Bank Ct Mahwah, NJ 07436

Cherry, Jim *(212) 807-6914* NY, NY

PAGE 68

Chester, Harry *(212) 752-0570* 501 Madison Ave NY, NY 10022

Chironna, Ronald *(718) 720-6142* 135 Sturges St Staten Island, NY 10314

Chow, Tad *(718) 946-8519* 179 Bay 35th St Brooklyn, NY 11214

Christopher, Tom *(212) 986-3282* 51 E 42nd St NY, NY 10017

Chwast, Jacqueline *(212) 246-7342* 462 W 58th St NY, NY 10019

Chwast, Seymour *(212) 674-8080* 215 Park Ave So NY, NY 10003

Ciardiello, Joe *(718) 727-4757* 2182 Clove Rd Staten Island, NY 10305

Ciccarelli, Gary *(212) 682-2462* 353 W 53rd St NY, NY 10019

Ciesiel, Christine G *(212) 982-9461* 101 MacDougal St NY, NY 10012

Ciss, Julius *(212) 473-8747* 145 E 22nd St NY, NY 10010

Clark, Jane *(212) 243-4412* 48 W 21st St NY, NY 10010

Clarke, Robert *(212) 581-4045* 159 W 53rd St NY, NY 10019

Cloteaux, Francois *(212) 679-1358* 333 E 30th St NY, NY 10016

Cober, Alan E *(914) 941-8696* Croton Dam Rd Ossining, NY 10562

PAGE 6-7

Cody, Brian *(212) 644-2020* 866 UN Plaza NY, NY 10017

Coe, Sue *(212) 825-9405* 105 Broad St NY, NY 10004

Cohen, Adam *(212) 924-5941* 74 Charles St NY, NY 10014

Cole, Olivia *(212) 838-0050* 19 E 48th St NY, NY 10017

Collier, John *(212) 490-2450* 501 Fifth Ave NY, NY 10017

PAGE 37

Collier, Roberta *(212) 532-0928* 201 E 28th St NY, NY 10016

Colon, Ernie *(212) 254-4996* 43 E 19th St NY, NY 10003

Colton, Keita *(212) 686-3514* 165 E 32nd St NY, NY 10016

Cone, William *(212) 874-7074* 140 West End Ave NY, NY 10023

Conner, Mona *(718) 636-1527* 1 Montgomery Pl Brooklyn, NY 11215

Conrad, Jon *(212) 677-9100* 853 Broadway NY, NY 10003

Conway, Michael *(212) 369-0019* 316 E 93rd St NY, NY 10128

Cook, David *(212) 867-8092* 60 E 42nd St NY, NY 10165

Cook, Esky *(312) 329-1370* 405 N Wabash Chicago, IL 60611

Cooper, Cheryl *(212) 486-9644* 515 Madison Ave NY, NY 10022

Cooper, Floyd *(212) 644-2020* 866 UN Plaza NY, NY 10017

Cooperstein, Sam *(212) 864-4064* 677 West End Ave NY, NY 10025

Corben, Richard *(212) 254-4996* 43 E 19th St NY, NY 10003

Cornelius, Ray-Mel *(212) 683-1362* 121 Madison Ave NY, NY 10016

Cornell, Jeff *(212) 489-8777* 24 W 57th St NY, NY 10019

Cornell, Laura *(212) 534-0596* 118 E 93rd St NY, NY 10128

Corvi, Donna *(212) 925-9622* 568 Broadway NY, NY 10012

Couch, Greg *(718) 625-1298* 112 Willow St Brooklyn, NY 11201

Courtney, Richard *(212) 254-4996* 43 E 19th St NY, NY 10003

Cove, Tony *(212) 953-7088* 60 E 42nd St NY, NY 10165

Craft, Kuniko *(203) 542-5018* Brocklebank RDF #1 Norfolk, CT 06058

Crawford, Margery *(212) 686-6883* 237 E 31st St NY, NY 10016

Crawford, Robert *(212) 674-8080* 215 Park Ave So NY, NY 10003

PAGE 54

Crawford, Ronald *(718) 768-6194* 354 22nd St Brooklyn, NY 11215

Creed, Cora *(718) 633-7753* 651 Vanderbilt St Brooklyn, NY 11218

CREWS, DONALD *(718) 636-5773* 653 Carroll St Brooklyn, NY 11215

CRISTIANO, RUDY *(212) 398-9540* 62 W 45th St NY, NY 10036

CROSTHWAITE, ROYD *(212) 355-0910* 50 E 50th St NY, NY 10022

CRUSE, HOWARD

(718) 639-4951 88-11 34th Ave Jackson Heights, NY 11372

CRUZ, JOSE *(212) 674-8080* 215 Park Ave So NY, NY 10003

CRUZ, RAY *(212) 475-0440* 194 Third Ave NY, NY 10003

CSATARI, JOE *(212) 986-5680* 420 Lexington Ave NY, NY 10170

CUEVOS, STILLERMAN, PLOTKIN

(212) 661-7149 230 E 44th St NY, NY 10017

CUMMINGS, PAT *(718) 834-8584* 28 Tiffany Pl Brooklyn, NY 11231

CUMMINGS, TERRENCE *(212) 586-4153* 210 W 64th St NY, NY 10023

CUNNINGHAM, ROBERT M *(203) 903-4545* 177 Waverly Pl NY, NY 10014

CURRY, TOM *(212) 980-8061* 333 E 49th St NY, NY 10017

CUSACK, MARGARET *(718) 237-0145* 124 Hoyt St Brooklyn, NY 11217

CUSHWA, TOM *(212) 228-2615* 303 Park Ave So NY, NY 10010

d

D'ANDREA, BERNARD *(212) 355-0910* 50 E 50th St NY, NY 10022

D'ANDREA, DOMENICK *(212) 355-0910* 50 E 50th St NY, NY 10022

D'ONOFRIO, ALICE *(212) 644-2020* 866 UN Plaza NY, NY 10017

DACEY, BOB *(212) 489-8777* 24 W 57th St NY, NY 10019

DALE, ROBERT *(212) 535-2505* 1573 York Ave NY, NY 10028

DALLISON, KEN *(212) 889-3337* 108 E 35th St NY, NY 10016

DALY, SEAN *(212) 668-0031* 85 South St NY, NY 10038

DAMORE, GEORGAN *(212) 775-1810* 280 Madison Ave NY, NY 10016

DANIEL, FRANK *(212) 532-0928* 201 E 28th St NY, NY 10016

DANIELS, BEAU & ALAN *(212) 489-8777* 24 W 57th St NY, NY 10019

DANIELS, SHELLEY *(718) 636-1046* 132 Berkeley Pl Brooklyn, NY 11217

DANIELS, SID *(212) 673-6520* 12 E 22nd St NY, NY 10010

DARDEN, HOWARD *(212) 398-9540* 62 W 45th St NY, NY 10036

DASTE, LARRY *(212) 532-0928* 201 E 28th St NY, NY 10016

DAVIDSON, EVERETT *(212) 682-1490* 60 E 42nd St NY, NY 10165

DAVIS, ALLEN *(718) 463-0966* 141-10 25th Rd Flushing, NY 11354

DAVIS, HARRY *(212) 674-5832* 189 E 3rd St NY, NY 10009

DAVIS, JACK *(212) 889-3337* 108 E 35th St NY, NY 10016

DAVIS, NELLE *(212) 807-7737* 20 E 17th St NY, NY 10003

DAVIS, PAUL *(212) 460-9644* 14 E 4th St NY, NY 10012

DAY, BETSY *(212) 644-2020* 866 UN Plaza NY, NY 10017

DEARAUJO, BETTY *(212) 532-0928* 201 E 28th St NY, NY 10016

DEAS, MICHAEL *(718) 852-5630* 39 Sidney Pl Brooklyn, NY 11201

DEEL, GUY *(212) 867-8092* 60 E 42nd St NY, NY 10165

DEGEN, PAUL *(212) 925-3053* 81 Greene St NY, NY 10012

DEGRAFFENRIED, JACK *(212) 206-0322* 18 E 16th St NY, NY 10003

DEIBLER, GORDON *(212) 323-8022* 1 Wrld Trade Ctr NY, NY 10048

DEJESUS, JAMIE *(212) 799-2231* 15 W 72nd St NY, NY 10023

DEL ROSSO, RICHARD *(212) 974-1059* 303 W 42nd St NY, NY 10036

DELATTRE, GEORGETTE *(212) 247-6850* 100 Central Park So NY, NY 10019

DELESSERT, ETIENNE *(203) 435-0061* Box 1689 Lakeview, CT 06039

DELVALLE, DANIEL *(212) 838-0050* 19 E 48th St NY, NY 10017

DEMAREST, CHRIS *(212) 925-3053* 81 Greene St NY, NY 10012

DEMICHIELL, ROBERT *(212) 769-9192* 226 W 78th St NY, NY 10024

DENARO, JOSEPH *(212) 206-0322* 18 E 16th St NY, NY 10003

DENEEN, JIM *(212) 986-5680* 420 Lexington Ave NY, NY 10170

DERIJK, WALT *(212) 254-4996* 43 E 19th St NY, NY 10003

DESCHAMPS, BOB *(212) 889-3337* 108 E 35th St NY, NY 10016

DESCOMBES, ROLAND *(212) 355-0910* 50 E 50th St NY, NY 10022

DESEVE, PETER *(212) 627-5533* 461 W 21st St NY, NY 10011

DESIGN LOIMINCHAY *(212) 608-2880* 210 Canal St NY, NY 10013

DETRICH, SUSAN *(718) 237-9174* 253 Baltic St Brooklyn, NY 11201

DEVLIN, BILL *(212) 889-3337* 108 E 35th St NY, NY 10016

DEWEY, KENNETH F *(212) 986-5680* 420 Lexington Ave NY, NY 10170

DIAMANTIS, KITTY *(212) 838-0050* 19 E 48th St NY, NY 10017

DIAMOND, RUTH *(212) 243-3188* 95 Horatio St NY, NY 10014

DICIANNI, RON *(212) 697-8525* 420 Lexington Ave NY, NY 10170

DIEHL, DAVID *(212) 242-8897* 222 W 20th St NY, NY 10011

DIETZ, JIM *(212) 686-3514* 165 E 32nd St NY, NY 10016

DILAKIAN, HOVIK *(212) 925-0491* 111 Wooster St NY, NY 10012

DILLON, LEO & DIANE *(718) 624-0023* 221 Kane St Brooklyn, NY 11231

DINNERSTEIN, HARVEY

(718) 783-6879 933 President St Brooklyn, NY 11214

DION, MADGE *(914) 698-1027* 320 Palmer Terrace Mamaroneck, NY 10543

DIRCKS, DAVID *(212) 260-7892* 295 Park Ave So NY, NY 10010

DITTRICH, DENNIS *(212) 864-5971* 42 W 72nd St NY, NY 10023

DIVINCENZO, DENNIS *(212) 673-1600* 27 Bleecker St NY, NY 10012

DODDS, GLENN *(212) 679-3630* 392 Central Park West NY, NY 10025

DODGE, BILL *(212) 867-8092* 60 E 42nd St NY, NY 10165

DOMINGO, RAY *(212) 889-3337* 108 E 35th St NY, NY 10016

DONIGER, NANCY *(212) 475-7901* 361 E 10th St NY, NY 10009

DONNER, CARROLL *(212) 254-0069* 830 Broadway NY, NY 10003

DONZE, LISA *(718) 956-9082* Astoria, NY 11106

DOQUETTE, STEVE *(212) 398-9540* 62 W 45th St NY, NY 10036

Doret, Michael *(212) 929-1688* 12 E 14th St NY, NY 10003

Doret/ Smith Studios *(212) 929-1688* 12 E 14th St NY, NY 10003

Doty, Curt *(718) 797-5115* 4 S Portland Ave Brooklyn, NY 11217

Downes, Nicholas *(718) 875-0086* PO Box 107 Brooklyn, NY 11231

Drescher, Henrik *(212) 777-6077* 151 First Ave NY, NY 10003

Drovetto, Richard *(212) 861-0927* 355 E 72nd St NY, NY 10021

Dryden, Patty *(212) 475-0440* 194 Third Ave NY, NY 10003

PAGE 30

Duarte, Mary Young *(212) 674-4513* 350 First Ave NY, NY 10010

Dubanevich, Arlene *(212) 644-2020* 866 UN Plaza NY, NY 10017

Dudash, C. Michael *(212) 755-1365* 211 E 51st St NY, NY 10022

PAGE 64-65

Dudzinski, Andrzej *(212) 628-6959* 52 E 81st St NY, NY 10028

Duerk, Chris *(212) 683-7729* 259 E 33rd St NY, NY 10016

Dunnick, Regan *(813) 951-2691* 41 Union Sq W NY, NY 10003

Dyess, John *(212) 243-1333* 156 Fifth Ave NY, NY 10010

e

Eagel, Cameron *(212) 929-5590* 41 Union Sq NY, NY 10003

Eastman, Norm & Bryant

(212) 697-8525 420 Lexington Ave NY, NY 10170

Eggert, John *(212) 986-5680* 420 Lexington Ave NY, NY 10170

Egielski, Richard *(212) 255-9328* 463 West St NY, NY 10014

Ehlert, Lois *(212) 644-2020* 866 UN Plaza NY, NY 10017

Eisner, Gil *(212) 595-2023* 310 W 86th St NY, NY 10024

Ellis, Dean *(212) 254-7590* 30 E 20th St NY, NY 10003

Elmer, Richard *(212) 522-1051* 504 E 11th St NY, NY 10009

Ely, Richard *(212) 757-8987* 150 W 55th St NY, NY 10019

Emerson, Carmela *(718) 224-4251* 217-11 54th Ave Bayside, NY 11364

Emmett, Bruce *(718) 636-5263* 285 Park Pl Brooklyn, NY 11238

Endewelt, Jack *(212) 877-0575* 50 Riverside Dr NY, NY 10024

English, Mark *(212) 755-1365* 211 E 51st St NY, NY 10022

PAGE 60-61

Enik, Ted *(212) 620-5972* 82 Jane St NY, NY 10014

Ennis, John *(914) 762-9403* 75 Stone Ave Ossining, NY 10562

Enos, Randall *(203) 227-4785* 11 Court of Oaks Wesport, CT 06880

Enric *(212) 688-1080* 43 E 19th St NY, NY 10014

Ensor, Barbara *(212) 619-6103* 90 Fulton St NY, NY 10038

Erickson, Mary Anne *(212) 929-7964* 154 Eighth Ave NY, NY 10011

Ettlinger, Doris *(212) 226-0331* 73 Leonard St NY, NY 10013

Eutemy, Loring *(212) 741-0140* 51 Fifth Ave NY, NY 10003

Evans, Jan *(212) 677-9100* 853 Broadway NY, NY 10003

Evcimen, Al *(212) 889-2995* 305 Lexington Ave NY, NY 10016

Ewing, Carolyn *(212) 532-0928* 201 E 28th St NY, NY 10016

f

Fanelli, Carolyn *(212) 533-9829* 19 Stuyvesant Oval NY, NY 10009

Farina, Michael *(212) 206-0322* 18 E 16th St NY, NY 10003

Farmakis, Andreas *(212) 758-5280* 835 Third Ave NY, NY 10022

Farrell, Sean *(212) 949-6081* 245 E 44th St NY, NY 10017

Fascione, Sabina *(212) 475-0440* 194 Third Ave NY, NY 10003

Fasolino, Teresa *(212) 741-2539* 58 W 15th St NY, NY 10011

PAGE 18-19

Faulkner, Matt *(718) 858-1724* 435 Clinton St Brooklyn, NY 11231

Faust, Clifford *(212) 581-9461* 322 W 57th St NY, NY 10019

FeBland, David *(212) 580-9299* 670 West End Ave NY, NY 10025

Fernandes, Stanislaw *(212) 533-2648* 35 E 12th St NY, NY 10003

Fernandez, Fernando *(212) 254-4996* 43 E 19th St NY, NY 10003

Fernandez, George *(212) 867-8092* 60 E 42nd St NY, NY 10165

Fertig, Howard *(718) 468-3627* 75-15 210th St Bayside, NY 11364

Fichera, Maryanne *(212) 689-8670* 120 E 34th St NY, NY 10016

Filippucci, Sandra *(212) 477-8732* 270 Park Ave So NY, NY 10010

Fine, Robert *(212) 254-4996* 43 E 19th St NY, NY 10003

Fiore, Peter *(718) 358-9018* 10-11 162nd St College Point, NY 11357

Fiorentino, Al *(212) 644-2020* 866 UN Plaza NY, NY 10017

Fischer, Rick *(212) 645-6772* 156 Fifth Ave NY, NY 10010

Fitzgerald, Frank *(212) 722-6793* PO Box 6113 NY, NY 10128

Flaherty, David *(212) 262-6536* 650 Ninth Ave NY, NY 10036

Flanagan, Dan *(718) 499-5253* 427 15th St Brooklyn, NY 11215

Fleming, Ron/Graphic Assoc

(212) 682-1490 60 E 42nd St NY, NY 10165

Flesher, Vivienne *(212) 475-0440* 194 Third Ave NY, NY 10003

PAGE 31

Forbes, Bart *(212) 490-2450* 501 Fifth Ave NY, NY 10017

PAGE 35

Forest, Sandra *(212) 580-8510* 315 Central Park W NY, NY 10025

Foster, B Lynne *(212) 740-7011* 540 Ft Washington Ave NY, NY 10033

Foster, Pat (Ms) *(212) 685-4580* 6 E 36th St NY, NY 10016

Foster, Stephen Design *(212) 967-2533* 145 W 28th St NY, NY 10001

Fox, Barbara *(212) 245-7564* 301 W 53rd St NY, NY 10019

Francis, Judy *(212) 866-7204* 110 W 96th St NY, NY 10025

Fraser, Betty *(212) 247-1937* 240 Central Park So NY, NY 10019

Fraser, Douglas *(201) 420-1836* 216 Hudson St Hoboken, NJ 07030

Freas, John *(212) 682-2462* 353 W 53rd St NY, NY 10019

Freelance Solutions *(212) 490-3334* 369 Lexington Ave NY, NY 10017

Freeman, Irving *(212) 674-6705* 145 Fourth Ave NY, NY 10003

Freeman, Tom *(212) 247-1130* 157 W 57th St NY, NY 10019

Fresh, Mark *(212) 674-5556* 1421 First Ave NY, NY 10009

Fretz, Frank *(212) 644-2020* 866 UN Plaza NY, NY 10017

Fricke, Warren *(212) 799-2231* 15 W 72nd St NY, NY 10023

Fried, Janice *(212) 398-0067* 51 W 46th St NY, NY 10036

Friedman, Barbara *(212) 242-4951* 29 Bank St NY, NY 10014

Friedman, Jon *(212) 644-2020* 866 UN Plaza NY, NY 10017

Friedman, Wendy *(212) 431-8824* 136 Grand St NY, NY 10013

Froom, Georgia *(212) 944-0330* 62 W 39th St NY, NY 10018

Fuchs, Bernie *(212) 752-8490* 50 E 50th St NY, NY 10022

Funtastic Studios *(212) 239-8245* 506 W 42nd St NY, NY 10036

Furukawa, Mel *(212) 349-3225* 116 Duane St NY, NY 10007

g

Gabriel, Don *(212) 254-4996* 43 E 19th St NY, NY 10003

Gabriele, Antonio J *(212) 986-5680* 420 Lexington Ave NY, NY 10170

Gadino, Victor *(212) 534-7206* 1601 Third Ave NY, NY 10028

Gaetano, Nicholas *(212) 674-5749* 821 Broadway NY, NY 10003

Gala, Tom *(212) 986-5680* 420 Lexington Ave NY, NY 10170

Gale, Cynthia *(212) 860-5429* 229 E 88th St NY, NY 10128

Galkin, Simon *(212) 838-0050* 19 E 48th St NY, NY 10017

Gallardo, Gervasio *(212) 355-0910* 50 E 50th St NY, NY 10022

Galub, Meg *(212) 757-3506* 405 W 57th St NY, NY 10019

Gambale, David *(212) 391-1830* 1500 Broadway NY, NY 10036

Gampert, John *(718) 441-2321* PO Box 219 Kew Gardens, NY 11415

Garner, David *(212) 874-3147* 175 W 87th St NY, NY 10024

Garrick, Jacqueline *(212) 628-1018* 333 E 75th St NY, NY 10021

Garrido, Hector *(212) 986-5680* 420 Lexington Ave NY, NY 10170

Garrison, Barbara *(212) 348-6382* 12 E 87th St NY, NY 10128

Gates, Donald *(212) 838-0050* 19 E 48th St NY, NY 10017

Gayler, Anne *(212) 734-7060* 418 E 75th St NY, NY 10021

Gehm, Charles *(212) 697-8525* 420 Lexington Ave NY, NY 10170

Geller, Amy *(718) 786-5277* 11-15 45th Ave Long Island City, NY 11101

Genova, Joe *(212) 682-1490* 60 E 42nd St NY, NY 10165

Gentile, John & Anthony

(212) 757-1966 850 Seventh Ave NY, NY 10019

Geras, Audra *(212) 490-2450* 501 Fifth Ave NY, NY 10017

Gershinowitz, George

(718) 596-1492 PO Box 204 Chelsea Stn NY, NY 10011

Gersten, Gerry *(212) 752-8490* 50 E 50th St NY, NY 10022

Giavis, Ted *(212) 986-5680* 420 Lexington Ave NY, NY 10170

Giglio, Mark *(212) 645-4124* 143 Waverly Pl NY, NY 10014

Giglio, Richard *(212) 724-8118* 2231 Broadway NY, NY 10024

Gillot, Carol *(212) 353-1174* 67 E 11th St NY, NY 10003

Giorgio, Nate *(212) 206-0322* 18 E 16th St NY, NY 10003

Giovanopoulos, Paul *(212) 661-0850* 216 E 45th St NY, NY 10017

Giusti, Robert *(212) 421-0050* 135 E 54th St NY, NY 10022

page 12-13

Glaser, Milton *(212) 889-3161* 27 W 67th St NY, NY 10023

Gold, Marcy *(212) 685-4974* 200 E 28th St NY, NY 10016

Goldstrom, Robert *(212) 421-0050* 336 E 54th St NY, NY 10022

page 47

Goodell, Jon *(212) 644-2020* 866 UN Plaza NY, NY 10017

Goodman, Paula *(212) 243-1333* 156 Fifth Ave NY, NY 10010

Goodrich, Carter *(212) 787-9184* 134 W 87th St NY, NY 10024

Gordon, Rebecca *(212) 989-5762* 201 W 16th St NY, NY 10011

Gore, Elissa *(212) 567-2161* 583 W 215th St NY, NY 10034

Gorey, Edward *(212) 288-8010* 15 E 76th St NY, NY 10021

Gorton, Julia *(212) 825-0190* 85 South St NY, NY 10038

Gothard, David *(212) 925-3053* 81 Greene St NY, NY 10012

Gottfried, Max *(718) 441-9868* 82-60 116th St Kew Gardens, NY 11418

Gottlieb, Penelope *(212) 679-8525* 420 Lexington Ave NY, NY 10170

Gourley, Robin *(212) 219-9391* 225 Lafayette St NY, NY 10012

Gowdy, Carolyn *(212) 925-3053* 81 Greene St NY, NY 10012

Grace, Alexa *(212) 254-4424* 70 University Pl NY, NY 10003

Graddon, Julian *(212) 243-4412* 48 W 21st St NY, NY 10010

Graham, Mariah *(212) 580-8061* 670 West End Ave NY, NY 10025

Graham, Thomas *(718) 680-2975* 408 77th St Brooklyn, NY 11209

Grajek, Tim *(212) 995-2129* 184 E 2nd St NY, NY 10009

Grant, William *(718) 996-3555* 4114 Highland Ave Brooklyn, NY 11224

Grashow, David *(212) 925-3053* 81 Greene St NY, NY 10012

Grashow, James *(203) 938-9195* 14 Diamond Hill Rd W. Redding, CT 06896

Gray, Doug *(212) 799-2231* 15 W 72nd St NY, NY 10023

Gray, John *(718) 447-6466* 264 Van Duzer St Staten Island, NY 10304

Gray, Susan *(212) 675-2243* 42 W 12th St NY, NY 10011

Grebu, Devis *(212) 688-1080* 43 E 19th St NY, NY 10014

Greenstein, Susan *(718) 373-4475* 4915 Surf Ave Brooklyn, NY 11224

Gregoretti, Rob *(718) 229-5647* 240-13 Hanford St Douglaston, NY 11362

Greif, Gene *(212) 966-0470* 270 Lafayette St NY, NY 10012

Greifinger, Mel *(212) 391-1830* 1500 Broadway NY, NY 10036

Greiner, Larry *(212) 982-2428* 63 E 7th St NY, NY 10003

Griesbach/Martucci *(718) 622-1831* 35 Sterling Pl Brooklyn, NY 11217

Griffel, Barbara *(718) 631-1753* 23-45 Bell Blvd Bayside, NY 11360

Griffin, James *(212) 867-8092* 60 E 42nd St NY, NY 10165

Grimmett, Douglas *(212) 627-8216* 467 Sixth Ave NY, NY 10011

Grinko, Andy *(212) 732-5308* 125 Cedar St NY, NY 10006

Gross, Mort *(212) 686-4788* 2 Park Ave NY, NY 10016

Grossman, Dina *(718) 789-3350* 28 St James Pl Brooklyn, NY 11205

Grossman, Robert *(212) 925-1965* 19 Crosby St NY, NY 10013

Grossman, Wendy *(212) 262-4497* 355 W 51st St NY, NY 10019

Grote, Rich *(212) 889-2400* 381 Park Ave So NY, NY 10016

page 32

Guarnaccia, Steven *(212) 645-9610* 430 W 14th St NY, NY 10011

Guitar, Jeremy *(212) 644-2020* 866 UN Plaza NY, NY 10017

Gumen, Murad *(718) 478-7267* 33-25 90th St Jackson Heights, NY 11372

Gunn, Robert *(212) 532-0928* 201 E 28th St NY, NY 10016

Gurbo, Walter *(212) 775-1810* 55 Hudson St NY, NY 10013

Gurney, John Steven *(718) 462-5073* 523 E 16th St Brooklyn, NY 11226

Gusson, Steven *(718) 852-7791* 105 Bergen St Brooklyn, NY 11201

h

Haas, Arie *(212) 398-9540* 62 W 45th St NY, NY 10036

Hack, Konrad *(212) 644-2020* 866 UN Plaza NY, NY 10017

Hahn, Marika *(212) 580-7896* 11 Riverside Dr NY, NY 10023

Hall, Deborah Ann
(718) 896-3152 105-28 65th Ave Forest Hills, NY 11375

Hall, Joan *(212) 243-6059* 155 Bank St NY, NY 10014

Hallgren, Gary *(212) 947-1054* 231 W 29th St NY, NY 10001

Hamann, Brad *718) 287-6086* 330 Westminster Rd Brooklyn, NY 11218

Hampton, Blake *(212) 398-9540* 62 W 45th St NY, NY 10036

Hamrick, Chuck *(212) 986-5680* 420 Lexington Ave NY, NY 10170

Hannon, Mark *(212) 243-1333* 156 Fifth Ave NY, NY 10010

Hardy, Fran *(212) 473-8747* 145 E 22nd St NY, NY 10010

Harrington, Glenn *(212) 686-3514* 165 E 32nd St NY, NY 10016

page 53

Harris, Diane Teske *(212) 719-9879* 342 Madison Ave NY, NY 10173

Harrison, William *(212) 206-0322* 18 E 16th St NY, NY 10003

Hart, Veronika *(212) 682-1490* 60 E 42nd St NY, NY 10165

Harvey, Paul *(203) 381-9836* 475B Commanche Ln Stratford, CT 06497

Harvey, Ray *(212) 867-8092* 60 E 42nd St NY, NY 10165

Harwood, Laurel *(212) 689-3515* 1239 Broadway NY, NY 10001

Hays, Michael *(718) 852-2731* 43 Cheever Pl Brooklyn, NY 11231

Heapps, Bill *(718) 726-2193* 2441 41st St Long Island City, NY 11103

Heck, Cathy *(915) 686-9343* 333 E 30th St NY, NY 10016

Hedin, Donald *(212) 247-1130* 157 W 57th St NY, NY 10019

Heindel, Robert *(212) 755-1365* 211 E 51st St NY, NY 10022

Heiner, Joe & Kathy *(212) 475-0440* 194 Third Ave NY, NY 10003

Hejja, Attila *(212) 986-5680* 420 Lexington Ave NY, NY 10170

Heller, Debbie *(212) 580-0917* 601 West End Ave NY, NY 10024

Heller, Karen *(212) 866-5879* 300 W 108th St NY, NY 10025

Helman, Marc *(212) 262-5039* 425 W 46th St NY, NY 10036

Henderson, Alan *(212) 243-0693* 31 Jane St NY, NY 10014

Henderson, Meryl *(212) 838-0050* 19 E 48th St NY, NY 10017

Henry, Paul *(212) 799-2231* 15 W 72nd St NY, NY 10023

Herbert, Jonathan
(718) 383-1251 1205 Manhattan Ave Brooklyn, NY 11222

Herbick, David *(718) 852-6450* 5 Montague Terrace Brooklyn, NY 11201

Herder, Edwin *(212) 867-8092* 60 E 42nd St NY, NY 10165

Hering, Al *(718) 789-7685* 277 Washington Ave Brooklyn, NY 11205

Herman, Rolla *(212) 226-1510* 462 Greenwich St NY, NY 10013

Herman, Tim *(212) 677-9100* 853 Broadway NY, NY 10003

Hernandez, Richard *(212) 732-3474* 144 Chambe:s St NY, NY 10007

Herrmann, Hal *(212) 752-8490* 50 E 50th St NY, NY 10022

Hess, Dick *(203) 542-5529* 310 Litchfield Rd Norfolk, CT 06058

Hess, Mark *(212) 421-0050* 135 E 54th St NY, NY 10022

page 10-11

Hewitt, Margaret *(718) 436-2039* 31 Ocean Pkwy Brooklyn, NY 11218

Hill, Amy *(212) 925-0491* 111 Wooster St NY, NY 10012

Himler, Ron *(212) 644-2020* 866 UN Plaza NY, NY 10017

Hiroko *(718) 896-2712* 67-12 Yellowstone Blvd Foreset Hills, NY 11375

Hirschfeld, Al *(212) 534-6172* 122 E 95th St NY, NY 10128

Hoffman, Ginnie *(212) 889-3337* 108 E 35th St NY, NY 10016

Hoffman, Rosekrans *(212) 644-2020* 866 UN Plaza NY, NY 10017

Hofkin, Bonnie *(212) 787-6384* 204 W 80th St NY, NY 10024

Hofmekler, Ori *(212) 829-9838* 166 Second Ave NY, NY 10003

Hogarth, Paul *(212) 925-3053* 81 Greene St NY, NY 10012

Holland, Brad *(212) 226-3675* 96 Greene St NY, NY 10012

Holland, Gary *(212) 877-9165* 140 W 86th St NY, NY 10024

Holliman, Richard *(212) 243-2750* 425 W 23rd St NY, NY 10011

Holm, John *(212) 682-2462* 353 W 53rd St NY, NY 10019

HOLST, JOANI *(718) 236-6214* 1519 81st St Brooklyn, NY 11228

HOM & HOM *(212) 242-6367* 470 W 23rd St NY, NY 10011

HONG, MIN JAE *(212) 674-4320* 422 E 14th St NY, NY 10009

HOOKS, MITCHELL *(212) 737-1853* 321 E 83rd St NY, NY 10028

HORTENS, WALTER *(212) 838-0014* 154 E 64th St NY, NY 10021

HOSNER, WILLIAM *(212) 677-9100* 853 Broadway NY, NY 10003

HOSTOVICH, MICHAEL *(212) 580-2175* 127 W 82nd St NY, NY 10024

HOVLAND, GARY *(212) 877-9165* 140 W 86th St NY, NY 10024

HOWARD, JOHN *(212) 832-7980* 336 E 54th St NY, NY 10022

HOWELL, KATHLEEN *(212) 644-2020* 866 UN Plaza NY, NY 10017

HOWLAND, GARY *(212) 877-9165* 140 W 86th St NY, NY 10024

HUANG, MEI-KU *(212) 532-0928* 201 E 28th St NY, NY 10016

HUB, THE *(212) 675-8500* 16 E 16th St NY, NY 10003

HUBERT, LAURENT *(212) 661-0850* 216 E 45th St NY, NY 10017

HUERTA, CATHERINE *(212) 682-1490* 60 E 42nd St NY, NY 10165

HUERTA, GERALD *(203) 656-0505* 45 Corbin Dr Darien, CT 06820

HUFFMAN, TOM *(212) 819-0211* 130 W 47th St NY, NY 10036

HUGHES, MARY ELLEN *(212) 288-8375* 403 E 70th St NY, NY 10021

HULING, PHIL *(212) 673-0839* 33 E 22nd St NY, NY 10010

HULL, CATHY *(212) 683-8559* 165 E 66th St NY, NY 10021

HUNT, JIM *(212) 677-9100* 853 Broadway NY, NY 10003

HUNTER, STAN *(212) 355-0910* 50 E 50th St NY, NY 10022

HUSTON, STEVEN *(212) 799-2231* 15 W 72nd St NY, NY 10023

HUYSSEN, ROGER *(203) 656-0200* 45 Corbin Dr Darien, CT 5838

i - j

IDELSON, JOYCE *(606) 269-2190* 11 Riverside Dr NY, NY 10023

IGARASHI, SATORU *(212) 242-8897* 222 W 20th St NY, NY 10011

IMAGE BANK, THE *(212) 529-6700* 111 Fifth Ave NY, NY 10003

PAGE 69

INCISA, MONICA *(212) 752-1554* 141 E 56th St NY, NY 10022

INOUE, IZUMI *(212) 473-8330* 323 Park Ave So NY, NY 10010

ISKOWITZ, JOEL *(212) 986-5680* 420 Lexington Ave NY, NY 10170

IVENS, ROSALIND *(718) 499-8285* 483 13th St Brooklyn, NY 11215

JABEN, SETH *(212) 242-3181* 54 W 21st St NY, NY 10010

JABEN, SETH *(212) 807-0840* 95 Horatio St NY, NY 10014

JAKESEVIC, NENAD *(212) 686-3514* 165 E 32nd St NY, NY 10016

JAMIESON, DOUG *(718) 565-6034* 42-20 69th St Woodside, NY 11377

JAMPEL, JUDITH *(212) 873-5234* 148 Columbus Ave NY, NY 10023

JASPER, JACKIE *(212) 686-3514* 165 E 32nd St NY, NY 10016

JEFFERS, KATHY *(212) 475-1756* 106 E 19th St NY, NY 10003

JENNIS, PAUL *(212) 986-5680* 420 Lexington Ave NY, NY 10170

JETTER, FRANCES *(212) 580-3720* 390 West End Ave NY, NY 10024

JEZIERSKI, CHET *(212) 355-0910* 50 E 50th St NY, NY 10022

JINKS, JOHN *(212) 675-2961* 690 Greenwich St NY, NY 10014

JOBE, JODY *(212) 795-4941* 875 W 181st St NY, NY 10033

JOHNSON, DAVID A *(212) 683-1362* 121 Madison Ave NY, NY 10016

JOHNSON, DOUG *(212) 260-1880* 45 E 19th St NY, NY 10011

JOHNSON, JULIE *(212) 697-6170* 155 E 38th St NY, NY 10016

JOHNSON, KRISTIN *(212) 594-2343* 441 W 37th St NY, NY 10018

JOHNSON, LONNIE SUE *(212) 873-7749* 162 W 72nd St NY, NY 10023

JOHNSTON, DAVID MCCALL *(212) 355-0910* 50 E 50th St NY, NY 10022

JONES, BOB *(212) 986-5680* 420 Lexington Ave NY, NY 10170

JONES, RANDY *(212) 677-5387* 323 E 10th St NY, NY 10009

JONES, TAYLOR *(212) 838-0050* 19 E 48th St NY, NY 10017

JOSEPH, PAULA *(212) 242-6137* 16 W 16th St NY, NY 10011

JOUDREY, KEN *(201) 659-8875* 746 Park Ave Hoboken, NJ 07030

JUHASZ, VICTOR *(212) 421-0050* 135 E 54th St NY, NY 10022

PAGE 15

JULIAN, CLAUDIA *(718) 891-7957* 2939 Ave Y Brooklyn, NY 11235

JUST, HAL *(212) 697-6170* 155 E 38th St NY, NY 10016

k

KAGANSKY, EUGENE *(718) 253-0454* 515 Ave I Brooklyn, NY 11204

KAHN, SANDRA

(212) 759-0630 PO Box 20141/Dag Hammrskld Ctr NY, NY 10017

KALISH, LIONEL *(212) 228-6587* 30 E 10th St NY, NY 10003

KALLE, CHRIS *(212) 644-2020* 866 UN Plaza NCY, NY 10017

KALOUSTIAN, ROSANNE

(718) 428-4670 208-19 53rd Ave Bayside, NY 11364

KANAREK, MICHAEL *(212) 243-4412* 48 W 21st St NY, NY 10010

KANTRA, MICHELLE *(212) 684-6700* 40 W 27th St NY, NY 10001

KAPLAN, MARK *(212) 243-1333* 156 Fifth Ave NY, NY 10010

KAPPES, WERNER *(212) 673-2484* 134 W 26th St NY, NY 10001

KARCHIN, STEVE *(212) 755-1365* 211 E 51st St NY, NY 10022

PAGE 66

KARLIN, BERNIE *(212) 687-7636* 41 E 42nd St NY, NY 10017

KARLIN, NURIT *(212) 838-0050* 19 E 48th St NY, NY 10017

KATSIN, NANCY *(212) 213-0709* 17 E 31st St NY, NY 10016

KATZ, LES *(718) 284-4779* 451 Westminster Rd Brooklyn, NY 11218

KAUFMAN, CURT *(212) 873-9841* 215 W 88th St NY, NY 10024

KAUFTHEIL/ROTHSCHILD *(212) 633-0222* 220 W 19th St NY, NY 10011

KELENY, EARL *(212) 486-9644* 515 Madison Ave NY, NY 10022

KELLEY, BARBARA *(718) 788-2465* 555 10th St Brooklyn, NY 11215

KELLEY, MARK *(212) 644-2020* 866 UN Plaza NY, NY 10017

KELLY, GARY *(212) 683-1362* 121 Madison Ave NY, NY 10016

KELLY, SUSANNAH *(212) 206-8960* 77 Perry St NY, NY 10014

KENDRICK, DENNIS *(212) 924-3085* 99 Bank St NY, NY 10014

KERNAN, PATRICK *(212) 581-2069* 413 W 48th St NY, NY 10036

KEYES, STEVEN *(212) 206-0322* 18 E 16th St NY, NY 10003

KIBBEE, GORDON *(212) 989-7074* 6 Jane St NY, NY 10014

KIEFFER, CHRISTA *(212) 644-2020* 866 UN Plaza NY, NY 10017

KILMER, DAVID *(212) 986-5680* 420 Lexington Ave NY, NY 10170

KIMURA, HIRO *(718) 638-0372* 145 Washington Ave Brooklyn, NY 11205

KINGSTON, JAMES *(212) 685-2520* 31 E 31st St NY, NY 10016

KIRK, DANIEL *(212) 825-0190* 85 South St NY, NY 10038

PAGE 58

KLAVINS, ULDIS *(212) 867-8092* 60 E 42nd St NY, NY 10165

KLEIN, DAVID G *(718) 788-1818* 257 Winsdor Pl Brooklyn, NY 11218

KLEIN, RENEE *(718) 727-0723* 164 Daniel Low Terr Staten Island, NY 10301

KLEIN/ALLEN STUDIO

(718) 727-0723 164 Daniel Low Terr Staten Island, NY 10301

KLING, CULLA *(212) 546-2138* 777 Third Ave NY, NY 10017

KLUGLEIN, KAREN *(212) 684-2974*

KNETTELL, SHARON *(212) 889-3337* 108 E 35th St NY, NY 10016

KNIGHT, JACOB *(212) 661-0850* 216 E 45th St NY, NY 10017

KOBAYASHI, ANN *(718) 622-6031* 146 Berkeley Pl Brooklyn, NY 11217

KOJOYIAN, ARMEN *(718) 797-5179* 52 Clark St Brooklyn, NY 11201

KONDO, YUKIO *(212) 532-0928* 201 E 28th St NY, NY 10016

KOREN, EDWARD *(212) 925-3053* 81 Greene St NY, NY 10012

KOTZKY, BRIAN

(718) 353-5480 132-42 Booth Memorial Ave Flushing, NY 11355

KOVALCIK, TERRY *(212) 620-7772* 48 W 20th St NY, NY 10011

KRAMER, CARVETH *(212) 661-0850* 216 E 45th St NY, NY 10017

KRETSCHMANN, KARIN *(212) 724-5001* 323 W 75th St NY, NY 10023

KRONEN, JEFF *(212) 475-3166* 231 Thompson St NY, NY 10012

KRUMEICH, TAD *(212) 243-1333* 156 Fifth Ave NY, NY 10010

KUBINYI, LASZLO *(201) 833-4428* 226 E 53rd St NY, NY 10022

KUESTER, BOB *(212) 682-2462* 353 W 53rd St NY, NY 10019

KUKALIS, ROMAS *(212) 986-5680* 420 Lexington Ave NY, NY 10170

KUNSTLER, MORT *(212) 355-0910* 50 E 50th St NY, NY 10022

KUNZ, ANITA *(212) 787-1340* NY, NY

PAGE 52

KUPER, PETER *(212) 864-5729* 250 W 99th St NY, NY 10025

KURMAN, MIRIAM *(212) 580-1649* 422 Amsterdam NY, NY 10024

KURSAR, RAY *(212) 873-5605* 1 Lincoln Plaza NY, NY 10023

KURTZMAN, EDWARD *(212) 953-7088* 60 E 42nd St NY, NY 10165

KURTZMAN, HARVEY *(212) 206-0322* 18 E 16th St NY, NY 10003

l - m

LACEY, LUCILLE *(718) 296-1813* 77-07 Jamaica Ave Woodhaven, NY 11421

LACKNER, PAUL *(212) 838-0050* 19 E 48th St NY, NY 10017

LACKOW, ANDY *(212) 472-8898* 1325 Third Ave NY, NY 10021

LADAS, GEORGE *(212) 673-2208* 157 Prince St NY, NY 10012

LAKEMAN, STEVEN *(212) 877-8888* 115 W 85th St NY, NY 10024

LAMUT, SONJA *(212) 686-3514* 165 E 32nd St NY, NY 10016

LANDIS, JOAN *(212) 989-7074* 6 Jane St NY, NY 10014

PAGE 41

LANDRY, ALICE *(212) 398-9540* 62 W 45th St NY, NY 10036

LANG, CECILY *(212) 206-1251* 19 Jones St NY, NY 10014

LANG, GARY *(212) 697-8525* 420 Lexington Ave NY, NY 10170

LANGENSTEIN, MICHAEL *(212) 964-9637* 56 Thomas St NY, NY 10013

LAPADULA, TOM *(212) 532-0928* 201 E 28th St NY, NY 10016

LAPINSKI, JOE *(212) 677-9100* 853 Broadway NY, NY 10003

LAPORTE, MICHELE *(718) 499-2178* 579 Tenth St Brooklyn, NY 11215

LARRAIN, SALLY MARSHALL *(212) 838-0050* 19 E 48th St NY, NY 10017

LASHER, MARY ANN *(212) 682-1490* 60 E 42nd St NY, NY 10165

LASLO, LARRY *(212) 737-2340* 179 E 71st St NY, NY 10021

LAURENCE, KAREN *(212) 661-0850* 216 E 45th St NY, NY 10017

LAUTER, RICHARD *(212) 867-8092* 60 E 42nd St NY, NY 10165

LAZURE, CATHERINE *(212) 690-1867* 593 Riverside Dr NY; NY 10031

LE-TAN, PIERRE *(212) 925-3053* 81 Greene St NY, NY 10012

LEBBAD, JAMES A *(212) 645-5260* 1133 Broadway NY, NY 10010

LEDER, DORA *(212) 644-2020* 866 UN Plaza NY, NY 10017

LEHR, PAUL *(212) 355-0910* 50 E 50th St NY, NY 10022

LEMERISE, BRUCE *(212) 989-0749* 410 W 24th St NY, NY 10011

LEONARD, RICHARD *(212) 243-6613* 212 W 17th St NY, NY 10011

LEONARD, TOM *(212) 644-2020* 866 UN Plaza NY, NY 10017

LESH, DAVID *(212) 581-8338* 18 McKinley St Rowayton, CT 06853

PAGE 38-39

LESSER, ROBERT *(212) 228-1371* 412 E 11th St NY, NY 10009

LESSER, RON *(212) 697-8525* 420 Lexington Ave NY, NY 10170

LEVIN, ARNIE *(212) 719-9879* 342 Madison Ave NY, NY 10173

LEVINE, ANDY *(718) 956-8539* 30-85 36th St Long Islnd City, NY 11103

LEVINE, BETTE *(212) 682-1490* 60 E 42nd St NY, NY 10165

LEVINE, DAVID *(212) 529-1790* 67 Irving Pl NY, NY 10003

LEVINE, RENA *(718) 642-7339* 200 Bethel Loop Brooklyn, NY 11239

LEVINE, RON *(212) 787-7415* 1 W 85th St NY, NY 10024

LEVY, FRANCK *(212) 557-8256* 305 E 40th St NY, NY 10016

LEWIN, TED *(718) 622-3882* 152 Willoughby Ave Brooklyn, NY 11205

LEWIS, HOWARD B *(212) 243-3954* 246 W 22nd St NY, NY 10011

LEWIS, TIM *(718) 638-2413* 184 St John's Pl Brooklyn, NY 11217

LEXA, SUSAN *(212) 644-2020* 866 UN Plaza NBYC, NY 10017

LIAO, SHARMEN *(818) 458-7699* 914 Arroyo Terr Alhambra, CA 91801

LIBERATORE, GAETANO *(212) 254-4996* 43 E 19th St NY, NY 10003

LIEBERMAN, RON *(212) 947-0653* 109 W 28th St NY, NY 10001

LIEPKE, SKIP *(212) 755-1365* 211 E 51st St NY, NY 10022

PAGE 62-63

LILLY, CHARLES *(718) 803-3442* 24-01 89th St E Elmhurst, NY 11369

LINDBERG, JEFFREY *(718) 492-1114* 449 50th St Brooklyn, NY 11220

LINDGREN, GORAN *(212) 838-0050* 19 E 48th St NY, NY 10017

LINDLOF, ED *(212) 682-2462* 353 W 53rd St NY, NY 10019

LINE, LEMUEL *(212) 355-0910* 50 E 50th St NY, NY 10022

LIPPMAN, PETER *(212) 865-1823* 410 Riverside Dr NY, NY 10025

LIPSTEIN, MORISSA *(212) 838-0050* 19 E 48th St NY, NY 10017

LITTLE APPLE ART *(718) 499-7045* 409 Sixth Ave Brooklyn, NY 11215

LLOYD, PETER *(212) 206-0322* 18 E 16th St NY, NY 10003

LOCKWOOD, TODD *(212) 682-1490* 60 E 42nd St NY, NY 10016

LODIGENSKY, TED *(212) 206-0322* 18 E 16th St NY, NY 10003

LoGRIPPO, ROBERT *(212) 355-0910* 50 E 50th St NY, NY 10022

LORENZ, LEE *(212) 889-3337* 108 E 35th St NY, NY 10016

LOVITT, ANITA *(212) 628-8171* 308 E 78th St NY, NY 10021

LOW, WILLIAM *(718) 436-2039* 31 Ocean Pkwy Brooklyn, NY 11218

LUCE, BEN *(212) 255-8193* 5 E 17th St NY, NY 10003

LULEVITCH, TOM *(212) 362-3318* 101 W 69th St NY, NY 10023

LUSTIG, LORETTA *(212) 838-0050* 19 E 48th St NY, NY 10017

LYALL, DENNIS *(212) 986-5680* 420 Lexington Ave NY, NY 10170

LYNCH, JEFF *(212) 986-5680* 420 Lexington Ave NY, NY 10170

MACCOMBIE, TURI *(212) 532-0928* 201 E 28th St NY, NY 10016

MACK, STAN *755-4945 (212)* 226 E 53rd St NY, NY 10022

MADDEN, DON *644-2020 (212)* 866 U N Plaza NY, NY 10017

MAFFIA, DANIEL *(201) 871-0435* 44 N Dean St Englewood, 07631

MAGDICH, DENNIS *(212) 697-8525* 420 Lexington Ave NY, NY 10170

MAGNUSON, DIANA *(212) 696-4680* 461 Park Ave So NY, NY 10016

MAHON, RICH *(212) 206-0322* 18 E 16th St NY, NY 10003

MAHONEY, RON *(212) 682-2462* 353 W 53rd St NY, NY 10019

MAHURIN, MATT *(212) 529-5275* 77 Bleeker St NY, NY 10012

MAITZ, DON *(212) 355-0910* 50 E 50th St NY, NY 10022

MALAN, DEE *(212) 532-0928* 201 E 28th St NY, NY 10016

MALONIS, TINA *(718) 565-8209* 34-44 71st St Jackson Hts, 11372

MANGAL *697-6170 (212)* 155 E 38th St NY, NY 10016

MANGIAT, JEFFREY *(212) 986-5680* 420 Lexington Ave NY, NY 10170

MANOS, JIM *986-3282 (212)* 51 E 42nd St NY, NY 10017

MANTEL, RICHARD *(212) 929-5590* 41 Union Sq W NY, NY 10003

MANTEL, RICHARD *(212) 889-2254* 114 E 32nd St NY, NY 10016

MANYUM, WALLOP *(718) 476-1478* 37-40 60th St Woodside, 11377

MARCELLINO, FRED STUDIO *(212) 532-0150* 432 Park Ave So NY, NY 10016

MARCHETTI, LOU *(212) 986-5680* 420 Lexington Ave NY, NY 10170

MARCIULIANO, FRANK *(212) 697-8525* 420 Lexington Ave NY, NY 10170

MARDON, ALLAN *(212) 889-3337* 108 E 35th St NY, NY 10016

MARGULIES, ROBERT *(212) 219-9621* 561 Broadway NY, NY 10012

MARICH, FELIX *(212) 677-9100* 853 Broadway NY, NY 10003

MARINELLI, ROBERT *(718) 979-4018* 165 Bryant Ave Staten Island, NY 10306

MARRIDEJOS, FERNANDO *(212) 724-7339* 130 W 67th St NY, NY 10023

MARTIN, JOHN *(212) 490-2450* 501 Fifth Ave NY, NY 10017

PAGE 34

MARTINEZ, EDWARD *(212) 986-5680* 420 Lexington Ave NY, NY 10170

MARTINEZ, JOHN *(212) 775-1810* 280 Madison Ave NY, NY 10016

MARTINEZ, SERGIO *(212) 254-4996* 43 E 19th St NY, NY 10003

MARTINOT, CLAUDE *(212) 473-3137* 145 Second Ave NY, NY 10003

MARVIN, FRED *(212) 254-4996* 43 E 19th St NY, NY 10003

MASI, GEORGE *(212) 925-0491* 111 Wooster St NY, NY 10012

MASLEN, BARBARA *(212) 645-5325* 45 W 18th St NY, NY 10011

MASON, BRICK *(212) 777-4297* 349 E 14th St NY, NY 10003

MASON, TOD *(212) 838-0050* 19 E 48th St NY, NY 10017

MATHEWUSE, JAMES *(212) 247-1130* 157 W 57th St NY, NY 10019

MATHIEU, JOSEPH *(212) 925-3053* 81 Greene St NY, NY 10012

MATSUYOSHI, AKIO *(212) 683-5621* PO Box 1150 NY, NY 10276

MATTELSON, MARVIN *(212) 684-2974* 37 Cary Rd Great Neck, NY 11021

PAGE 49

MAXWELL, BROOKIE *(212) 475-6909* 53 Irving Pl NY, NY 10003

MAY, DARCY *(212) 532-0928* 201 E 28th St NY, NY 10016

MAZUR, RUBY (MR) *(212) 734-2950* 300 E 75th St NY, NY 10021

McARTHUR, DENNIS *(718) 559-0029* 170-44 130th Ave Jamaica, NY 11434

McCLINTOCK, WENDELL *953-7088* 60 E 42nd St NY, NY 10165

McCOLLUM, RICK *(212) 489-8777* 24 W 57th St NY, NY 10019

McConnell, Gerald *(212) 505-0950* 10 E 23rd St NY, NY 10010

McCormack, Geoffrey *(212) 986-5680* 420 Lexington Ave NY, NY 10170

McCreanor, Mike *2(212) 43-1333* 156 Fifth Ave NY, NY 10010

McCreary, Jane *(212) 644-2020* 866 UN Plaza NY, NY 10017

McDaniel, Jerry *(212) 697-6170* 155 E 38th St NY, NY 10016

McGinnis, Robert *637-5055* 13 Arcadia Rd Greenwich, 06870

McKeating, Eileen *(718) 638-0760* 862 Union St Brooklyn, 11215

McKenzie, Crystal *(212) 598-4567* 30 E 20th St NY, NY 10003

McKie, Roy *(212) 989-5186* 75 Perry NY, NY 10014

McLaughlin, Gary *(212) 697-8525* 420 Lexington Ave NY, NY 10170

McLean, Wilson *(212) 473-5554* 902 Broadway NY, NY 10010

PAGE 4-5

McMullan, James *(212) 473-5083* 222 Park Ave So NY, NY 10003

McNeel, Richard *(212) 674-8080* 215 Park Ave So NY, NY 10003

McPheeters, Neal *(212) 799-7021* 16 W 71st St NY, NY 10023

Mead, Kimble Pendleton

(718) 768-3632 125 Prospect Park West Brooklyn, NY 11215

Mehlman, Elwyn *(212) 889-3337* 108 E 35th St NY, NY 10016

Meisel, Ann *(212) 986-5680* 420 Lexington Ave NY, NY 10170

Meisel, Paul *(212) 226-5463* 90 Hudson St NY, NY 10013

Meisler, Meryl *(718) 499-9836* 553 8th St Brooklyn, NY 11215

Mele, Gary *(201) 308-0936* 32 Harbor Circle Freehold, NJ 07728

Melendez, Robert *(212) 206-0322* 18 E 16th St NY, NY 10003

Merrell, Patrick *(212) 620-7777* 48 W 20th St NY, NY 10011

Messi, Enzo & Schmidt, Urs

(212) 473-8747 145 E 22nd St NY, NY 10010

Meyerowitz, Rick *(212) 989-7074* 6 Jane St NY, NY 10014

PAGE 42

Michaels, Bob *(212) 685-6225* 304 E 49 St NY, NY 10017

Michal, Marie *(212) 889-3337* 108 E 35th St NY, NY 10016

Michner, Ted *(212) 986-5680* 420 Lexington Ave NY, NY 10170

Midda, Sara *(212) 925-3053* 81 Greene St NY, NY 10012

Mihaesco, Eugene *(212) 692-9271* 25 Tudor City Pl NY, NY 10017

Mikos, Mike *(212) 986-5680* 420 Lexington Ave NY, NY 10170

Milbourn, Patrick *(212) 989-4594* 327 W 22nd St NY, NY 10011

Milicic, Michael *(212) 927-2353* 570 Ft Washington Ave NY, NY 10033

Miller, Cliff *(212) 867-8092* 60 E 42nd St NY, NY 10165

Millington, Hunter *(212) 645-8688* 49 W 11th St NY, NY 10011

Milne, Jonathon *(212) 986-5680* 420 Lexington Ave NY, NY 10170

Minor, Wendell *(212) 691-6925* 277 W 4th St NY, NY 10014

PAGE 16

Miro *(212) 867-8092* 60 E 42nd St NY, NY 10165

Mitchell, Celia *(718) 626-4095* 30-25 Steinway St Astoria, NY 11103

Mitra, Annie *(212) 330-6444* 237 W 15th St NY, NY 10011

Mitsuhashi, Yoko *(212) 683-7312* 43 E 29th St NY, NY 10016

Miyamoto, Linda *(212) 596-4787* PO Box 2310 Brooklyn, NY 11202

Mones-Mateu *(212) 254-4996* 43 E 19th St NY, NY 10003

Montesano, Sam *(212) 867-8092* 60 E 42nd St NY, NY 10165

Montgomery, Marilyn *(212) 775-1810* 280 Madison Ave NY, NY 10016

Montiel, David *(212) 989-7426* 115 W 16th St NY, NY 10011

Moraes, Greg *(212) 867-8092* 60 E 42nd St NY, NY 10165

Morgan, Jacqui *(212) 463-8488* 692 Greenwich St NY, NY 10014

PAGE 44-45

Morgen, Barry *(212) 595-6835* 337 W 87th St NY, NY 10024

Morris, Frank *(212) 799-2231* 15 W 72nd St NY, NY 10023

Morrison, Don *(212) 697-6170* 155 E 38th St NY, NY 10016

Morse, Bill *(212) 682-1490* 60 E 42nd St NY, NY 10165

Moss, Geoffrey *(212) 472-9474* 315 E 68th St NY, NY 10021

Mossey, Belinda *(718) 499-2588* 526 2nd St Brooklyn, NY 11215

Mukai, Dennis *(212) 391-1830* 1500 Broadway NY, NY 10036

Mulcaby, Karen *(212) 714-2550* 130 Jane St NY, NY 10014

Murakami, Maho *(718) 446-3204* 34-21 61st St Woodside, NY 11377

Murawski, Alex *(212) 889-3337* 108 E 35th St NY, NY 10016

Murdocca, Sal *(212) 838-0050* 19 E 48th St NY, NY 10017

Myers, David L *(212) 989-5260* 228 Bleecker St NY, NY 10014

Myers, Lou *(914) 737-2307* 58 Lakeview Ave W Peekskill, NY 10566

n - o

Nagaoka, Shusei *(212) 799-2231* 15 W 72nd St NY, NY 10023

Nahigan, Alan *(718) 274-4042* 33-08 31st Ave Long Island City, NY 11106

Najaka, Marlies *(212) 580-0058* 241 Central Park W NY, NY 10024

Nascimbene, Yan *(212) 645-6772* 156 Fifth Ave NY, NY 10010

Nazz, James *(212) 228-9713* 159 Second St NY, NY 10003

Neff, Leland *(212) 724-1884* 506 Amsterdam Ave NY, NY 10024

Nelson, Bill *(212) 683-1362* 121 Madison Ave NY, NY 10016

Nemirov, Meredith *(718) 389-5972* 110 Kent St Brooklyn, NY 11222

Nessim, Barbara *(212) 677-8888* 63 Greene St NY, NY 10012

Neubecker, Robert *(212) 219-8435* 395 Broadway NY, NY 10013

PAGE 50

Neumann, Ann *(212) 431-7141* 444 Broome St NY, NY 10013

Newton, Richard *(212) 490-2450* 501 Fifth Ave NY, NY 10017

Neyman-Levikova, Marina *(212) 697-6170* 155 E 38th St NY, NY 10016

Ng, Michael *(718) 461-8264* 58-35 155th St Flushing, NY 11355

Nicastre, Michael *(212) 697-8525* 420 Lexington Ave NY, NY 10170

Nicholas, Jess *(212) 206-0322* 18 E 16th St NY, NY 10003

Nicklaus, Carol *(212) 644-2020* 866 UN Plaza NY, NY 10017

Nicotra, Rosanne *(212) 697-8525* 420 Lexington Ave NY, NY 10170

Nitzburg, Andrew *(212) 686-3514* 165 E 32nd St NY, NY 10016

Noftsinger, Pamela *(212) 316-4241* 600 W 111th St NY, NY 10025

Noonan, Julia *(718) 622-9268* 873 President St Brooklyn, NY 11215

North, Russ *(212) 242-6300* 40 W 20th St NY, NY 10011

Nosek, Laslo *(212) 362-7376* 440 West End Ave NY, NY 10024

Nosz Studio Inc *(212) 362-7376* 440 West End Ave NY, NY 10024

Notarile, Chris *(212) 986-5680* 420 Lexington Ave NY, NY 10170

Novak, Justin *(212) 243-1333* 156 Fifth Ave NY, NY 10010

O'Brien, Tim *(212) 953-7088* 60 E 42nd St NY, NY 10165

Oberheide, Heide
(718) 622-7056 295 Washington Ave Brooklyn, NY 11205

Ochagavia, Carlos *(212) 355-0910* 50 E 50th St NY, NY 10022

Odom, Mel *(212) 724-9320* 252 W 76th St NY, NY 10023

Oelbaum, Fran *(212) 391-1830* 1500 Broadway NY, NY 10036

Olanoff, Greg *(212) 867-8092* 60 E 42nd St NY, NY 10165

Olbinski, Rafal *(212) 242-6367* 470 W 23rd St NY, NY 10011

Olitsky, Eve *(212) 678-1045* 235 W 102nd St NY, NY 10025

Olson, Richard A *(212) 925-1820* 85 Grand St NY, NY 10013

Ortiz, Jose Luis *(212) 877-3081* PO Box 6678 NY, NY 10128

Osaka, Rick *(718) 956-0015* 14-22 30th Dr Long Island City, NY 11102

Osborn, Stephen *(212) 775-1810* 280 Madison Ave NY, NY 10016

Otnes, Fred *(203) 938-2829* 26 Chalburn Rd W Redding, CT 06896

p

Pace, Don *(718) 748-7651* 9303 Shore Rd Brooklyn, NY 11217

Palaez, Joan *(212) 254-4996* 43 E 19th St NY, NY 10003

Pantuso, Mike *(212) 534-3511* 350 E 89th St NY, NY 10128

Pappas, Joanne *(718) 788-7689* 401 20th St Brooklyn, NY 11215

Paragraphics *(718) 965-2231* 427 3rd St Brooklyn, NY 11215

Paraskevas, Mickey *(212) 929-5590* 41 Union Sq NY, NY 10003

Pardy, Cyndy *(212) 391-1830* 1500 Broadway NCY, NY 10036

Parker, Robert Andrew *(212) 925-3053* 81 Greene St NY, NY 10012

Parsons, John *(212) 697-8525* 420 Lexington Ave NY, NY 10170

Paslavsky, Evan
(212) 759-3985 510-7 Main St N Roosevelt Islnd, NY 10044

Passarelli, Charles *(212) 682-2462* 353 W 53rd St NY, NY 10019

Pasternak, Robert *(212) 675-0002* 114 W 27th St NY, NY 10001

Paul, Tony *(212) 307-6188* 467 W 57th St NY, NY 10019

Payne, C F *(212) 683-1362* 121 Madison Ave NY, NY 10016

Peak, Matt *(212) 867-8092* 60 E 42nd St NY, NY 10165

Peak, Robert *(212) 752-8490* 50 E 50th St NY, NY 10022

Pearson, Jim *(212) 644-2020* 866 UN Plaza NY, NY 10017

Pechanel, Vladimir
(718) 729-3973 34-43 Crescent St Long Island City, NY 11106

Pedersen, Judy *(212) 226-3675* 96 Greene St NY, NY 10012
page 48

Peele, Lynwood *(212) 799-3305* 344 W 88th St NY, NY 10024

Pelavin, Daniel *(212) 929-2706* 46 Commerce St NY, NY 10014

Pelikan, Judy *(212) 570-9069* 200 E 78th St NY, NY 10021

Penberthy, Mark *(212) 219-2664* 47 Greene St NY, NY 10013

Pendleton, Roy *(212) 674-8080* 215 Park Ave So NY, NY 10003

Percivalle, Rosanne *(212) 243-6589* 430 W 14th St NY, NY 10014

Perez, Maria *(212) 807-8730* 119 W 23rd St NY, NY 10011

Perez, Vince *(212) 254-4996* 43 E 19th St NY, NY 10003

Perini, Benny *(718) 622-4578* 932 President St Brooklyn, NY 11215

Personality Inc *(212) 490-2450* 501 Fifth Ave NY, NY 10017

Peters, Bob *(212) 889-3337* 108 E 35th St NY, NY 10016

Peterson, Cheryl *(212) 925-3053* 81 Greene St NY, NY 10012

Peterson, Robin *(212) 724-3479* 411 West End Ave NY, NY 10024

Petragnani, Vincent *(212) 677-9100* 853 Broadway NY, NY 10003

Petruccio, Steven *(212) 532-0928* 201 E 28th St NY, NY 10016

Pettingill, Ondre *(212) 942-1993* 2 Ellwood St NY, NY 10040

Phillips, Barry *(212) 489-8777* 24 W 57th St NY, NY 10019

Pierson, Mary Louise *(212) 315-3516* 310 W 56th St NY, NY 10019

Pietrobono, Janet *(212) 245-7300* 147 Sterling Pl Brooklyn, NY 11217

Piglia, Paola *(212) 941-1305* 28 Cliff St NY, NY 10003

Pincus, Harry *(212) 925-8071* 160 Sixth Ave NY, NY 10012

Pinkney, Debbie *(212) 775-1810* 280 Madison Ave NY, NY 10016

Pinkney, Jerry *(212) 889-3337* 108 E 35th St NY, NY 10016

Pinturov *(212) 799-2231* 15 W 72nd St NY, NY 10023

Pisano, Al *(212) 213-3204* 22 W 38th St NY, NY 10016

Piscopia, Joe *(718) 384-2206* 114 Beadel St Brooklyn, NY 11222

Podevin, Jean-Francois *(212) 964-4244* NY, NY
page 56

Podwill, Jerry *(212) 255-9464* 108 W 14th St NY, NY 10011

Pogue, Deborah Bazzel *(212) 243-4412* 48 W 21st St NY, NY 10010

Poladian, Girair *(212) 529-7878* 42 E 23rd St NY, NY 10010

Polenghi, Evan *(718) 499-3214* 159 25th St Brooklyn, NY 11232

Pollack, Scott *(212) 517-3599* 333 E 66th St NY, NY 10021

Popp, Wendy *(212) 807-0840* 95 Horatio St NY, NY 10014

Porter, Frederick *(212) 243-1333* 156 Fifth Ave NY, NY 10010

Powell, Ivan *(212) 741-2539* 58 W 15th St NY, NY 10011

Powers, Christine *(203) 966-1417* 198 Berkeley Pl Brooklyn, NY 11217

Powers, Tom *(212) 243-1333* 156 Fifth Ave NY, NY 10010

Prato, Rodica *(212) 683-1362* 154 W 57th St NY, NY 10019

Punchatz, Don Ivan *(212) 989-7074* 6 Jane St NY, NY 10014

Purdom, Bill *(212) 988-4566* 780 Madison Ave NY, NY 10021

Pyk, Jan *(212) 838-0050* 19 E 48th St NY, NY 10017

q - r

Quartuccio, Dom *(212) 661-1173* 5 Tudor City Pl NY, NY 10017

Quon, Mike Design Office *(212) 226-6024* 568 Broadway NY, NY 10012

Racz, Michael *(718) 956-0980* 18-36 26th Rd Astoria, NY 11102

Radigan, Bob *(212) 775-1810* 280 Madison Ave NY, NY 10016

Ragland, Greg *(212) 513-7218* 258 Broadway NY, NY 10007

PAGE 51

Raglin, Tim *(212) 873-0538* 138 W 74th St NY, NY 10023

Rainbow Grinder *(212) 775-1810* 55 Hudson St NY, NY 10013

Rane, Walter *(212) 867-8092* 60 E 42nd St NY, NY 10165

Rea, John *(212) 546-1384* 300 W 23rd St NY, NY 10011

Realo, Perry A *(212) 254-5635* 155 E 2nd St NY, NY 10009

Reay, Richard *(212) 884-2317* 515 W 236th St Bronx, NY 10463

Reddin, Paul *(718) 965-0647* 120 Windsor Pl Brooklyn, NY 11215

Reed, Chris *(212) 677-7198* 14 E 4th St NY, NY 10012

Reed, Herb *(212) 243-1333* 156 Fifth Ave NY, NY 10010

Reid, Charles *(203) 255-1917* 81 Clapboard Hill Rd Greens Farms, CT 06436

Reim, Melanie *(212) 749-0177* 214 Riverside Dr NY, NY 10025

Reinert, Kirk *(212) 867-8092* 60 E 42nd St NY, NY 10165

Reingold, Alan *(212) 697-6170* 155 E 38th St NCY, NY 10016

Reingold, Michael

(718) 981-1999 121 Heberton Ave Staten Island, NY 10302

Renfro, Ed *(212) 879-3823* 250 E 83rd St NY, NY 10028

Reott, Paul *(718) 426-1928* 51-10 Van Horn St Elmhurst, NY 11373

Reynolds, Scott *(212) 239-0009* 308 W 30th St NCY, NY 10001

Rice, John *(212) 243-1333* 156 Fifth Ave NY, NY 10010

Rich, Anna M *(718) 604-0121* 777 St Marks Ave Brooklyn, NY 11213

Rich, Norman *(212) 733-5140* 2557 Marion Ave Bronx, NY 10458

Richards, Linda *(212) 673-1600* 27 Bleecker St NY, NY 10012

Ridgeway, Ron *(212) 714-0130* 330 W 42nd St NY, NY 10036

Rigie, Mitch *(212) 807-6627* 41 Union Sq W NY, NY 10003

Rigo, Martin *(212) 254-4996* 43 E 19th St NY, NY 10003

Risko, Robert *(212) 989-6987* 201 W 11th St NY, NY 10014

Rixford, Ellen *(212) 697-6170* 155 E 38th St NY, NY 10016

Roberts, Phil *(212) 986-5680* 420 Lexington Ave NY, NY 10170

Robinson, Charles *(212) 644-2020* 866 UN Plaza NY, NY 10017

Robinson, Lenor *(212) 734-0944* 201 E 69th St NCY, NY 10021

Rodriguez, Robert *(212) 490-2450* 501 Fifth Ave NY, NY 10017

Rogers, Lilla *(718) 624-6862* 483 Henry St Brooklyn, NY 11231

Roman, Barbara *(212) 362-1374* 345 W 88th St NY, NY 10024

Romer, Dan *(718) 768-3632* 125 Prospect Park W Brooklyn, NY 11215

Romero, Javier *(212) 206-9175* 529 W 42nd St NY, NY 10036

Root, Barry *(212) 741-2589* 58 W 15th St NY, NY 10001

Roper, Bob *(718) 898-8591* 43-17 55th St Woodside, NY 11377

Rosen, Terry *(212) 580-4784* 101 W 81st St NY, NY 10024

Rosenblum, Richard *(212) 279-2068* 392 Fifth Ave NY, NY 10018

Rosenfeld, Mort *(212) 986-5680* 420 Lexington Ave NY, NY 10170

Rosenthal, Doug *(212) 475-9422* 24 Fifth Ave NY, NY 10011

Rosenthal, Marc *(518) 766-4191* 230 Clinton St Brooklyn, NY 11201

Rosenzweiz, Myra *(212) 362-9871* 310 W 90th St NY, NY 10024

Rosner, Meryl *(212) 254-7668* 21 Grammercy Pk NY, NY 10003

Ross Culbert Holland & Lavery

(212) 206-0044 15 W 20th St NY, NY 10011

Ross, Barry *(212) 663-7386* 211 W 102nd St NY, NY 10025

Ross, Bronwen *(212) 644-2020* 866 UN Plaza NY, NY 10017

Ross, Ian *(212) 685-4178* 106 Lexington Ave NY, NY 10016

Ross, Richard *(212) 675-8800* 204 W 20th St NY, NY 10011

Rothman, Mike *(212) 362-3302* 21 W 74th St NY, NY 10023

Roy, Frederick *(212) 255-0775* 205 W 14th St NY, NY 10011

Ruddell, Gary *(212) 206-0322* 18 E 16th St NY, NY 10003

Rudenjack, Phyllis *(212) 772-2813* 245 E 72nd St NY, NY 10021

Ruff, Donna *(212) 627-9858* 595 West End Ave NY, NY 10024

Ruffins, Reynold *(212) 627-5220* 15 W 20th St NY, NY 10011

Ruiz, Artie *(212) 254-4996* 43 E 19th St NY, NY 10003

Runda, Ron *(212) 867-8092* 60 E 42nd St NY, NY 10165

Russell, Billy D *(212) 873-7975* 483 Columbus Ave NY, NY 10024

Russell, Melissa *(212) 502-3976* 350 E 89th St NY, NY 10128

Rutherford, Stephen *(718) 857-5253* 69 Fifth Ave Brooklyn, NY 11217

Ryan, Terry *(212) 688-1080* 330 W 4th St NY, NY 10014

S

Sabanosh, Michael *(212) 947-8161* 433 W 34th St NY, NY 10001

Sabin, Robert *(212) 867-8092* 60 E 42nd St NY, NY 10165

Saffioti, Lino *(718) 224-3170* 61-15 218th St Bayside, NY 11364

Saksa Art & Design *(212) 255-5539* 41 Union Sq W NY, NY 10003

Saldutti, Denise *(212) 255-9328* 463 West St NY, NY 10014

Salina, Joe *(212) 682-1490* 60 E 42nd St NY, NY 10165

Samuels, Mark *(212) 777-8580* 25 Minetta Ln NY, NY 10014

Sanders, Jane *(718) 786-3505* 47-51 40th St Sunnyside, NY 11104

Sanjulian *(212) 688-1080* 43 E 19th St NY, NY 10014

Santoro, Christopher *(212) 532-0928* 201 E 28th St NY, NY 10016

Sargent, Claudia K *(718) 461-8280* 15-38 126th St Queens, NY 11356

Saris, Anthony *(212) 831-6353* 103 E 86th St NY, NY 10028

Sauber, Rob *(212) 986-5680* 420 Lexington NY, NY 10170

Sauriel, Brian *(212) 986-5680* 420 Lexington Ave NY, NY 10170

Sawka, Jan *(212) 682-2462* 353 W 53rd St NY, NY 10019

Saxon, Charles *(203) 227-7806* 158 Hills Point Rd Westport, CT 06880

Schaare, Harry *(212) 867-8092* 60 E 42nd St NY, NY 10165

Schaedler, Sally *(212) 243-1333* 156 Fifth Ave NY, NY 10010

Schaer, Miriam *(212) 673-4926* 522 E 5th St NY, NY 10009

Schaller, Tom *(212) 362-5524* 2255 Broadway NY, NY 10024

Schanzer, Roz *(212) 696-4680* 461 Park Ave So NY, NY 10016

Scheld, Betsy *(212) 260-0062* 429 E 65th St NY, NY 10021

Scheuer, Phil *(212) 620-0728* 126 Fifth Ave NY, NY 10011

Schmidt, Bill *(212) 867-8092* 60 E 42nd St NY, NY 10165

Schmidt, Chuck *(212) 677-9100* 853 Broadway NY, NY 10003

Schneegass, Martinu *(212) 860-6643* 35 Carmine St NY, NY 10014

Schongut, Emanuel *(212) 929-5590* 41 Union Sq NY, NY 10003

Schottland, Miriam *(212) 242-6367* 470 W 23rd St NY, NY 10011

Schreiber, Dana *(718) 638-3505* 89 James Pl Brooklyn, NY 11238

Schreier, Joshua *(212) 925-0472* 466 Washington St NY, NY 10013

Schumacher, Michael *(212) 682-2462* 353 W 53rd St NY, NY 10019

Schumacher, Ward *(212) 475-0440* 194 Third Ave NY, NY 10003

page 29

Schumer, Arlen *(212) 254-8242* 313 E Sixth St NY, NY 10003

Schwab, Michael *(212) 490-2450* 501 Fifth Ave NY, NY 10017

page 33

Schwartz, Daniel *(212) 533-0237* 48 E 13th St NY, NY 10003

Schwartz, Joanie *(212) 213-1282* 22 E 36th St NY, NY 10016

Schwarz, Jill Karla *(212) 227-2444* 80 N Moore St NY, NY 10013

Scott, Bob *(212) 684-2409* 106 Lexington Ave NY, NY 10016

Scott, Robert *(301) 535-3741* 250 W 16th St St NY, NY 10011

Scrofani, Joe *(212) 682-2462* 353 W 53rd St NY, NY 10019

Seaver, Jeffrey *(212) 741-2279* 130 W 24th St NY, NY 10011

Segal, John *(212) 662-3278* 324 W 101st St NY, NY 10025

Seltzer, Isadore *(212) 741-2539* 58 W 15th St NY, NY 10011

page 22-23

Sempe, J J *(212) 925-3053* 81 Greene St NY, NY 10012

Sentnor, Robert *(212) 884-7048* 3871 Sedgwick Ave Bronx, NY 10463

Shafer, Ginger *(212) 989-7697* 113 Washington Pl NY, NY 10014

Shahinian, Brenda *(212) 925-3053* 81 Greene St NY, NY 10012

Shannon, David *(212) 529-5319* 81 Second Ave NY, NY 10003

Shap, Sandra *(212) 677-9100* 853 Broadway NY, NY 10003

Sharpe, JIm *(203) 226-9984* 21 Ten O'Clock Lane Weston, NY 16883

Shea, Mary Anne *(212) 929-7964* 154 Eighth Ave NY, NY 10011

Shega, Marla *(212) 682-1490* 60 E 42nd St NY, NY 10165

Shenefield, Barbara *(212) 254-1946* 223 Sullivan St NY, NY 10012

Sherman, Mary *(212) 686-3514* 165 E 32nd St NY, NY 10016

Sherman, Maurice *(212) 679-7350* 209 E 23rd St NY, NY 10010

Shields, Charles *(212) 755-4945* 226 E 53rd St NY, NY 10022

Shohet, Marti *(212) 627-1299* 26 W 17th St NY, NY 10011

Shub, Steve *(212) 243-4412* 48 W 21st St NY, NY 10010

Siciliano, Gerald *(718) 636-4561* 261 Fourth Ave Brooklyn, NY 11215

Siegel, Norm *(212) 980-8061* 333 E 49th St NY, NY 10017

Silverman, Burton *(212) 799-3399* 324 W 71st St NY, NY 10023

page 17

Singer, Alan D *(718) 797-4083* 70 Prospect Park W Brooklyn, NY 11215

Singer, Paul Design *(718) 499-8172* 494 14th St Brooklyn, NY 11215

Skardinski, Stan *(212) 532-0928* 201 E 28th St NY, NY 10016

Sketch Pad Studio, The *(212) 989-7074* 6 Jane St NY, NY 10014

Skolsky, Mark *(212) 799-2231* 15 W 72nd St NY, NY 10023

Skopp, Jeniffer *(718) 789-2983* 1625 Emmons Ave Brooklyn, NY 11235

Slack, Chuck *(212) 682-1490* 60 E 42nd St NY, NY 10165

Slackman, Charles B *(212) 758-8233* 320 E 57th St NY, NY 10022

Slavin, Fran *(718) 403-9643* 452 Myrtle Ave Brooklyn, NY 11205

Sloan, William *(212) 463-7025* 236 W 26th St NY, NY 10001

Slvavec, Diane *(212) 867-8092* 60 E 42nd St NY, NY 10165

Smalley, Guy *(212) 683-0339* 183 Madison Ave NY, NY 10016

Smith, Brett *(212) 682-2462* 353 W 53rd St NY, NY 10019

Smith, Doug *(212) 683-1362* 121 Madison Ave NY, NY 10016

Smith, Elwood H.

***(914) 876-2358* 2 Locust Grove Rd Rhinebeck, NY 12572**

page 57

Smith, Gary *(212) 243-4412* 48 W 21st St NY, NY 10010

Smith, Joseph *(212) 825-1475* 159 John St NY, NY 10038

Smith, Laura *(212) 206-9162* 12 E 14th St NY, NY 10003

Smith, Mary Anne *(212) 420-0204* 44 E 1st St NY, NY 10003

Smith, Trudi *(212) 644-2020* 866 UN Plaza NY, NY 10017

Smith, Vicki *(212) 475-1671* 504 E 5th St NY, NY 10009

Smollin, Mike *(212) 986-5680* 420 Lexington Ave NY, NY 10170

Smythe, Danny *(212) 677-9100* 853 Broadway NY, NY 10003

Sneberger, Dan *(212) 867-8092* 60 E 42nd St NY, NY 10165

Sobel, Phillip Eric *(718) 476-3841* 80-15 41st Ave Elmhurst, NY 11373

Soderlind, Kirsten *(212) 925-0491* 111 Wooster St NY, NY 10012

Solie, John *(212) 986-5680* 420 Lexington Ave NY, NY 10170

Solomon, Debra *(212) 662-5619* 536 W 111th St NY, NY 10025

Soloski, Tommy *(212) 787-7142* 49 W 85th St NY, NY 10024

Solowedel, Kip *(212) 986-5680* 420 Lexington Ave NY, NY 10170

Sorel, Ed *(212) 966-3949* 156 Franklin St NY, NY 10013

Sottung, George *(212) 986-5680* 420 Lexington Ave NY, NY 10170

Spacak, Peter *(212) 505-6802* 611 Broadway NY, NY 10012

Spalenka, Greg *(212) 741-9064* 165 Perry St NY, NY 10014

Sparks, Richard *(203) 866-2002* 2 West Rocks Rd Norwalk , CT 06851

Spector, Joel *(212) 254-3527* 130 E 16th St NY, NY 10003

Spollen, Chris *(718) 979-9695* 362 Cromwell Ave Staten Island, NY 10305

Sposato, John *(212) 477-3909* 43 E 22nd St NY, NY 10010

Stabin, Victor *(212) 243-7688* 100 W 15th St NY, NY 10011

Stahl, Nancy *(212) 475-0440* 194 Third Ave NY, NY 10003

Page 28

Stallard, Peter *(212) 682-1490* 60 E 42nd St NY, NY 10165

Staples, Matthew *(212) 279-7935* 141 W 36th St NY, NY 10018

Starace, Tom *(212) 228-8674* 2 Stuyvesant Oval NY, NY 10009

Stavrinos, George *(212) 724-1557* 76 W 86th St NY, NY 10024

Page 55

Steadman, Barbara *(212) 684-6326* 330 E 33rd St NY, NY 10016

Steadman, E T *(212) 242-6367* 470 W 23rd St NY, NY 10011

Steiner, Frank *(212) 867-8092* 60 E 42nd St NY, NY 10165

Stephens, Lynn *(212) 787-6195* 52 W 87th St NY, NY 10024

Sternglass, Arno *(212) 675-5667* 622 Greenwich St NY, NY 10014

Sterrett, Jane *(212) 929-2566* 160 Fifth Ave NY, NY 10010

Stewart, Arvis *(212) 644-2020* 866 UN Plaza NY, NY 10017

Stewart, Pat *(212) 352-0928* 201 E 28th St NCY, NY 10016

Stillerman, Robbie *(212) 661-7149* 230 E 44th St NY, NY 10017

Stillman, Susan *(212) 724-5634* 126 W 71st St NY, NY 10023

Stone, Gilbert *(212) 741-2539* 58 W 15th St NY, NY 10011

Strachan, Bruce *(718) 383-1264* 999 Lorimer St Brooklyn, NY 11222

Streeter, Sabina *(212) 254-7436* 141 Wooster St NY, NY 10012

Suares, J C *(212) 682-1490* 60 E 42nd St NY, NY 10165

Suh, John *(212) 953-7088* 60 E 42nd St NY, NY 10165

Sullivan, Suzanne Hughes

(212) 496-0162 225 Central Pk W NY, NY 10024

Sutter, David *(516) 267-8507* Box 1538 Amagansett, NY 11930

Sweeney, Jerry *(412) 391-4471* 339 Blvd of Allies Pittsburg, PA 15222

Sweny, Stephen *(212) 532-4072* 217 E 29th St NY, NY 10016

Szabo, Gustav *(212) 362-7376* 440 West End Ave NY, NY 10024

Szilagyi, Mary *(212) 666-7578* 410 Central Park W NY, NY 10025

Szpura, Beata *(718) 424-8440* 48-02 69th St Woodside, NY 11377

Szumowski, Tom *(212) 682-1490* 60 E 42nd St NY, NY 10165

Szygiel, Jas *(212) 686-3514* 165 E 32nd St NY, NY 10016

t - u

Taba, Eugene *(212) 730-0101* 1185 Sixth Ave NY, NY 10036

Taback, Simms *(212) 627-5220* 15 W 20th St NY, NY 10011

Taleporos, Plato *(212) 689-3138* 333 E 23rd St NY, NY 10010

Tankersley, Paul *(212) 924-0015* 29 Bethune St NY, NY 10014

Tauss, Herbert *(914) 424-3765* So. Mtn. Pass Garrison, NY 10524

Tauss, Marc *(212) 410-2827* 484 W 43rd St NY, NY 10036

Taylor, Doug *(212) 674-6346* 106 Lexington Ave NY, NY 10016

Taylor, Katrina *(212) 661-0850* 216 E 45th St NY, NY 10017

Tedesco, Michael *(718) 596-4179* 120 Boerum Pl Brooklyn, NY 11201

Terreson, Jeffrey *(212) 986-5680* 420 Lexington Ave NY, NY 10170

Theakston, Greg *(212) 799-2231* 15 W 72nd St NY, NY 10023

Thompson, Bill *(212) 206-0322* 18 E 16th St NY, NY 10003

Thompson, John *(212) 989-7074* 6 Jane St NY, NY 10014

Page 43

Thompson, Thierry *(212) 986-5680* 420 Lexington Ave NY, NY 10170

Thonnessen, Sabina *(212) 254-7436* 141 Wooster St NY, NY 10012

Thorpe, Peter *(212) 477-0131* 254 Park Ave So NY, NY 10010

Tiani, Alex *(212) 391-1830* 1500 Broadway NY, NY 10036

Page 46

Tierney, Tom *(212) 532-0928* 201 E 28th St NY, NY 10016

Tinkelman, Murray

(914) 737-5960 75 Lakeview Ave W Peekskill, NY 10566

Tod-Kat Studios *(212) 682-2462* 353 W 53rd St NY, NY 10019

Torpedo Studios *(212) 502-3976* 350 E 89th St NY, NY 10128

Travers, Robert *(212) 867-8092* 60 E 42nd St NY, NY 10165

Trondsen, Bob *(212) 867-8092* 60 E 42nd St NY, NY 10165

Trossman, Michael *(212) 799-6852* 411 West End Ave NY, NY 10024

Trull, John *(212) 535-5383* 1573 York Ave NY, NY 10028

Tsugami, Kyuzo *(212) 243-1333* 156 Fifth Ave NY, NY 10010

Tunstull, Glenn *(718) 834-8529* 47 State St Brooklyn, NY 11201

Turk, Steve *(818) 705-0660* 4120 Cold Stream Terrace Tarzana, CA 91356

Tuttle, Jean *(212) 967-6442* 227 W 29th St NY, NY 10001

Uram, Lauren *(718) 789-7717* 251 Washington Ave Brooklyn, NY 11205

V - W

Vaccaro, Lou *(212) 644-2020* 866 UN Plaza NY, NY 10017

Vahid *(212) 206-0322* 18 E 16th St NY, NY 10003

Vainisi, Jenny *(212) 477-3086* 225 E 10th St NY, NY 10003

Valla, Victor *(212) 867-8092* 60 E 42nd St NY, NY 10165

Varlet-Martinelli *(212) 391-1830* 1500 Broadway NY, NY 10036

Vaux, Jacquie Marie *(212) 686-3514* 165 E 32nd St NY, NY 10016

Vecchio, Carmine *(212) 683-2679* 200 E 27th St NY, NY 10016

Velasquez, Eric *(212) 866-2209* 226 W 113th St NY, NY 10026

Ventura, Dana *(212) 244-4270* 134 W 32nd St NY, NY 10001

Victor, Joan B *(212) 988-2773* 863 Park Ave NY, NY 10021

Villa, Roxanne *(718) 797-0348* 31 Strong Pl Brooklyn, NY 11231

Viskupic, Gary *(212) 684-2974*

Vitsky, Sally *(212) 489-8777* 24 W 57th St NY, NY 10019

Viviano, Sam *(212) 242-1471* 25 W 13th St NY, NY 10011

Vogt, Elaine *(212) 988-6430* 242 E 83rd St NY, NY 10028

Vollath, Gunther *(212) 243-1333* 156 Fifth Ave NY, NY 10010

Vosk, Alex *(212) 737-2314* 521 E 82nd St NY, NY 10028

Voth, Gregory *(212) 807-9766* 231 W 20th St NY, NY 10011

Wajdowicz, Jurek *(212) 807-8144* 1123 Broadway NY, NY 10010

Wald, Carol *(212) 288-8010* 15 E 76th St NY, NY 10021

Waldman, Michael *(212) 239-8245* 506 W 42nd St NY, NY 10036

Walker, Jeff *(212) 867-8092* 60 E 42nd St NY, NY 10165

Walker, John S *(212) 242-3435* 47 Jane St NY, NY 10014

Wall, Pam/Airstream *(212) 682-1490* 60 E 42nd St NY, NY 10165

Waller, Charles *(212) 989-5843* 35 Bethune St NY, NY 10014

Wallner, Alexandra & John
(212) 644-2020 866 UN Plaza NY, NY 10017

Walsh, Terry *(212) 243-4412* 48 W 21st St NY, NY 10010

Wanamaker, Jo Ann *(212) 724-1786* 225 W 86th St NY, NY 10024

Ward, Donna *(212) 838-0050* 19 E 48th St NY, NY 10017

Warhola, James
(718) 937-6467 23-11 40th Ave Long Island City, NY 11101

Wasserman, Randi *(212) 254-0468* 28 W 11th St NY, NY 10011

Wasson, Cameron *(718) 875-8277* 4 S Portland Ave Brooklyn, NY 11217

Weaver, Robert *(212) 254-4289* 42 E 12th St NY, NY 10003

Weiman, Jon *(212) 787-3184* 147 W 85th St NY, NY 10024

Weinstein, Morey *(212) 260-6702* 35 E 20th St NY, NY 10003

Weisbecker, Philippe *(212) 966-6051* 476 Broadway NY, NY 10013

Weisser, Carl *(718) 834-0952* 38 Livingston St Brooklyn, NY 11201

Weissman, Sam *(212) 840-3300* 2510 Fenton Ave Bronx, NY 10469

Welker, Gaylord *(212) 673-1600* 27 Bleecker St NY, NY 10012

Wells, Skip *(212) 242-5563* 244 W 10th St NY, NY 10014

White, Charles III *(212) 929-5990* 41 Union Sq W NY, NY 10003

White, Richard A
(718) 783-3244 250 Washington Ave Brooklyn, NY 11205

Whitehead, Samuel B
(718) 965-2047 206 Eighth Ave Brooklyn, NY 11215

Whitehouse, Debora *(212) 840-8223* 1457 Broadway NY, NY 10036

Whitesides, Kim *(212) 490-2450* 501 Fifth Ave NY, NY 10017

Wiemann, Roy *(212) 431-3793* POB 271/Prince St Sta NY, NY 10012

Wilcox, David *(212) 421-0050* 135 E 54th St NY, NY 10022
PAGE 14

Wilkinson, Bill *(212) 697-6170* 155 E 38th St NY, NY 10016

Wilkinson, Chuck *(212) 989-7074* 6 Jane St NY, NY 10014
PAGE 67

Willardson + Assoc *(212) 475-0440* 194 Third Ave NY, NY 10003

Williams, Elizabeth *(212) 517-4593* 349 E 82nd St NY, NY 10028

Williams, Oliver *(212) 674-1903* 141 Fifth Ave NY, NY 10010

Williams, Richard *(212) 741-2539* 58 W 15th St NY, NY 10011

Wilshire, Mary *(212) 463-8980* 217 E 85th St NY, NY 10028

Wilson, Amanda *(212) 260-7567* 346 E 20th St NCY, NY 10003

Wilson, Deborah C *(212) 532-5205* 339 E 33rd St NY, NY 10016

Wilson, Gahan *(203) 227-7806* 158 Hills Point Rd Westport, CT 06880

Wilson, Harvey *(718) 857-8525* 316 Clinton Ave Brooklyn, NY 11205

Wind, Bodhi *(212) 254-4996* 43 E 19th St NY, NY 10003

Winkowski, Fred *(212) 724-3136* 48 W 71st St NY, NY 10023

Winterrowd, Turk *(212) 966-0031* 62 E Broadway NY, NY 10002

Winters, Nina *(212) 877-3089* 20 W 77th St NY, NY 10024

Wohlberg, Ben *(212) 254-9663* 43 Great Jones St NY, NY 10012

WOLFE, BRUCE ***(212) 475-0440*** **194 Third Ave NY, NY 10003**

PAGE 26-27

WOLFF, PUNZ *(212) 254-5705* 151 E 20th St NY, NY 10003

WOLFGANG, SHERRI *(212) 254-8242* 313 E 6th St NY, NY 10003

WOLLMAN, PAUL *(212) 682-1490* 60 E 42nd St NY, NY 10165

WOMERSLEY, DAVID *(212) 986-5680* 420 Lexington Ave NY, NY 10170

WOOD, CLARE *(718) 783-3734* 54 Berkeley Pl Brooklyn, NY 11217

WOOD, PAGE *(212) 243-4412* 48 W 21st St NY, NY 10010

WOODEND, JAMES *(212) 697-8525* 420 Lexington Ave NY, NY 10170

WOODMAN, JOWILL *(212) 765-8406* 334 W 49th St NY, NY 10019

WRAY, WENDY *(212) 475-0440* 194 Third Ave NY, NY 10003

WYATT, KATHY *(212) 254-4996* 43 E 19th St NY, NY 10003

WYNNE, PATRICIA *(212) 865-1059* 446 Central Pk W NY, NY 10025

y - z

YALOWITZ, PAUL ***(212) 532-0859*** **215 E 26th St NY, NY 10010**

PAGE 59

YANKUS, MARC *(212) 242-2860* 1133 Broadway NY, NY 10010

YEE, JOSIE *(212) 925-0491* 111 Wooster St NY, NY 10012

YELDHAM, RAY *(212) 986-5680* 420 Lexington Ave NY, NY 10170

YEMI *(212) 627-1269* 77 W 15th St NY, NY 10011

YIANNIAS, VICKI *(212) 391-1830* 1500 Broadway NY, NY 10036

YIP, JENNIE *(718) 236-0349* 6103 Twentieth Ave Brooklyn, NY 11204

YORK, JUDY *(212) 686-3514* 165 E 32nd St NY, NY 10016

YORKE, OLIVER *(718) 965-0609* 525-A Sixth Ave Brooklyn, NY 11215

YOUNG, LISA *(212) 864-5673* 545 W 111th St NY, NY 10025

YULE, SUSAN HUNT *(212) 226-0439* 176 Elizabeth St NY, NY 10012

ZACHAROW, M CHRISTOPHER

(212) 460-5739 109 Waverly Pl NY, NY 10011

ZAGORSKI, STANISLAW *(212) 532-2348* 142 E 35th St NY, NY 10016

ZAID, BARRY *(212) 889-3337* 108 E 35th St NY, NY 10016

ZAMCHICK, GARY *(212) 213-5096* 137 E 25th St NY, NY 10010

ZANN, NICKY *(212) 724-5027* 155 W 68th St NY, NY 10023

ZELDICH, ARIEH *(212) 644-2020* 866 UN Plaza NY, NY 10017

ZICK, BRIAN *(212) 475-0440* 194 Third Ave NY, NY 10003

ZIERING, BOB *(212) 873-0034* 151 W 74th St NY, NY 10023

ZIMIC, TRICIA *(212) 598-4228* 341 E 6th St NY, NY 10003

ZIMMERMAN, JERRY *(212) 620-7777* 48 W 20th St NY, NY 10011

ZIMMERMAN, ROBERT *(212) 477-0131* 254 Park Ave So NY, NY 10010

ZUDECK, MICHAEL *(212) 929-5590* 41 Union Sq NY, NY 10003

ZWARENSTEIN, ALEX *(212) 799-2231* 15 W 72nd St NY, NY 10023

ILLUSTRATION REPRESENTATIVES

a - f

AMERICAN ARTISTS *(212) 682-2462* 353 W 53rd St NY, NY 10019

ANTON, JERRY *(212) 679-4562* 107 E 38th St NY, NY 10016

ART FARM, THE *(212) 688-4555* 420 Lexington Ave NY, NY 10017

ARTCO/GAIL THURM *(212) 889-8777* 24 W 57th St NY, NY 10019

ARTISTS ASSOCIATES ***(212) 755-1365*** **211 E 51st St NY, NY 10022**

PAGE 60-66

ARTON ASSOCIATES *(212) 661-0850* 216 E 45th St NY, NY 10017

ASCIUTTO ART REPS *(212) 838-0050* 19 E 48th St NY, NY 10017

AZZARA, LOUISE *(212) 674-8114* 131 E 17th St NY, NY 10003

BADIN, ANDY *(212) 532-1222* 1538 W 38th St NY, NY 10018

BAHM, DARWIN ***(212) 989-7074*** **6 Jane St NY, NY 10014**

PAGE 40-43; 67

BAKER, SALLY *(212) 825-9405* 105 Broad St NY, NY 10004

BAKER, VALERIE *(212) 807-9754* 152 W 25th St NY, NY 10001

BARRACCA, SAL ASSOCIATES

(212) 889-2400 **381 Park Ave So NY, NY 10016**

PAGE 32

BERNSTEIN & ANDRIULLI *(212) 682-1490* 60 E 42nd St NY, NY 10165

BOOTH, TOM INC *(212) 243-2750* 425 W 23rd St NY, NY 10011

BRINDLE, CAROLYN *(212) 534-4177* 203 E 89th St NY, NY 10028

BRODY, SAM *(212) 758-0640* 12 E 46th St NY, NY 10017

BROWNE, PEMA LTD *(212) 369-1925* 185 E 85th St NY, NY 10028

BRUCK, JS *(212) 247-1130* 322 W 57th St NY, NY 10019

BRUCK, NANCY *(212) 645-1547* 302 W 12th St NY, NY 10014

CHISLOVSKY, CAROL *(212) 677-9100* 853 Broadway NY, NY 10003

COHEN, BRUCE *(212) 620-7839* 54 W 16th St NY, NY 10011

COLLIGNON, DANIELE ***(212) 391-1830*** **1500 Broadway NY, NY 10036**

PAGE 46

CONLON, JEAN *(212) 966-9897* 461 Broome St NY, NY 10013

CREATIVE FREELANCER *(212) 398-9540* 62 W 45th St NY, NY 10036

CREATIVE TALENT *(212) 243-7869* 62 LeRoy St NY, NY 10014

CULLOM, ELLEN *(212) 925-1121* 55 E 9th St NY, NY 10003

DEDELL, JAQUELINE INC. ***(212) 741-2539*** **58 W 15th St NY, NY 10011**

PAGE 18-23

DES VERGES, DIANA *(212) 691-8674* 73 Fifth Ave NY, NY 10003

DIPARISI, PETER *(212) 840-8225* 54 W 39th St NY, NY 10018

DREXLER, SHARON *(718) 284-4779* 451 Westminster Rd Brooklyn, NY 11218

ERLACHER, BILL *(212) 755-1365* 211 E 51st St NY, NY 10022

PAGE 60-66

FISHBACK, LEE *(212) 929-2951* 350 W 21st St NY, NY 10011

FRASER, GAYLENE *(212) 475-5911* 211 Thompson St NY, NY 10012

g - l

GARGAGLIANO, TONY *(212) 661-0850* 216 E 45th St NY, NY 10017

GELB, ELIZABETH *(212) 222-1218* 856 West End Ave NY, NY 10025

GODFREY, DENNIS *(212) 807-0840* 95 Horatio St NY, NY 10014

GOLDMAN, DAVID *(212) 807-6627* 41 Union Sq W NY, NY 10003

GOMBERG, SUSAN *(212) 473-8747* 145 E 22nd St NY, NY 10010

GORDON, BARBARA ASSOCIATES LTD.

***(212) 686-3514* 165 E 32nd St NY, NY 10016**

PAGE 53

GOTHAM ART AGENCY *(212) 989-2737* 1123 Broadway NY, NY 10010

GRIEN, ANITA *(212) 697-6170* 155 E 38th St NY, NY 10016

GRIFFITH, VALERIE *(212) 675-2089* 10 Sheridan Sq NY, NY 10014

HANKINS & TEGENBORG LTD *(212) 867-8092* 60 E 42nd St NY, NY 10165

HARMON, ROD *(212) 245-8935* 254 W 51st St NY, NY 10019

HAYES, KATHY ASSOCIATES *(212) 925-4340* 131 Spring St NY, NY 10012

HK PORTFOLIO *(203) 454-4687* 248 Newtown Turnpike Weston, CT 06883

HOLMBERG, IRMELI *(212) 775-1810* 280 Madison Ave NY, NY 10016

HUSAK, JOHN *(212) 463-7025* 236 W 26th St NY, NY 10001

HYMERS, MAUREEN *(212) 807-6914* NY, NY

PAGE 68

JOHNSON, BUD & EVELYNE *(212) 532-0928* 201 E 28th St NY, NY 10016

JOSEPH MINDLIN & MULVEY *(212) 243-1333* 156 Fifth Ave NY, NY 10010

JOSEPH, DEBORAH *(212) 243-1333* 156 Fifth Ave NY, NY 10010

KAHN, HARVEY ASSOCIATES INC *(212) 752-8490* 50 E 50th St NY, NY 10022

KANE, BARNEY & FRIENDS *(212) 206-0322* 18 E 16th St NY, NY 10003

KASAK, HARRIET *(203) 454-4687* 458 Newtown Trnpk Weston, CT 06883

KAUSS, JEAN-GABRIEL *(212) 370-4300* 122 E 42nd ST NY, NY 10168

KEATING, PEGGY *(212) 691-4654* 30 Horatio St NY, NY 10014

KIM *(212) 679-5628* 209 E 25th St NY, NY 10010

KIMCHE, TANIA *(212) 242-6367* 470 W 23rd St NY, NY 10011

KIRCHOFF-WOHLBERG INC *(212) 644-2020* 866 UN Plaza NY, NY 10017

LANDER, JANE ASSOCIATES *(212) 679-1358* 333 E 30th St NY, NY 10016

LAVATY, JEFF & FRANK *(212) 355-0910* 50 E 50th St NY, NY 10022

LEFF, JERRY *(212) 697-5825* 420 Lexington Ave NY, NY 10170

LEGRAND, JEAN YVES & ASSOCIATE *(212) 724-598* 41 W 84th StNY,NY 10024

LINDGREN, PAT *(212) 929-5590* 41 Union Sq NY, NY 10003

LOCKE, JOHN STUDIOS INC *(212) 288-8010* 15 E 76th St NY, NY 10021

LOTT, PETER & GEORGE *(212) 687-4185* 60 E 42nd St NY, NY 10165

LYNCH, ALAN *(212) 255-6530* 155 Sixth Ave NY, NY 10013

m - r

MANASSE, MICHELE *(212) 873-3797* 1960 Broadway NY, NY 10023

MATTELSON, JUDY *(212) 684-2974* 37 Cary Rd Great Neck, NY 11021

PAGE 49

MCGILL, STEPHEN *(212) 463-7025* 236 W 26th St NY, NY 10001

MENDELSOHN, RICHARD *(212) 682-2462* 353 W 53rd St NY, NY 10019

MENDOLA, JOE *(212) 986-5680* 420 Lexington Ave NY, NY 10170

MILLER, SUSAN *(212) 905-8400* 1641 Third Ave NY, NY 10028

MINTZ, LES *(212) 925-0491* 111 Wooster St NY, NY 10012

MORGAN, VICKI ASSOCIATES

***(212) 475-0440* 194 Third Ave NY, NY 10003**

PAGE 26-31

MOSKOWITZ, MARIAN *(212) 719-9879* 342 Madison Ave NY, NY 10173

MOSS, EILEEN *(212) 980-8061* 333 E 49th St NY, NY 10017

NEAIL, PAMELA R ASSOCIATES *(212) 673-1600* 27 Bleecker St NY, NY 10012

NEW YORK PORTFOLIO DEPOT *(212) 989-8588* 41 Union Sq NY, NY 10003

NEWBORN, MILTON ASSOCIATES

***(212) 421-0050* 135 E 54th St NY, NY 10022**

PAGE 8-15

NEWMAN, LISA *(212) 787-1340* NY, NY

PAGE 52

PALMER, JEFF *(203) 222-8777* 227 Godfrey Rd Weston, CT 06883

PALULIAN, JOANNE *(212) 581-8338* 18 McKinley St Rowayton, CT 6853

PAGE 38-39

PENNY & STERMER GROUP *(212) 243-4412* 48 W 21st St NY, NY 10010

PERON, BEA *(212) 255-3440* 5 W 19th St NY, NY 10011

PICKARD, MAGGIE

***(914) 876-2358* 2 Locust Grove Rd Rhinebeck, NY 12572**

PAGE 57

PETERSEN, VICTORIA *(212) 799-7021* 16 W 71st St NY, NY 10023

PRITCHETT, TOM *(212) 688-1080* 330 W 4th St NY, NY 10014

PUHALSKI, RON & ASSOCIATES

(212) 242-2860 1133 Broadway NY, NY 10010

PUSHPIN ASSOCIATES *(212) 674-8080* 215 Park Ave So NY, NY 10003

PAGE 54

RAPP, GERALD & CULLEN *(212) 889-3337* 108 E 35th St NY, NY 10016

Renard Represents Inc ***(212) 490-2450*** **501 Fifth Ave NY, NY 10017**

PAGE 33-37

Ridgeway, Karen *(212) 714-0147* 330 W 42nd St NY, NY 10036

Riley, Edward T *(212) 925-3053* 81 Greene St NY, NY 10012

Roman, Helen Associates Inc

(212) 874-7074 140 West End Ave NY, NY 10023

S - Z

Seigel, Fran *(212) 486-9644* 515 Madison Ave NY, NY 10022

SI International *(212) 254-4996* 43 E 19th St NY, NY 10003

Siegel, Tema *(212) 696-4680* 461 Park Ave So NY, NY 10016

Sigman, Joan ***(212) 421-0050*** **336 E 54th St NY, NY 10022**

PAGE 47

Solomon, Richard *(212) 683-1362* 121 Madison Ave NY, NY 10016

Sonneville, Dane *(212) 603-9530* Box 20415 Greeley Stn NY, NY 10001

Spiers, Herb *(212) 254-4996* 43 E 19th St NY, NY 10003

Stogo, Don *(212) 490-1034* 310 E 46th St NY, NY 10017

Taborda, Carlos *(212) 734-1903* 344 E 85th St NY, NY 10028

Thomas, Brenda & Associates

(212) 873-7236 127 W 79th St NY, NY 10024

Thurm, Gail *(212) 489-8777* 24 W 57th St NY, NY 10019

Tise, Katherine *(212) 570-9069* 200 E 78th St NY, NY 10021

Valen, Herb *(203) 227-07806* 158 Hills Pt Rd Westport, CT 6880

Ward, Wendy *(212) 684-0590* 200 Madison Ave NY, NY 10016

Lettering & Design

a

Abramson, Michael R Studio

(212) 683-1271 21 E 40th St NY, NY 10016

Adams, Gaylord Design *(212) 683-4625* 401 E 34th St NY, NY 10016

Adams, Scott Design *(212) 420-8866* 118 E 25th St NY, NY 10010

Adlemann, Morton *(212) 564-8528* 30 W 32nd St NY, NY 10001

Adler, Stan Associates *(212) 719-1944* 1140 Sixth Ave NY, NY 10036

Adzema, Diane *(212) 982-5657* 17 Bleecker St NY, NY 10012

Aeschlima Design *(212) 685-1585* 307 Fifth Ave NY, NY 10016

AKM Associates *(212) 687-7636* 41 E 42nd St NY, NY 10017

Album Graphics Inc *(212) 489-0793* 1776 Broadway NY, NY 10019

Alexander, Martha *(212) 360-1123* 1065 Park Ave NY, NY 10128

Aliman, Elie *(212) 925-9621* 134 Spring St NY, NY 10012

Allied Graphics Arts *(212) 730-1414* 1515 Broadway NY, NY 10036

Amorello, Frank Assoc *(212) 779-1442* 114 E 32nd St NY, NY 10016

Anagraphics *(212) 279-2370* 104 W 29th St NY, NY 10001

Anspach Grossman Portugal

(212) 692-9000 711 Third Ave NY, NY 10017

Anthony, Robert *(212) 673-3011* 10 E 23rd St NY, NY 10010

Antler & Baldwin Graphics *(212) 751-2031* 7 E 47th St NY, NY 10017

Appelbaum Company *(212) 213-1130* 176 Madison Ave NY, NY 10016

Arnold, Robert *(212) 989-7049* 149 W 14th St NY, NY 10011

Aron, Michael & Co *(212) 627-4054* 20 W 20th St NY, NY 10011

Art Department *(212) 391-1826* 2 W 46th St NY, NY 10036

Artery Graphic *(212) 807-8429* 1133 Broadway NY, NY 10010

b

Bacon, Paul *(212) 247-4760* 881 Seventh Ave NY, NY 10019

Balch, Barbara *(212) 242-0026* 1 Union Sq NY, NY 10003

Barmache, Leon Design *(212) 759-3840* 226 E 54th St NY, NY 10022

Barry David Berger & Assoc

(212) 477-4100 9 E 19th St NY, NY 10003

Barry, Jim *(212) 873-6787* 69 W 68th St NY, NY 10023

Becker Hockfield Design Assoc

(212) 684-0496 35 E 21st St NY, NY 10010

Bell, James Graphic Design

(718) 638-8900 692 Washington Ave Brklyn, NY 11238

Bennett, Suzanne & Assoc

212) 564-8050 875 Sixth Ave NY, NY 10001

Bernhardt/Fudyma *(212) 889-9337* 133 E 36th St NY, NY 10016

Besalel, Ely *(212) 759-7820* 235 E 49th St NY, NY 10017

Bessen & Tully & Lee *(212) 213-1911* 220 E 23rd St NY, NY 10010

Biniasz, Paul ***(212) 979-0025*** **305 Prospect Pl Brooklyn, NY 11238**

PAGE 73

Binns, Betty Graphic Design

(212) 679-9200 31 E 28th St NY, NY 10016

Biondo, Charles Design Assoc

(212) 645-5300 389 W 12th St NY, NY 10014

Blackburn, Bruce & Assoc

(212) 777-5375 331 Park Ave So NY, NY 10010

Bloch, Garulich & Whelan, Inc

(212) 473-7033 333 Park Ave So NY, NY 10010

Bonnell Design Assoc *(212) 757-4420* 409 W 44th St NY, NY 10036

Bordnick, Jack & Assoc *(212) 563-1544* 224 W 35th St NY, NY 10001

Botero, Samuel Assoc *(212) 935-5155* 150 E 58th St NY, NY 10155

Bradford, Peter *(212) 982-2090* 11 E 22nd St NY, NY 10010

Brainchild Designs *(212) 420-1222* 108 E 16th St NY, NY 10003

Bree/Taub Design *(212) 334-5200* 97 Crosby St NY, NY 10012

Breinberg, Aaron *(212) 243-4929* 1123 Broadway NY, NY 10010

Brown, Alastair Assoc *(212) 213-8719* 419 Park Ave So NY, NY 10016

Brown, Kirk *(718) 346-8281* 1092 Blake Ave Brooklyn, NY 11208

Brunetti Design Studio

(718) 278-3667 4220 25th Ave Astoria, NY 11103

Buckley Designs Inc *(212) 861-0626* 310 E 75th St NY, NY 10021

By Design *(212) 684-0388* 14 E 38th St NY, NY 10016

Byrne Design *(212) 807-6671* 133 W 19th St NY, NY 10011

c

Cain, David *(212) 633-0258* 200 W 20th St NY, NY 10011

Calfo Assoc *(212) 627-3800* 20 W 20th St NY, NY 10011

Caliber Design Planning *(212) 944-0808* 40 W 38th St NY, NY 10018

Cannan, Bill & Co Inc *(212) 563-1004* 529 W 42nd St NY, NY 10036

Caravello Studios *(212) 620-0620* 165 W 18th St NY, NY 10011

Carbone/Smolan Assoc *(212) 807-0011* 170 Fifth Ave NY, NY 10010

Carlo Assoc *(212) 420-1110* 900 Broadway NY, NY 10003

Carnase Inc, Tom *(212) 777-1500* 30 E 21st St NY, NY 10010

PAGE 78

Celedonia Design *(212) 223-0233* 145 E 49th St NY, NY 10017

Chajet Design Group Inc *(212) 684-3669* 148 E 40th St NY, NY 10016

Charles, Irene Assoc *(212) 765-8000* 270 Madison Ave NY, NY 10016

Chermayeff & Geismar *(212) 532-4499* 15 E 26th St NY, NY 10010

Chu, HL & Co Ltd *(212) 889-4818* 39 W 29th St NY, NY 10001

Church, Wallace Assoc *(212) 755-2903* 330 E 48th St NY, NY 10017

Cisler, Jon *(212) 995-8933* 148 W 4th St NY, NY 10012

PAGE 79

Cliffer, Jill *(212) 691-7013* 9 E 16th St NY, NY 10003

Cohen, Norman Design *(212) 679-3906* 201 E 28th St NY, NY 10016

Colangelo, Ted Assoc *(212) 909-9012* 909 Third Ave NY, NY 10022

Comart Assoc *(212) 714-2550* 360 W 31st St NY, NY 10001

Condon, J & M *(212) 242-7811* 126 Fifth Ave NY, NY 10011

Congdon/MacDonald *(212) 697-9300* 420 Lexington Ave NY, NY 10170

Cooney, R.A. *(212) 995-8001* 35 E 21st St NY, NY 10010

Corchia Woliner Assoc *212) 977-9778* 130 W 56th St NY, NY 10019

Corey & Co *(212) 924-4311* 155 Sixth Ave NY, NY 10013

Corpographics Inc *(212) 483-9065* 47 West St NY, NY 10016

Corporate Annual Reports Inc

(212) 889-2450 112 E 31st St NY, NY 10016

Corporate Graphics Inc *(212) 599-1820* 655 Third Ave NY, NY 10017

Cosgrove Assoc Inc *(212) 889-7202* 233 E 31st St NY, NY 10016

Cotler, Sheldon Inc *(212) 719-9590* 80 W 40th St NY, NY 10018

Cotton, Jim Graphic Comm

(212) 563-3022 13 W 36th St NY, NY 10018

Cousins Designs Inc *(212) 431-8222* 599 Broadway NY, NY 10012

CPM 95 Inc *(212) 924-3815* 95 Fifth Ave NY, NY 10003

Creamer Dickson Basford

(212) 887-8010 1633 Broadway NY, NY 10019

Creative Directors, The *(212) 929-2929* 72 Fifth Ave NY, NY 10011

Creative Source, The *(212) 302-0059* 123 W 44th St NY, NY 10036

Cruz & Slowik Associates Inc

(212) 764-6593 246 W 38th St NY, NY 10018

Csoka Benato Fleurant Inc

(212) 242-6777 134 W 26th St NY, NY 10001

Cuevas, Robert *(212) 661-7149* 230 E 44th St NY, NY 10017

Curry, David Design Inc *(212) 753-9848* 338 E 53rd St NY, NY 10022

Curtis Design Inc *(212) 685-0670* POB 461 Armonk, NY 10504

Cygnus Productions *(212) 391-1099* 1114 Sixth Ave NY, NY 10036

d

Daniels Design *(212) 935-6777* 145 E 49th St NY, NY 10017

Danne, Richard *(212) 645-7400* 126 Fifth Ave NY, NY 10011

David, Stuart *(212) 866-6089* 12 W 95th St NY, NY 10025

Davis Delaney Arrow Inc *(212) 686-2500* 141 E 25th St NY, NY 10010

Deharak & Poulin Assoc *(212) 929-5445* 320 W 13th St NY, NY 10014

Delano Goldman & Young *(212) 697-7820* 320 E 46th St NY, NY 10017

Delgado Design *(212) 645-0097* 22 W 21st St NY, NY 10010

Delphan Company *(212) 371-6700* 515 Madison Ave NY, NY 10022

Demartin Marona Cranstoun Down

(212) 682-9044 630 Third Ave NY, NY 10017

Demartino/Schultz *(212) 513-0300* 233 Broadway NY, NY 10007

Desantis Design *(212) 725-2655* 116 E 27th St NY, NY 10016

Design Arm, The *(212) 354-8181* 45 W 45th St NY, NY 10036

Design Associates *(212) 505-1493* 295 Park Ave So NY, NY 10010

Design Magic *(212) 505-8308* 218 E 17th St NY, NY 10003

Design Source *(212) 475-8080* 218 E 17th St NY, NY 10003

DESIGNED TO PRINT *(212) 924-2090* 130 W 25th St NY, NY 10001

DESIGNERS THREE *(212) 221-5900* 25 W 43rd St NY, NY 10036

DESIGNFRAME *(212) 924-2426* 1 Union Sq NY, NY 10003

DESKEY ASSOC *(212) 967-3360* 45 W. 36th St NY, NY 10018

DEUTSCH DESIGN *(212) 684-4478* 166 Lexington Ave NY, NY 10016

DIAMOND ART STUDIO *(212) 685-6622* 11 E 36th St NY, NY 10016

DICKENS, HOLLY *(212) 682-1490* 60 E 42nd St NY, NY 10165

DIFRANZA/WILLIAMSON INC *(212) 463-8302* 16 W 22nd St NY, NY 10011

DINAND PIERRE DESIGN *(212) 751-3086* 37 W 57th St NY, NY 10019

DIRECTIONS INC *(212) 370-1133* 201 E 37th St NY, NY 10016

DISPIGNA, TONY *(212) 674-2647* 215 Park Ave So NY, NY 10003

DIXON & PARCELS ASSOC *(212) 697-2522* 521 Fifth Ave NY, NY 10175

DONOVAN & GREEN INC *(212) 725-2233* 1 Madison Ave NY, NY 10010

DORET, MICHAEL *(212) 929-1688* 12 E 14th St NY, NY 10003

DOUGLAS, BARRY DESIGN *(212) 734-4137* 300 E 71st St NY, NY 10021

DOWNEY WEEKS & TOOMEY

(212) 564-8260 519 Eighth Ave NY, NY 10018

DRATE , SPENCER *(212) 620-4672* 160 Fifth Ave NY, NY 10010

DUBINS, MILT DESIGNER INC *(212) 691-0232* 353 W 22nd St NY, NY 10011

DUBROW, OSCAR ASSOC *(212) 688-0698* 18 E 48th St NY, NY 10017

DWYER & HOWELL *(212) 986-7108* 420 Lexington Ave NY, NY 10017

e - f

EDGAR, LAUREN *(212) 673-6060* 36 E 20th St NY, NY 10003

EDGE, DENNIS DESIGN *(212) 679-0927* 36 E 38th St NY, NY 10016

EHLERS, LESLIE DESIGN *(212) 219-1868* 225 Lafayette St NY, NY 10012

EISENMAN & ENOCK *(212) 349-7100* 157 Chambers St NY, NY 10007

EMERSON/WAJDOWICZ STUDIOS

212) 807-8144 1123 Broadway NY, NY 10010

ENGLAND-LEVITT, DEBORAH *(212) 989-0253* 210 W 17th St NY, NY 10011

ETC COMMUNICATIONS GROUP

(212) 996-4551 POB 7046 Yorkville Finance St NY, NY 10128

ETHERIDGE, PALOMBO, SEDEWITZ

(212) 944-2530 1500 Broadway NY, NY 10036

FAILING, KENDRICK G DESIGN

(212) 677-5764 80 Fourth Ave NY, NY 10003

FALKINS, RICHARD DESIGN *(212) 840-3045* 15 W 44th St NY, NY 10036

FAVILLE GRAPHICS *(212) 944-8241* 25 W 39th St NY, NY 10018

FEUCHT, FRED DESIGN GROUP INC

(914) 769-5005 88 Mountain Rd Pleasantville, NY 10570

FINEBERG ASSOCIATES *(212) 734-1220* 333 E 68th St NY, NY 10021

FIORENTINO & LEIBE ASSOC *(212) 243-2236* 134 W 26th St NY, NY 10001

FITZNER, YVONNE *(212) 988-4039* 231 E 76th St NY, NY 10021

PAGE 76

FLAGG, HOLLY DESIGN *(212) 734-5790* 103 E 84th St NY, NY 10028

FLORVILLE, PATRICK DESIGN *(212) 475-2278* 928 Broadway NY, NY 10010

FORMAN, YALE DESIGNS INC *(212) 799-1665* 11 Riverside Dr NY, NY 10023

FOSTER, STEPHEN DESIGN

***(212) 967-2533* 145 W 28th St NY, NY 10001**

PAGE 75

FRIDAY SATURDAY SUNDAY INC

(212) 779-8788 210 E 15th St NY, NY 10003

FRIEDMAN, SI ASSOC *(212) 755-0258* 141 E 55th St NY, NY 10022

FULTON & PARTNERS *(212) 695-1625* 330 W 42nd St NY, NY 10036

g

GALE, CYNTHIA *(212) 860-5429* 229 E 88th St NY, NY 10128

GALE, ROBERT A INC *(212) 535-4791* 970 Park Ave NY, NY 10028

GARDNER, BEAU ASSOC INC

(212) 832-2426 541 Lexington Ave NY, NY 10022

GASTNER, JOANNE *(212) 686-0860* 201 E 30th St NY, NY 10016

GERSIN, ROBERT P ASSOC *(212) 777-9500* 11 E 22nd St NY, NY 10010

GERSTMAN & MEYERS INC *(212) 586-2535* 60 W 55th St NY, NY 10019

GIANNINOTO ASSOC INC *(212) 759-5757* 133 E 54th St NY, NY 10022

GIOVANNI DESIGN ASSOC *(212) 972-2145* 230 E 44th St NY, NY 10017

GIPS & BALKIND & ASSOC *(212) 421-5888* 244 E 58th St NY, NY 10022

GIRVIN, TIM *(212) 490-2450* 501 Fifth Ave NY, NY 10017

PAGE 77

GLASER, MILTON *(212) 889-3161* 207 E 32nd St NY, NY 10016

GLASMAN DESIGN ASSOCIATES *(212) 679-6016* 38 E 29th St NY, NY 10016

GLASSER, ROBERTA GRAPHIC DESIGN

(212) 599-0988 213 E 38th St NY, NY 10016

GLAZER & KALAYJIAN *(212) 687-3099* 301 E 45th St NY, NY 10017

GLUCKMAN, ERIC *(212) 697-3670* 60 E 42nd St NY, NY 10017

GLUSKER GROUP *(212) 757-4438* 154 W 57th St NY, NY 10019

GOETZ GRAPHICS *(212) 679-4250* 60 Madison Ave NY, NY 10010

GOLDBERG, CARIN DESIGN *(212) 226-1366* 270 Lafayette St NY, NY 10012

GOLDMAN, NEAL ASSOC INC *(212) 687-5058* 230 Park Ave NY, NY 10169

GORBATY, NORMAN DESIGN *(212) 684-1665* 14 E 38th St NY, NY 10016

GORMAN, CHRIS ASSOCIATES

(212) 983-3375 305 Madison Ave NY, NY 10165

GOTLIB, GEORGES INC *(212) 627-7777* 156 Fifth Ave NY, NY 10010

Graef, Wm. *(212) 868-3239* 347 W 36th St NY, NY 10018

Graphic Art Resource Assoc
(212) 929-0017 257 W 10th St NY, NY 10014

Graphic Center, The *(212) 686-6585* 60 Madison Ave NY, NY 10016

Graphic Chart & Map Co *(212) 463-0190* 236 W 26th St NY, NY 10001

Graphic Expression, The *(212) 759-7788* 330 E 59th St NY, NY 10022

Graphic Horizons *(212) 219-2040* 100 Sixth Ave NY, NY 10013

Graphic Options *(212) 687-8520* 122 E 42nd St NY, NY 10168

Graphic Solutions Inc *(212) 995-9600* 35 E 21st St NY, NY 10010

Graphics By Nostradamus *(212) 581-1362* 250 W 57th St NY, NY 10017

Graphics For Industry *(212) 889-6202* 8 W 30th St NY, NY 10001

Graphics To Go *(212) 889-9337* 133 E 36th St NY, NY 10016

Green, Douglas *(212) 752-6284* 251 E 51st St NY, NY 10022

Greenboam & Casey *(212) 564-3450* 575 Eighth Ave NY, NY 10018

Griffler Designs *(212) 794-2625* 17 E 67th St NY, NY 10021

Griswold Heckel & Kelly
(212) 254-1900 257 Park Ave So NY, NY 10010

Group One *(212) 686-4040* 128 E 31st St NY, NY 10016

Grunfeld Graphics *(212) 431-8700* 80 Varick St NY, NY 10013

Gucciardo & Shapokas *(212) 683-9378* 244 Madison Ave NY, NY 10016

h

Hall, Carla Design Group
(212) 799-4850 261 W 85th St NY, NY 10024

Handelman, Stuart Graphic
(212) 674-7131 565 Fifth Ave NY, NY 10017

Handler Group Inc *(212) 391-0951* 55 W 45th St NY, NY 10036

Harmon Kemp *(212) 929-0226* 95 Fifth Ave NY, NY 10003

Harris, Ned Associates *(212) 714-9770* 45 W 34th St NY, NY 10001

Haydee Design Studio *(212) 242-3110* 27 W 20th St NY, NY 10014

Hecker, Mark Studio *(212) 620-9050* 321 W 11th St NY, NY 10014

Heimall, Bob Inc *(212) 245-4525* 250 W 57th St NY, NY 10019

Herstein & Schecterson Inc
(212) 889-3950 274 Madison Ave NY, NY 10016

Hibbard, R P Inc *(212) 921-0240* 1120 Sixth Ave NY, NY 10036

HNA Group *(212) 685-8668* 307 Fifth Ave NY, NY 10016

Hoashi, Jitsuo *(212) 697-7208* 50 E 42nd St NY, NY 10017

Holzsager, Mel Associates Inc
(212) 741-7373 275 Seventh Ave NY, NY 10001

Hopkins, Will Group *(212) 242-3238* 80 Fifth Ave NY, NY 10011

HUB Graphics Corp *(212) 675-8500* 18 E 16th St NY, NY 10003

Huerta, Gerard Inc *(203) 656-0505* 45 Corbin Dr Darien, CT 06820

Huttner & Hillman *(212) 463-0776* 19 W 21st St NY, NY 10011

i - k

Image Communications Inc *(212) 807-9677* 85 Fifth Ave NY, NY 10003

Image Network *(212) 877-2517* 645 West End Ave NY, NY 10025

Infield & D'Astolfo *(212) 924-9206* 49 W 24th St NY, NY 10010

Inkwell Inc *(212) 279-2066* 5 W 30th St NY, NY 10001

Intersight Design Inc *(212) 696-0700* 419 Park Ave So NY, NY 10016

Jaffe Communications Inc *(212) 697-4310* 122 E 42nd St NY, NY 10168

Jaffee, Lee Ann Design *(212) 627-1205* 12 W 18th St NY, NY 10011

Jastrom-Edstrom *(212) 889-0210* 32 E 31st St NY, NY 10016

Jonson Pirtle Pedersen Alcorn
(212) 353-0101 35 E 20th St NY, NY 10003

Juris Graphic *(212) 255-0303* NY, NY

Kacik Design *(212) 753-0031* 201 E 56th St NY, NY 10022

Kaeser &Wilson Design *(212) 563-2455* 330 Seventh Ave NY, NY 10001

Kahn, Al Group *(212) 580-3517* 221 W 82nd St NY, NY 10024

Kahn, Donald *(212) 889-8898* 39 W 29th St NY, NY 10001

Kallir Phillips Ross Inc *(212) 878-3700* 605 Third Ave NY, NY 10158

Kanai, Kiyoshi *(212) 679-5542* 115 E 30th St NY, NY 10016

Kass Communications *(212) 868-3133* 505 Eighth Ave NY, NY 10018

Kass, Milton Assoc Inc *(212) 874-0418* 1966 Broadway NY, NY 10023

Katz, Marjorie Design Inc *(212) 685-8416* 630 Park Ave NY, NY 10016

Keithley & Assoc *(212) 807-8388* 32 W 22nd St NY, NY 10010

Kissiloff Assoc Inc *(212) 421-8448* 330 W 42nd St NY, NY 10036

Klaboe & Siwek Assoc *(212) 362-6666* 2315 Broadway NY, NY 10024

KLN Publishing Services Inc *(212) 686-8200* 36 E 30th St NY, NY 10016

Klumb, E Christopher *(212) 679-2552* 192 Lexington Ave NY, NY 10016

Kneapler, John Design *(212) 463-9774* 48 W 21st St NY, NY 10011

Koff, Zale S Graphics *(212) 255-6788* 435 Hudson St NY, NY 10014

Kollberg-Johnson Assoc Inc
(212) 686-3648 254 Fifth Ave NY, NY 10001

Koppel & Scher Inc *(212) 627-9330* 156 Fifth Ave NY, NY 10011

Kramer Associates *(212) 582-4530* 119 W 57th St NY, NY 10019

Kunz, Willi Assoc *(212) 799-4300* 2112 Broadway NY, NY 10023

l

Lacy, N Lee *(212) 633-0303* 230 W 17th St NY, NY 10011

Lamplight Group, The *(212) 682-6270* 342 Madison Ave NY, NY 10173

Landman, K Design *(212) 924-4254* 156 Fifth Ave NY, NY 10011

Landor Assoc *(212) 751-6961* 46 E 61st NY, NY 10021

Laundy/Rogers Design *(212) 929-1555* 322 Eighth Ave NY, NY 10001

Lauren Associates *(212) 463-8909* 7 W 22nd St NY, NY 10010

Lazin & Katalan Design *(212) 242-7611* 227 W 17th St NY, NY 10011

LCL Design Assoc Inc *(212) 758-2604* 120 E 56th St NY, NY 10022

Leach, Richard Design *(212) 869-0972* 62 W 39th St NY, NY 10018

Lebbad, James A *(212) 645-5260* 1133 Broadway NY, NY 10010

Lee & Young Communications

(212) 689-4000 One Park Ave NY, NY 10016

Lesley-Hille Inc *(212) 677-7570* 32 E 21st St NY, NY 10010

Lester & Butler *(212) 889-0578* 437 Fifth Ave NY, NY 10016

Leutwyler Associates *(212) 689-0480* 155 E 31st St NY, NY 10016

Levine, Gerald *(212) 986-1068* 370 Lexington Ave NY, NY 10017

Levine, William V & Assoc *(212) 683-7177* 31 E 28th St NY, NY 10016

Levirne, Joel *(212) 869-8370* 151 W 46th St NY, NY 10036

Lewin Design Associates *(212) 255-6456* 240 W 23rd St NY, NY 10011

Lichtenberg, Al Graphic *(212) 679-5370* 10 E 40th St NY, NY 10016

Lieber, Anna *(212) 874-2874* 324 W 87th St NY, NY 10024

Liebert Studios Inc *(212) 686-4520* 6 E 39th St NY, NY 10016

Lika Association *(212) 490-3660* 160 E 38th St NY, NY 10016

Lind Brothers Inc *(212) 924-9280* 111 Eighth Ave NY, NY 10011

Lister Butler Inc *(212) 889-0578* 437 Fifth Ave NY, NY 10016

Lloyd, William Assoc *(212) 686-1766* 76 Madison Ave NY, NY 10016

Lubliner/Saltz *(212) 679-9810* 183 Madison Ave NY, NY 10016

Luby, Jody Graphic *(212) 473-1922* 808 Broadway NY, NY 10003

Lukasiewicz Design Inc *(212) 581-3344* 119 W 57th St NY, NY 10019

Lundgren, Ray Graphics *(212) 370-1686* 122 E 42nd St NY, NY 10017

Luth & Katz Inc *(212) 644-5777* 40 E 49th St NY, NY 10017

m

M & Co Design Group *(212) 243-0082* 50 W 17th St NY, NY 10011

Maggio, Ben Assoc Inc *(212) 697-8600* 420 Lexington Ave NY, NY 10017

Maisner, Bernard *(212) 475-5911* 211 Thompson St NY, NY 10012

page 71

Manners, Lee & Assoc *(212) 227-9292* 114 Liberty St NY, NY 10006

Marckrey Design Group Inc *(212) 620-7077* 7 W 18th St NY, NY 10011

Marker II Studio *(212) 982-1390* 270 Park Ave So NY, NY 10010

Marshall, Frank Graphic *(212) 463-0127* 100 Fifth Ave NY, NY 10010

Mauro, C L & Assoc *(212) 868-3940* 12 W 31st St NY, NY 10001

Mauro, Frank Assoc *(212) 719-5570* 18 W 45th St NY, NY 10036

Mayer Visual Communications

(212) 686-1717 245 Fifth Ave NY, NY 10016

Mayo-Infurna Design *(212) 888-7883* 10 E 21st St NY, NY 10010

McDonald, B & Assoc *(212) 645-7555* 1123 Broadway NY, NY 10010

McGovern & Pivoda *(212) 840-2912* 39 W 38th St NY, NY 10018

McMullen, James Inc *(212) 473-5083* 222 Park Ave So NY, NY 10003

Mendola Design *(212) 986-5680* 420 Lexington Ave NY, NY 10170

Miho, Tomoko Co *(212) 288-2070* 1045 Fifth Ave NY, NY 10028

Miller, Paul D Enterprises *(212) 777-2229* 14 Fifth Ave NY, NY 10011

Miller, Irving D Inc *(212) 755-4040* 641 Lexington NY, NY 10022

Mitchell, E M Inc. *(212) 986-5595* 820 Second Ave NY, NY 10017

Mittleman, Frederick Design *(212) 689-7911* 112 E 36 St NY, NY 10016

Mizerek Advertising *(212) 986-5702* 48 E 43 St NY, NY 10017

Mochli, Erich Design *(212) 645-1520* 1123 Broadway NY, NY 10010

Modern Arts Packaging *(212) 221-6300* 38 W 39th St NY, NY 10018

Modi & Beckler Design *(212) 695-1220* 19 W 34th St NY, NY 10001

Mokarry, Jim *(718) 788-4756* 311 Eighth St Brooklyn, NY 11215

Mont, Howard Associates Inc

(212) 683-4360 132 E 35th St NY, NY 10016

Moskoff & Associates *(212) 333-2015* 154 W 57th St NY, NY 10019

MR Graphic Inc *(212) 679-5555* 165 Madison Ave NY, NY 10016

Muir, Cornelius, Moore *(212) 463-7715* 79 Fifth Ave NY, NY 10003

Murtha Desola Finsilver Fiore

(212) 832-4770 800 Third Ave NY, NY 10022

Myers, David *(212) 989-5260* 228 Bleeker St NY, NY 10014

n - p

Nak Inc *(212) 505-9290* 36 E 22nd St NY, NY 10010

Nelson, Louis Associates *(212) 620-9191* 80 University Pl NY, NY 10003

Nemser, Robert *(212) 832-9595* 330 W 42nd St NY, NY 10036

Newman Design Associates

(212) 226-9801 133 Mulberry St NY, NY 10013

Newman, Harvey Associates

(212) 685-8668 307 Fifth Ave NY, NY 10016

Nicholson Design *(212) 206-1530* 148 W 24th St NY, NY 10011

Nobart NY Inc *(212) 475-5522* 33 E 18th St NY, NY 10003

Noneman & Noneman Design

(212) 473-4090 230 E 18th St NY, NY 10003

North, Charles W Studio *(212) 242-6300* 40 W 20th St NY, NY 10011

Notovitz & Perrault Design Inc

(212) 677-9700 47 E 19th St NY, NY 10003

Novus Visual Communicaions Inc

(212) 689-2424 18 W 27th St NY, NY 10001

O'Neil, Brian Design *(212) 691-1510* 95 Fifth Ave NY, NY 10003

Oak Tree Graphics Inc *(212) 398-9355* 570 Seventh Ave NY, NY 10018

Offenhartz, Harvey Inc *(212) 463-8308* 16 W 22nd St NY, NY 10011

Olsen Muscara Design *(212) 684-4580* 60 Madison Ave NY, NY 10010

Ong & Associates *(212) 633-0202* 11 W 19th St NY, NY 10011

Oz Communications *(212) 686-8200* 36 E 30th St NY, NY 10016

page Arbitrio Resen Ltd *(212) 421-8190* 305 E 46th St NY, NY 10017

Palladino, Tony *(212) 751-0068* 400 E 56th St NY, NY 10022

Paris, Tony *(212) 686-6150* 137 E 25th St NY, NY 10010

Patel, Harish Design Associates

(212) 686-7425 218 Madison Ave NY, NY 10016

Peckolick & Partners *(212) 532-6166* 108 E 31st St NY, NY 10016

Pedob, Al *(212) 242-0708* 150 Varick St NY, NY 10013

Pelavin, Daniel *(212) 929-2706* 46 Commerce St NY, NY 10014

Pellegrini & Associates *(212) 686-4481* 16 E 40th St NY, NY 10016

Pencils Portfolio Inc *(212) 355-2468* 333 E 49th St NY, NY 10016

Penraat Jaap Associates

(212) 873-4541 315 Central Pk W NY, NY 10025

Pentagram Design Ltd *(212) 683-7000* 212 Fifth Ave NY, NY 10010

Pento, Paul Inc *(212) 757-9337* 301 W 53rd St NY, NY 10019

Perlman Withers Design *(212) 935-2552* 305 E 46th St NY, NY 10017

Perlow, Paul *(212) 758-4358* 123 E 54th St NY, NY 10022

PAGE 72

Peterson Blythe & Cato *(212) 557-5566* 216 E 45th St NY, NY 10017

Pettis, Valerie *(212) 683-7382* 88 Lexington Ave NY, NY 10016

Pinnacle Graphics Inc *(212) 666-3610* 310 Riverside Dr NY, NY 10025

Pisarkiewicz Design *(212) 239-7345* 298 Fifth Ave NY, NY 10001

Platinum Design *(212) 750-5070* 123 E 54th St NY, NY 10022

Plumb Design Group Inc *(212) 505-2073* 57 E 11th St NY, NY 10003

Podob, Al *(212) 697-6643* 9 E 46th St NY, NY 10017

Polito, Angela *(212) 242-0708* 150 Varick St NY, NY 10013

Pop Shots Corporate Design

(212) 807-0172 71 W 23rd St NY, NY 10011

Prendergast, J W & Associates

(212) 687-8805 605 Third Ave NY, NY 10016

Projects In Knowledge *(212) 683-4820* 53 E 34th St NY, NY 10016

Puiying/Emmanuel/Misenas

(914) 528-8908 1679 Lawrence Rd Mohegan Lake, NY 10547

Purpura & Kisner *(212) 807-7445* 61 Jane St NY, NY 10014

Pushpin Group *(212) 674-8080* 215 Park Ave So NY, NY 10003

q - r

Quadrant Communications Co

(212) 421-0544 595 Madison Ave NY, NY 10022

Quon, Mike Design *(212) 226-6024* 568 Broadway NY, NY 10012

Ralf Shockey Associates

(212) 686-5160 295 Madison Ave NY, NY 10017

Ratzkin, Lawrence *(212) 279-1314* 392 Fifth Ave NY, NY 10018

RD Graphics *(212) 889-5612* 151 Lexington NY, NY 10017

Regn-Califano Inc *(212) 239-0380* 330 W 42nd St NY, NY 10036

Resource Manhattan *(212) 644-3850* 14 E 60th St NY, NY 10022

Robbins Tocker & Prince *(212) 645-7770* 80 Eighth Ave NY, NY 10011

Rogers Seidman Design *(212) 741-4687* 20 W 20th St NY, NY 10011

Rogers, Richard Inc *(212) 685-3666* 300 E 33rd St NY, NY 10016

Romero, Javier *(212) 564-3991* 529 W 42nd St NY, NY 10036

Ross Culbert Holland & Lavery

(212) 206-0044 15 W 20th St NY, NY 10011

Rouya, Es *(718) 392-5887* 45-19 42nd St LIC, NY 11104

Russell, Anthony *(212) 255-0650* 170 Fifth Ave NY, NY 10010

Russo, Rocco Anthony

(212) 213-4710 184 Lexington Ave NY, NY 10016

s

Saiki & Associates *(212) 255-0466* 154 W 18th St NY, NY 10011

Saks, Arnold *(212) 861-4300* 350 E 81st St NY, NY 10028

Saksa Art & Design *(212) 255-5539* 41 Union Sq W NY, NY 10003

Salisbury & Salisbury *(212) 575-0770* 15 W 44th St NY, NY 10036

Salpeter, Pagnaucci Inc *(212) 683-3310* 142 E 37th St NY, NY 10016

Saltzman, Mike Group *(212) 929-4655* 27 W 20th St NY, NY 10011

Sandgren Associates Inc *(212) 679-4650* 79 Madison Ave NY, NY 10016

Santoro Design *(212) 714-9207* 503 W 27th St NY, NY 10001

Sawyer, Arnie Studio *(212) 685-4927* 15 W 28th St NY, NY 10001

Saxton Communications Group

(212) 867-2210 124 E 40th St NY, NY 10016

Scanell, Peter *(212) 947-3822* 145 W 28th St NY, NY 10001

Schaefer-Cassety Inc *(212) 840-0175* 42 W 39th St NY, NY 10018

Schechter Group Inc *(212) 752-4400* 212 E 49th St NY, NY 10017

Scott, Louis Associates *(212) 924-3334* 16 W 22nd St NY, NY 10010

SCR Design Organization *(212) 421-3500* 1114 First Ave NY, NY 10021

Shapiro, Ellen Graphics *(212) 460-8544* 141 Fifth Ave NY, NY 10010

Shareholders Reports Inc *(212) 686-9099* 600 Third Ave NY, NY 10016

Shaw, Paul *(212) 666-3738* 110 Morningside Dr NY, NY 10027

PAGE 81

Shaw, Susan Design *(212) 929-7255* 126 Fifth Ave NY, NY 10013

Sherin & Matejka Inc *(212) 686-8410* 404 Park Ave So NY, NY 10016

Shreeve, Draper Design *(212) 675-7534* 28 Perry St NY, NY 10014

Siegel & Gale *(212) 730-0101* 1185 Sixth Ave NY, NY 10036

Silverman Bob Design *(212) 371-6472* 216 E 49th St NY, NY 10017

Sloan, William *(212) 463-7025* 568 Broadway NY, NY 10012

Slover, Susan Design *(212) 431-0093* 584 Broadway NY, NY 10012

Small Kaps Associates *(212) 683-0339* 40 E 34th St NY, NY 10016

Smart Design *(212) 807-8150* 7 W 18th St NY, NY 10011

Smith, Edward Design *(212) 255-1717* 1133 Broadway NY, NY 10010

Sobb & Associates *(212) 260-1653* 175 Fifth Ave NY, NY 10010

Sochynsky, Ilona *(212) 686-1275* 200 E 36th St NY, NY 10016

Solay/Hunt *(212) 840-3313* 28 W 44th St NY, NY 10036

Sposato, John *(212) 477-3909* 43 E 22nd St NY, NY 10010

PAGE 80

Star, Thomas & Associates *(212) 532-6506* 23 E 37th St NY, NY 10016

Stetson, Turner Associates

(315) 475-2138 241 W Fayette St Syracuse, NY 13202

Stevens, John *(516) 579-5352* 68 Rita Dr East Meadow, NY 11554

PAGE 74

Stillman, Linda *(212) 410-3225* 1556 Third Ave NY, NY 10128

Strignano, J R *(212) 751-8626* 300 E 59th St NY, NY 10022

Studio 42 *(212) 354-7298* 1472 Broadway NY, NY 10036

Sukon/Decarolis *(212) 627-4100* 355 Lexington Ave NY, NY 10017

Swatek & Romanoff Design Inc

(212) 807-0236 156 Fifth Ave NY, NY 10010

Syn-Comm Group *(212) 838-0262* 12 E 53rd St NY, NY 10022

t - V

Taurins Designs Associates

(212) 679-5955 280 Madison Ave NY, NY 10016

Tauss, Jack George *(212) 279-1658* 484 W 43rd St NY, NY 10036

Taylor & Ives *(212) 921-9300* 1001 Sixth Ave NY, NY 10018

Taylor, Stan *(212) 685-4741* 6 E 39th St NY, NY 10016

Teague, Walter Dorwin Associates

(212) 686-5300 95 Madison Ave NY, NY 10016

Tercovich, Douglas Associates

(212) 838-4800 575 Madison Ave NY, NY 10022

Tobias, William *(212) 741-1712* 6 W 18th St NY, NY 10011

Tscherny, George Design *(212) 734-3277* 238 E 72nd St NY, NY 10021

Typeshop, The *(212) 354-8181* 45 W 45th St NY, NY 10036

Ultra Arts Inc *(212) 679-7493* 150 E 35th St NY, NY 10016

Valk, Jon *(212) 889-4490* 245 E 24th St NY, NY 10010

Vecchio, Carmine *(212) 683-2679* 200 E 27th St NY, NY 10016

W - Z

Viewpoint Graphics *(212) 685-0560* 10 Park Ave NY, NY 10016

Vignelli Associates *(212) 244-1919* 475 Tenth Ave NY, NY 10018

Visual Accents Corp *(212) 777-7766* 30 Irving Pl NY, NY 10003

Walter Dorwin Teague *(212) 686-5300* 95 Madison Ave NY, NY 10016

Walz, Kevin Design *(212) 477-2211* 141 Fifth Ave NY, NY 10010

Wasserman, Bruce & Associates

(212) 226-4500 568 Broadway NY, NY 10012

Waters, John Associates *(212) 807-0717* 3 W 18th St NY, NY 10011

Waters, Pamela Studio *(212) 362-2870* 320 W 13th St NY, NY 10014

Webster, Robert Inc *(212) 677-2966* 331 Park Ave So NY, NY 10010

Wechsler & Partners *(212) 686-1370* 112 E 31st St NY, NY 10016

Weed, Eunice Associates

(212) 725-4933 370 Lexington Ave NY, NY 10017

Weissman, Simone Graphic

(212) 924-3366 300 W 23rd St NY, NY 10011

Whelan Design Office *(212) 967-4404* 158 W 29th St NY, NY 10001

White, Pamela Jaber *(212) 496-1179* 7 1/2 W 75th St NY, NY 10023

Whitehouse & Co *(212) 206-1080* 18 E 16th St NY, NY 10003

Whole Works, The *(212) 575-0765* 28 W 44th St NY, NY 10036

Widman & Co *(212) 683-3700* 12 E 41st St NY, NY 10017

Wijtvliet, Ine *(212) 319-4444* 440 E 56th St NY, NY 10022

Williams, Bryan & Associates

(212) 674-1277 118 E 25th St NY, NY 10010

Williams, Stuart *(212) 586-4793* 319 W 48th St NY, NY 10036

Wilson, Rex Co *(212) 594-3646* 330 Seventh Ave NY, NY 10001

Wizard Graphics Inc *(212) 686-8200* 36 E 30th St NY, NY 10016

Wolf, Henry *(212) 472-2500* 167 E 73rd St NY, NY 10021

Wolff, Rudi Inc *(212) 873-5800* 135 Central Park W NY, NY 10023

Wood, Alan *(212) 889-5195* 274 Madison Ave NY, NY 10016

Word-Wise *(212) 246-0430* 325 W 45th St NY, NY 10036

Works *(212) 696-1666* 45 W 27th St NY, NY 10001

Wozney, Greg Design *(212) 620-7776* 48 W 20th St NY, NY 10011

Yasumura & Associates *(212) 685-5000* 292 Madison Ave NY, NY 10017

Yoshimura/Fisher Graphic Design

(212) 431-4776 284 Lafayette St NY, NY 10012

Young Goldman Young *(212) 697-7820* 320 E 46th St NY, NY 10017

Your Corporate Look *(212) 682-2555* 60 E 42nd St NY, NY 10017

Zahor & Bender *(212) 532-7475* 200 E 33rd St NY, NY 10016

Zimmerman & Foyster *(212) 674-5337* 22 E 21st St NY, NY 10010

INDEX TO TAB 2

PHOTOGRAPHY

FASHION & BEAUTY

PEOPLE

PORTRAITURE

Photographers & *Representatives*

All Photography Listings, TAB 5

INDEX TO TAB 2

PHOTOGRAPHY
FASHION & BEAUTY
PEOPLE
PORTRAITURE

PHOTOGRAPHERS & *Representatives*

All Photography Listings, Tab 5

PHOTOGRAPHY: PEOPLE FASHION 2

Alan Kaplan Photography (212) 982-9500

ALFRED HITCHCOCK ONCE SAID . . .

Represented by **Bernstein & Andriulli, Inc.** (212) 682-1490

Represented by
Bernstein & Andriulli, Inc.
60 E. 42 St.
New York, New York 10165
(212) 682-1490
(212) 286-1890 FAX

...NO BORING BITS HERE.

Color Separations Quality House of Graphics (718) 784-7400
Represented by Bernstein & Andriulli, Inc. (212) 682-1490
OXMOX Design

... THAT MOVIES WERE JUST LIKE LIFE, ONLY WITH THE BORING BITS REMOVED.
ALAN KAPLAN ONCE SAID ...
Alan Kaplan Photography (212) 982-9500

Alan Kaplan
7 E. 20 St.
New York, New York 10003
(212) 982-9500

Represented by **Bernstein & Andriulli, Inc.** (212) 682-1490

Alan Kaplan Photography (212) 982-9500

isabel snyder 212 • 608 1945

Neil Selkirk
212 243-6778

Represented by Jim Zaccaro

Neil Selkirk
212 243-6778

Represented by Jim Zaccaro

CAREYES, MY LOVE
ON MEXICO'S PACIFIC COAST, THE DAYS, THE NIGHTS AND THE CLOTHES ARE SOFT, EASY AND ROMANTIC

/87 august dm 7,50 sfr 7,50
HARPER'S
BAZAAR
DEUTSCHE AUSGABE
MODE AUS PARIS:
KURZ, KNAPP, KOKETT
EROTISCHE SIGNALE
WAS MÄNNER VERFÜHRT
INSELGLÜCK:
KARIBISCHE HOTELS FÜR HONEYMOONERS
DIE UNZERTRENNLICHEN: PROMINENTE LOVE-STORIE

UMBERTO GINOCCHIETTI
Düsseldorf Kö-Center tel. 0211/13.30.00

URSULA CONZEN
4000 DÜSSELDORF · BILKER STRASSE 5 · TEL. 0211/132041-42

It takes two to tango-- and two tones to create a modern, elegant look.
Double-breasted wool suit jacket, about $580; matching trousers, about $300; both by Mario Valentino. Cotton shirt by Agnes B., about $85. Leather slip-ons by Susan Bennis Warren Edwards. Her cotton gown by Patrick Kelly.

SANTE D'ORAZIO

REPRESENTED BY
MARLON STOLTZMAN
67 EAST 11TH STREET #602
NEW YORK NEW YORK 10003
TEL 212/777-5757 FAX 477-5217

PIERO GEMELLI

REPRESENTED BY

MARLON STOLTZMAN

67 EAST 11TH ST. #602

NEW YORK CITY 10003

TEL 212/777-5757

FAX 477-5217

DAVID HARRY STEWART

PHOTOGRAPHER ■ 100 CHAMBERS ST ■ NY, NY 10007 ■ 212-619-7783

S T E P H A N I E

STEPHANIE • PHOTOGRAPHY
277 WEST TENTH STREET, NEW YORK, NY 10014
212.929.1029
REPRESENTED BY
NEW YORK • VINCENT J. APARO • 212.877.5439
LOS ANGELES • VIRGINIA J. APARO • 213.434.8065

Peter & Karine at Welwyn preserve June 14, 1988
Photographed by Mark Ledzian 2125634589

MARK LEDZIAN (212) 563-4589

PELLISSIER

M A R E S C A

TO SEE ADDITIONAL IMAGES PLEASE REFER TO THE BLACK BOOK

M A R E S C A

236 W. 26th ST. • NEW YORK, N.Y. 10001 • 212/620 • 0955

MISTRETTA

Martin Mistretta Inc., 220 West 19th Street, New York, N.Y. 10011 212 • 675-1547
Represented by Ellen Dillon • 675-1548

Barbara Bordnick 39 East 19th Street New York (212) 533-1180

LARRY DALE GORDON

LARRY DALE GORDON
REPRESENTATION:

NEW YORK/CHICAGO/DETROIT
NOB HOVDE/PAT HERRON
212/753-0462

LOS ANGELES
FOX & CLARK
213/653-6484

LONDON
DEREK HARMAN
441/352-7635

SHEER ENERGY PANTYHOSE.
SO YOUR LEGS CAN KEEP UP WITH THE REST OF YOU.
L'eggs Sheer Energy® pantyhose refreshes and soothes with every move you make.
The springy yarn hugs your legs so they'll feel as lively as you do. All day. All night.

CHRIS
CALLIS
STUDIO INC.

Fifth Avenue New York NY 10003 Represented by Melissa Ekblom: (212) 996-0912

CHRISTOPHER MICAUD

REPRESENTED BY:
JUDY CASEY INC. • NINETY SIX FIFTH AVENUE • NEW YORK, NEW YORK • 10011 • 212-255-3252

TORKIL GUDNASON

REPRESENTED BY:

JUDY CASEY INC. • NINETY SIX FIFTH AVENUE • NEW YORK, NEW YORK • 10011 • 212-255-3252

CALLIOPE

REPRESENTED BY:

JUDY CASEY INC. • NINETY SIX FIFTH AVENUE • NEW YORK, NEW YORK • 10011 • 212-255-3252

JOSÉ PICAYO

CONTACT PICAYO AT:
JUDY CASEY INC. • NINETY SIX FIFTH AVENUE • NEW YORK, NEW YORK • 10011 • 212-255-3252

MICHAEL PATEMAN

MICHAEL PATEMAN STUDIO, 155 EAST 35 STREET, NEW YORK 10016, TELEPHONE (212) 685-6584
REPRESENTED BY NORA DAVIES, TELEPHONE (212) 628-6657 REEL ON REQUEST

MICHAEL PATEMAN

MICHAEL PATEMAN STUDIO, 155 EAST 35 STREET, NEW YORK 10016, TELEPHONE (212) 685-6584
REPRESENTED BY NORA DAVIES, TELEPHONE (212) 628-6657 REEL ON REQUEST

FOR MORE IMAGES SEE CREATIVE BLACK BOOK

■ 13 LAIGHT ST., NY 10013 ■ (212) 219-1613
■ CHICAGO– VINCE KAMIN ■ (312) 787-8834

■ REVLON, MADEMOISELLE, COSMOPOLITAN, EBONY, STERLING OPTICAL, PORT AUTHORITY, BORDEN'S, SANDOZ, WESTVACO, NEC, VOGUE BUTTERICK, DuPONT, SCOPE ■

RIC SOMEKH

TINA MUCCI
P H O T O G R A P H Y

119 WEST 23RD STREET, NEW YORK, NY 10011, (212) 206-9402

N I C K   R O Z S A   [2 1 2]   7 3 4 · 5 6 2 9

represented by Pat Herron · 212 · 683 · 9039

kip meyer

Nob Hovde Associates · 212 · 753 · 0462

FEVER

Photography by Kip Meyer

Some people have fantastic voices and sometimes the girls even scream. Pubs have competitions and there are singers who become local heros, people who never even dreamed they could sing. But the other side of the coin are the worst singer of the year night. Joanne Arbiter runs the backing tape side of the business and has a

GUICE

Brad Guice Photography
Telephone/212/206-0966
Represented by Janice Moses
Telephone/212/779-7929

Robert Whitman Photography 1181 Broadway New York, New York 10001 212 • 213 • 6611

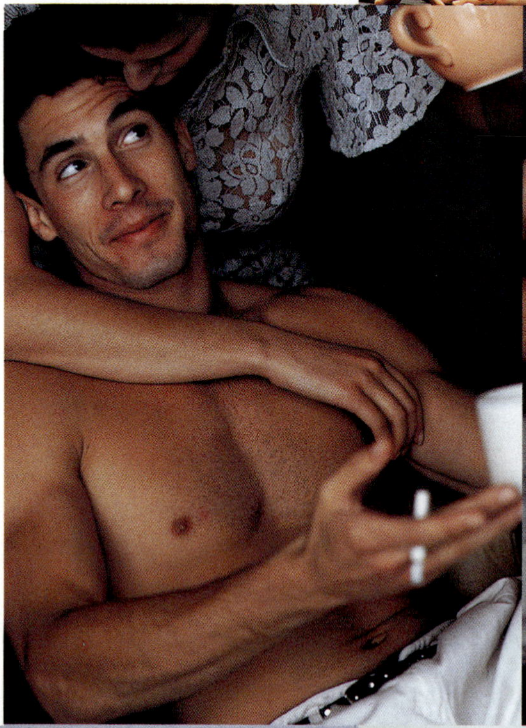

Cyndy Warwick

PHOTOGRAPHY

144 EAST 22ND STREET

NEW YORK CITY 10010

212-420-4760

291 CHURCH STREET NEW YORK CITY 10013 REPRESENTED BY CHUCK DORR (212) 431-5858

PALMA KOLANSKY

291 CHURCH STREET NEW YORK CITY 10013 REPRESENTED BY CHUCK DORR (212) 431-5858

IMPORTED
ELEPHANT
MALT LIQUOR
IMPORTED

POST
NO
BILLS

DENNIS
CHALKIN
STUDIO
INC

5 East 16th Street
New York, New York 10003
212•929•1036

Represented by Barbara Umlas
212•534•4008

nicholas melillo photographer 118 west 27th st n.y., n.y. 10001 • 212 691 7612

JAMES STILES

PHOTOGRAPHY
212 • 627 • 1766

FOR PORTFOLIO CONTACT
EDWARD SARTAN AT: SOURCE FORCE
212 · 643 · 3100

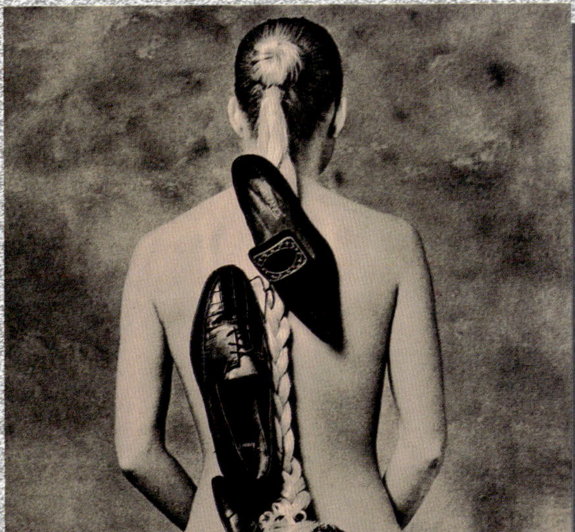

STEPHEN GREEN-ARMYTAGE

171 West 57th St.
New York, NY 10019
(212) 247-6314

Representative:
Ted Wasserman
(212) 867-5360.

STEPHEN GREEN-ARMYTAGE

171 West 57th St.
New York, NY 10019
(212) 247-6314

Representative:
Ted Wasserman
(212) 867-5360.

Richard Blinkoff

PHOTOGRAPHY

147 WEST 15TH STREET / NYC 10011 / 212-620-7883

REPRESENTED BY VICKIE SPAETH: 718-520-8632

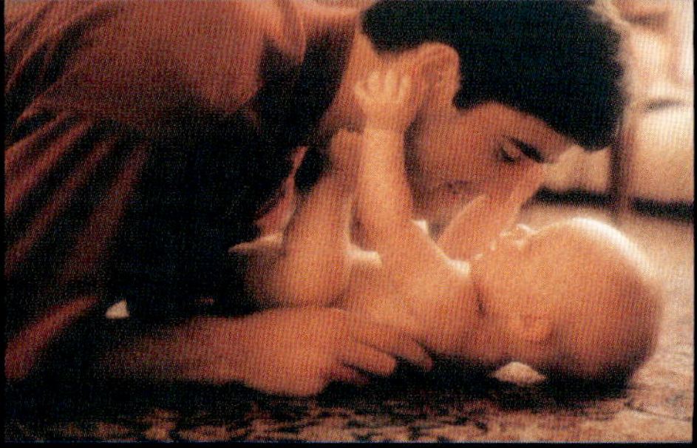

BRUCE BYERS PHOTOGRAPHY

Represented by Gary Lerman • 212-683-5777 • Studio • 212-242-5846

JAN COBB

PHOTOGRAPHY, LTD
5 W 19 ST NYC 10011
212.255.1400
REPRESENTED BY, GARY LERMAN
212.683.5777

ARMA'S KIDS

TOM ARMA STUDIO 38 WEST 26 STREET NEW YORK, N.Y. 10010 (212) 243-7904

REPRESENTED BY ADRIENNE RUBIN

KEN NAHOUM 212 · 219 · 0592

Buster
POINDEXTER

REVLON
UNFORGETTABLE

NANCY BROWN

6 W. 20 ST., N.Y., N.Y. 10011
(212) 924-9105
ASMP APA STOCK: IMAGE BANK
REP IN CHICAGO: DOUG BROOKS (312) 642-3208

FOR HALSA SHAMPOO

NANCY BROWN

6 W. 20 ST., N.Y., N.Y. 10011
(212) 924-9105
ASMP APA STOCK: IMAGE BANK
REP IN CHICAGO: DOUG BROOKS (312)642-3208

BUCK

Bruce Buck

39 West 14th Street, NY, NY 10011 212-645-1022

ROB FRASER

P h o t o g r a p h y

New York City (212) 779-1285 Represented by Marian Vitale (212) 683-4225

Still photography that moves.

HAIR AND MAKEUP BY STAN KRAMER

KAN PHOTOGRAPHY INC.
122 WEST 26 STREET, N.Y.C.

AGENT GEORGE WATSON 212-645-8616 STUDIO 212-989-1083

J. BARRY
ROURKE
578 BROADWAY
NEW YORK 10012
(212) 226-7113
STOCK/THE
STOCK
MARKET

Maureen Lambray New York City (212) 879-3960

KELLY MCGILLIS PLAYBOY MAGAZINE

JOHN SHEA GIORGIO ARMANI CLOTHING

Stylist: Rose Smith, Hair and makeup: James Reda.

Maureen Lambray New York City (212) 879-3960

LORI CARSON

L'OREAL MAKEUP

Stylist: Rose Smith, Hair and makeup: Leonardo DeVega

KatieGray
145 Hudson Street, 14th Floor
New York, New York 10013
(212) 226-0223

PHOTOGRAPHY

212.928.4199

joshua sheldon

BALDWIN

REPRESENTED BY BILL STOCKLAND & MAUREEN MARTEL
212·972·4747

BALDWIN

REPRESENTED BY BILL STOCKLAND & MAUREEN MARTEL
212·972·4747

A nice balance of color
and black and white
PHOTOGRAPHY
212
947-7883
BODI
BODI PRODUCTIONS
340 W. 39 ST. NYC 10018
Drop off portfolio available. Call (212) 947-7883

mercedes

NED HARVEY

• 129 •
West 22nd Street
New York City
10011
(212) 807-7043

K A Z · C H I B A

r e p r e s e n t e d · b y · j e a n – y v e s · l e g r a n d · 2 1 2 · 7 2 4 · 5 9 8 1

TICE ALEXANDER/HG © 1988 CHRIS SANDERS

CHRIS SANDERS

130 WEST 23RD STREET NEW YORK CITY 10011 212 645 6111

CLOCKWISE FROM TOP LEFT: SENGA MORTIMER/HG, HANNO AHRENS/HG, ADAM PURPLE/ROLLING STONE, SPALDING GREY/BRITISH ELLE © 1988 CHRIS SANDERS

CHRIS SANDERS

130 WEST 23RD STREET NEW YORK CITY 10011 212 645 6111

Sharp

WILL
RYAN
STUDIO
16 EAST 17 STREET
NEW YORK CITY 10003
242-6270

My pictures speak for themselves.

To speak with me, contact...

JON FISHER STUDIOS
236 West 27th Street
New York, NY 10001

212-206-6311

Le Moyne Page

310 East Fourty Sixth · New York City · 10017 · 212·286·9159

Emmilou Harris · Warner Bros. Records

Jean Beauvoir · CBS Records

Jermaine Jackson · Arista Records

V-magazine

Caroline Greyshock

578 Broadway #707 · N.Y.C. 10012 · 212 · 226 · 7563

millicom · annual report

INDEX TO TAB 3

PHOTOGRAPHY
STILL-LIFE
FOOD / INTERIORS
SPECIAL EFFECTS

Photographers & *Representatives*

All
Photography Listings,
TAB 5

INDEX TO TAB 3

PHOTOGRAPHY

STILL-LIFE

FOOD / INTERIORS

SPECIAL EFFECTS

PHOTOGRAPHERS & *Representatives*

ALL PHOTOGRAPHY LISTINGS, TAB 5

PHOTOGRAPHY: STILL LIFE INTERI 3

NORA SCARLETT
REPRESENTED BY
BARBARA UMLAS
(212) 534-4OO8

© Nora Scarlett 1988

Nora Scarlett
Represented By
Barbara Umlas
(212) 534-4008

Colin Cooke

380 Lafayette Street, NYC 10003-6923
(212) 254-5090   Telefax (212) 979-9524

craig cutler
photography

39 walker street
new york, n.y. 10013
212 · 966 · 1652

represented by
MARZENA
212 · 772 · 2522

Domino

CONVERSE
ALL STAR

MAZZEO

212·627·3766

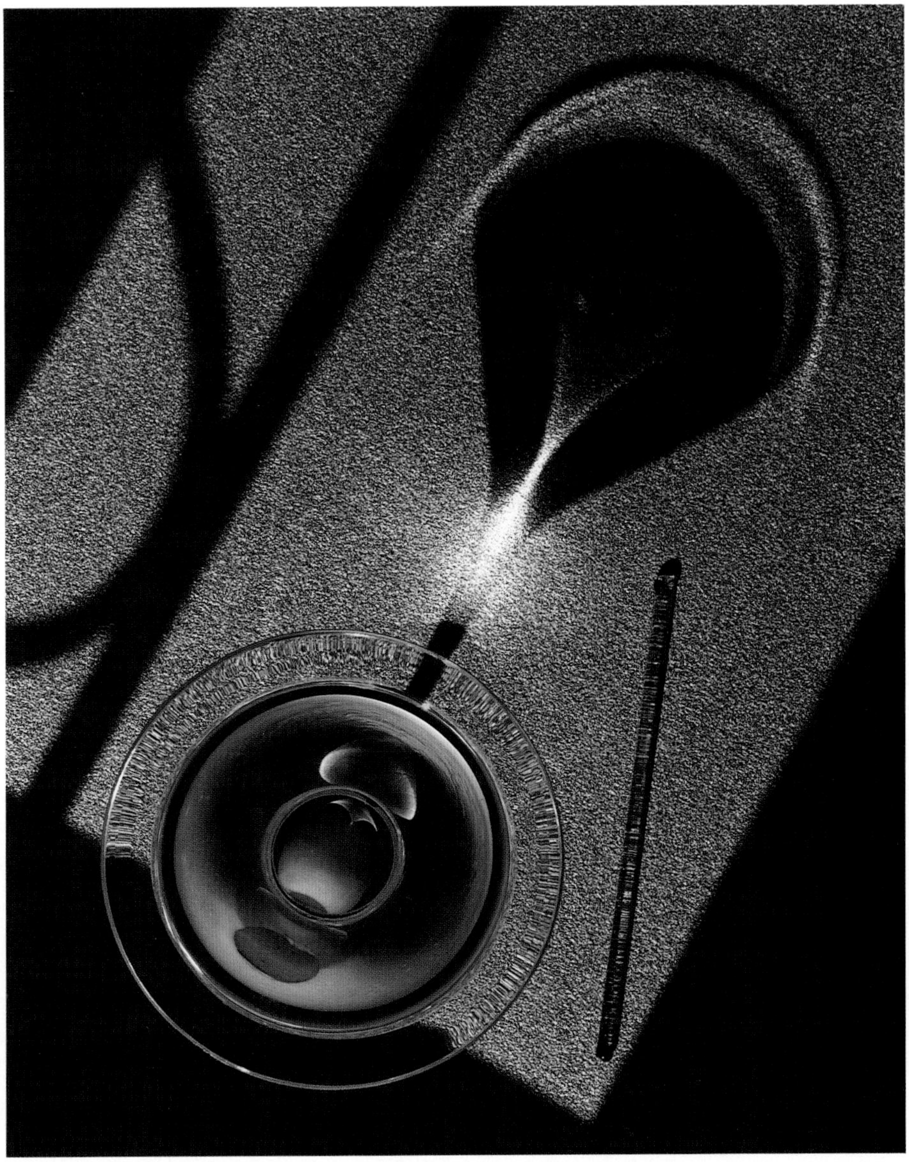

MICHAEL MAZZEO · PHOTOGRAPHY · 119 WEST 23RD STREET · NEW YORK, NEW YORK 10011

john bechtold

Represented by: Gary Lerman (919) 683-5777

PIERRE CHANTEAU STUDIO

209 WEST 38 STREET/PENTHOUSE/NYC/10018—212/221/5860 • AGENT/VICKI SPAETH—718/520/8632

RITA MAAS

119 WEST 23RD STREET N.Y.C., N.Y. 10011 212 • 645 • 9120
REPRESENTED BY ANITA GREEN 212 • 674 • 4788

RITA
MAAS

119 WEST 23RD STREET N.Y.C., N.Y. 10011 212•645•9120
REPRESENTED BY ANITA GREEN 212•674•4788

CHARLES MASTERS

ST. JOHN ASSOCIATES
308 EAST 59TH ST. NYC 10022
TELEPHONE (212) 308-7744

REPRESENTED BY MARY LARKIN

ESTĒE LAUDER
TOP PRIORITIES
YOUTH-DEW

ESTĒE LAUDER
Polished Performance Liquid Makeup
Fond de Teint Fluide
SIGNATURE

Grolsch
LAGER BEER
A real masterpiece from Holland.

EGG PLANT
BLACK BEAUTY
75¢
The Chas. C. Hart Seed Co.
WETHERSFIELD, CONN 06109

LYNN ST. JOHN

ST. JOHN ASSOCIATES
308 EAST 59TH ST. NYC 10022
TELEPHONE (212) 308-7744

REPRESENTED BY MARY LARKIN

E L I Z A B E T H W A T T

p h o t o g r a p h y . N. Y. C. . (2 1 2) 9 2 9 - 8 5 0 4

ZENITH

Royal

Martex • Designframe Inc.

S. D. Warren • Heller Breene

©TORU OCHI

RU OCHI 109 WEST 27TH STREET NEW YORK, N.Y. 10001 TEL.212-807-7711

© 1988 TOHRU NAKAMURA
Tohru Nakamura Studio
112 GREENE STREET, NEW YORK, NY 10012 REPRESENTED BY DARIO SACRAMONE 212·929·0487

BILLY
TOY SURPRISE
ROY ROGERS
paddle
47
EARTH BOMBS MARS
DONALD DUCK
Cola
PEZ

GUICE

Brad Guice Photography
Telephone / 212 / 206-0966
Represented by Janice Moses
Telephone / 212 / 779-7929

Buck

SPACE GUN
American
ARITHM
GUICE
Brad Guice Photography
Telephone/212/206-0966
Represented by Janice Moses
Telephone/212/779-7929

Give the bi

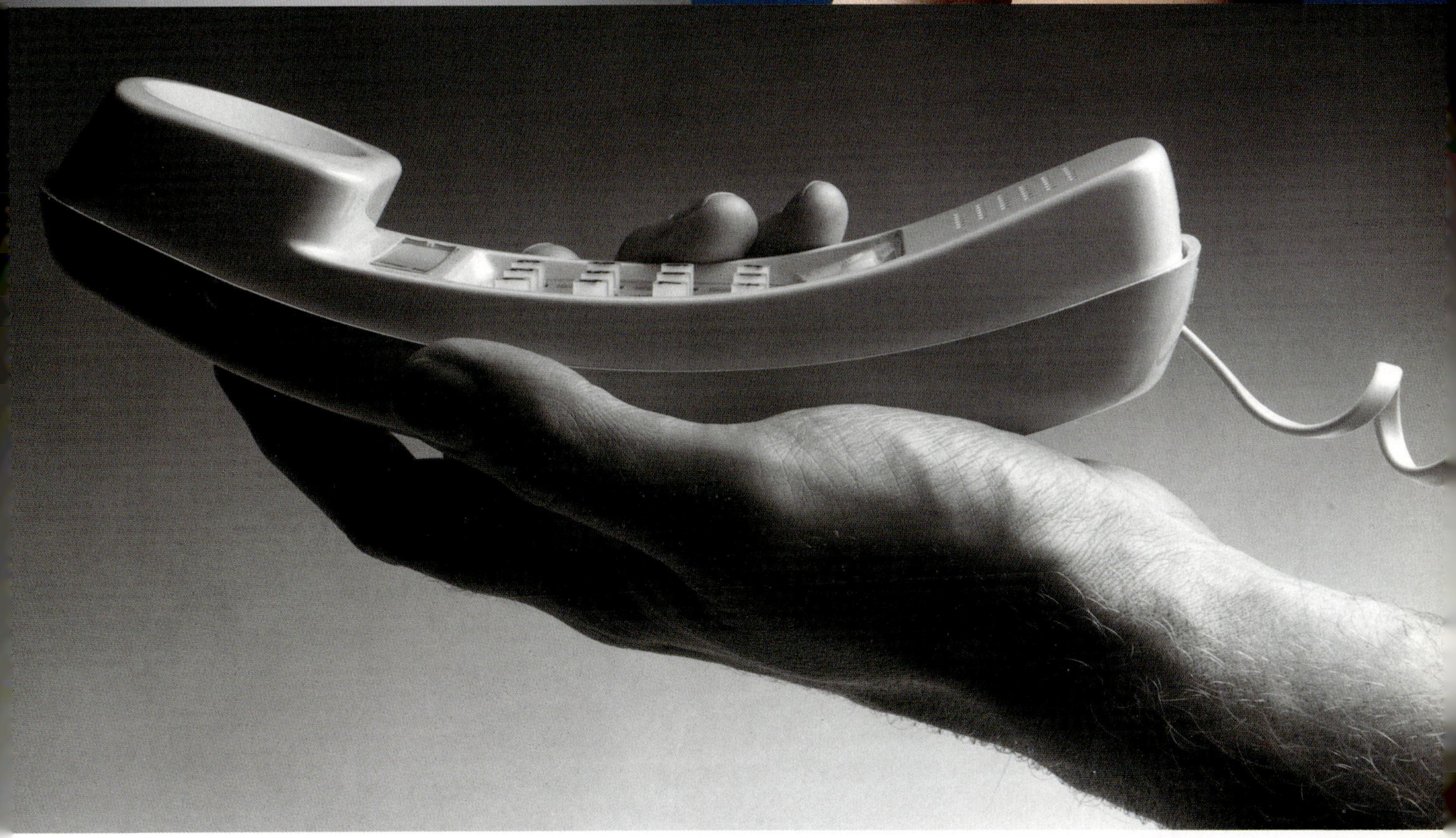

uy a little hand.

Dick Frank Studios, Inc. 11 West 25th St., N.Y., N.Y. (212) 242-4648 or Ted Wasserman (212) 867-5360

Salaverry
PHILIP SALAVERRY 133 W. 22 N.Y.C. 10011 (212) 807-0896
REPRESENTED BY: BILL DELANY (212) 683-8331

Salaverry
PHILIP SALAVERRY 133 W. 22 N.Y.C. 10011 (212) 807-0896
REPRESENTED BY: BILL DELANY (212) 683-8331

CLAYTON PRICE

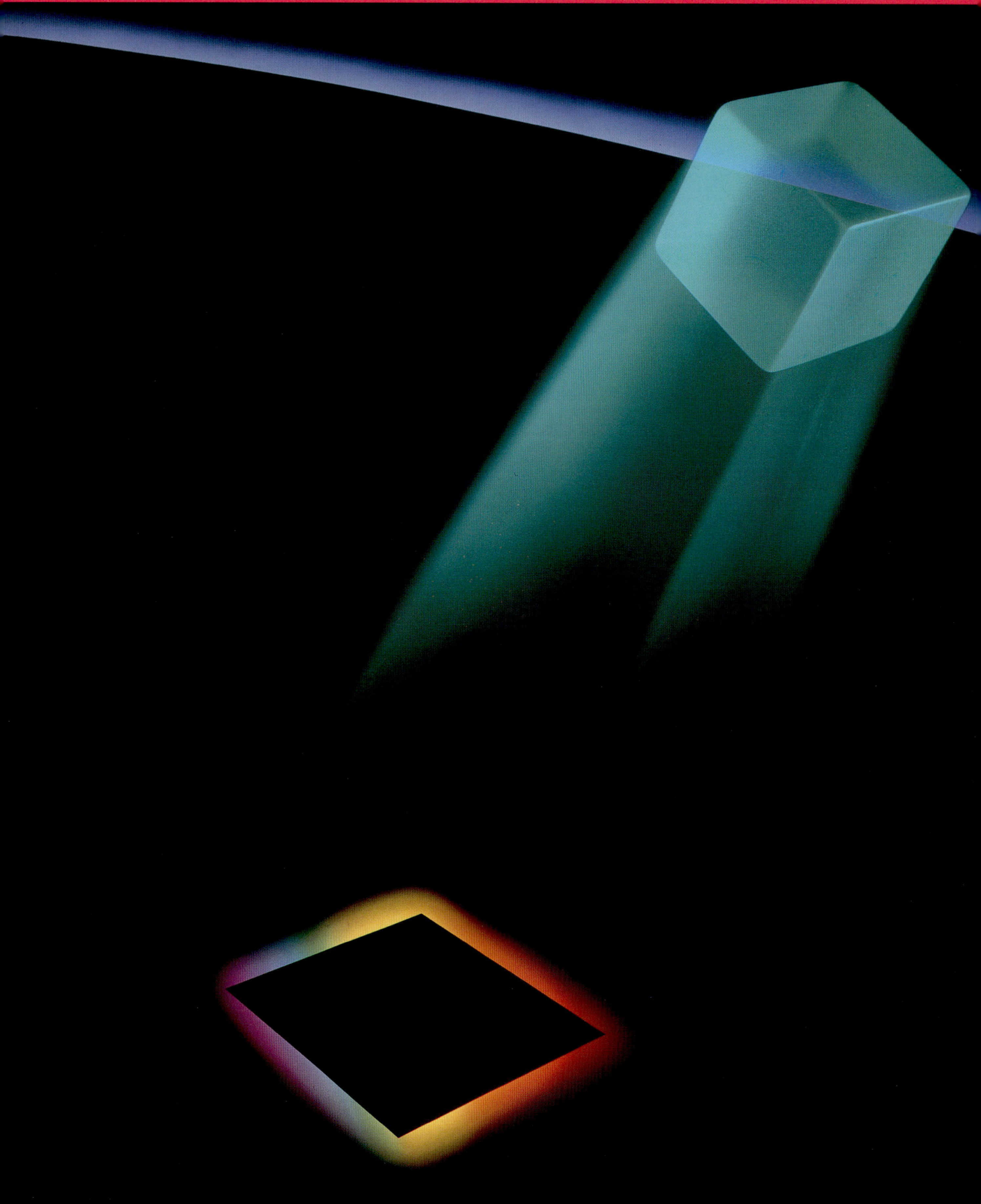

MAKES MAGIC.

KEN ANDREWLAVAGE / DUNLOP TIRES

SAM COOPERSTEIN / U.S. POSTAL SERVICE

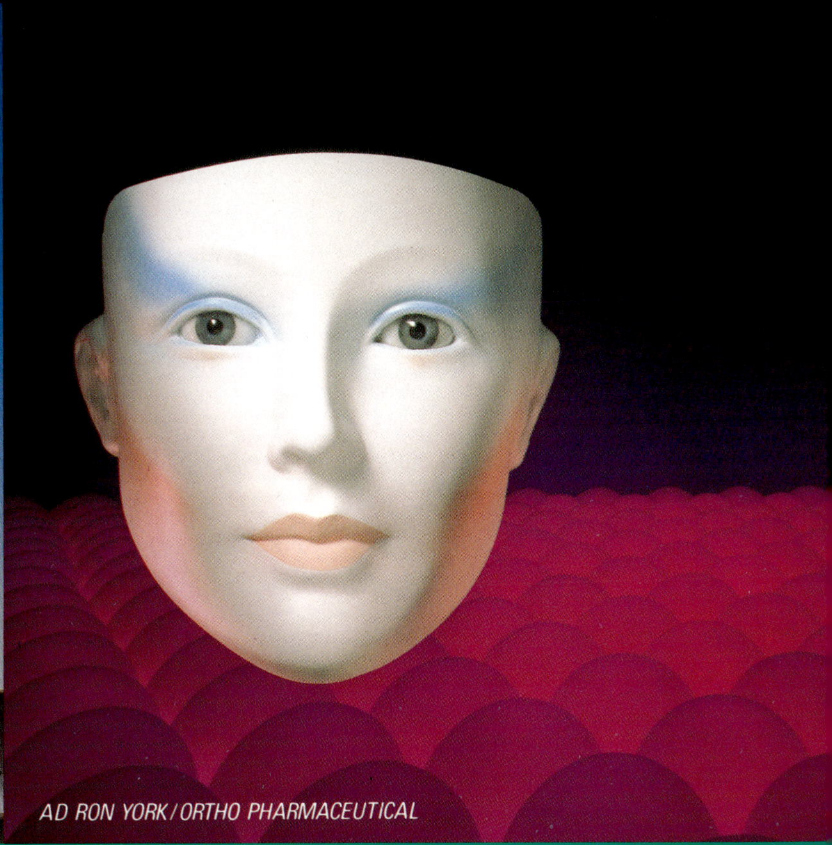

AD RON YORK / ORTHO PHARMACEUTICAL

205 WEST 19 ST. N.Y. N.Y. 10011 212-929-7721

KENRO IZU

Kenro Izu · Photography / Jean Conlon · Representative · 212 966 9897

ROSE'S
LIME JUICE

AARON M.

PETTINATO
PHOTOGRAPHY
42 GREENE STREET, NEW YORK, NY 10013 (212) 226-9380
REPRESENTED BY GLORIA VALENTINE (212) 725-1596

PRESCRIPTIVES / PRESCRIPTIVES /

TEA

N T H I N

CONTACT ANITA GREEN: (212) 674-4788 • STUDIO: (212) 594-0144 • FAX: (212) 643-0043

ROBERTO BROSAN

873 BROADWAY, NEW YORK, NEW YORK 10003 212 473-1471

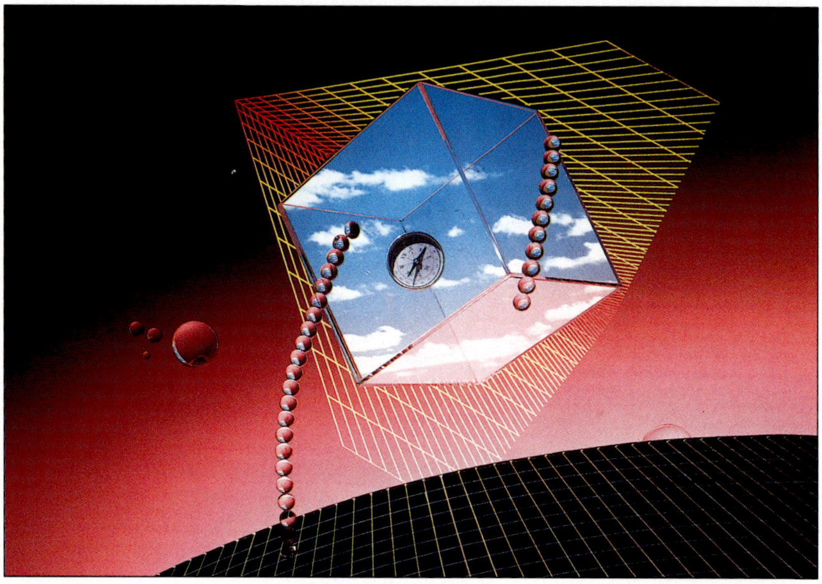

ROBERTO BROSAN

873 BROADWAY, NEW YORK, NEW YORK 10003 212 473-1471

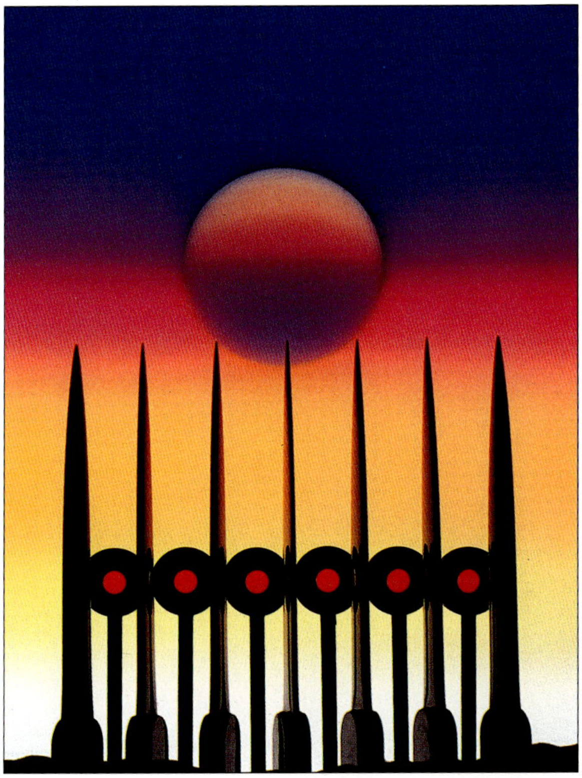

MISTRETTA

Martin Mistretta Inc., 220 West 19th Street, New York, N.Y. 10011 212 • 675-1547
Represented by Ellen Dillon • 675-1548

MISTRETTA

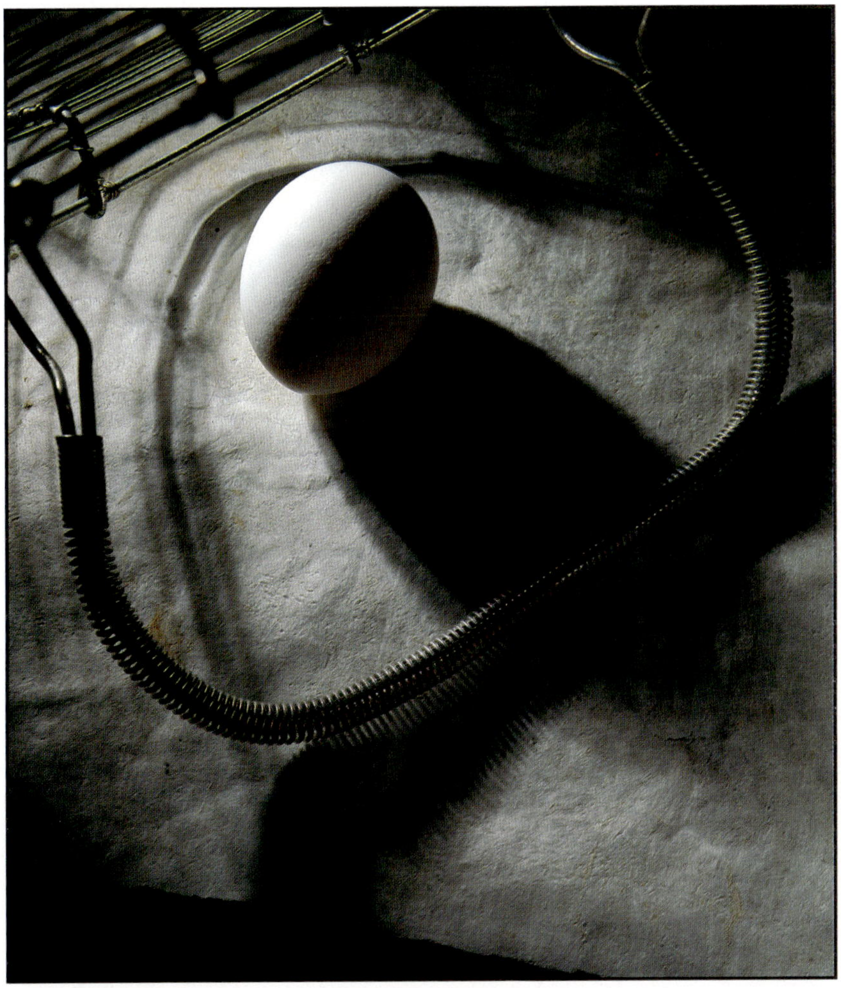

Martin Mistretta Inc., 220 West 19th Street, New York, N.Y. 10011 212 • 675-1547
Represented by Ellen Dillon • 675-1548

ANDY SPREITZER PHOTOGRAPHER

225 East 24th Street, New York City (212) 685-9669

ANDY SPREITZER
PHOTOGRAPHER

225 East 24th Street, New York City (212) 685-9669

RICK MULLER

2 1 2 9 6 7 3 1 7 7

EJP

face soap
regular
strength
CLINIQUE
SKIN SUPPLIES
FOR MEN

Eric
Jacobson
photography
39 West 29th Street
New York, New York 10001 212-696-4279

BRIAN **HAGIWARA**
504 LA GUARDIA PL
NEW YORK NY 10012
212 · 674 · 6026

TOM CONRAD / BROWN & WILLIAMSON

JORDAN SCHAPPS / NY MAG.

LARRY BERCOW
344 W. 38 ST. NYC 10018
212·629·9000

KEITH WEINMAN / WM. ESTY

LYNN SUGARMAN

LYNN SUGARMAN STUDIO
40 WEST 22 STREET
NEW YORK, NEW YORK 10010
212 · 691 · 3245
REPRESENTATION:
PAT HERRON 212 · 683 · 9039
NOB HOVDE ASSOCIATES
212 · 753 · 0462

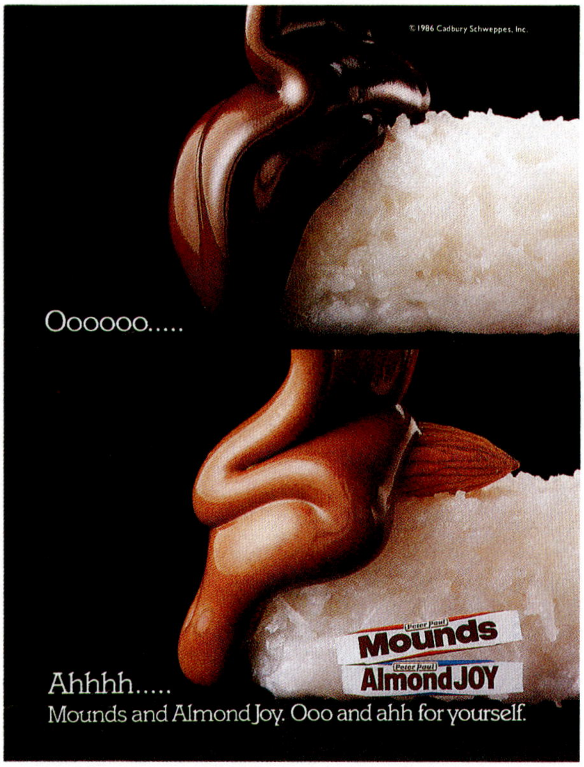

VITTORIO SACCO

Represented by Bernstein & Andriulli, Inc.
(212) 682-1490

VITTORIO SACCO

Represented by Bernstein & Andriulli, Inc.
(212) 682-1490

YSATIS
de
GIVENCHY
PARIS

ROBERT TARDIO

Photography Ltd.

19 West 21st Street
New York, NY 10010
212·463-9085
Fax: 212·807-8831

Represented by
Marian Vitale 212·683-4225

JUNG • LEE

2
1
2
•
8
0
7
•
8
1
0
7

132 WEST 21st STREET
NEW YORK, N.Y. 10011

Anthony Verde 133 *Mulberry Street, New York, NY* 10013 (212) 219-1152

Anthony Verde 133 *Mulberry Street, New York, NY* 10013 (212) 219-1152

THE DIFFICULT BARRY BLACKMAN DOES RIGHT AWAY.

THE IMPOSSIBLE TAKES A LITTLE LONGER.

BARRY BLACKMAN
He wrote the book on special effects.

150 5th Avenue New York, N.Y. 10011 (212) 627-9777.

McCAVERA

McCAVERA

KITTINGER FURNITURE

TOM McCAVERA 212 714 9122. REPRESENTED BY BERNSTEIN & ANDRIULLI, INC. 212 682 1490.

J.P. STEVENS & CO.

MIEROP DESIGN

CITIBANK

McCAVERA

TOM McCAVERA 212 714 9122. REPRESENTED BY BERNSTEIN & ANDRIULLI, INC. 212 682 1490

JON HOLDERER

119 WEST 23rd STREET, NEW YORK 10011 (212) 620-4260

JON HOLDERER

119 WEST 23rd STREET, NEW YORK 10011 (212) 620-4260

SUSANNE BUCKLER
PHOTOGRAPHY
344 West 38th Street
New York, NY 10018
Represented by
Harriet Meixler
(212) 868-0078

INDEX TO TAB

4

PHOTOGRAPHY

ARCHITECTURE

LANDSCAPE / LOCATION

Photographers & *Representatives*

All

Photography Listings,

TAB 5

INDEX TO TAB

4

PHOTOGRAPHY

ARCHITECTURE

LANDSCAPE / LOCATION

Photographers & *Representatives*

All

Photography Listings,

TAB 5

DAVID
McGLYNN

718 • 626 • 9427

PETER KING WEIDLEIN
122 WEST TWENTY SIXTH STREET, NEW YORK, NEW YORK 10001

212•989•5498

fax 212•929•7275

PETER KING WEIDLEIN

122 WEST TWENTY SIXTH STREET, NEW YORK, NEW YORK 10001

212•989•5498

fax 212•929•7275

WIDELINE

Buvez
Coca-Cola

LARRY DALE GORDON

LARRY DALE GORDON
REPRESENTATION:

NEW YORK/CHICAGO/DETROIT
NOB HOVDE/PAT HERRON
212/753-0462

LOS ANGELES
FOX & CLARK
213/653-6484

LONDON
DEREK HARMAN
441/352-7635

LARRY DALE GORDON

LARRY DALE GORDON
REPRESENTATION:

NEW YORK/CHICAGO/DETROIT
NOB HOVDE/PAT HERRON
212/753-0462

LOS ANGELES
FOX & CLARK
213/653-6484

LONDON
DEREK HARMAN
441/352-7635

JOHN STUART

80 VARICK ST. NYC 10013 212 966 6783

JOHN STUART

80 VARICK ST. NYC 10013 212 966 6783

L E N J E N S H E L

212 316-7809

INDEX TO TAB

5

INDEX TO TAB

5

G1308

G1256

G1385

G1449

COMSTOCK

Stock Photography

Toll Free: 800-225-2727

In New York: 212-353-8600

Fax: 212-353-3383

Telex: 6503209858

COMSTOCK • The Comstock Building • Dept G
30 Irving Place • New York, NY 10003
132 page color catalog available on request.

G1504

G1362

G1322

G1319

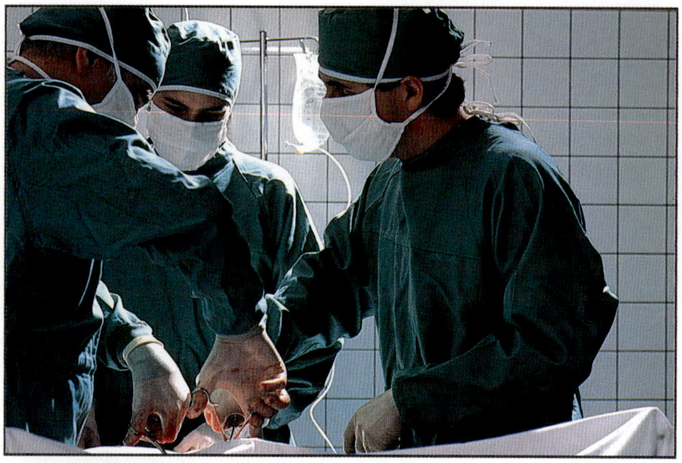

G1607

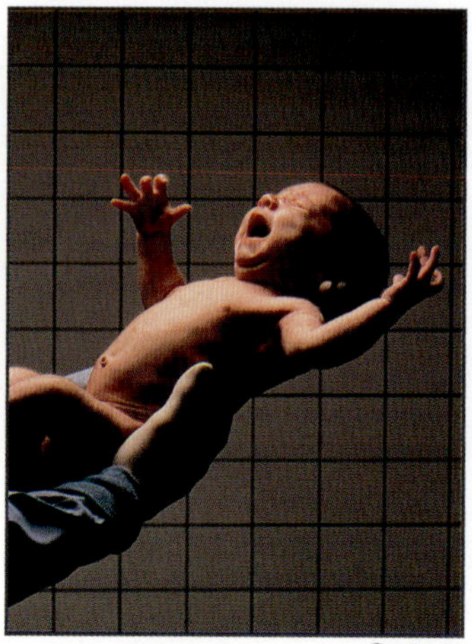

G1313

G829

G1743

G1770

G1731

G1801

COMSTOCK

Stock Photography

Toll Free: 800-225-2727

In New York: 212-353-8600

Fax: 212-353-3383

Telex: 6503209858

COMSTOCK • The Comstock Building • Dept. G
30 Irving Place • New York, NY 10003
132 page color catalog available on request.

G1785

G1826

G1879

G1818

G1730

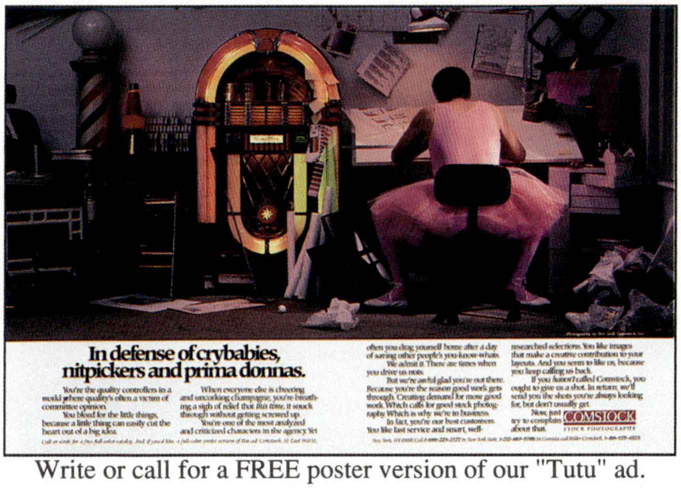

Write or call for a FREE poster version of our "Tutu" ad.

© Galen Rowell
World Trave
People
Transportat
U.S. Cities
FPG Stock
Historical
Special Effe
Industry
Landscapes
Sports
50's Color
FPG International
251 Park Ave South, NY, NY 10010
212. 777. 4210

PHOTOGRAPHY

a

ABATELLI, GARY *(212) 243-1034* 80 Charles St NY, NY 10014

ABEL, JIM *(212) 460-5374* 112 E 19th St NY, NY 10003

ABRAMOWITZ, ELLEN *(212) 686-2409* 166 E 35th St NY, NY 10016

ABRAMOWITZ, JERRY *(212) 420-9500* 680 Broadway NY, NY 10012

ABRAMSON, MICHAEL *(212) 941-1970* 15 Renwick St NY, NY 10013

ACEVEDO, MELANIE *(212) 439-6059* 336 E 77th St NY, NY 10021

ADAMO, JEFF *(212) 866-4886* 50 W 93rd St NY, NY 10025

ADAMS, EDDIE *(212) 929-1080* 40 W 24th St NY, NY 10010

ADAMS, GEORGE G. *(212) 391-1345* 15 W 38th St NY, NY 10010

ADDEO, EDWARD *(212) 206-1686* 151 W 19th St NY, NY 10011

ADELMAN, BOB *(212) 736-0537* 151 W 28th St NY, NY 10001

ADELMAN, MENACHEM ASSOC *(212) 675-1202* 156 Fifth Ave NY, NY 10010

ADLER, ARNIE *(212) 304-2443* 70 Park Terrace W NY, NY 10034

AGOR, ALEXANDER *(718) 531-0720* 108-28 Flatlands 7 St Brooklyn, NY 11236

AHARONI, OUDI *(212) 777-0847* 704 Broadway NY, NY 10003

AICH, CLARA *(212) 686-4220* 218 E 25th St NY, NY 10016

ALBERT, JADE *(212) 242-0940* 59 W 19th St NY, NY 10011

ALBERTS, ANDREA *(212) 242-5794* 100 Fifth Ave NY, NY 10011

ALCORN, RICHARD *(212) 866-1161* 160 W 95th St NY, NY 10025

ALEXANDER, ROBERT *(212) 684-0180* 50 W 29th St NY, NY 10001

ALEXANDERS, JOHN W *(212) 734-9166* 308 E 73rd St NY, NY 10021

ALLISON, DAVID *(212) 460-9056* 42 E 23rd St NY, NY 10010

ALPER, BARBARA *(212) 316-6518* 202 W 96th St NY, NY 10025

ALPERN/LUKOSKI *(212) 724-5017* 250 W 88th St NY, NY 10024

ALT, HOWARD *(212) 490-7868* 314 E 41st St NY, NY 10017

AMATO, PAUL *(212) 541-4787* 881 Seventh Ave NY, NY 10019

AMBROSE, KEN *(212) 757-2676* 1650 Broadway NY, NY 10028

AMPLO, NICK *(212) 741-2799* 271 1/2 W 10th St NY, NY 10014

AMRINE, JAMIE *(212) 243-2178* 30 W 22nd St NY, NY 10010

ANDREWS, BERT *(212) 662-6732* PO Box 20707 NY, NY 10025

ANTHONY, DON *(718) 317-6340* 79 Prall Ave Staten Isl, NY 10312

ANTONIO/STEPHEN PHOTO *(212) 674-2350* 45 E 20th St NY, NY 10003

APPLE, RICHARD *(212) 966-6782* 80 Varick St NY, NY 10013

ARAKAWA, NOBU *(212) 475-0206* 40 E 21st St NY, NY 10010

ARANITA, JEFFREY *(718) 625-7672* 60 Pineapple St Brooklyn, NY 11201

ARDITO, PETER *(212) 941-1561* 596 Broadway NY, NY 10012

ARESU/GOLDRING STUDIO *(212) 334-9494* 568 Broadway NY, NY 10012

ARKY, DAVID *(212) 242-4760* 57 W 19th St NY, NY 10011

ARLAK, VICTORIA *(212) 879-0250* 40 East End Ave NY, NY 10028

ARMA, TOM *(212) 243-7904* 38 W 26th St NY, NY 10010

PAGE 14; 66-67

ARNDT/BOWER *(212) 866-1902* 400 Central Park W NY, NY 10025

ARSLANIAN, OVAK *(212) 255-1519* 344 W 14th St NY, NY 10014

ASHE, BILL *(212) 695-6473* 534 W 35th St NY, NY 10001

ASHLEY, PAT *(212) 473-6180* 920 Broadway NY, NY 10011

ASTOR, JOSEF *(212) 307-5588* 154 W 57th St NY, NY 10019

ATKIN, JONATHAN *(212) 242-5218* 23 E 17th St NY, NY 10003

AUBRY, DANIEL *(212) 598-4191* 365 First Ave NY, NY 10010

AUSTER, EVAN *(212) 517-9776* 215 E 68th St NY, NY 10021

AUSTER, WALTER *(212) 627-8448* 18 E 16th St NY, NY 10003

AVA, BETH *(212) 966-4407* 87 Franklin St NY, NY 10013

AVEDIS *(212) 685-5888* 381 Park Ave So NY, NY 10016

AVEDON, RICHARD *(212) 879-6325* 407 E 75th St NY, NY 10021

AXON, RED *(212) 532-6317* 17 Park Ave NY, NY 10016

AZZATO, HANK *(212) 929-9455* 348 W 14th St NY, NY 10014

AZZI, ROBERT *(212) 481-6900* 116 E 27th St NY, NY 10016

b

BAASCH, DIANE *(212) 724-2123* 41 W 72nd St NY, NY 10023

BABCHUCK, JACOB *(212) 929-8811* 132 W 22nd St NY, NY 10011

BABUSHKIN, MARK *(212) 239-6630* 110 W 31st St NY, NY 10001

BACK, JOHN *(212) 243-6347* 15 Sheridan Sq NY, NY 10014

BAHRT, IRV *(212) 661-5260* 310 E 46th St NY, NY 10017

BAILLIE, ALLAN & GUS FRANCISCO
(212) 683-0418 220 E 23rd St NY, NY 10010

BAKER, CHRIS *(212) 678-4871* 310 Greenwich St NY, NY 10011

BAKER, CHUCK *(212) 517-9060* 1630 York Ave NY, NY 10028

BAKER, GLORIA *(212) 222-2866* 415 Central Park W NY, NY 10025

BAKER, JOE *(212) 925-6555* 35 Wooster St NY, NY 10013

BAKERMAN, NELSON *(212) 489-1647* 342 W 56th St NY, NY 10019

BALDWIN, JOEL *(212) 308-5991* 350 E 55th St NY, NY 10022

PAGE 82-83

BALE, J R *(212) 627-1489* 130 W 25th St NY, NY 10001

BALIOTTI, DAN *(212) 627-9039* 6 W 18th St NY, NY 10011

BANCROFT, MONTY *(212) 807-8650* 161 W 15th St NY, NY 10011

BAPTISTE, BETH *(212) 691-5674* 263A W 19th St NY, NY 10011

BARASH, HOWARD *(212) 242-6182* 349 W 11th St NY, NY 10014

BARATTA, NICHOLAS *(212) 239-0999* 450 W 31st St NY, NY 10001

Barba, Dan *(212) 420-8611* 201 E 16th St NY, NY 10003

Barber, James *(212) 598-4500* 873 Broadway NY, NY 10003

Barboza, Tony *(212) 529-5027* 853 Broadway NY, NY 10003

Barcellona, Marianne *(212) 463-9717* 175 Fifth Ave NY, NY 10010

Barclay, Bob Studios *(212) 255-3440* 5 W 19th St NY, NY 10011

Barkentin, George *(212) 243-2174* 15 W 18th St NY, NY 10011

Barnell, Joe *(212) 633-0101* 10 W 20th St NY, NY 10011

Barnett, Peggy *(212) 673-0500* 26 E 22nd St NY, NY 10010

Barns, Larry *(212) 242-8833* 21 W 16th St NY, NY 10011

Barr, Neal *(212) 765-5760* 222 Central Park So NY, NY 10019

Barrett, John *(212) 517-5210* 164 E 66th St NY, NY 10021

Barrett, John E *(212) 777-7309* 40 E 20th St NY, NY 10003

Barrick, Rick *(212) 741-2304* 12 E 18th St NY, NY 10003

Barrow, Scott *(212) 736-4567* 214 W 30th St NY, NY 10001

Barrows, Wendy *(212) 685-0799* 205 E 22nd St NY, NY 10010

Barton, Paul *(212) 533-1422* 101 W 18th St NY, NY 10011

Basilion, Nick *(212) 645-6568* 150 Fifth Ave NY, NY 10011

Bates, Art *(212) 799-3388* 154 W 70th St NY, NY 10023

Batlin, Lee *(212) 685-9492* 37 E 28th St NY, NY 10016

Baum, Charles *(212) 724-8013* 320 West End Ave NY, NY 10023

Baumann, Jennifer *(212) 633-0161* 682 Sixth Ave NY, NY 10010

Baumel, Ken *(212) 929-7550* 175 Fifth Ave NY, NY 10010

Bealmear, Brad *(212) 675-8060* 54 Barrow St NY, NY 10014

Bean, John *(212) 242-8106* 5 W l9th St NY, NY 10011

Bechtold, John *(212) 679-7630* 117 E 31st St NY, NY 10016

PAGE 112

Beck, Arthur *(212) 691-8331* 119 W 22nd St NY, NY 10011

Becker, Jonathan *(212) 929-3180* 450 West 24th St NY, NY 10011

Beebe, Rod *(212) 996-8926* 334 E 93rd St NY, NY 10128

Begleiter, Steven *(212) 334-5262* 38 Greene St NY, NY 10013

Belinsky, Jon *(212) 627-1246* 119 E 17th St NY, NY 10003

Beller, Janet *(212) 334-0281* 225 Varick St NY, NY 10014

Belott, Robert *(212) 924-1503* 236 W 26th St NY, NY 10001

Benedict, William *(212) 697-4460* 5 Tudor City NY, NY 10017

Bensimon, Gilles *(212) 966-5770* 110 Greene St NY, NY 10012

Bercow, Larry *(212) 629-9000* 344 W 38th St NY, NY 10018

PAGE 162-163

Berenholtz, Richard

***(212) 222-1302* 600 W 111th St NY, NY 10025**

PAGE 184-185

Berger, Joseph *(212) 685-7191* 121 Madison Ave NY, NY 10016

Bergman, Beth *(212) 724-1867* 150 West End Ave NY, NY 10023

Bergren, John *(212) 627-5292* 27 W 20th St NY, NY 10011

Berkun, Phil *(718) 237-2648* 199 Amity St Brooklyn, NY 11201

Berkwit, Lane *(212) 889-5911* 262 Fifth Ave NY, NY 10001

Berman, Brad *(718) 383-8950* 295 Ecksford St Brooklyn, NY 11222

Berman, Howard *(212) 473-3366* 5 E 19th St NY, NY 10003

Bernson, Carol *(212) 473-3884* 119 Fifth Ave NY, NY 10003

Bernstein, Alan *(212) 254-1355* 365 First Ave NY, NY 10010

Bernstein, Audrey *(212) 243-9373* 142 W 24th St NY, NY 10011

Bernstein, Bill *(212) 925-6853* 59 Thompson St NY, NY 10012

Bersell, Barbara *(212) 734-9049* 12 E 86th St NY, NY 10128

Bester, Roger *(212) 645-5810* 55 Van Dam St NY, NY 10013

Betz, Charles *(212) 675-4760* 138 W 25th St NY, NY 10001

Bevan, David *(212) 582-5045* 536 W 50th St NY, NY 10019

Bevilacqua, Joe *(212) 490-0355* 202 E 42nd St NY, NY 10017

Biddle, Geoffrey *(212) 505-7713* 5 E 3rd St NY, NY 10003

Bies, William *(718) 278-0236* 21-29 41st St LIC, NY 11105

Big City Productions *(212) 473-3366* 5 E 19th St NY, NY 10003

Bijur, Hilda *(212) 737-4458* 190 E 72nd St NY, NY 10021

Biondo, Michael *(212) 353-9377* 23 Second Ave NY, NY 10003

Bisbee, Terry *(212) 242-4762* 290 W 12th St NY, NY 10014

Bishop, David *(212) 929-4355* 251 W 19th St NY, NY 10011

Blachut, Dennis *(212) 947-4270* 145 W 28th St NY, NY 10001

Blackman, Barry *(212) 627-9777* 150 Fifth Ave NY, NY 10011

PAGE 174-175

Blackman, Jeffrey *(718) 769-0986* 2323 E 12th St Brooklyn, NY 11229

Blackstock, Ann *(212) 695-2525* 400 W 43rd St NY, NY 10036

Blake, Rebecca *(212) 695-6438* 35 W 36th St NY, NY 10018

Blanch, Andrea *(212) 888-7912* 434 E 52nd St NY, NY 10022

Blechman, Jeff *(212) 226-0006* 591 Broadway NY, NY 10012

Blecker, Charles *(212) 242-8390* 350 Bleecker St NY, NY 10014

Blinkoff, Richard *(212) 620-7883* 147 W 15th St NY, NY 10011

PAGE 60-61

Blitz, Irvin *(212) 219-9744* 114 Spring St NY, NY 10012

Block, Helen *(718) 788-1097* 385 14th St Brooklyn, NY 11215

Block, Ira Photography *(212) 242-2728* 215 W 20th St NY, NY 10011

Bloom, Teri *(212) 475-2274* 300 Mercer St NY, NY 10003

Blosser, Robert *(212) 662-0107* 741 West End Ave NY, NY 10025

Bobbe, Leland *(212) 685-5238* 51 W 28th St NY, NY 10001

Bodi Studios *(212) 947-7883* 340 W 39th St NY, NY 10018

PAGE 84-85

BODICK, GAY *(212) 772-8584* 11 E 80th St NY, NY 10021

BOGERTMAN, RALPH INC *(212) 889-8871* 34 W 28th St NY, NY 10001

BOISSEAU, JOSEPH *(212) 519-8672* 105 E 223rd St Bronx, NY 10466

BOLESTA, ALAN *(212) 873-1932* 11 Riverside Dr NY, NY 10023

BOLJONIS, STEVEN *(212) 740-0003* 555 Ft Washington Ave NY, NY 10033

BOMAN, ERIC *(212) 460-5212* NY, NY

BONOMO, LOUIS *(212) 242-4630* 118 W 27th St NY, NY 10001

BORDNICK, BARBARA *(212) 533-1180* 39 E 19th St NY, NY 10003

PAGE 25

BOROWSKI, STEVE *(212) 627-7642* 36 W 20th St NY, NY 10011

BOSCH, PETER *(212) 925-0707* 477 Broome St NY, NY 10013

BOSZKO, RON *(212) 541-5504* 140 W 57th St NY, NY 10019

BOTTOMLEY, JIM *(212) 677-9646* 125 Fifth Ave NY, NY 10003

BOWMAN, ERIC *(212) 460-5212* NY, NY

BOYLE, JEFFREY *(212) 686-5277* 200 E 33rd St NY, NY 10016

BRACCO, BOB *(212) 228-0230* 43 E 19th St NY, NY 10003

BRADING, MARTIN *(212) 255-3252* 96 Fifth Ave NY, NY 10011

BRADY, STEVE *(212) 213-6024* 507 E 30th St NY, NY 10016

BRAKHA, MOSHE *(212) 645-7946* NY, NY

BRANDT, PETER *(212) 242-4289* 73 Fifth Ave NY, NY 10003

PAGE 86-87

BRAUN, YENACHEM *(212) 873-1985* 666 West End Ave NY, NY 10025

BRAVERMAN, ALAN *(212) 674-1925* 139 Fifth Ave NY, NY 10010

BREDEL, WALTER *(212) 228-8565* 21 E 10th St NY, NY 10003

BREITROSE, HOWARD *(212) 242-7825* 443 W 18th St NY, NY 10011

BRELLO, RON *(212) 982-0490* 400 Lafayette St NY, NY 10003

BRENNER, GEORGE *(212) 691-7436* 15 W 24th St NY, NY 10010

BRENNER/LENNON *(516) 752-0610* 24 So Mall Plainview, NY 11803

BRESKIN, MICHAEL *(212) 925-2858* 324 Lafayette NY, NY 10012

BRETT, CLIFTON *(212) 675-6236* 51 W 14th St NY, NY 10011

BREWSTER, DON *(212) 874-0548* 235 West End Ave NY, NY 10023

BREY, ALBERT *(212) 941-1180* 225 Lafayette St NY, NY 10012

BRILL STUDIO *(212) 885-0802* 270 City Island Ave City Isl, NY 10464

BRILL, JAMES *(212) 645-9414* 160 W 16th St NY, NY 10011

BRITTON, PETER *(212) 737-1664* 315 E 68th St NY, NY 10021

BROCHMANN, KRISTEN E *(212) 989-6319* 236 W 27th St NY, NY 10001

BRODY, BOB *(212) 741-0013* 5 W 19th NY, NY 10011

BRONSTEIN, STEVE *(212) 473-3366* 5 E 19th St NY, NY 10003

BROOKE, RANDY *(212) 677-2656* 179 E 3rd St NY, NY 10009

BROSAN, ROBERTO *(212) 473-1471* 873 Broadway NY, NY 10003

PAGE 150-151

BROWN, CYNTHIA *(212) 564-1625* 455 W 34th St NY, NY 10001

BROWN, NANCY *(212) 924-9105* 6 W 20th St NY, NY 10011

PAGE 70-71

BROWN, OWEN STUDIO *(212) 947-9470* 134 W 29th St NY, NY 10001

BRUDERER, ROLF *(212) 684-4890* 443 Park Ave So NY, NY 10016

BRUNO BURKLIN *(212) 420-0208* 873 Broadway NY, NY 10003

BRUNO PHOTO *(212) 925-2929* 43 Crosby St NY, NY 10012

BRUNSWICK, CECILE *(212) 222-2088* 127 W 96th St NY, NY 10025

BRY, KNUT *(212) 925-8333* 568 Broadway NY, NY 10012

BRYCE, SHERMAN E *(212) 580-9639* 269 W 90th St NY, NY 10024

BRYSON, JOHN *(212) 755-1321* 12 E 62nd St NY, NY 10021

BUCETA, JAIME *(212) 807-8485* 56 W 22nd St NY, NY 10010

BUCK, BRUCE *(212) 645-1022* 39 W 14th St NY, NY 10011

PAGE 72

BUCKLER, SUSANNE *(212) 279-0043* 344 W 38th St NY, NY 10018

PAGE 180

BUCKMASTER, ADRIAN *(212) 799-7318* 332 W 87th St NY, NY 10022

BUCKNER, BILL *(212) 941-1204* 38 Greene St NY, NY 10003

BULLATY, SONJA *(212) 663-2122* 336 Central Park W NY, NY 10025

BUONNANO, RAY *(212) 675-7680* 237 W 26th St NY, NY 10001

BURKHART, VANNI *(212) 925-8333* 568 Broadway NY, NY 10012

BURNETTE, DAVID *(212) 683-2002* NY, NY

BURNIE, ELLEN FORBES *(212) 219-1091* 19 Hubert St NY, NY 10013

BURNS, TOM *(212) 927-4678* 534 W 35th St NY, NY 10001

BURQUEZ, FELIZARDO *(718) 274-6139* 22-63 38th St Astoria, NY 11105

BURRELL, FRED *(212) 691-0808* 54 W 21st St NY, NY 10010

BUSS, GARY *(212) 645-0928* 250 W 14th St NY, NY 10011

PAGE 97

BUTCHER, ROBERT *(212) 371-7659* NY, NY

BUTLER, DENNIS *(212) 686-5084* 200 E 37th St NY, NY 10016

BUTLER, ROBERT *(212) 982-8051* 400 Lafayette St NY, NY 10003

BYERS, BRUCE *(212) 242-5846* 11 W 20th St NY, NY 10011

PAGE 64

C

CADGE, JEFF *(212) 246-6155* 341 W 47th St NY, NY 10036

CAILOR/RESNICK *(212) 977-4300* 237 W 54th St NY, NY 10019

CALICCHIO, TOM *(212) 473-8990* 30 E 21st St NY, NY 10010

CALLIOPE *(212) 255-3252* NY, NY

PAGE 32

CALLIS, CHRIS *(212) 243-0231* 91 Fifth Ave NY, NY 10003

PAGE 28-29

CAMERA COMMUNICATIONS *(212) 925-2722* 110 Greene St NY, NY 10012

CAMERON PHOTO *(212) 675-0089* 78 Fifth Ave NY, NY 10011

CAMP, E J *(212) 475-6267* 20 E 10th St NY, NY 10003

CAMPBELL, BARBARA *(212) 929-5620* 138 W 17th St NY, NY 10011

CAMPOS, JOHN *(212) 675-0601* 132 W 21st St NY, NY 10011

CANADY, PHILIP *(212) 737-3855* 1411 Second Ave NY, NY 10021

CANNON, GREGORY *(212) 228-3190* 876 Broadway NY, NY 10003

CANTOR, PHIL *(212) 243-1143* 75 Ninth Ave NY, NY 10011

CARDACINO, MICHAEL *(212) 947-9307* 20 Ridge Rd Douglaston, NY 11363

CARGASACCHI, GIANNI *(212) 206-0410* NY, NY

CARRINO, JOHN *(212) 243-3623* 160 Fifth Ave NY, NY 10010

CARRON, LES *(212) 255-8250* 15 W 24th St NY, NY 10010

CARSON, DONALD *(212) 807-8987* 115 W 23rd St NY, NY 10011

CARTER, DWIGHT *(212) 627-1266* 11 W 17th St NY, NY 10011

CASHIN, ART *(212) 255-3440* 5 W 19th St NY, NY 10011

CASTELLI, CHARLES *(212) 620-5536* 41 Union Sq W NY, NY 10003

CASTILLO, LUIS A *(718) 834-1380* 60 Pineapple St Brooklyn, NY 11201

CAULFIELD, PATRICIA *(212) 362-1951* 115 W 86th St NY, NY 10024

CAVERLY, KAT *(212) 757-8388* 414 W 49th St NY, NY 10016

CEARLEY, GUY *(212) 260-3084* 460 Grand St NY, NY 10002

CELNICK, EDWARD *(212) 420-9326* 36 E 12th St NY, NY 10003

CEMENTI, JOSEPH *(212) 924-7770* 133 W 19th St NY, NY 10011

CENICOLA, TONY STUDIO *(212) 420-9798* 32 Union Sq E NY, NY 10003

CESARVERA *(212) 582-1501* 162 W 56th St NY, NY 10019

CHAKMAKJIAN, PAUL *(212) 563-3195* 35 W 36th St NY, NY 10018

CHALK, DAVID *(212) 874-9042* 157 Hudson St NY, NY 10013

CHALKIN, DENNIS *(212) 929-1036* 5 E 16th St NY, NY 10003

PAGE 52-53

CHAN, AMOS T.S. *(212) 219-0574* 480 Broadway NY, NY 10013

CHAN, JOHN *(212) 534-4390* 1469 Lexington Ave NY, NY 10128

CHANEY, SCOTT *(212) 924-8440* 11 W 20th St NY, NY 10011

CHANTEAU, PIERRE *(212) 221-5860* 209 W 38th St NY, NY 10018

PAGE 113

CHAPMAN, MIKE *(212) 966-9542* 543 Broadway NY, NY 10012

CHARLES, BILL *(212) 627-8012* 148 W 23rd St NY, NY 10011

CHARLES, FREDERICK *(212) 505-0686* 254 Park Ave So NY, NY 10010

CHARLES, LISA *(212) 807-8600* 119 W 23rd St NY, NY 10011

CHATELAIN, ALEX *(212) 966-5678* 205 Mulberry St NY, NY 10012

CHAULK, DAVID *(212) 925-4203* 157 Hudson St NY, NY 10013

CHAUNCY, KIM *(212) 242-2400* 123 W 13th St NY, NY 10011

CHECANI, RICHARD *(212) 645-8634* 1133 Broadway NY, NY 10016

CHELSEA PHOTO/GRAPHICS *(212) 206-1780* 641 Sixth Ave NY, NY 10011

CHEN, PAUL INC *(212) 674-4100* 133 Fifth Ave NY, NY 10003

CHERNIN, BRUCE *(212) 496-0266* 330 W 86th St NY, NY 10024

CHESTNUT, RICHARD *(212) 255-1790* 236 W 27th St NY, NY 10001

PAGE 122-123

CHIBA, KAZ *(212) 674-7575* 303 Park Ave So NY, NY 10010

PAGE 89

CHIN, TED *(212) 691-7612* 118 W 27th St NY, NY 10001

CHIN, WALTER *(212) 924-6760* 160 Fifth Ave NY, NY 10010

CHRISTENSEN, PAUL H *(212) 279-2838* 286 Fifth Ave NY, NY 10001

CHRYNWSKI, WALTER *(212) 675-1906* 154 W 18th St NY, NY 10011

CHURCH, DIANA *(212) 736-4116* 31 W 31st St NY, NY 10001

CIPOLLA, KAREN *(212) 619-6114* 103 Reade St NY, NY 10013

CIRONE, BETTINA *(212) 888-7649* 57 W 58th St NY, NY 10019

CLARKE, KEVIN *(212) 460-9360* 900 Broadway NY, NY 10003

CLAYTON, TOM *(212) 431-3377* 568 Broadway NY, NY 10012

CLEMENTI, JOSEPH ASSOC *(212) 924-7770* 133 W 19th St NY, NY 10011

CLOUGH, TERRY *(212) 255-3040* 147 W 25th St NY, NY 10001

CLYMER, JONATHAN *(718) 482-5493* 146 W 29th St NY, NY 10001

COBB, JAN *(212) 255-1400* 5 West 19th St NY, NY 10011

PAGE 65

COBIN, MARTIN *(212) 758-5742* 145 E 49th St NY, NY 10017

COCHRAN, GEORGE *(212) 689-9054* 381 Park Ave So NY, NY 10016

COGGIN, ROY *(212) 929-6262* 64 W 21st St NY, NY 10010

COHEN, JAMES *(212) 719-2790* 580 Eighth Ave NY, NY 10018

COHEN, JOEL *(212) 691-5129* 27 E 13th St NY, NY 10003

COHEN, LAWRENCE PHOTO *(212) 967-4376* 247 W 30th St NY, NY 10001

COHEN, MARC DAVID *(212) 741-0015* 5 W 19th NY, NY 10011

COHEN, ROBERT *(212) 206-0410* NY, NY

COHN, RIC *(212) 924-4450* NY, NY

COLABELLA, VINCENT *(212) 949-7456* 304 E 41st St NY, NY 10017

COLEMAN, GENE *(212) 691-4752* 250 W 27th St NY, NY 10001

COLEN, CORRINE *(212) 431-7425* 519 Broadway NY, NY 10012

COLES, MONTY *(212) 688-4364* 699 Madison Ave NY, NY 10021

COLLETTI, STEVE *(212) 972-2218* 200 Park Ave NY, NY 10166

COLLINS, ARLENE *(212) 431-9117* 64 N Moore St NY, NY 10013

COLLINS, BENTON *(212) 254-7247* 873 Broadway NY, NY 10003

COLLINS, CHRIS *(212) 633-1670* 35 W 20th St NY, NY 10011

COLLINS, SHELDON *(212) 242-0076* 27 W 24th St NY, NY 10010

COLLITON, PAUL *(212) 619-6102* 310 Greenwich St NY, NY 10013

COLTON, ROBERT *(212) 831-3953* 1700 York Ave NY, NY 10028

Comte, Michel (212) 370-4300 235 E 40th St NY, NY 10016

Connors, William (212) 490-3801 310 E 46th St NY, NY 10017

Contact Press Images (212) 481-6910 116 E 27th St NY, NY 10016

Contarsy, Ron (212) 995-8850 611 Broadway NY, NY 10012

Cook, Irvin (212) 925-6216 534 W 43rd St NY, NY 10036

Cook, Rod (212) 995-0100 29 E 19th St NY, NY 10003

Cooke, Colin (212) 254-5090 380 Lafayette St NY, NY 10003

page 102-103

Cooper, Martha (212) 222-5146 310 Riverside Dr NY, NY 10025

Cope, Gil (212) 929-1777 135 W 26th St NY, NY 10001

Corbett, Jane (212) 505-1177 303 Park Ave So NY, NY 10010

Corman, Richard (212) 255-3252 96 Fifth Ave NY, NY 10011

Cornish, Dan (212) 226-3183 594 Broadway NY, NY 10012

Corporate Photographers Inc

(212) 964-6515 45 John St NY, NY 10038

Cosimo (212) 206-1818 43 W 13th St NY, NY 10011

Couzens, Larry (212) 620-9790 16 E 17th St NY, NY 10003

Cowan, Frank (212) 675-5960 5 E 16th St NY, NY 10003

Cox, David (212) 925-0734 25 Mercer St NY, NY 10013

Crampton, Nancy (212) 254-1135 35 W 9th St NY, NY 10011

Crocker, Ted (212) 686-8684 117 E 30th St NY, NY 10016

Croner, Ted (212) 685-3944 15 W 28th St NY, NY 10001

Cronin, Casey (212) 334-9253 115 Wooster St NY, NY 10012

Crum, John R (212) 463-8663 124 W 24th St NY, NY 10011

Cserna, George (212) 477-3472 80 Second Ave NY, NY 10003

Culberson, Earl (212) 473-3366 5 E 19th St NY, NY 10003

Cunningham, Peter (212) 475-4866 214 Sullivan St NY, NY 10012

Curatola, Tony (212) 243-5478 18 E 17th St NY, NY 10003

Cutler, Craig (212) 966-1652 39 Walker St NY, NY 10013

page 108-109

Czaplinski, Czeslaw (718) 389-9606 90 Dupont St Brooklyn, NY 11222

d

D'Addio, James (212) 645-0267 41 Union Sq W NY, NY 10003

Daley, James D (212) 925-7192 568 Broadway NY, NY 10012

Daly, Jack (212) 695-2726 247 W 30th St NY, NY 10001

Dantuono, Paul (212) 683-5778 433 Park Ave So NY, NY 10016

Dantzic, Jerry (718) 789-7478 910 President St Brooklyn, NY 11215

Dauman, Henri (212) 860-3804 4 E 88th St NY, NY 10128

Davidson, Bruce (212) 966-9200 72 Spring St NY, NY 10012

Davidson, Darwin K (212) 242-0095 32 Bank Street NY, NY 10014

Davis, Dick (212) 751-3276 400 E 59th St NY, NY 10022

Davis, Don (212) 989-2820 61 Horatio St NY, NY 10014

Davis, Hal (212) 769-9099 130 W 79th St NY, NY 10024

Davis, Lynn (212) 206-0737 108 W 18th St NY, NY 10011

Davis, Richard (212) 675-2428 17 E 16th St NY, NY 10003

Day, Bob (212) 475-7387 29 E 19th St NY, NY 10003

Day, Olita (212) 673-9354 239 Park Ave So NY, NY 10003

De Zanger, Arie (212) 354-7327 80 W 40th St NY, NY 10018

De Zitter, Harry (212) 989-7074 6 Jane St NY, NY 10014

Decanio, Steve (212) 594-0593 448 W 37th St NY, NY 10018

DeFever, Cyril (212) 233-7177 157 Chambers St NY, NY 10007

DeFrancis, Peter (212) 966-1357 424 Broome St NY, NY 10013

DeGrado, Drew (212) 302-2760 250 W 40th St NY, NY 10018

Degrado, Drew (212) 302-2760 250 W 40th St NY, NY 10018

DeLeone, Katrina (212) 714-9777 286 Fifth Ave NY, NY 10010

DeLessio, Len (212) 206-8725 7 E 17th St NY, NY 10003

DeMarchelier, Patrick (212) 924-3561 162 W 21st St NY, NY 10011

DeMelo, Antonio (212) 929-0507 126 W 22nd St NY, NY 10011

DeMilt, Ronald (212) 228-5321 873 Broadway NY, NY 10003

Denker, Deborah (212) 219-9263 460 Greenwich St NY, NY 10013

Denner, Manuel (212) 947-6220 249 W 29th St NY, NY 10001

Dennis, Lisl (212) 532-8226 135 E 39th St NY, NY 10016

Denson, Walt (212) 642-8211 NY, NY

DePaul, Raymond (212) 769-2550 252 W 76th St NY, NY 10023

DePra, Nancy (212) 242-0252 15 W 24th St NY, NY 10011

DeRosa, Peter (212) 864-3007 117 W 95th St NY, NY 10025

Derr, Stephen (212) 246-5920 420 W 45th St NY, NY 10036

Des Fontaines, Thierry (212) 925-5909 66 Crosby St NY, NY 10012

DeSanto, Thomas (212) 967-1390 116 W 29th St NY, NY 10001

DeToy, Ted (212) 988-1869 511 E 78th St NY, NY 10021

Deutsch, Jack (212) 799-7179 165 W 83rd St NY, NY 10024

DeVito, Bart (212) 421-0377 43 E 30th St NY, NY 10016

Diadul, Robert (212) 966-5770 110 Greene St NY, NY 10012

Diamond, Joe (212) 316-5295 915 West End Ave NY, NY 10025

Dian, Russell (212) 722-4348 432 E 88th St NY, NY 10128

Diaz, Jorge (212) 675-4783 142 W 24th St NY, NY 10011

Dibue, Robert (212) 206-0860 40 W 20th St NY, NY 10011

Dicran Studio (212) 695-6438 35 W 36th St NY, NY 10018

DiFranza Williamson Photography (212) 463-8302 NY, NY

DiMartini, Sally (516) 329-1236 137 Riverside Dr NY, NY 10024

DiMicco/Ferris Studio *(212) 627-4074* 40 W 17th St NY, NY 10011

D'Innocenzo, Paul *(212) 925-9622* 568 Broadway NY, NY 10012

Dipetto, John *(212) 935-4762* 245 E 54th St NY, NY 10022

Dodge, Jeff *(212) 620-9652* 133 Eighth Ave NY, NY 10011

Dolgins, Alan *(212) 741-2270* NY, NY

Dominis, John *(212) 841-2340* 252 W 102nd St NY, NY 10025

Donaho, Linda *(212) 966-5770* 110 Greene St NY, NY 10012

Donnelly, Mike *(212) 688-4364* 699 Madison Ave NY, NY 10021

D'Orazio, Sante *(212) 777-5757* 66 Crosby St NY, NY 10012

page 12-13

Dorf, Myron Jay *(212) 255-2020* 205 W 19th St NY, NY 10011

Dorot, Didier *(212) 206-1608* 48 W 21st St NY, NY 10010

Dorrance, Scott *(212) 529-4030* 131 E 23rd St NY, NY 10010

Doubilet, David *(212) 348-5011* 1040 Park Ave NY, NY 10028

Drabkin, Si Studios Inc *(718) 279-4512* Brooklyn, NY

Drew, Rue Faris *(212) 794-8994* 177 E 77th St NY, NY 10021

Druskis, Laima *(212) 889-2997* NY, NY

Dubler, Douglas *(212) 410-6300* 162 E 92nd St NY, NY 10128

Duchaine, Randy *(212) 243-4371* 200 W 18th St NY, NY 10011

Ducote, Kimberly *(212) 989-3680* 410 W 23rd St NY, NY 10011

Dugdale, John *(212) 219-8234* 17 Cleveland Pl NY, NY 10012

Duke, Dana *(212) 260-3334* 620 Broadway NY, NY 10012

Duke, Randy *(212) 292-1226* 235 E 149th St Bronx, NY 10451

Dunand, Frank *(212) 686-3478* 18 W 27th St NY, NY 10001

Dunkley, Richard *(212) 206-0410* NY, NY

Dunning, Hank *(212) 675-6040* 50 W 22nd St NY, NY 10010

Dunning, Robert & Deane *(212) 688-0788* 57 W 58th St NY, NY 10019

Duomo Photo Inc *(212) 243-1150* 133 W 19th St NY, NY 10011

Durrance, Dick *(212) 749-6382* 175 W 92nd St NY, NY 10025

e

Eagan, Timothy *(212) 737-0256* NY, NY

Ealovega, Chuck *(212) 683-2002* NY, NY

Eastep, Wayne *(212) 686-8404* 443 Park Ave So NY, NY 10016

Eberstadt, Fred *(212) 794-9471* 791 Park Ave NY, NY 10021

Eckstein, Ed *(212) 685-9342* 234 Fifth Ave NY, NY 10001

Edahl, Edward *(212) 929-2002* 236 W 27th St NY, NY 10001

Edgeworth, Anthony *(212) 679-6031* 130 Madison Ave NY, NY 10016

Edwards, Gregory *(212) 879-4339* 30 East End Ave NY, NY 10028

Eggers, Claus *(212) 243-6811* 160 Fifth Ave NY, NY 10010

Eguiguren, Carlos *(212) 888-6732* 139 E 57th St NY, NY 10022

Ehrenpreis, Dave *(212) 242-1976* 156 Fifth Ave NY, NY 10010

Eisenberg, Steve *(212) 563-2061* 448 W 37th St NY, NY 10018

Elbers, Johan *(212) 929-5783* 18 E 18th St NY, NY 10003

Elgort, Arthur *(212) 219-8775* 136 Grand St NY, NY 10013

Elios-Zunini Studio *(212) 228-6827* 142 W 4th St NY, NY 10012

Ellis, Ray *(718) 282-6449* 176 Westminster Rd Brooklyn, NY 11218

Ellis, Roz *(212) 627-7040* 127 W 24th St NY, NY 10011

Elmer, Jo *(212) 369-7077* 200 E 87th St NY, NY 10165

Elmore, Steve *(212) 472-2463* 60 E 42nd St NY, NY 10028

Elness, Jack *(212) 242-5045* 236 W 26th St NY, NY 10001

Elz, Barry *(212) 962-0037* 68 Thomas St NY, NY 10013

Emberling, David *(212) 473-5130* 9 E 19th St NY, NY 10003

Emil, Pamela *(212) 749-4716* 327 Central Park W NY, NY 10025

Endress, John Paul *(212) 736-7800* 254 W 31st St NY, NY 10001

Engel, Mort Studio *(212) 889-8466* 260 Fifth Ave NY, NY 10001

Englander, Maury *(212) 242-9777* 43 Fifth Ave NY, NY 10003

Englehardt, Duk *(212) 226-6490* 80 Varick St NY, NY 10013

Epstein, Mitch *(212) 535-8699* NY, NY

Epstein, Robert *(212) 691-5860* 160 Fifth Ave NY, NY 10010

Epstein, S Karin *(212) 496-5592* 610 West End Ave NY, NY 10024

Erdmann, Robert *(212) 777-5757* 67 E 11th St NY, NY 10003

Erwitt, Eliot *(212) 799-6767* NY, NY

Essel, Robert *(212) 877-5228* 39 W 71st St NY, NY 10023

Estrada, Sigrid *(212) 673-4300* 902 Broadway NY, NY 10010

Everly, Bart *(212) 924-1510* 156 Fifth Ave NY, NY 10010

f

Falocco, John *(212) 532-4571* 135 E 26th St NY, NY 10010

Farber, Robert *(212) 486-9090* 188 E 64th St NY, NY 10021

Faria, Rui *(212) 243-6343* 304 Eighth Ave NY, NY 10001

Farrell, Bill *(212) 683-1425* 343 E 30th St NY, NY 10016

Farrell, John William *(212) 460-9001* 189 Second Ave NY, NY 10003

Favero, Jean P *(212) 683-9188* 208 Fifth Ave NY, NY 10010

Feibel, Theodor *(718) 897-2445* 102-10 66th Rd Forest Hills, NY 11375

Feinstein, Gary *(212) 242-3373* 19 E 17th St NY, NY 10003

Feintuch, Harvey *(718) 339-0301* 1440 E 14th St Brooklyn, NY 11230

Feldman, Andy *(718) 788-6585* 195 11th St Brooklyn, NY 11215

Feller, Nora *(212) 307-5923* 269 W 25th St NY, NY 10001

Fellerman, Stan *(212) 243-0027* 152 W 25th St NY, NY 10001

Fellman, Sandi *(212) 925-5187* 548 Broadway NY, NY 10012

Ferrante, Terry *(212) 683-7240* 555 Third Ave NY, NY 10016

Ferri, Mark *(212) 431-1356* 463 Broome St NY, NY 10013

Fetter, Frank *(212) 249-3138* 400 E 78th St NY, NY 10021

Feurer, Hans *(212) 924-6760* 160 Fifth Ave NY, NY 10010

Fields, Bruce *(212) 431-8852* 71 Greene St NY, NY 10012

Filari, Katrina *(212) 279-2838* 286 Fifth Ave NY, NY 10001

Finkelman, Allan *(212) 684-3487* 118 E 28th St NY, NY 10016

Finlay, Alastair *(212) 645-6430* NY, NY

Finley, Calvin *(212) 533-6820* NY, NY

Firman, John *(212) 794-2794* 434 E 75th St NY, NY 10021

Fischer, Carl *(212) 794-0400* 121 E 83rd St NY, NY 10028

Fishbein, Chuck *(212) 532-4452* 276 Fifth Ave NY, NY 10001

Fisher, Jon *(212) 206-6311* 236 W 27th St NY, NY 10001

PAGE 94

Fishman, Chuck *(212) 242-3987* 69 1/2 Morton St NY, NY 10014

Fishman, Robert *(212) 620-7976* 153 W 27th St NY, NY 10011

Fiur, Lola Troy *(212) 861-1911* 360 E 65th St NY, NY 10021

Flash Flood Enterprises

(212) 627-7157 PO Box 1955/Old Chelsea Sta NY, NY 10011

Flatow, Carl *(212) 683-8688* 20 E 30th St NY, NY 10016

Floret, Evelyn *(212) 472-3179* 3 E 80th St NY, NY 10021

Floyd, Bob *(212) 684-0795* PO Box 216 NY, NY 10156

Flying Camera *(212) 619-0808* 114 Fulton St NY, NY 10038

Flynn, Matt *(212) 927-2985* 99 W 27th St NY, NY 10001

Flynn, Richard *(212) 243-0834* 306 W 4th St NY, NY 10014

Fonteyne, Carel *(212) 370-4300* 235 E 40th St NY, NY 10016

Forastieri, Marili *(212) 431-1840* 426 W Broadway NY, NY 10012

Ford, Carol *(212) 334-4662* 80 Varick St NY, NY 10013

Forelli, Chip *(212) 564-1835* 316 Fifth Ave NY, NY 10001

Forrest, Bob *(212) 288-4458* 273 Fifth Ave NY, NY 10016

Foto Shuttle Japan *(212) 586-5304* NY, NY

Foulke, Douglas *(212) 243-0822* 28 W 25th St NY, NY 10010

Fox, Jeffrey *(212) 620-0147* 6 W 20th St NY, NY 10011

Foxx, Stephanie *(212) 580-9158* 274 W 71st St NY, NY 10023

Frajndlich, Abe *(212) 995-8648* 30 E 20th St NY, NY 10003

Frame, Bob *(212) 431-6707* 225 Lafayette St NY, NY 10012

Francais, Isabelle *(212) 678-7508* 873 Broadway NY, NY 10003

Francekevich, Al *(212) 691-7456* 73 Fifth Ave NY, NY 10003

Frances, Scott *(212) 749-8026* 175 Fifth Ave NY, NY 10010

Francisco, Gus *(212) 683-0418* 220 E 23rd St NY, NY 10010

Francki, Jo *(212) 838-3170* 420 E 54th St NY, NY 10022

Frank, Dick *(212) 242-4648* 11 W 25th St NY, NY 10010

PAGE 136-137

Frankian, Paul *(212) 675-1654* 59 W 19th St NY, NY 10011

Fraser, Douglas *(212) 777-8404* 9 E 19th St NY, NY 10003

Fraser, Rob *(212) 779-1285* 211 Thompson St NY, NY 10012

PAGE 73

Frazier, David *(212) 279-0003* 245 W 29th St NY, NY 10001

Freed, Leonard *(212) 966-9200* 72 Spring St NY, NY 10012

Freni, Al *(212) 679-2533* 381 Park Ave So NY, NY 10016

Fried, Richard *(212) 929-1052* 430 W 14th St NY, NY 10014

Friedman, Benno *(212) 255-6038* 26 W 20th St NY, NY 10011

Friedman, Jerry *(212) 505-5600* 873 Broadway NY, NY 10003

Friedman, Steve *(212) 864-2662* 545 W 111th St NY, NY 10025

Friedman, Walter *(212) 874-5287* 58 W 68th St NY, NY 10023

Froomer, Brett *(212) 533-3113* 7 E 20th St NY, NY 10003

Funk, Mitchell *(212) 988-2886* 500 E 77th St NY, NY 10162

Furones, Claude *(212) 683-0622* 40 Waterside Plaza NY, NY 10010

Fusco, Paul *(212) 966-9200* 72 Spring St NY, NY 10012

g

Gainey, Tim *(212) 243-1503* 114 W 27th St NY, NY 10001

Gairy, John *(212) 242-5805* 11 W 17th St NY, NY 10011

Galante, Dennis *(212) 463-0938* 133 W 22nd St NY, NY 10011

Gallucci, Ed *(212) 226-2215* 568 Broadway NY, NY 10012

Galton, Beth *(212) 242-2266* 130 W 25th St NY, NY 10001

Ganges, Halley *(212) 868-1810* 35 W 36th St NY, NY 10018

Gans, Hank *(212) 683-0622* 40 Waterside Plaza NY, NY 10010

Gardner, Tony *(212) 683-2002* NY, NY

Garetti, John *(212) 505-0304* 140 W 22nd St NY, NY 10011

Garik, Alice *(718) 499-1456* 173 Windsor Pl Brooklyn, NY 11215

Garn, Andrew *(212) 353-8434* 207 Eighth Ave NY, NY 10011

Garrett, William *(212) 243-2750* 52 W 9th St NY, NY 10011

Gatehouse, Don *(212) 517-8979* 356 E 89th St NY, NY 10128

Geller, Bonnie *(212) 864-5922* 57 W 93rd St NY, NY 10025

Gelsobello, Paul *(212) 947-0317* 245 W 29th St NY, NY 10007

Gemelli, Piero *(212) 777-5757* 67 E 11th St NY, NY 10003

PAGE 15

Generico, Tony *(212) 627-9755* 130 W 25th St NY, NY 10001

Gentieu, Penny *(212) 691-1994* 87 Barrow St NY, NY 10014

George, Michael *(212) 627-5868* 525 Hudson St NY, NY 10014

Geradi, Marcia *(212) 243-8400* 448 W 16th St NY, NY 10011

Gerstein, Jesse *(212) 370-4300* 235 E 40th St NY, NY 10016

Gesar, Aram *(212) 228-1852* 417 Lafayette St NY, NY 10003

Gescheidt, Alfred *(212) 889-4023* 175 Lexington Ave NY, NY 10016

Ghergo, Christina *(212) 243-6811* 160 Fifth Ave NY, NY 10010

Gidion Inc *(212) 627-4769* 140 W 22nd St NY, NY 10011

Gigli, Oberdo *(212) 463-0372* 231 W 11th St NY, NY 10013

Gigli, Ormond *(212) 758-2860* 327 E 58th St NY, NY 10022

Gilbert, Thom *(212) 243-2750* 438 W 37th St NY, NY 10018

Gillardin, Andre *(212) 675-2950* 6 W 20th St NY, NY 10011

Gillette, Bruce *(212) 807-9207* 142 W 26th St NY, NY 10001

Giordano, John A *(212) 477-3273* 60 E 9th St NY, NY 10006

Giovanni, Raeanne *(212) 673-7199* 311 E 12th St NY, NY 10003

Giraldi, Frank *(212) 840-8225* 54 W 39th St NY, NY 10018

Giraldo, Anita *(212) 431-1193* 83 Canal St NY, NY 10002

Gladstone, Gary *(212) 777-7772* 237 E 20th St NY, NY 10003

Glancz, Jeff *(212) 741-2504* 38 W 21st St NY, NY 10010

Glassman, Carl *(212) 732-2458* 80 N Moore St NY, NY 10013

Glaviano, Marco *(212) 924-6760* 160 Fifth Ave NY, NY 10010

Glinn, Burt *(212) 877-2210* 41 Central Park W NY, NY 10023

Globus Brothers *(212) 243-1008* 44 W 24th St NY, NY 10010

Goble, Brian *(212) 460-8329* 365 First Ave NY, NY 10010

Goff, Lee *(212) 223-0716* 32 E 64th St NY, NY 10021

Gold, Bernie *(212) 677-0311* 873 Broadway NY, NY 10003

Gold, Charles *(212) 242-2600* 56 W 22nd St NY, NY 10010

Goldberg, Les *(212) 925-8333* 568 Broadway NY, NY 10012

Goldman, Richard *(212) 675-3021* 36 W 20th St NY, NY 10010

Goldring, Barry *(212) 334-9494* 568 Broadway NY, NY 10012

Goldsmith, Lynn *(212) 736-4602* 241 W 36th St NY, NY 10018

Goldstein, Art *(212) 966-2682* 101 Wooster St NY, NY 10012

Goll, Charles R *(212) 628-4881* 404 E 83rd St NY, NY 10028

Golob, Stanford *(212) 532-7166* 40 Waterside Plz NY, NY 10010

Gonzalez, Manuel *(212) 242-2202* 127 W 26th St NY, NY 10011

Goodman, John *(212) 243-2750* 425 W 23rd St NY, NY 10011

Goodman, Michael *(212) 889-4060* NY, NY

Gordon, Andrew *(212) 807-9758* 48 W 22nd St NY, NY 10010

Gordon, Brad *(212) 206-7758* 259 W 12th St NY, NY 10011

Gordon, Joel *(212) 254-1688* 112 Fourth Ave NY, NY 10003

Gordon, Larry Dale *(212) 753-0462* NY, NY

Page 26-27;186-189

Gorin, Bart *(212) 683-3743* 1160 Broadway NY, NY 10001

Gorodnitzki, Diane *(212) 724-6259* 160 W 71st St NY, NY 10023

Gotfryd, Bernard *(718) 261-8039* 46 Wendover Rd Forest Hills, NY 11375

Gottlieb, Dennis *(212) 620-7050* 137 W 25th St NY, NY 10001

Gould, Jeff *(718) 897-0610* 98-41 64th Rd Rego Park, NY 11374

Gould, Peter *212) 675-3707* 22 E 17th St NY, NY 10003

Gove, Geoffrey *(212) 260-6051* 117 Waverly Pl NY, NY 10011

Gozo Studio *(212) 620-8115* 40 W 17th St NY, NY 10011

Graff, Randolph *(212) 254-0412* 160 Bleecker St NY, NY 10012

Graflin, Jill *(212) 529-6700* 111 Fifth Ave NY, NY 10003

Grant, Robert *(212) 925-1121* 62 Greene St NY, NY 10012

Graphic Media *(212) 696-0880* 12 W 27th St NY, NY 10001

Graves, Tom *(212) 683-0241* 136 E 36th St NY, NY 10016

Gray, Katie *(212) 226-0223* 145 Hudson St NY, NY 10013

Page 80

Gray, Mitchell *(212) 226-0223* 145 Hudson St NY, NY 10013

Gray, Robert *(212) 807-7121* 36 W 20th St NY, NY 10011

Green, Allen *(212) 534-1718* 1641 Third Ave NY, NY 10128

Green, Richard *(212) 242-5282* 18 E 17th St NY, NY 10010

Green-Armytage, Stephen

***(212) 247-6314* 171 W 57th St NY, NY 10019**

Page 58-59

Greenberg, Joel *(212) 285-0979* 265 Water St NY, NY 10038

Greene, Jim *(212) 674-1631* 20 W 20th St NY, NY 10011

Greene, Joshua *(212) 243-2750* 448 W 37th St NY, NY 10018

Greenwald, Seth *(718) 802-1531* 195 Adams St Brooklyn, NY 11201

Gregoire, Peter *(212) 967-4969* 448 W 37th St NY, NY 10018

Gregory, John *(212) 529-9424* 39 E 19th St NY, NY 10003

Gregory, Kevin *(212) 807-9859* 237 W 26th St NY, NY 10001

Grehan, Farrell *(212) 677-3999* 5 E 22nd St NY, NY 10010

Greyshock, Caroline *(212) 226-7563* 578 Broadway NY, NY 10012

Page 96

Griffiths, Philip Jones *(212) 966-9200* 72 Spring St NY, NY 10012

Grignaschi, Renato *(212) 925-8333* 568 Broadway NY, NY 10012

Grill, Tom *(212) 353-8600* 30 Irving Pl NY, NY 10003

Gross, Cy *(212) 243-2556* 59 W 19th St NY, NY 10011

Gross, David *(212) 688-4729* 922 Third Ave NY, NY 10022

Gross, Garry *(212) 807-7141* 235 W 4th St NY, NY 10014

Gross, Geoffrey *(212) 645-5193* 119 W 23rd St NY, NY 10011

Gross, Pat *(212) 427-9396* 315 E 86th St NY, NY 10028

Grossman, Eugene *(212) 962-6795* 80 N Moore St NY, NY 10013

Grossman, Henry *(212) 580-7751* 37 Riverside Dr NY, NY 10023

Grotell, Al *(212) 349-3165* 170 Park Row NY, NY 10038

Gruen, John *(212) 242-8415* 20 W 22nd St NY, NY 10010

GSCHEIDLE, GERHARD E *(212) 666-0748* 792 Columbus Ave NY, NY 10025

GUATTI, ALBANO *(212) 674-2230* 250 Mercer St NY, NY 10012

GUDNASON, TORKIL *(212) 255-3252* NY, NY

PAGE 31

GUICE, BRAD *(212) 206-0966* 132 W 21st St NY, NY 10011

PAGE 44-45; 130-133

GUROVITZ, JUDY *(212) 988-8685* 207 E 74th St NY, NY 10021

GUYAUX, JEAN-MARIE *(212) 529-5395* 29 E 19th St NY, NY 10003

GUZMAN *(212) 691-5162* 78 Fifth Ave NY, NY 10011

h

HAAR, THOMAS *(212) 929-9054* 463 West St NY, NY 10014

HAAS, KENNETH *(212) 255-0707* 15 Sheridan Square NY, NY 10014

HAFT, EMILY *(212) 517-5123* 435 E 65th St NY, NY 10021

HAGEN, BOYD *(212) 244-2436* 448 W 37th St NY, NY 10018

HAGGERTY, DAVID *(212) 879-4141* 17 E 67th St NY, NY 10021

HAGIWARA, BRIAN *(212) 674-6026* 504 La Guardia Pl NY, NY 10012

PAGE 161

HAIMANN, TODD *(212) 391-0810* 26 W 38th St NY, NY 10018

HALARD, FRANCOIS *(212) 370-4300* 235 E 40th St NY, NY 10016

HALASKA, JAN *(718) 389-8923* PO Box 6611 FDR Sta NY, NY 10022

HALING, GEORGE *(212) 736-6822* 231 W 29th St NY, NY 10001

HALL, CLAYTON *(212) 629-8659* 165 W 29th St NY, NY 10001

HAMILTON, KEITH *(212) 982-3375* 749 FDR Dr NY, NY 10009

HAMILTON, MARK *(212) 691-3504* 119 W 23rd St NY, NY 10011

HAMMOND, MAURY *(212) 460-9990* 9 E 19th St NY, NY 10003

HANLON, GARY *(212) 206-9144* 40 W 20th St NY, NY 10011

HANSEN, BARBARA *(212) 822-1676* 1954 Bronxdale Ave Bronx, NY 10462

HANSEN, CONSTANCE *(212) 691-5162* 78 Fifth Ave NY, NY 10011

HANSON, KENT *(212) 777-2399* 147 Bleecker St NY, NY 10012

HARDIN, TED *(212) 242-2958* 119 W 23rd St NY, NY 10011

HARRINGTON, GRACE *(212) 246-1749* 312 W 48th St NY, NY 10036

HARRIS, MICHAEL *(212) 255-3377* 18 W 21st St NY, NY 10010

HARRIS, RONALD G *(212) 255-2330* 119 W 22nd St NY, NY 10011

HARRISON, HOWARD *(212) 989-9233* 20 W 20th St NY, NY 10011

HARTMAN, HARRY *(212) 675-5454* 61 W 23rd St NY, NY 10010

HARTMANN, ERICH *(212) 966-9200* 72 Spring St NY, NY 10012

HARVEY, NED *(212) 807-7043* 129 W 22nd St NY, NY 10011

PAGE 88

HASHI STUDIO *(212) 675-6902* 49 W 23rd St NY, NY 10010

HASHIMOTO *(212) 645-1221* 153 W 27th St NY, NY 10001

HATHON, ELIZABETH *(212) 219-0685* 8 Greene St NY, NY 10013

HAUSMAN, GEORGE *(212) 686-4810* 1181 Broadway NY, NY 10001

HAVILAND, BRIAN *(212) 481-4132* 34 E 30th St NY, NY 10016

HAYES, KERRY *(718) 442-4804* 35 Taft Ave Staten Isl, NY 10301

HAYNES, RICHARD *(212) 872-1927* 383 Madison Ave NY, NY 10017

HAYWARD, BILL *(212) 966-6490* 596 Broadway NY, NY 10012

HEDRICH, DAVID *(212) 924-3324* 7 E 17th St NY, NY 10003

HEERY, GARY *(212) 966-6364* 577 Broadway NY, NY 10012

HEGE, LASZLO *(718) 706-0833* 13 E 30th St NY, NY 10016

HEIBERG, MILTON *(212) 741-6405* 71 W 23rd St NY, NY 10010

HEIN, GEORGE *(212) 741-3211* 13 E 16th St NY, NY 10003

HEIR, STUART *(212) 337-8779* NY, NY

HEISLER, GREGORY *(212) 777-8100* 568 Broadway NY, NY 10012

HELLERSTEIN, STEPHEN A *(212) 645-0508* 56 W 22nd St NY, NY 10010

HELMS, BILL *(212) 759-2079* 1175 York Ave NY, NY 10021

HEMSAY, YVONNE

(212) 549-0095 4520 Henry Hudson Pkwy Riverdale, NY 10471

HENDERSON, AKEMI *(212) 581-3630* 44 W 54th St NY, NY 10019

HENZE, DON STUDIO *(212) 689-7375* 139 W 29th St NY, NY 10001

HERON, MICHAL *(212) 787-1272* 28 W 71st St NY, NY 10023

HERR, H BUFF *(212) 595-4783* 56 W 82nd St NY, NY 10024

HERRENBRUCK, DAVID *(212) 967-5550* 119 Fifth Ave NY, NY 10003

HESS, BRAD *(212) 684-3131* 1201 Broadway NY, NY 10001

HEUBERGER, WILLIAM *(312) 242-1532* 28 W 25th St NY, NY 10010

HEYERT, ELIZABETH *(212) 594-1008* 251 W 30th St NY, NY 10001

HILL, PAT *(212) 532-3479* 37 W 26th St NY, NY 10010

HILLER, GEOFFREY *(212) 873-0555* 601 W 113th St NY, NY 10025

HINE, SKIP *(212) 691-5903* 34 W 17th St NY, NY 10011

HING/ NORTON *(212) 683-4258* 24 W 30th St NY, NY 10001

HIRO *(212) 580-8000* 50 Central Park W NY, NY 10023

HIRST, MICHAEL *(914) 666-2993* 1150 Sixth Ave NY, NY 10036

HISPARD, MARC *(212) 370-4300* 235 E 40th St NY, NY 10016

HITZ, BRAD *(212) 929-1432* 95 Horatio St NY, NY 10014

HOCHMAN, ALLEN STUDIO *(212) 777-8404* 9-11 E 19 St NY, NY 10003

HODGSON, DAVID *(212) 864-6941* 550 Riverside Dr NY, NY 10027

HOELTZELL, SID *(212) 255-0303* 156 Fifth Ave NY, NY 10010

HOGAN, DAVID *(212) 369-4575* 352 E 91st St NY, NY 10128

HOLBROOKE, ANDREW *(212) 889-5995* 50 W 29th St NY, NY 10001

HOLDERER, JON *(212) 620-4260* 119 W 23rd St NY, NY 10011

PAGE 178-179

HOLDORF, THOMAS *(212) 532-4571* 135 E 26th St NY, NY 10010

HOLLAND, ROBIN *(212) 431-5351* 430 Greenwich St NY, NY 10013

HOLLYMAN, TOM *(212) 867-2383* 300 E 40th St NY, NY 10016

HOLTZMAN PHOTOGRAPHY *(212) 242-7985* 269 W 11th St NY, NY 10014

HOLZ, GEORGE *(212) 505-5607* 400 Lafayette St NY, NY 10003

HOOPER, THOMAS *(212) 691-0122* 126 Fifth Ave NY, NY 10011

HOPKINS, DOUGLAS *(212) 243-1774* 636 Sixth Ave NY, NY 10011

HOPKINS, STEPHEN *(212) 460-5022* 57 E 11th St NY, NY 10003

HOPSON, GARETH *(212) 535-3800* 22 E 21st St NY, NY 10010

HORI, RICHARD *(212) 645-8333* 119 W 23rd St NY, NY 10011

HOROWITZ, ROSS M *(212) 206-9216* 206 W 15th St NY, NY 10011

HOROWITZ, RYSZARD *(212) 243-6440* 137 W 25th St NY, NY 10003

HOROWITZ, TED *(203) 454-8766* 214 Wilton Rd Westport, CT 6880

HORST *(212) 751-4937* 188 E 64th St NY, NY 10021

HORTH, ANTHONY *(212) 925-8333* 568 Broadway NY, NY 10012

HORVATH, JIM *(212) 741-0300* 95 Charles St NY, NY 10014

HOUZE, PHILIPPE LOUIS *(212) 614-0435* 123 Prince St NY, NY 10012

HOWARD, KEN *(718) 388-9610* 50-52 Dobbin St Brooklyn, NY 11222

HOWARD, ROSEMARY *(212) 473-5552* 902 Broadway NY, NY 10010

HUANG, MING *(718) 262-0220* 3174 44th St LIC, NY 11103

HUET, JOHN *(212) 532-4571* 135 E 26th St NY, NY 10010

HUGHES, PINDER *(212) 662-5105* 536 W 111th St NY, NY 10025

HUIBREGTSE, JIM *(212) 925-3351* 14 Jay St NY, NY 10013

HUME, ADAM *(212) 794-1754* 231 E 76th St NY, NY 10021

HUNTZINGER, BOB *(212) 645-9035* 34 Renwick St NY, NY 10013

HURWITZ, HARRISON *(212) 213-4820* 379 Park Ave So NY, NY 10016

HUSZAR *(212) 532-3772* 377 Park Ave So NY, NY 10016

HYATT, MORTON *(212) 226-6880* 13 Laight St NY, NY 10013

HYMAN, BARRY *(212) 879-3294* 319 E 78th St NY, NY 10021

HYMAN, PAUL *(212) 255-1532* 236 W 26th St NY, NY 10001

i

IANUZZI, TOM *(212) 563-1987* 488 W 37th St NY, NY 10018

ICHI *(212) 254-4810* 303 Park Ave So NY, NY 10010

IHARA *(212) 219-9363* 568 Broadway NY, NY 10012

IKEDA, SHIG *(212) 924-4744* 636 Sixth Ave NY, NY 10011

ILLOGRAPHY *(212) 219-0244* 49 Crosby St NY, NY 10012

IMAGE MAKERS *(212) 533-4498* 310 E 23rd St NY, NY 10010

IMRIE, RICHARD *(212) 752-8174* 245 E 58th St NY, NY 10022

ING, FRANCIS *(212) 279-5022* 112 W 31st St NY, NY 10001

INTRATER, ROBERTA *(718) 462-4004* 1212 Beverly Rd Brooklyn, NY 11218

IRISH, LEN *(212) 242-2237* 11 W 17th St NY, NY 10011

IRWIN, WILLIAM *(718) 237-2598* 70 Remsen St Brooklyn, NY 11201

ISAACS, NORMAN *(212) 243-5547* 277 W 11th St NY, NY 10014

ISGAR, SCOTT *(212) 675-1349* 50 W 22nd St NY, NY 10010

ISHIMURO, EISUKE *(212) 255-9198* 130 W 25th St NY, NY 10001

ISSERMANN, DOMINIQUE *(212) 370-4300* 235 E 40th St NY, NY 10016

IVANY, SANDRA *(212) 580-1501* 6 W 90th St NY, NY 10024

IZU, KENRO *(212) 254-1002* 140 W 22nd St NY, NY 10011

PAGE 142-143

j

JACOBS, MARTIN *(212) 475-1160* 34 E 23rd St NY, NY 10010

JACOBS, ROBERT *(212) 683-3629* 116 Lexington Ave NY, NY 10016

JACOBSON, ALAN *(212) 265-0170* 250 W 49th St NY, NY 10019

JACOBSON, ERIC *(212) 696-4279* 39 W 29th St NY, NY 10001

PAGE 158-159

JANEART LTD *(212) 691-9701* 161 W 15th St NY, NY 10011

JANN, GAIL *(212) 861-4335* 352 E 85th St NY, NY 10028

JANOFF, DEAN *(212) 807-0816* 514 W 24th St NY, NY 10011

JAWITZ, LOUIS H *(212) 929-0008* 13 E 17th St NY, NY 10003

JEFFERY, RICHARD *(212) 255-2330* 119 W 22nd St NY, NY 10011

JEFFREY, LANCE *(212) 582-1501* 162 W 56th St NY, NY 10019

JEFFRY, ALIX *(212) 979-9712* NY, NY

JENKINSON, MARK *(212) 929-7457* 130 Barrow St NY, NY 10014

JENSEN, PETER M *(212) 725-1973* NY, NY

JENSHEL, LEN *(212) 316-7809* 309 W 93rd St NY, NY 10025

PAGE 192

JENSSEN, BUDDY *(212) 686-0865* 34 E 29th St NY, NY 10016

JOEL, SETH PHOTOGRAPHY *(212) 685-3179* 440 Park Ave So NY, NY 10016

JOERN, JAMES *(212) 260-8025* 125 Fifth Ave NY, NY 10003

JOHANSKY, PETER *(212) 242-7013* 27 W 20th St NY, NY 10011

JONES, AARON *(212) 953-0088* 17 E 45th St NY, NY 10017

JONES, CHRIS *(212) 685-0679* 240 E 27th St NY, NY 10006

JONES, SPENCER *(212) 941-8165* 23 Leonard St NY, NY 10013

JONES, STEVE PHOTO *(212) 929-3641* 120 W 25th St NY, NY 10001

JOSEPH, MERYL *(212) 861-5057* 158 E 82nd St NY, NY 10028

JOUANY, CHRISTOPHER *(212) 777-5757* 67 E 11th St NY, NY 10003

JURADO, LOUIS *(212) 242-7480* 170 Fifth Ave NY, NY 10010

k

KACHATURIAN, ARMEN *(212) 334-0986* 330 Broome St NY, NY 10002

KAHAN, ERIC *(212) 243-9727* 36 W 20th St NY, NY 10011

KAHN, R T *(212) 988-1423* 156 E 79th St NY, NY 10021

KAHN, STEVE *(212) 619-7932* 60 Thomas St NY, NY 10013

KALINSKY, GEORGE *(212) 563-8095* 4 Penn Plz NY, NY 10001

KAMP, ERIC *(718) 896-7780* 98-120 Queens Blvd Forest Hills, NY 11374

KAMSLER, LEONARD *(212) 242-4678* 140 Seventh Ave NY, NY 10011

KAN PHOTOGRAPHY *(212) 989-1083* 122 W 26th St NY, NY 10001

PAGE 74-75; 106-107

KANA, TITUS *(212) 473-5550* 876 Broadway NY, NY 10003

KANAKIS, MICHAEL *(212) 807-8232* 144 W 27th St NY, NY 10001

KANE, ART *(212) 925-7334* 568 Broadway NY, NY 10012

KANE, PETER T *(212) 924-4968* 236 W 26th St NY, NY 10001

KANE, THOMAS *(212) 475-6383* 351 E 12th St NY, NY 10003

KANIKLIDIS, JAMES *(718) 338-0931* 1270 E 18th St Brooklyn, NY 11230

KAPLAN, ALAN *(212) 982-9500* 7 E 20th St NY, NY 10003

PAGE 1-8

KAPLAN, PETER B *(212) 995-5000* 7 E 20th St NY, NY 10003

KAPLAN, PETER J *(212) 222-1193* 924 West End Ave NY, NY 10025

KARALES, JAMES H *(212) 799-2483* 147 W 79th St NY, NY 10024

KASOFF, BRIAN *(212) 243-4880* 28 W 25th St NY, NY 10001

KASSABIAN PHOTOGRAPHY *(212) 421-1950* 127 E 59th St NY, NY 10022

KASTEN, BARBARA *(212) 627-5229* 251 W 19th St NY, NY 10011

KATCHIAN, SONIA *(212) 586-5304* NY, NY

KATRINA *(212) 279-2838* 286 Fifth Ave NY, NY 10011

KATVAN, MOSHE *(212) 242-4895* 40 W 17th St NY, NY 10011

KATZ, PAUL *(212) 684-4395* 381 Park Ave So NY, NY 10016

KATZENSTEIN, DAVID *(212) 529-9460* 21 E 4th St NY, NY 10003

KAUFMAN, ELLIOTT *(212) 496-0860* 255 W 90th St NY, NY 10024

KAUFMAN, JEFF *(718) 779-5753* 6353 Harring St Forest Hills, NY 11374

KAUFMAN, MICKY *(212) 255-1976* 144 W 27th St NY, NY 10001

KAUFMAN, TED *(212) 685-0349* 121 Madison Ave NY, NY 10016

KAWA, JANUSZ *(212) 431-1212* 134 Reade St NY, NY 10013

KAWACHI, YUTAKA *(212) 929-4825* 33 W 17th St NY, NY 10011

KAWALERSKI, TED *(212) 242-0198* 7 Evergreen Way N. Tarrytown, NY 10591

KAYE, NANCY *(212) 645-6463* 77 Seventh Ave NY, NY 10011

KAYSER, ALEX *(212) 431-8518* 211 W Broadway NY, NY 10013

KEAVENY, FRANCIS *(212) 481-9187* 260 Fifth Ave NY, NY 10001

KEEGAN, MARCIA *(212) 953-9023* 140 E 46th St NY, NY 10017

KEEVE, DOUGLAS *(212) 777-5405* 114 E 13th St NY, NY 10003

KELLER, TOM *(212) 472-3667* 440 E 78th St NY, NY 10021

KELLEY, CHARLES W JR *(212) 686-3879* 649 Second Ave NY, NY 10016

KELLEY, DAVID *(212) 869-7896* 265 W 37th St NY, NY 10018

KELLNER, JEFF *(212) 475-3719* 16 Waverly Pl NY, NY 10003

KEN, DAVID *(212) 633-1122* 222 W 23rd St NY, NY 10011

KENNEDY, DONALD J *(212) 206-7740* 521 W 23rd St NY, NY 10011

KENT, KAREN *(212) 962-6793* 29 John St NY, NY 10038

KHORNAK, LUCILLE *(212) 593-0933* 425 E 58th St NY, NY 10022

KILKELLY, JAMES *(212) 496-2291* 30 W 73rd St NY, NY 10023

KINGSFORD, MICHAEL *(212) 475-0553* 874 Broadway NY, NY 10003

KINMONTH, ROB *(212) 475-6370* 85 E 10th St NY, NY 10003

KIRK, BARBARA *(212) 734-3233* 447 E 65th St NY, NY 10021

KIRK, MALCOLM *(212) 744-3642* 12 E 72nd St NY, NY 10021

KIRK, RUSSELL *(212) 206-1446* 31 W 21st St NY, NY 10010

KIRKPATRICK, CHARLA *(212) 249-6285* NY, NY

KISS, BOB *(212) 505-6650* 29 E 19th St NY, NY 10003

KITCHEN, DENNIS *(212) 674-7658* 80 Fourth Ave NY, NY 10003

KITTLE, KIT *(212) 673-0596* 511 E 20th St NY, NY 10010

KLAUSS, CHERYL *(212) 431-3569* 463 Broome St NY, NY 10013

KLEIN, ARTHUR *(718) 278-0457* 35-42 80th St Jackson Heights, NY 11372

KLEIN, MATTHEW *(212) 255-6400* 104 W 17th St NY, NY 10011

KLEIN, ROBERT *(212) 580-0381* 215 W 90th St NY, NY 10024

KLIGGE, ROBERT *(212) 226-7113* 578 Broadway NY, NY 10012

KLONSKY, ARTHUR *(212) 691-9701* 161 W 15th St NY, NY 10011

KLOSTER, DORIS *(212) 925-2480* 451 Broome St NY, NY 10013

KNOTT, KIM *(212) 206-0737* 108 W 18th St NY, NY 10011

KOHLI, EDDY *(212) 924-6760* 160 Fifth Ave NY, NY 10010

KOHLMAN, LYNN *(212) 608-7070* 122 Chambers St NY, NY 10007

KOLANSKY, PALMA *(212) 431-5858* 291 Church St NY, NY 10013

PAGE 50-51

KOMAR, GREG *(212) 685-0275* 30 Waterside Sq NY, NY 10010

KOPELOW, PAUL *(212) 689-0685* 135 Madison Ave NY, NY 10016

KOPPELMAN, JOZEF *(718) 645-3548* 1717 Ave N Brooklyn, NY 11230

KORSH, KEN *(212) 685-8864* 118 E 28th St NY, NY 10016

KOSOFF, BRIAN *(212) 243-4880* 28 W 25th St NY, NY 10010

KOUDIS, NICK *(212) 475-2802* 40 E 23rd St NY, NY 10010

KOUIRNIS, BILL *(212) 696-5674* 381 Park Ave So NY, NY 10016

KOZAN, DAN *(212) 691-2288* 32 W 22nd St NY, NY 10010

KOZLOWSKI, MARK *(212) 684-7487* 39 W 28th St NY, NY 10001

KOZYRA, JAMES *(212) 431-1911* 568 Broadway NY, NY 10012

KRAMER, BILL *(212) 242-7007* 33 W 17th St NY, NY 10011

KRAMER, DANIEL *(212) 873-7777* 110 W 86th St NY, NY 10024

KRAMER, NATHANIEL *(212) 925-8333* 568 Broadway NY, NY 10012

KRASOWITZ, MIKE *(212) 861-4207* 330 E 76th St NY, NY 10021

Kratochvil, Antonin *(212) 947-1589* 448 W 37th St NY, NY 10018

Krauskopf, Sara *(201) 420-1120* 404 Adams St Hoboken, NJ 07030

Krein, Jeffrey *(212) 741-5207* 119 W 23rd St NY, NY 10011

Krementz, Jill *(212) 688-0480* 228 E 48th St NY, NY 10017

Krieger, Harold *(212) 758-6389* NY, NY

Kristofik, Robert *(212) 534-5541* 334 E 90th St NY, NY 10128

Kroll, Eric *(212) 684-2465* 118 E 28th St NY, NY 10016

Kron, Dan *(212) 463-9333* 154 W 18th St NY, NY 10011

Krongard, Steve *(212) 689-5634* 212A E 26th St NY, NY 10010

Krotki, Saul *(212) 724-4823* 170 West End Ave NY, NY 10023

Kuehn, Karen *(212) 406-3005* 49 Warren St NY, NY 10007

Kugler, Dennis *(212) 677-3826* 43 Bond St NY, NY 10012

Kuhn, Ann Spanos *(212) 685-1774* 1155 Broadway NY, NY 10001

Kupinski, Steven *(212) 206-1446* 31 W 21st St NY, NY 10010

l

Labar, Elizabeth *(212) 929-7463* 327 W 18th St NY, NY 10011

Lachenauer, Paul *(212) 529-7059* 876 Broadway NY, NY 10003

Lambray, Maureen *(212) 879-3960* NY, NY

page 78-79

LaMonica, Chuck *(212) 673-4848* 121 E 24th St NY, NY 10010

Langley, David *(212) 581-3930* 536 W 50th St NY, NY 10019

Lanker, Brian *(212) 944-2853* 20 W 46th St NY, NY 10036

Laperruque, Scott *(212) 227-3587* 157 Chambers St NY, NY 10007

Larrain, Gilles *(212) 925-8494* 95 Grand St NY, NY 10013

Lassek, Art *(212) 870-0831* 92 Jefferson St Hoboken, NJ 07030

Laszlo Studio *(212) 736-6690* 28 W 39th St NY, NY 10018

Lategan, Barry *(212) 228-6850* 502 LaGuardia Pl NY, NY 10012

Lattari, Tony *(212) 947-7488* 448 W 37th St NY, NY 10018

Laubmeyer, Klaus *(212) 598-4066* 150 Thompson St NY, NY 10012

Laurance, Bruce Studio *(212) 947-3451* 253 W 28th St NY, NY 10001

Laure, Jason *(212) 691-7466* 8 W 13th St NY, NY 10011

Laurence, Mary *(212) 903-4025* PO Box 1763 NY, NY 10150

Lavine, Arthur *(212) 348-2642* 1361 Madison Ave NY, NY 10128

Lawrence, Christopher *(212) 807-8028* 12 E 18th St NY, NY 10003

Lax, Ken *(212) 228-6191* 239 Park Ave So NY, NY 10003

Layman, Alex *(212) 989-5845* 6 W 18th St NY, NY 10011

Le Moyne, page *(212) 286-9159* 310 E 46th St NY, NY 10017

Leach, David *(212) 228-1234* 75 Spring St NY, NY 10012

LeBaube, Guy *(212) 986-6981* 310 E 46th St NY, NY 10017

Lecash, Leon *(212) 967-0827* 284 Fifth Ave NY, NY 10001

Lederman, Ed *(212) 685-8612* 166 E 34th St NY, NY 10016

Leduc, Lyle *(212) 697-9216* 320 E 42nd St NY, NY 10017

Ledzian, Mark *(212) 563-4589* 245 W 29th St NY, NY 10001

page 18-19

Lee, Jung *(212) 807-8107* 132 W 21st St NY, NY 10011

page 170-171

Lee, Vincent *(212) 254-7888* 155 Wooster St NY, NY 10012

Lee, Wellington *(718) 760-2762* 305 Broadway NY, NY 10007

Lefkowitz, Lester *(212) 627-8088* 370 Lexington Ave NY, NY 10017

Lefler, David *(212) 691-5860* 160 Fifth Ave NY, NY 10010

Legrand, Michel *(212) 807-9754* 152 W 25th St NY, NY 10001

Lehman, Amy *(212) 535-7457* 210 E 75th St NY, NY 10021

Leibovitz, Annie *(212) 206-0737* 108 W 18th St NY, NY 10011

Leicmon, John *(212) 675-3219* 200 W 15th St NY, NY 10011

Leighton, Thomas *(212) 370-1835* 321 E 43rd St NY, NY 10017

Leiter, Saul *(212) 475-6034* 111 E 10th St NY, NY 10003

Lennard, Erica *(212) 947-9019* 519 W 26th St NY, NY 10001

Lennard, Jonathan *(212) 529-9875* NY, NY

Lenore, Dan *(212) 967-7115* 249 W 29th St NY, NY 10001

Leo, Donato *(212) 685-5527* 866 Sixth Ave NY, NY 10001

Leonian, Phillip *(212) 989-7670* 220 E 23rd St NY, NY 10010

Lerner, Richard *(212) 481-4135* 807 Sixth Ave NY, NY 10001

Lesinski, Martin *(718) 624-8475* 49 Willow St Brooklyn, NY 11201

Levin, James *(212) 734-0315* 1570 First Ave NY, NY 10028

Levine, Jonathan *(212) 673-4698* 11 W 9th St NY, NY 10011

LeVine, Nancy *(212) 473-0015* 41 Fifth Ave NY, NY 10003

Levinson, Ken *(212) 254-6180* 35 East 10th St NY, NY 10003

Levy, Franck *(212) 557-8256* 305 E 40th St NY, NY 10016

Levy, Peter *(212) 691-6600* 119 W 22nd St NY, NY 10011

Levy, Richard *(212) 243-4220* 5 W 19th St NY, NY 10011

Lewin, Gideon *(212) 921-5558* 25 W 39th St NY, NY 10018

Lewin, Ralph *(212) 580-0482* 156 W 74th St NY, NY 10023

Lewis, Robert *(212) 475-6564* 333 Park Ave So NY, NY 10010

Lewis, Ross *(212) 691-6878* 460 W 24th St NY, NY 10011

Lieberman, Allen *(212) 925-8874* 480 Broadway NY, NY 10013

Ligeti Inc *(212) 246-8949* 415 W 55th St NY, NY 10019

Lindner, Steven *(212) 683-1317* 18 W 27th St NY, NY 10001

Lippman, Marsha *(212) 832-0321* 220 E 63rd St NY, NY 10021

Lipton, Trina *(212) 533-3148* 60 E 8th St NY, NY 10003

Little, Christopher *(212) 691-1024* 4 W 22nd St NY, NY 10010

Lloyd, Harvey *(212) 533-4498* 310 E 23rd St NY, NY 10010

Loete, Mark *(212) 571-2235* 33 Gold St NY, NY 10038

Loew, Anthony *(212) 226-1999* 503 Broadway NY, NY 10012

Logan, Kevin *(212) 206-0539* 119 W 23rd St NY, NY 10011

Lombardi, Frederick *(212) 568-0740* 180 Pinehurst Ave NY, NY 10033

Lombroso, Dorit *(212) 219-8722* 67 Vestry St NY, NY 10013

Lomeo, Angelo *(212) 663-2122* 336 Central Park W NY, NY 10025

Lonsdale, William J *(718) 788-6652* 35 Orange St Brooklyn, NY 11201

Loomis, Just *(212) 924-6760* 160 Fifth Ave NY, NY 10010

Loppacher, Peter *(212) 929-1322* 56 Jane St NY, NY 10014

Lorenz, Albert *(516) 354-5530* 49 Floral Park Floral Park, NY 11001

Lorenz, Robert *(212) 505-8483* 80 Fourth Ave NY, NY 10003

Love, Robin *(212) 777-3113* 676 Broadway NY, NY 10012

Lovi, Steve *(212) 431-1212* 134 Reade St NY, NY 10013

Lowe, Jacques *(212) 227-3298* 138 Duane St NY, NY 10013

Lubianitsky, Leonid *(212) 391-0197* 1013 Sixth Ave NY, NY 10018

Lucka, Klaus *(212) 255-2424* 101 Fifth Ave NY, NY 10003

Luftig, Allan *(212) 533-4113* 873 Broadway NY, NY 10003

Lulow, William *(212) 873-5380* 302 W 86th St NY, NY 10024

Lupino, Mike *(212) 691-2197* 78 Fifth Ave NY, NY 10011

Lupino, Stephan *(212) 334-6474* 543 Broadway NY, NY 10012

Luria, Dick *(212) 929-7575* 5 E 16th St NY, NY 10003

Lusk, Frank *(212) 679-1441* 25 E 37th St NY, NY 10016

Luttenberg, Gene *(212) 620-8112* 20 W 22nd St NY, NY 10010

Lypides, Chris *(212) 741-1911* 119 W 23rd St NY, NY 10011

m

Maas, Rita *(212) 645-9120* 119 W 23rd St NY, NY 10011

page 114-115

Macedonia, Carmine *(212) 889-8520* 866 Sixth Ave NY, NY 10001

Mack, Donald *(212) 246-6086* 69 W 55th St NY, NY 10019

Mackiewicz, Jim *(212) 689-0766* 208 E 28th St NY, NY 10016

MacLaren, Mark *(212) 674-8615* 430 E 20th St NY, NY 10009

MacPherson, Andrew *(212) 255-3252* 96 Fifth Ave NY, NY 10011

MacWeeney, Alen Inc *(212) 473-2500* 171 First Ave NY, NY 10003

Madere, John *(212) 966-4136* 75 Spring St NY, NY 10012

Madoka *(212) 431-1015* 476 Broadway NY, NY 10013

Magni, Tiziano *(212) 688-4364* 699 Madison Ave NY, NY 10021

Mahurin, Matt *(212) 529-5275* 77 Bleeker St NY, NY 10012

Maisel, Jay *(212) 431-5013* 190 Bowery NY, NY 10012

Malabrigo, Mark *(212) 420-8087* 28 E 4th St NY, NY 10003

Malignon, Jacques *(212) 532-7727* 34 W 28th St NY, NY 10001

Maloof, Karen *(212) 678-7737* 110 W 94th St NY, NY 10025

Manarchy, Dennis *(212) 807-6286* 107 W 25th St NY, NY 10001

Mandarino, Tony *(212) 686-2866* 114 E 32nd St NY, NY 10016

Mangia, Tony *(212) 889-6340* 11 E 32nd St NY, NY 10016

Mani, Monsor *(212) 582-4240* NY, NY

Manna, Lou *(212) 683-8689* 20 E 30th St NY, NY 10016

Manno, John *(212) 243-7353* 20 W 22nd St NY, NY 10010

Maplethorpe, Robert *(212) 206-0737* 108 W 18th St NY, NY 10011

Marchese, Carole *(212) 627-5562* 91 Bedford St NY, NY 10014

Marchese, Jim *(212) 242-1087* 200 W 20th St NY, NY 10011

Marco, Phil *(212) 929-8082* 104 Fifth Ave NY, NY 10011

Marcus, Helen *(212) 879-6903* 120 E 75th St, NY 10021

Marcusson, Eric E *(212) 924-5437* 85 Barrow St, NY 10014

Maresca, Frank *(212) 620-0955* 236 W 26th St, NY 10001

page 22-23

Margerin, Bill *(212) 645-1532* 41 W 25th St, NY 10010

Markus, Kurt *(212) 431-1212* 134 Reade St, NY 10013

Marshall, Alec *(914) 779-0022* 1 Midland Gardens, Bronxville 10708

Marshall, Elizabeth *(212) 463-7884* 200 Central Pk So , NY 10019

Marshall, Lee *(212) 799-9717* 201 W 89th St, NY 10024

Martin, Bard *(212) 929-6712* 142 W 26th St, NY 10001

Martin, Bill Photographic *(212) 645-9550* 110 W 17th St, NY 10023

Martin, Butch *(201) 486-3049* 75 Hussa St, Linden 07036

Martinez, Oscar *(212) 673-0932* 303 Park Ave So, NY 10010

Marvullo/Photomontage *(212) 564-6501* 141 W 28th St, NY 10001

Marx, Richard *(212) 929-8880* 130 W 25th St, NY 10001

Masca *(212) 929-4818* 109 W 26th St, NY 10001

Maser, Wayne *(212) 953-0088* 17 E 45th St, NY 10017

Mason, Donald *(212) 675-3809* 101 W 18th St, NY 10011

Massey, Philip *(212) 928-8210* 475 W 186th St, NY 10033

Masters, Charles *(212) 308-7744* 308 E 59th St, NY 10022

page 116-117

Masullo, Ralph *(212) 929-4825* 33 W 17th St , NY 10011

Masunaga, Ryuzo *(212) 807-7012* 119 W 22nd St, NY 10011

Mathews, Barbara Lynn *(212) 691-0823* 16 Jane St, NY 10014

Mathews, Bruce Photo *(212) 529-7909* 95 E 7th St, NY 10009

Matsuo, Toshi *(212) 532-1320* 105 E 29th St, NY 10016

Matthews, Cynthia *(212) 288-7349* 200 E 78th St, NY 10021

Maucher, Arnold *(212) 206-1535* 154 W 18th St, NY 10011

Maynard, Chris *(212) 255-8204* 297 Church St, NY 10013

Mazzeo, Michael *(212) 627-3766* 119 W 23rd St, NY 10011

page 110-111

McCabe, David *(212) 874-7480* 39 W 67th St, NY 10023

McCabe, Robert *(212) 677-1910* 117 E 24th St, NY 10010

McCarthy, Jo Anna *(212) 255-5150* 535 Greenwich St, NY 10016

McCarthy, Margaret *(212) 696-5971* 31 E 31st St, NY 10016

McCartney, Susan *(212) 533-0660* 902 Broadway, NY 10022

McCavera, Tom *(212) 714-9122* 450 W 31st St, NY 10001

page 176-177

McDermott, Brian *(212) 675-7273* 48 W 21st St, NY 10010

McFarland, Nancy & Lowell *(212) 691-2600* 50 W 23rd St, NY 10010

McGee, Tony *(212) 925-8333* 568 Broadway, NY 10012

McGlynn, David *(718) 626-9427* 18-23 Astoria Blvd, LIC 11102

page 181

McGoon, James *(212) 473-7680* 317 E 18th St, NY 10003

McGrath, Norman *(212) 799-6422* 164 W 79th St, NY 10024

McKiernan, Scott *(212) 645-3784* 27 W 24th St, NY 10010

McKinley, Barry *(212) 243-1102* 277 W 10th St, NY 10014

McLaughlin, Glenn *(212) 645-7028* 6 W 20th St, NY 10011

McLaughlin-Gill, Frances *(212) 664-7637* 454 W 46th St, NY 10036

McLoughlin, James *(212) 206-8207* 148 W 24th St 5th Fl, NY 10011

McMullen, Mark *(212) 243-6343* 304 Eighth Ave, NY 10001

McNally, Brian T *(212) 744-1263* 234 E 81st St, NY 10028

McNally, Joe *(212) 219-1014* 305 W 98th St, NY 10025

McNamara, David *(212) 226-6770* 568 Broadway, NY 10012

McQueen, Hamilton *(212) 689-7367* 373 Park Ave So, NY 10016

McSpirit, Jerry *(212) 879-2332* 413 E 82nd St, NY 10028

Mead, Chris *(212) 619-5616* 108 Reade St, NY 10003

Megna, Richard *(212) 473-5770* 210 Forsyth St, NY 10002

Meier, Raymond *(212) 807-6286* 438 Broome St, NY 10012

Meisel, Steven *(212) 206-0737* 108 W 18th St, NY 10011

Meiselas, Susan *(212) 966-9200* 72 Spring St, NY 10012

Melford, Michael *(212) 473-3095* 141 Fifth Ave, NY 10003

Melillo, Nicholas *(212) 691-7612* 118 W 27th St, NY 10001

page 54-55

Mella, Michael *(212) 777-6012* 217 Thompson St, NY 10012

Mellon *(212) 691-4166* 69 Perry St, NY 10014

Meltzer, Irwin & Assoc *(212) 807-7464* 50 W 17th St, NY 10011

Memo Studio *(212) 787-1658* 39 W 67th St, NY 10023

Menashe, Abraham *(212) 254-2754* 306 E 5th St, NY 10003

Menda, George *(212) 431-7440* 568 Broadway, NY 10012

Menken, Howard Studios *(212) 924-4240* 119 W 22nd St, NY 10011

Mensch, Barbara *(212) 349-8170* 274 Water St, NY 10038

Meola, Eric *(212) 255-5150* 535 Greenwich St, NY 10013

Merle, Michael G *(212) 741-3801* 5 Union Square W, NY 10003

Mervar, Louis *(212) 354-8024* 29 W 38th St, NY 10018

Metzner, Shelia *(212) 865-1222* 310 Riverside Dr, NY 10025

Meyer, Kip *(212) 683-9039* 80 Madison Ave, NY 10016

page 42-43

Meyerowitz, Joel *(212) 242-0740* 151 W 19th St, NY 10011

Micaud, Christopher *(212) 473-7266* 143 Ave B, NY 10009

page 30

Michaelson, Eric *(212) 223-0948* 136 Grand St, NY 10013

Michals, Duane *(212) 473-1563* 109 E 19th St, NY 10003

Michelson, Eric T *(212) 687-6190* 101 Lexington Ave, NY 10016

Milbauer, Dennis *(212) 532-3702* 15 W 28th St, NY 10001

Miljakovich, Helen *(212) 242-0646* 114 Seventh Ave, NY 10011

Miller, Bert *(212) 567-7947* 30 Dongan Pl, NY 10040

Miller, Bill Photo *(212) 674-8026* 36 E 20th St, NY 10003

Miller, Donald L *(212) 496-2830* 295 Central Park W, NY 10024

Miller, Eileen *(212) 944-1507* 28 W 38th St, NY 10018

Miller, Myron *(212) 242-3780* 23 E 17th St, NY 10003

Miller, Sue Ann *(212) 645-5172* 16 W 22nd St, NY 10010

Ming Photo *(212) 213-1166* 1200 Broadway, NY 10001

Ming, Lung J. Studio *(212) 254-8570* 110 E 23rd St, NY 10010

Minh Studio *(212) 477-0649* 200 Park Ave So, NY 10003

Minks, Marlin *(718) 507-9513* 34-43 82nd St, Jackson Hts 11372

Mistretta, Martin *(212) 675-1547* 220 W 19th St, NY 10011

page 24; 152-153

Mitchell, Andrew *(718) 783-6727* 220 Berkeley Pl, Brooklyn 11217

Mitchell, Benn *(212) 255-8686* 119 W 23rd St, NY 10010

Mitchell, Diane *(212) 877-7624* 175 W 73rd St, NY 10023

Mitchell, Jack *(212) 737-8940* 356 E 74th St, NY 10021

Molacek, Rudy *(212) 598-4473* NY, NY

Molkenthin, Michael *(212) 594-0144* 31 W 31st St, NY 10001

page 148-149

Momy, Michele *(212) 582-1501* 162 W 56th St, NY 10019

Moore, Carla *(212) 633-0300* 11 W 19th St, NY 10011

Moore, Chris *(212) 242-0553* 20 W 22nd St, NY 10010

Moore, Jimmy *(212) 674-7150* 38 E 19th St, NY 10003

Moore, Truman *(212) 533-3655* 873 Broadway, NY 10003

Moran, Nancy *(212) 505-9620* 143 Greene St, NY 10012

Morello, Joe *(212) 684-2340* 40 W 28th St, NY 10001

Moretz, Charles *(212) 714-1357* 529 W 42nd St, NY 10036

Morgan, Jeff *(212) 924-4000* 27 W 20th St, NY 10011

Morris, Bill *(212) 685-7354* 34 E 29th St , NY 10016

Morris, Leonard *(212) 473-8485* 200 Park Ave So , NY 10003

Morrison, Ted *(212) 279-2838* 286 Fifth Ave, NY 10001

Morsch, Roy J *(212) 679-5537* 1200 Broadway , NY 10001

Morsillo, Les *(212) 219-8009* 17 Laight St, NY 10013

Morton, Keith *(212) 889-6643* 39 W 29th St, NY 10001

Moscati, Frank *(212) 255-3434* 5 E 16th St, NY 10003

Moskowitz, Sonia *(212) 877-6883* 5 W 86th St , NY 10024

Mougin, Claude *(212) 691-7895* 227 W 17th St, NY 10011

Mucchi, Fabio *(212) 620-0167* 5 W 20th St, NY 10011

Mucci, Tina *(212) 206-9402* 119 W 23rd St, NY 10011

PAGE 40

Mueller, Deano *(212) 645-6244* 435 W 23rd St, NY 10011

Mullane, Fred *(212) 580-4045* 415 Madison Ave, NY 10017

Muller, Rick *(212) 967-3177* 23 W 31st St, NY 10001

PAGE 156-157

Muller, Rudy *(212) 679-8124* 318 E 39th St, NY 10016

Munro, Gordon *(212) 889-1610* 381 Park Ave So, NY 10016

Munson, Russell *(212) 226-8875* 458 Broadway, NY 10013

Muresan, Jon *(212) 242-1227* 56 W 22nd St, NY 10010

Murray, Robert *(212) 226-6860* 149 Franklin St, NY 10013

Myers, Robert J *(212) 249-8085* 407 E 69th St, NY 10021

Myriad Communications Inc *(212) 564-4340* 208 W 30th St, NY 10001

n

Naar, Jon *(212) 752-4625* 230 E 50th St, NY 10022

Nadelson, Jay *(212) 226-4266* 116 Mercer St, NY 10012

Nahoum, Ken *(212) 219-0592* 95 Greene St, NY 10012

PAGE 68-69

Naideau, Harold *(212) 691-2942* 233 W 26th St, NY 10001

Nakamura, Tohru *(212) 334-8011* 112 Greene St, NY 10012

PAGE 128

Nakano, George *(212) 228-9370* 8 1/2 MacDougal Alley, NY 10011

Namuth, Hans *(212) 691-3220* 20 W 22nd St, NY 10010

Nanfra, Victor *(212) 687-8920* 222 E 46th St, NY 10017

Nardi, Bob *(212) 219-8298* 568 Broadway, NY 10012

Nardiello, Carl *(212) 242-3106* 143 W 20th St, NY 10011

Nathan, Simon *(212) 873-5560* 275 W 96th St, NY 10025

Nault, Corky *(212) 807-7310* 251 W 19th St, NY 10011

Needham, Steven Marc *(212) 206-1914* 6 W 18th St , NY 10011

Neff, Leland *(212) 633-1122* 222 W 23rd St, NY 10011

Neil, Joe *(212) 691-1881* 150 Fifth Ave , NY 10011

Neleman, Hans *(212) 645-5832* 348 W 14th St, NY 10014

Nelken, Dan *(212) 532-7471* 43 W 27th St, NY 10001

Nelson, Michael *(212) 924-2892* 7 E 17th St , NY 10003

Nemeth Studio *(212) 686-3272* 220 E 23rd St , NY 10010

Nesbit, Charles *(212) 807-1855* 64 Greene St, NY 10012

Neumann, Peter *(212) 420-9538* 30 E 20th St NY, NY 10003

Newler, Michael *(212) 242-2449* 119 W 23rd St NY, NY 10011

Newman, Arnold *(212) 877-4510* 39 W 67th St NY, NY 10023

Newman, Marvin E *(212) 219-1228* 227 Central Park W NY, NY 10024

Newton, Helmut *(212) 206-0737* 108 W 18th St NY, NY 10011

Ney, Nancy *(212) 260-4300* 108 E 16th St NY, NY 10003

Ng, Norman Kaimen *(212) 982-3230* 36 E 20th St NY, NY 10003

Niccolini, Dianora *(212) 564-4953* 2 W 32nd St NY, NY 10001

Nicholas, Peter *(212) 529-5560* 29 Bleecker St NY, NY 10012

Nicholson, Nick *(212) 362-8418* 121 W 72nd St NY, NY 10023

Nicolaysen, Ron *(212) 947-5167* 448 W 37th St NY, NY 10018

Niederman, Mark *(212) 362-3902* 230 W 72nd St NY, NY 10023

Niefield, Terry *(212) 686-8722* 12 W 27th St NY, NY 10001

Nilsen, Geoffrey *(212) 226-3260* 463 Broome St NY, NY 10013

Nisnevich, Lev *(212) 219-0535* 133 Mulberry St NY, NY 10013

Nivelle, Serge *(212) 473-2802* 145 Hudson St NY, NY 10013

Niwa-Ogrudek Ltd *(212) 982-7120* 17 W 17th St NY, NY 10011

Noble, Richard *(212) 807-6286* 107 W 25th St NY, NY 10001

Nobu *(212) 633-1122* 222 W 23rd St NY, NY 10011

Nons, Leonard *(212) 741-3990* 5 Union Sq W NY, NY 10003

Noren, Catherine *(212) 627-7805* 15 Barrow St NY, NY 10014

Norman, Helen *(212) 532-4571* 135 E 26th St NY, NY 10010

Novick, Elizabeth *(212) 226-3013* 54 Bleeker St NY, NY 10012

Nystrom, Dick *(212) 431-6793* 158 Spring St NY, NY 10012

o

O'Connor, Michael *(212) 679-0396* 216 E 29th St NY, NY 10016

O'Connor, Thom *(212) 620-0723* 74 Fifth Ave NY, NY 10011

O'Neill, Michael *(212) 807-8777* 134 Tenth Ave NY, NY 10011

O'Reilly, Robert *(212) 832-8992* 311 E 50th St NY, NY 10022

Obremski, George *(212) 684-2933* 1200 Broadway NY, NY 10001

Ochi, Toru *(212) 807-7711* 109 W 27th St NY, NY 10001

PAGE 126-127

Oelbaum, Zeva ***(212) 864-7926*** **600 W 115th St NY, NY 10025**

PAGE 160

Ogata, Kei *(212) 688-4364* 699 Madison Ave NY, NY 10021

Ogden, Perry *(212) 206-0737* 108 W 18th St NY, NY 10018

Ogilvy, Stephen *(212) 505-9005* 876 Broadway NY, NY 10003

Ohara, Ken *(212) 255-0798* Pier 62/W 23rd St NY, NY 10011

Olivo, John *(212) 765-8812* 545 W 45th St NY, NY 10036

Olman, Bradley *(212) 243-0649* 15 W 24th St NY, NY 10010

Orenstein, Ronn *(212) 967-6075* 511 W 33rd St NY, NY 10001

Oringer, Hal *(212) 219-1588* 568 Broadway NY,NY 10012

O'Rourke, J Barry ***(212) 226-7113*** **578 Broadway NY, NY 10012**

PAGE 76-77

Ortner, Jon *(212) 873-1950* 64 W 87th St NY, NY 10024

Osonitsch, Robert *(212) 533-1920* 112 Fourth Ave NY, NY 10003

Otfinowski, Danuta *(212) 254-5799* 420 E 10th St NY, NY 10009

Otsuki, Toshi *(212) 594-1939* 241 W 36th St NY, NY 10018

Oudi *(212) 777-0847* 704 Broadway NY, NY 10003

Owens, Sigrid *(212) 686-5190* 221 E 31st St NY, NY 10016

Ozgen, Nebil *(212) 505-7770* 37 E 18th St NY, NY 10003

p

Paccione *(212) 691-8674* 73 Fifth Ave NY, NY 10003

Padys, Diane *(212) 972-4747* 17 E 45th St NY, NY 10017

Page, Lee ***(212) 286-9159*** **310 E 46th St NY, NY 10017**

PAGE 95

Page, LeMoyne ***(212) 286-9159*** **310 E 46th St NY, NY 10017**

PAGE 95

Pagliuso, Jean & Lee *(212) 873-6594* 315 Central Pk W NY, NY 10025

Pagnano, Patrick *(212) 475-2566* 217 Thompson St NY, NY 10012

Palmisano, Giorgio *(212) 431-7719* 309 Mott St NY, NY 10012

Palubniak, Jerry *(212) 645-2838* 144 W 27th St NY, NY 10001

Palubniak, Nancy *(212) 645-2838* 144 W 27th St NY, NY 10001

Papadopolous, Peter *(212) 675-8830* 78 Fifth Ave NY, NY 10011

Pappas, Tony *(212) 868-2032* 110 W 31st St NY, NY 10001

Paras, Michael N *(718) 278-6768* 28-40 34th St Astoria, NY 11103

Parks, Claudia *(212) 879-9841* 210 E 73rd St NY, NY 10021

Passmore, Nick *(212) 724-1401* 150 W 80th St NY, NY 10024

Pastner, Robert L *(212) 838-8335* 166 E 63rd St NY, NY 10021

Pateman, Michael ***(212) 685-6584*** **155 E 35th St NY, NY 10016**

PAGE 34-37

Peacock, Christian *(212) 645-9837* 126 W 22nd St NY, NY 10011

Pearson, Lee *(212) 691-0122* 126 Fifth Ave NY, NY 10011

Peden, John *(212) 255-2674* 155 W 19th St NY, NY 10011

Pederson, Rob *(212) 431-1212* 134 Reade St NY, NY 10013

Pederson/Erwin *(212) 929-9001* 76 Ninth Ave NY, NY 10011

Pedota, Jack *(212) 586-6436* 314 W 52nd St NY, NY 10019

Pellissier, Sam ***(212) 242-7222*** **22 W 21st St NY, NY 10010**

PAGE 20-21

Pemberton, John *(212) 532-9285* 377 Park Ave So NY, NY 10016

Pendleton, Bruce *(212) 921-0599* PO Box 1060 Forest Hills, NY 11375

Penn, Irving *(212) 880-8426* 89 Fifth Ave NY, NY 10003

Penny, Donald *(212) 243-6453* 505 W 23rd St NY, NY 10011

Peress, Gilles *(212) 966-9200* 72 Spring St NY, NY 10012

Perkell, Jeff *(212) 645-1506* 132 W 22nd St NY, NY 10011

Perweiler, Gary *(212) 254-7247* 873 Broadway NY, NY 10003

Peterson, Grant *(212) 475-2767* 568 Broadway NY, NY 10012

Peticolas, Kip *(212) 473-5770* 210 Forsyth St NY, NY 10002

Petoe, Denes *(212) 213-3311* 22 W 27th St NY, NY 10001

Pettinato, Anthony ***(212) 226-9380*** **42 Greene St NY, NY 10013**

PAGE 145

Pfeffer, Barbara *(212) 877-9913* 40 W 86th St NY, NY 10024

Pfizenmaier, Edward *(212) 475-0910* 42 E 23rd NY, NY 10010

Phillips, James *(212) 219-1799* 82 Greene St NY, NY 10012

Phillips, Robert *(212) 757-5190* 101 W 57th St NY, NY 10019

Picayo, Jose ***(212) 255-3252*** **NY, NY**

PAGE 33

Piel, Denis *(212) 925-8929* 458 Broadway NY, NY 10013

Pierce, Richard *(212) 947-8241* 241 W 36th St NY, NY 10018

Pilgreen, John *(212) 243-7516* 91 Fifth Ave NY, NY 10003

Pilossof, Judd *(212) 989-8971* 142 W 26th St NY, NY 10001

Pioppo, Peter *(212) 243-0661* 50 W 17th St NY, NY 10011

Pipinou, Tom *(212) 431-4518* 568 Broadway NY, NY 10012

Pisarello, Charlie *(212) 243-8441* 15 W 18th St NY, NY 10011

Piscioneri, Joe *(212) 533-7982* 333 Park Ave So NY, NY 10010

Pite, Jonathan *(212) 777-5484* 244 E 21st St NY, NY 10010

Pittman, Dustin *(212) 243-2956* 41 Union Sq W NY, NY 10003

Pizzolorusso, Chris *(212) 686-7175* 381 Park Ave So NY, NY 10016

Platt, Mark *(212) 475-1481* 41 E 20th St NY, NY 10003

Plimpton, Randy *(212) 603-9338* 401 W 48th St NY, NY 10036

Plotkin, Bruce *(212) 691-6185* 3 W 18th St NY, NY 10011

Pobereskin, Joseph *(212) 619-3711* 51 Warren St NY, NY 10007

Pobiner, Ted *(212) 679-5911* 381 Park Ave So NY, NY 10016

Polsky, Herb *(212) 730-0508* 1024 Sixth Ave NY, NY 10018

Popper, Andrew J *(212) 982-9713* 330 First Ave NY, NY 10009

Porcella, Phillip *(212) 912-1828* NY, NY

page 62-63

Porta, Art *(212) 685-1555* 29 E 32nd St NY, NY 10016

Portnoy, Neal *(212) 619-4661* 1 Hudson St NY, NY 10013

Porto, James *(212) 966-4407* 87 Franklin St NY, NY 10013

Poster, James Studio *(212) 206-4065* 210 Fifth Ave NY, NY 10010

Pottle, Jock *(212) 874-0216* 301 W 89th St NY, NY 10024

Powell, Dean *(212) 239-9760* 32 Union Sq E NY, NY 10003

Powers, Guy *(212) 563-3177* 534 W 43rd St NY, NY 10036

Pressman, Herb *(212) 683-5055* 137 E 30th St NY, NY 10016

Prezant, Steve *(212) 684-0822* 1181 Broadway NY, NY 10001

Pribula, Barry *(212) 777-7612* 59 First Ave NY, NY 10003

Price, Clayton J *(212) 929-7721* 205 W 19th St NY, NY 10011

page 140-141

Price, David *(212) 794-9040* 4 E 78th St NY, NY 10021

Priggen, Leslie *(212) 772-2230* 215 E 73rd St NY, NY 10021

Prozo, Marco *(212) 766-4490* 122 Duane St NY, NY 10013

Pruitt, David *(212) 807-0767* 156 Fifth Ave NY, NY 10010

Pruzan, Michael *(212) 686-5505* 1181 Broadway NY, NY 10001

Puhlmann, Rico *(212) 620-4211* 156 Fifth Ave NY, NY 10010

Purvis, Charles *(212) 619-8028* 84 Thomas St NY, NY 10013

q - r

Quat, Dan *(212) 945-1814* NY, NY

Raab, Michael *(212) 533-0030* 831 Broadway NY, NY 10003

Rajs, Jake *(212) 947-9403* 252 W 30th St NY, NY 10001

Rapoport, David *(212) 691-5528* 55 Perry St NY, NY 10014

Ratzkin, Lawrence *(212) 279-1314* 392 Fifth Ave NY, NY 10018

Rau, Andre *(212) 431-1212* 134 Reade St NY, NY 10013

Ravid, Joyce *(212) 477-4233* 12 E 20th St NY, NY 10003

Ray, Bill *(212) 222-7680* 350 Central Park W NY, NY 10025

Raymond, Lilo *(212) 362-9546* 212 E 14th St NY, NY 10003

Rea, Jimmy *(212) 627-1473* 151 W 19th St NY, NY 10011

Reed, Robert *(212) 243-2750* 540 Sixth Ave NY, NY 10011

Regan, Ken *(212) 989-2004* 6 W 20th St NY, NY 10011

Regen, David *(212) 533-5183* 227 E 11th St NY, NY 10003

Reichert, Robert *(212) 645-9515* 149 W 12th St NY, NY 10013

Reiher, Jim *(212) 925-8333* 568 Broadway NY, NY 10012

Reinhardt, Mike *(212) 541-4787* 881 Seventh Ave NY, NY 10019

Reinmiller, Mary Ann *(212) 243-4302* 163 W 17th St NY, NY 10011

Rentmeester, Co *(212) 757-4796* 4479 Douglas Ave Riverdale, NY 10471

Reznicki, Jack *(212) 925-0771* 568 Broadway NY, NY 10012

Rezny, Aaron *(212) 691-1894* 119 W 23rd St NY, NY 10011

Rezny, Abe

(212) 226-7747 28 Cadman Plz W Brooklyn Heights, NY 11201

Rhodes, Arthur *(212) 249-3974* 325 E 64th St NY, NY 10021

Ricucci, Vincent *(212) 691-5860* 59 W 19th St NY, NY 10011

Ries, Henry *(212) 689-3794* 204 E 35th St NY, NY 10016

Ries, Stan *(212) 533-1852* 48 Great Jones St NY, NY 10012

Riggs, Cole *(212) 481-6119* 39 W 29th St NY, NY 10001

Riley, David *(212) 741-3662* 152 W 25th St NY, NY 10001

page 129

Riley, Jon *(212) 532-8326* 12 E 37th St NY, NY 10016

Ritts, Herb *(212) 431-1212* 134 Reade St NY, NY 10013

Rivelli, William *(212) 254-0990* 303 Park Ave So NY, NY 10010

Rivera, Al *(212) 691-3930* 139 W 14th St NY, NY 10011

Robins, Lawrence *(212) 206-0436* 50 W 17th St NY, NY 10011

Robinson, Ceotis *(212) 663-1231* 4-6 W 101st St NY, NY 10025

Robinson, James *(212) 580-1793* 1255 Fifth Ave NY, NY 10029

Robison, Chuck *(212) 777-4894* 21 Stuyvesant Oval NY, NY 10009

Robledo, Maria *(212) 213-1517* 43 W 29th St NY, NY 10001

Rockfield, Bert *(212) 689-3900* 31 E 32nd St NY, NY 10016

Rodin, Christine *(212) 242-3260* 38 Morton St NY, NY 10014

Rohr, Robert *(212) 674-1519* 325 E 10th St NY, NY 10003

Rolo Photo *(212) 691-8355* 214 W 17th St NY, NY 10011

Rolston, Matthew *(212) 431-0993* NY, NY

Romanelli, Marc *(212) 865-5214* 244 Riverside Dr NY, NY 10025

Rose, Uli *(212) 988-8890* 1725 York Ave NY, NY 10128

Rosen, David *(212) 684-5193* 238 E 24th St NY, NY 10010

Rosenberg, Ken *(212) 362-3149* 514 West End Ave NY, NY 10024

Rosenthal, Barry *(212) 645-0433* 205 W 19th St NY, NY 10011

Rosenthal, Marshall M *(212) 807-1247* 231 W 18th St NY, NY 10011

Ross, Ken *(212) 213-9205* 80 Madison Ave NY, NY 10016

Ross, Mark *(212) 744-7258* 345 E 80th St NY, NY 10021

Ross, Steve *(718) 783-6451* 10 Montgomery Pl Brooklyn, NY 11215

Rossignol, Lara *(212) 243-2750* 344 E 63rd St NY, NY 10021

Rossum, Cheryl *(212) 628-3173* 310 E 75th St NY, NY 10021

Roth, Peter *(212) 662-3765* 8 W 19th St NY, NY 10011

Roth, Seth *(212) 620-7050* 137 W 25th St NY, NY 10012

Rothaus, Ede *(212) 989-8277* 34 Morton St NY, NY 10014

ROTHSTEIN, JEFFREY *(212) 966-5770* 110 Greene St NY, NY 10012

ROZSA, NICK *(212) 734-5629* 325 E 64th St NY, NY 10021

PAGE 41

RUBENSTEIN, RAEANNE *(212) 964-8426* 8 Thomas St NY, NY 10007

RUBIN, AL *(212) 674-4535* 250 Mercer St NY, NY 10012

RUBIN, DANIEL *(212) 989-2400* 126 W 22nd St NY, NY 10011

RUBINSTEIN, EVA *(212) 243-4115* 145 W 27th St NY, NY 10001

RUBYAN, ROBERT *(212) 460-9217* 270 Park Ave So NY, NY 10010

RUDNICK, JAMES *(718) 783-4156* 799 Union St Brooklyn, NY 11215

RUDOLPH, NANCY *(212) 989-0392* 35 W 11th St NY, NY 10011

RUGEN-KORY *(212) 777-3889* 150 E 18th St NY, NY 10003

RUGGERI, FRANCESCO *(212) 505-8477* 71 St Marks Pl NY, NY 10003

RYAN, WILL *(212) 242-6270* 16 E 17th St NY, NY 10003

PAGE 92-93

RYSINSKI, EDWARD *(212) 807-7301* 636 Sixth Ave NY, NY 10011

RYUZO *(212) 807-7012* 119 W 22nd St NY, NY 10011

S

SABAL, DAVID *(212) 242-8464* 20 W 20th St NY, NY 10001

SACCO, VITTORIO *(212) 929-9225* 126 Fifth Ave NY, NY 10011

PAGE 166-167

SACHA, BOB *(212) 749-4128* 370 Central Park W NY, NY 10025

SAHAIDA, MICHAEL *(212) 924-4545* 5 W 19th St NY, NY 10019

SAILORS, DAVID *(212) 505-9654* 123 Prince St NY, NY 10012

SAKAS, PETER *(212) 254-6096* 400 Lafayette St NY, NY 10003

SALAFF, FRED *(212) 246-3699* 322 W 57th St NY, NY 10019

SALAVERRY, PHILIP *(212) 807-0896* 133 W 22nd St NY, NY 10011

PAGE 138-139

SALVATI, JERRY *(212) 696-0454* 206 E 26th St NY, NY 10011

SALZANO, JIM *(212) 242-4820* 29 W 15th St NY, NY 10011

SAMARDGE, NICK *(212) 226-6770* 568 Broadway NY, NY 10012

SANCHEZ, ALFREDO *(718) 726-0182* 14-23 30th Dr LIC, NY 11102

SANDERS, CHRIS *(212) 645-6111* 130 W 23rd St NY, NY 10011

PAGE 90-91

SANDONE, A J *(212) 807-6472* 132 W 21st St NY, NY 10011

SANFORD, TOBEY *(212) 245-2736* 888 Eighth Ave NY, NY 10019

SARAPOCHIELLO, JERRY *(212) 219-8545* 47-A Beach St NY, NY 10013

SARTOR, VITTORIO *(212) 674-2994* 10 Bleecker St NY, NY 10012

SASSON, BOB *(212) 675-0973* 352 W 15th St NY, NY 10011

SATO PHOTO *(212) 741-0688* 152 W 26th St NY, NY 10001

SATTERWHITE, AL *(212) 219-0808* 80 Varick St NY, NY 10013

SATTERWHITE, STEVE *(212) 254-8844* 13 Avenue A NY, NY 10009

SAVIDES, HARRIS *(212) 260-6816* 648 Broadway NY, NY 10012

SAYLOR, H DURSTON *(212) 620-7122* 219 W 16th St NY, NY 10011

SCADUTO, LAWRENCE *(212) 410-9319* 328 E 93rd St NY, NY 10128

SCALORA, SUZA *(212) 643-0058* 3 W 30th St NY, NY 10001

PAGE 56

SCARLETT, NORA *(212) 741-2620* 37 W 20th St NY, NY 10011

PAGE 98-101

SCAVULLO, FRANCESCO *(212) 838-2450* 212 E 63rd St NY, NY 10021

SCHECTER, LEE *(212) 431-0088* 13-17 Laight St NY, NY 10013

SCHEER, STEPHEN *(212) 233-7195* 261 Broadway NY, NY 10007

SCHEIN, BARRY *(212) 432-6844* NY, NY

SCHENK, FRED *(212) 677-1250* 112 Fourth Ave NY, NY 10003

SCHIAVONE, CARMEN *(212) 496-6016* 271 Central Park W NY, NY 10024

SCHILLACI, MICHAEL *(212) 564-2364* 320 W 30th St NY, NY 10001

SCHILLER, JUDY *(212) 924-7612* 328 W 19th St NY, NY 10011

SCHINZ, MARINA *(212) 246-0457* 222 Central Park S NY, NY 10019

SCHLACHTER, TRUDY *(212) 741-3128* 160 Fifth Ave NY, NY 10010

SCHLIGHT, GREG *(212) 736-2957* 146 W 29th St NY, NY 10001

SCHMID, LOTHAR *(212) 431-1212* 134 Reade St NY, NY 10013

SCHNEIDER, JOSEF *(212) 265-1223* 119 W 57th St NY, NY 10019

SCHNEIDER, PETER *(212) 982-9040* 902 Broadway NY, NY 10010

SCHNEIDER, ROY *(212) 691-9588* 59 W 19th St NY, NY 10016

SCHRAGER, VICTOR *(212) 334-9575* NY, NY

SCHRAMM, FRANK E. III *(212) 807-1390* 59 Bank St NY, NY 10014

SCHRECK, BRUNO *(212) 254-3078* 873 Broadway NY, NY 10003

SCHULZE, FRED *(212) 242-0930* 38 W 21st St NY, NY 10010

SCHUPF, JOHN *(212) 226-2250* 568 Broadway NY, NY 10012

SCHURINK, YONAH *(212) 362-2860* 666 West End Ave NY, NY 10025

SCHUSTER, SHARON *(212) 734-0927* 320 W 90th St NY, NY 10024

SCHWARTZ, MARVIN *(212) 929-8916* 223 W 10th St NY, NY 10014

SCHWARTZ, SING SI *(212) 475-9222* 15 Gramercy Pk So NY, NY 10003

SCHWERIN, RON *(212) 228-0340* 889 Broadway NY, NY 10003

SCLIGHT, GREG *(212) 736-2957* 146 W 29th St NY, NY 10001

SCOCOZZA, VICTOR *(212) 686-9440* 117 E 30th St NY, NY 10016

SECUNDA, SHELDON *(212) 477-0241* 112 Fourth Ave NY, NY 10003

SEESSELBERG, CHARLES *(212) 807-8730* 119 W 23rd St NY, NY 10011

SEGHERS, CARROLL *(212) 679-4582* 441 Park Ave So NY, NY 10016

SEIDMAN, BARRY *(212) 255-6666* 85 Fifth Ave NY, NY 10003

SEIDNER, DAVID *(212) 744-0286* 12 E 86th St NY, NY 10028

SEITZ, SEPP *(212) 505-9917* 12 E 22nd St NY, NY 10010

Selby, Richard (212) 431-1719 113 Greene St NY, NY 10012

Seligman, Paul (212) 242-5688 163 W 17th St NY, NY 10011

Selkirk, Neil (212) 243-6778 515 W 19th St NY, NY 10011

PAGE 10-11

Seltzer, Abe (212) 807-0660 443 W 18th St NY, NY 10011

Seltzer, Kathleen (212) 475-0314 25 E 4th St NY, NY 10003

Sewell, Jim (212) 923-7686 720 W 181st St NY, NY 10033

Shaffer, Stan (212) 580-5522 NY, NY

Shaman, Harvey (718) 793-0434 109 81st Ave Kew Gardens, NY 11415

Shapiro, Pam (212) 967-2363 11 W 30th St NY, NY 10010

Share, Jed/Tokyo (212) 562-8931 Bronx, NY 10463

Sharko, Greg (718) 738-9694 103-56 103rd St Ozone Pk, NY 11417

Sharratt, Paul (212) 243-3281 20 W 20th St NY, NY 10011

Sheldon, Joshua (212) 928-4199 601 W 176th St NY, NY 10033

PAGE 81

Shelley, George (212) 473-0519 873 Broadway NY, NY 10003

Sherman, Guy (212) 675-4983 108 E 16th St NY, NY 10003

Shiki (212) 929-8847 119 W 23rd St NY, NY 10011

Shipley, Christopher (718) 626-9427 18-23 Astoria Blvd LIC, NY 11102

Shiraishi, Carl (212) 679-5628 137 E 25th St NY, NY 10010

Shung, Ken (212) 807-1449 236 W 27th St NY, NY 10001

Silano, Bill (212) 889-0505 138 E 27th St NY, NY 10016

Silbert, Layle (212) 677-0947 505 LaGuardia Pl NY, NY 10012

Silver, Larry (212) 807-9560 236 W 26th St NY, NY 10001

Simko, Robert (212) 369-6570 NY, NY

Simmons, Laurie (212) 206-0737 108 W 18th St NY, NY 10018

Simon, Peter Angelo (212) 925-0890 568 Broadway NY, NY 10012

Simpson, Coreen (212) 877-6210 599 West End Ave NY, NY 10025

Simpson, Jerry (212) 696-9738 28 W 27th St NY, NY 10001

Singer, Michelle (212) 969-9522 251 W 19th St NY, NY 10011

Sint, Steven (212) 463-8844 45 W 17th St NY, NY 10011

Sirdofsky, Arthur (212) 279-7557 112 W 31st St NY, NY 10001

Sirota, Peggy (212) 598-4473 NY, NY

Skalski, Ken (212) 777-6207 866 Broadway NY, NY 10003

Skelley, Ariel (212) 226-4091 80 Varick St NY, NY 10013

Skogsbergh, Ulf (212) 255-7536 5 E 16th St NY, NY 10003

Skolnik, Lewis (212) 239-1455 135 W 29th St NY, NY 10001

Skott, Michael (212) 686-4807 244 Fifth Ave NY, NY 10001

Slade, Chuck (212) 807-1153 12 E 14th St NY, NY 10003

Slavin, Fred (212) 627-2652 28 W 25th St NY, NY 10010

Slavin, Neal (212) 925-8167 62 Greene St NY, NY 10012

Sleppin, Jeff (212) 947-1433 3 W 30th St NY, NY 10001

Sloan-White, Barbara (212) 760-0057 372 Fifth Ave NY, NY 10018

Small, John (212) 645-4720 156 Fifth Ave NY, NY 10010

Smilow, Stanford (212) 685-9425 333 E 30th St NY, NY 10016

Smith, George (212) 989-4336 366 W 23rd St NY, NY 10011

Smith, Jeff (212) 674-8383 30 E 21st St NY, NY 10010

Smith, Kevin (212) 757-4812 446 W 55th St NY, NY 10019

Smith, Michael (212) 724-2800 140 Claremont NY, NY 10027

Smith, Rita (212) 580-4842 666 West End Ave NY, NY 10025

Smith, Robert Photo (212) 563-2535 421 Seventh Ave NY, NY 10001

Smith, Sean (212) 505-5688 365 First Ave NY, NY 10010

Smith, William E (212) 877-8456 498 West End Ave NY, NY 10024

Snedeker, Katherine (212) 684-0788 16 E 30th St NY, NY 10016

Snider, Lee (212) 873-6141 221 W 82nd St NY, NY 10024

Snyder, Isabel (212) 608-1945 149 Church St NY, NY 10007

PAGE 9

So Studio (212) 475-0090 34 E 23rd St NY, NY 10011

Sobel, Jane (212) 691-9701 161 W 15th St NY, NY 10011

Sochurek, Howard (212) 582-1860 680 Fifth Ave NY, NY 10019

Solomon, Paul (212) 760-1203 440 W 34th St NY, NY 10001

Solowinski, Ray (212) 757-7940 154 W 57th St NY, NY 10019

Soluri, Michael (212) 645-7999 95 Horatio St NY, NY 10014

Somekh, Ric (212) 219-1613 13 Laight St NY, NY 10013

PAGE 38-39

Soot, Olaf (212) 686-4565 419 Park Ave So NY, NY 10016

Sorce, Wayne (718) 237-0497 20 Henry St Brooklyn, NY 11201

Sorensen, Chris (212) 684-0551 PO Box 1760 NY, NY 10156

Sotres, Craig (212) 627-4599 40 W 17th St NY, NY 10011

Spatz, Eugene (212) 777-6793 264 Sixth Ave NY, NY 10014

Spear, Geoff (212) 243-2750 152 Wooster St NY, NY 10013

Specht, Diane (212) 877-8381 167 W 71st St NY, NY 10023

Speier, Leonard (212) 595-5480 190 Riverside Dr NY, NY 10024

Spelman, Steve (212) 242-9381 260 W 10th St NY, NY 10011

Spielman, Les (212) 947-3470 5 W 30th St NY, NY 10001

Spindel, David M (212) 989-4984 18 E 17th St NY, NY 10003

Spinelli, Frank (212) 243-8318 12 W 21st St NY, NY 10010

Spinelli, Paul (212) 410-3320 1619 Third Ave NY, NY 10128

Spiro, Edward (212) 947-7883 340 W 39th St NY, NY 10018

PAGE 144

Spreitzer, Andy (212) 685-9669 225 E 24th St NY, NY 10010

PAGE 154-155

Springston, Dan *(212) 689-0685* 135 Madison Ave NY, NY 10016

St. John, Lynn *(212) 308-7744* 308 E 59th St NY, NY 10022

page 118-119

Staedler, Lance *(212) 243-0935* 154 W 27th St NY, NY 10001

Stahman, Robert *(212) 679-1484* 1200 Broadway NY, NY 10024

Stambler, Wayne *(212) 925-8333* 568 Broadway NY, NY 10012

Standart, Joe *(212) 924-4545* 5 W 19th St NY, NY 10011

Stanton, Brian *(212) 678-7574* 175 Fifth Ave NY, NY 10010

Stanton, William *(212) 662-3571* 160 W 95th St NY, NY 10025

Stark, Philip *(212) 868-5555* 245 W 29th St NY, NY 10001

Steele, Kim *(212) 777-7753* 640 Broadway #7W NY, NY 10012

Steigman, Steve *(212) 473-3366* 5 E 19th St NY, NY 10003

Stein, Larry *(212) 219-9077* 568 Broadway NY, NY 10012

Steinbrenner, Karl *(212) 779-1120* 225 E 24th St NY, NY 10010

Steiner, Charles *(212) 777-0813* 61 Second Ave NY, NY 10003

Steiner, Christian *(212) 724-1990* 300 Central Park W NY, NY 10024

Stember, John *(212) 757-0067* 881 Seventh Ave NY, NY 10019

Stephanie *(212) 929-1029* 277 W 10th St NY, NY 10014

page 17

Stern, Anna *(212) 349-1134* 261 Broadway NY, NY 10007

Stern, Bert *(212) 925-5909* 330 E 39th St NY, NY 10016

Stern, Bob *(212) 889-0860* 12 W 27th St NY, NY 10001

Stern, Cynthia *(212) 925-2677* 515 Broadway NY, NY 10012

Stern, John *(212) 477-0656* 451 W Broadway NY, NY 10012

Stern, Laszlo *(212) 691-7696* 57 W 19th St NY, NY 10011

Sternfeld, Joel *(212) 517-3648* 353 E 77th St NY, NY 10021

Stetson, David *(212) 243-6811* 133 W 71st St NY, NY 10023

Stettner, Bill *(212) 460-8180* 118 E 25th St NY, NY 10010

Stevens, D David *(212) 677-2200* 175 Fifth Ave NY, NY 10010

Stewart, David Harry

***(212) 619-7783* 100 Chambers St NY, NY 10007**

page 16

Stiles, James *(212) 627-1766* 413-15 W 14th St NY, NY 10014

page 57

Stock, Dennis *(212) 966-9200* 72 Spring St NY, NY 10012

Stoecker Bergami Studios *(212) 929-6393* 34 W 15th St NY, NY 10011

Stone, Bob *(212) 682-1490* NY, NY

Stone, Erika *(212) 737-6435* 327 E 82nd St NY, NY 10028

Stratos, Jim *(212) 695-5674* 150 W 36th St NY, NY 10018

Strobe Studio, The *(212) 532-1977* 91 Fifth Ave NY, NY 10003

Strode, Mark *(718) 332-1241* 2026 E 29th St Brooklyn, NY 11229

Stroili, Elaine *(212) 879-8587* 416 E 85th St NY, NY 10028

Strongin, Jeanne *(212) 473-3718* 61 Irving Pl NY, NY 10003

Stuart, John *(212) 966-6783* 80 Varick St NY, NY 10013

page 190-191

Stucker, Hal *(718) 789-1180* 295 Washington Ave Brooklyn, NY 11205

Stupakoff, Otto *(212) 334-8032* 80 Varick St NY, NY 10013

Sugarman, Lynn *(212) 691-3245* 40 W 22nd St NY, NY 10010

page 164-165

Sun Photo *(212) 505-9585* 19 E 21st St NY, NY 10010

Sussman, Daniel *(212) 947-5546* 369 Seventh Ave NY, NY 10001

Sussman, David *(212) 675-5863* 138 W 25th St NY, NY 10001

Svensson, Steen *(212) 242-7272* 52 Grove St NY, NY 10014

Swedowsky, Ben *(212) 684-1454* 381 Park Ave So NY, NY 10016

Swick, Danille *(212) 777-0653* 276 First Ave NY, NY 10009

Symons, Abner *(212) 777-6660* 27 E 21st St NY, NY 10010

t

Tagniez, Anne *(212) 966-5770* 110 Greene St NY, NY 10012

Takeyama, Kimio *(212) 873-0908* 154 W 70th St NY, NY 10023

Tannenbaum, Ken *(212) 675-2345* 16 W 21st St NY, NY 10010

Tanous, Dorothy *(212) 255-9409* 652 Hudson St NY, NY 10014

Tapie, Gilles *(212) 688-4364* 699 Madison Ave NY, NY 10021

Tardio, Robert *(212) 463-9085* 19 W 21st St NY, NY 10010

page 168-169

Taufic, William *(212) 620-8143* 166 W 22nd St NY, NY 10011

Tauss, Marc *(212) 496-1179* 7 1/2 W 75th St NY, NY 10023

page 48

Taylor, Curtise *(212) 473-6886* 29 E 22nd St NY, NY 10010

Taylor, Jonathan *(212) 741-2805* 5 W 20th St NY, NY 10011

Tcherevkoff, Michel *(212) 228-0540* 873 Broadway NY, NY 10003

Teboul, Daniel *(212) 353-1040* 42 E 23rd St NY, NY 10010

Tedesco, Frank *(212) 629-4353* Union Sq W NY, NY 10003

Tegni, Ricardo *(212) 367-8972* 100 E Mosholu Pkwy So NY, NY 10458

Tenneson, Joyce *(212) 741-9371* 114 W 27th St NY, NY 10001

Terk, Neil *(212) 838-1213* 400 E 59th St NY, NY 10022

Tervenski, Steve *(212) 753-6990* 421 E 54th St NY, NY 10016

Tessler, Stefan *(212) 924-9168* 115 W 23rd St NY, NY 10011

Thiery, Franck *(212) 925-5909* 66 Crosby St NY, NY 10012

Thomas, Mark *(212) 741-7252* 141 W 26th St NY, NY 10001

page 134-135

Thompson, Eleanor *(212) 675-6773* 147 W 25th St NY, NY 10001

Thompson, Kenneth *(212) 348-3530* 220 E 95th St NY, NY 10128

Tighe, Michael *(212) 254-4252* 110 E 1st St NY, NY 10009

Tillinghast, Paul *(212) 741-3764* 20 W 20th St NY, NY 10011

Tillman, Denny *(212) 674-7160* 39 E 20th St NY, NY 10003

Today's Photos Inc *(212) 686-0071* 17 E 28th St NY, NY 10016

Togashi *(212) 929-2290* 36 W 20th St NY, NY 10011

Tooke, Hugh Hales *(212) 243-6608* 81 Horatio St NY, NY 10014

Tornberg-Coghlan Assoc *(212) 685-7333* 6 E 39th St NY, NY 10016

Toto, Joe *(212) 620-0755* 148 W 24th St NY, NY 10011

Tran, Clifford *(212) 777-5724* 525 E 14th St NY, NY 10009

Trautwein, Patrick *(212) 582-1501* 162 W 56th St NY, NY 10019

Truran, Bill *(212) 406-2440* 54 Green St NY, NY 10013

Trzeciak, Erwin *(212) 254-4140* 145 E 16th St NY, NY 10003

Tullis, Marcus *(212) 966-8511* 13-17 Laight St NY, NY 10013

Tully, Roger *(212) 947-3961* 341 W 38th St NY, NY 10018

Tung, Matthew *(212) 741-0570* 5 Union Sq W NY, NY 10003

Turbeville, Deborah *(212) 924-6760* 160 Fifth Ave NY, NY 10010

Turner, David *(212) 924-2255* NY, NY

Turner, Pete *(212) 765-1733* 154 W 57th St NY, NY 10019

Turner, Sam *(212) 777-8715* 321 E 21st St NY, NY 10010

Turbeville, Deborah *(212) 924-6760* 160 Fifth Ave NY, NY 10010

Tweedy-Holmes, Karen *212) 866-2289* 180 Claremont Ave NY, NY 10027

Tyler, Mark *(212) 962-3690* 233 Broadway NY, NY 10279

U - V

Uher, John *(212) 594-7377* 529 W 42nd St NY, NY 10036

Umans, Marty *(212) 995-0100* 29 E 19th St NY, NY 10003

Unangst, Andrew *(212) 889-4888* 381 Park Ave So NY, NY 10016

Ursillo, Catherine *(212) 722-9297* 1040 Park Ave NY, NY 10028

Urwuand, Dan *(212) 921-2730* 250 W 40th St NY, NY 10018

Vadukul, Max *(212) 570-0644* NY, NY

Valente, Jerry *(718) 389-0469* 193 Meserole Ave Brooklyn, NY 11222

Valentin, Augusto *(212) 888-1371* 202 E 29th St NY, NY 10016

Vallini Productions *(212) 674-6581* 43 E 20th St NY, NY 10003

Van Der Heyten, Frans *(212) 226-8302* 60-66 Crosby St NY, NY 10012

Van Otteren, Juliet *(212) 627-1958* 568 Broadway NY, NY 10012

Vandommel, Rudoplh *(212) 226-4226* 548 Broadway NY, NY 10012

Vanglintenkamp, Rik *(212) 945-1917* NY, NY

Varnedoe, Sam *(212) 679-1230* 12 W 27th St NY, NY 10001

Varon, Malcolm *(212) 473-5957* 125 Fifth Ave NY, NY 10003

Varriale, Jim *(212) 807-0088* 36 W 20th St NY, NY 10011

Vartoogian, Jack *(212) 663-1341* 262 W 107th St NY, NY 10025

Vega, Julio *(212) 645-1867* NY, NY

Veldenzer, Alan *(212) 420-8189* 160 Bleecker St NY, NY 10012

Vendikos, Tasso *(212) 206-6451* 59 W 19th St NY, NY 10011

Verde, Anthony *(212) 219-1152* 133 Mulberry St NY, NY 10013

page 172-173

Vest, Michael *(212) 532-8331* 40 W 27th St NY, NY 10001

Vhandy Productions *(212) 759-6150* 225-A E 59th St NY, NY 10022

Vickers, Camille *(212) 580-8649* 200 W 79th St NY, NY 10024

Victor, Thomas *(212) 777-6004* 131 Fifth Ave NY, NY 10003

Vidal, Bernard *(212) 629-3764* 450 W 31st St NY, NY 10001

Vidol, John *(212) 889-0065* 37 W 26th St NY, NY 10010

Viesti, Joe *(212) 734-4890* Box 20424 Cherokee Sta, NY 10028

Villanueva, Bill *(212) 924-2500* 5 E 17th St NY, NY 10003

Vine, David *(212) 505-8070* 873 Broadway NY, NY 10003

Vishniac, Roman *(212) 787-0997* 219 W 81st St NY, NY 10024

Visual Impact *(212) 243-8441* 15 W 18th St NY, NY 10011

Vitale, Peter *(212) 249-8412* 157 E 71st St NY, NY 10021

Vogel, Allen *(212) 675-7550* 348 W 14th St NY, NY 10014

Volkmann, Roy *(212) 889-7067* 260 Fifth Ave NY, NY 10001

Volpi, Rene *(212) 532-7367* 121 Madison Ave NY, NY 10016

Von Hassell, Agostino *(212) 242-7290* 277 W 10th St NY, NY 10014

Vos, Gene *(212) 714-1155* 440 Park Ave So NY, NY 10016

W - X

Wadler, Lois *(212) 777-5638* 341 E 6th St NY, NY 10003

Wagner Int'l Photos *(212) 661-6100* 216 E 45th St NY, NY 10017

Wagner, Daniel *(212) 532-8255* 50 W 29th St NY, NY 10001

Wagner, David *(212) 925-5149* 568 Broadway NY, NY 10012

Wahlund, Olof *(212) 929-9067* 7 E 17th St NY, NY 10003

Waine, Michael *(212) 533-4200* 873 Broadway NY, NY 10003

Waitesmith, Matthew *(212) 582-1501* 162 W 56th St NY, NY 10019

Waldo, Maje *(212) 255-3155* Box 1156 Cooper Sta NY, NY 10276

Waldron, William *(212) 226-0356* 463 Broome St NY, NY 10013

Wallace, Randall *(212) 242-2930* 43 W 13th St NY, NY 10011

Wallach, Louis *(212) 925-9553* 594 Broadway NY, NY 10012

page 146-147

Walsh, Bob *(212) 684-3015* 401 E 34th St NY, NY 10016

Waltzer, Bill *(212) 925-1242* 110 Greene St NY, NY 10012

Waltzer, Carl *(212) 475-8748* 873 Broadway NY, NY 10003

Walz, Barbra *(212) 242-7175* 143 W 20th St NY, NY 10011

WANG, JOHN STUDIO INC *(212) 982-2765* 30 E 20th St NY, NY 10003

WANG, TONY *(212) 213-4433* 118 E 28th St NY, NY 10016

WARCHOL, PAUL *(212) 431-3461* 133 Mulberry St NY, NY 10013

WARD, BOB *(212) 627-7005* NY, NY

WARKOV, AARON *(212) 529-0404* 38 E 23rd St NY, NY 10010

WARWICK, CYNDY *(212) 420-4760* 144 E 22nd St NY, NY 10010

PAGE 49

WATABE, HARUO *(212) 505-8800* 37 W 20th St NY, NY 10011

WATANABE, NANA *(212) 741-3248* 130 W 25th St NY, NY 10001

WATERMANN, GREG *(212) 966-5770* 110 Greene St NY, NY 10012

WATSON, ALBERT M *(212) 925-8552* 82 Greene St NY, NY 10012

WATSON, MICHAEL *(212) 620-3125* 133 W 19th St NY, NY 10011

WATT, ELIZABETH *(212) 929-8504* 141 W 26th St NY, NY 10001

PAGE 120-121

WATTS, CLIFF *(212) 629-8116* 360 W 36th St NY, NY 10018

WAXMAN, DANI *(212) 481-3579* 242 E 19th St NY, NY 10003

WEAKS, DAN *(212) 473-3366* 5 E 19th St NY, NY 10003

WEBB, ALEX *(212) 966-9200* 72 Spring St NY, NY 10012

WEBER, BRUCE *(212) 226-0814* NY, NY

WECKLER, CHAD *(212) 355-1135* 210 E 63rd St NY, NY 10021

WEIDLEIN, PETER *(212) 989-5498* 122 W 26th St NY, NY 10001

PAGE 182-183

WEINBERG, CAROL *(212) 206-8200* 40 W 17th St NY, NY 10011

WEINBERG, MICHAEL *(212) 691-1000* 5 E 16th St NY, NY 10003

WEINBERG, STEVE *(212) 254-9571* 47 E 19th St NY, NY 10003

WEINSTEIN, TODD *(212) 254-7526* 47 Irving Pl NY, NY 10003

WEISS, MICHAEL *(212) 929-4073* 10 W 18th St NY, NY 10011

WERNER, PERRY *(212) 379-7434* PO Box 3992 NY, NY 10185

WEST, BONNIE *(212) 929-3338* 156 Fifth Ave NY, NY 10010

WESTHEIMER, BILL *(212) 431-6360* 167 Spring St NY, NY 10012

WEXLER, MARK *(212) 564-7733* 400 W 43rd St NY, NY 10036

WHEATMAN, TRUCKIN *(212) 239-1081* 251 W 30th St NY, NY 10001

WHITAKER, ROSS *(212) 529-0404* 38 E 23rd St NY, NY 10010

WHITE, BILL *(212) 243-1780* 34 W 17th St NY, NY 10011

WHITE, JOEL *(212) 929-1777* 135 W 26th St NY, NY 10001

WHITE, JOHN *(212) 691-1133* 11 W 20th St NY, NY 10011

WHITE, STEVEN *(212) 686-0644* 218 E 32nd St NY, NY 10016

WHITE, TIMOTHY *(212) 777-5484* 244 E 21st St NY, NY 10010

WHITEHURST, WILLIAM *(212) 206-8825* 32 W 20th St NY, NY 10011

WHITELY PRESENTATIONS *(212) 490-3111* 60 E 42nd St NY, NY 10017

WHITMAN, ROBERT *(212) 213-6611* 1181 Broadway NY, NY 10001

PAGE 46-47

WHYTE, DOUGLAS *(212) 431-1667* 519 Broadway NY, NY 10012

WICK, WALTER *(212) 243-3448* 560 Broadway NY, NY 10012

WICKRATH, CLAUS *(212) 925-8333* 568 Broadway NY, NY 10012

WIEN, JEFFREY *(212) 243-7028* 160 Fifth Ave NY, NY 10010

WIER, JOHN ARTHUR *(212) 685-6021* 20 W 20th St NY, NY 10010

WIER, TERRY *(212) 685-6021* 20 W 20th St NY, NY 10010

WIESEHAHN, CHARLES *(212) 563-6612* 249 W 29th St NY, NY 10001

WILCOX, SHORTY/DPI *(212) 246-6367* 19 W 21st St NY, NY 10010

WILKES, STEPHEN *(212) 475-4010* 48 E 13th St NY, NY 10003

WILKS, HARRY *(212) 929-4772* 234 W 21st St NY, NY 10011

WILLIAMSON, RICHIE *(212) 807-0816* 514 W 24th St NY, NY 10011

WILLS, BRET *(212) 629-4878* 245 W 29th St NY, NY 10001

WILSON, MIKE *(212) 683-3557* 441 Park Ave So NY, NY 10016

WINSTEAD, JIMMY *(718) 789-2997* NY, NY

WOHL, MARTY *(212) 460-9269* 40 E 21st St NY, NY 10010

WOJCIK, JAMES *(212) 431-0108* 256 Mott St NY, NY 10012

WOLF, BRUCE *(212) 695-8042* 123 W 28th St NY, NY 10001

PAGE 124-125

WOLF, HENRY *(212) 472-2500* 167 E 73rd St NY, NY 10021

WOLFF, BRIAN R *(212) 465-8976* 560 W 43rd St NY, NY 10036

WOLFSON, ROBERT *(212) 924-1510* 156 Fifth Ave NY, NY 10010

WOLFSON, STEVE & JEFF *(212) 226-0077* 13-17 Laight St NY, NY 10013

WONG, DANIEL *(212) 260-7058* 652 Broadway NY, NY 10012

WONG, LESLIE *(212) 595-0434* 303 W 78th St NY, NY 10024

WOOD, MERRELL *(212) 868-0262* 319 W 38th St NY, NY 10018

WOOD, SUSAN *(212) 371-0679* 641 Fifth Ave NY, NY 10022

WOODWARD, HERBERT *(212) 685-4385* 555 Third Ave NY, NY 10016

WOOL, TOM *(212) 532-4571* 135 E 26th St NY, NY 10010

WORKMAN, WENDY *(718) 965-0257* 203 7th Ave Brooklyn, NY 11215

WORMSER, RICHARD L *(212) 928-0056* 800 Riverside Dr NY, NY 10032

WYMAN, RON *(212) 799-8281* 36 Riverside Dr NY, NY 10023

WYNN, DAN *(212) 535-1551* 170 E 73rd St NY, NY 10021

y - z

YALTER, MEMO *(718) 767-3330* 14-15 162nd St Whitestone, NY 11357

YAMASHIRO, TAD *(212) 473-7177* 224 E 12th St NY, NY 10003

YEE, TOM *(212) 947-5400* 141 W 28th St NY, NY 10001

YOAV *(212) 942-8185* 4523 Broadway NY, NY 10040

YOSHITOMO PHOTOGRAPHY *(212) 505-8800* 119 Fifth Ave NY, NY 10003

YOUNG, DONALD *(212) 593-0010* 166 E 61st St NY, NY 10021

YOUNG, JAMES *(212) 924-5444* 56 W 22nd St NY, NY 10010

Young, Rick *(212) 929-5701* 27 W 20th St NY, NY 10011

Youngblood, Lee *(212) 595-7913* 200 W 70th St NY, NY 10023

Zager, Howard *(212) 239-8082* 450 W 31st St NY, NY 10001

Zan *(212) 260-0271* 108 E 16th St NY, NY 10003

Zander, George *(212) 971-0874* 141 W 28th St NY, NY 10001

Zander, Peter *(212) 534-3125* 312 E 90th St NY, NY 10028

Zanetti, Gerald *(212) 473-4999* 36 E 20th St NY, NY 10003

Zapp, Carl *(212) 924-4240* 119 W 22nd St NY, NY 10011

Zegre, Francois *(212) 684-6517* 124 E 27th St NY, NY 10016

Zehnder, Bruno *(212) 840-1234* Box 5996 NY, NY 10163

Zenreich, Alan *(212) 807-1551* 78 Fifth Ave NY, NY 10011

Zeray, Peter *(212) 674-0332* 113 E 12th St NY, NY 10003

PAGE 104-105

Zeschin, Elizabeth *(212) 219-0326* 50 White St NY, NY 10013

Zimmerman, David *(212) 243-2718* 119 W 23rd St NY, NY 10011

Zimmerman, Marilyn *(212) 243-2718* 119 W 23rd St NY, NY 10011

Zingler, Joseph *(212) 226-3867* 18 Desbrosses St NY, NY 10013

Zitz, Peter *(212) 543-7896* 6126 Firestone Rd Riverdale, NY 10471

Zoiner, John *(212) 972-0357* 12 W 44th St NY, NY 10036

Zwiebel, Michael *(212) 477-5629* 42 E 23rd St NY, NY 10010

PHOTOGRAPHY REPRESENTATIVES

a - b

Abbey, Ken *(212) 947-7577* 421 Seventh Ave NY, NY 10001

Altamore, Bob *(212) 977-4300* 237 W 54th St NY, NY 10019

Anthony, Ed *(212) 924-7770* 133 W 19th St NY, NY 10011

Anton, Jerry *(212) 679-4562* 107 E 38th St NY, NY 10016

Aparo, Vincent *(212) 877-5439* 65 W 68th St NY, NY 10023

PAGE 17

Arnold, Peter Inc *(212) 481-1190* 1181 Broadway NY, NY 10001

Arroyo, Lou *(212) 486-9575* 245 E 63rd St NY, NY 10021

Art & Commerce *(212) 206-0737* 108 W 18th St NY, NY 10011

Ash, Michael *(212) 807-6286* 107 W 25th St NY, NY 10001

Azzara, Louise *(212) 674-8114* 131 E 17th St NY, NY 10003

Backer, Vic *(212) 620-0944* 30 W 26th St NY, NY 10010

Badin, Andy *(212) 532-1222* 1538 W 38th St NY, NY 10018

Bahm, Darwin *(212) 989-7074* 6 Jane St NY, NY 10014

Baker, Valerie *(212) 807-9754* 152 W 25th St NY, NY 10001

Bantry, Bryan *(212) 245-0200* 105 W 55th St NY, NY 10019

Barboza, Ken *(212) 505-8635* 853 Broadway NY, NY 10003

Barclay, R Francis *(212) 255-3440* 5 W 19th St NY, NY 10011

Baruch, Liz *(212) 752-8174* 245 E 58th St NY, NY 10022

Becker, Noel *(212) 757-8987* 150 W 55th St NY, NY 10019

Beidler, Barbara *(212) 535-2488* 235 E 73rd St NY, NY 10021

Beilin, Frank *(212) 751-3074* 405 E 56th St NY, NY 10022

Bernstein & Andriulli

_(212) 682-1490_ 60 E 42nd St NY, NY 10165

PAGE 1-8; 166-167; 176-177

Bevan, Paul *(212) 645-5832* 348 W 14th St NY, NY 10014

Black Star *(212) 679-3288* 450 Park Ave So NY, NY 10016

Black, Silver & Lord *(212) 580-4045* 415 Madison Ave NY, NY 10017

Blevins, Steve *(212) 888-1828* 1109 First Ave NY, NY 10021

PAGE 156-157

Bloncourt, Nelson *(212) 924-2255* 421 Hudson St NY, NY 10014

Blum, Felice S *(212) 929-2166* 79 W 12th St NY, NY 10011

Boghosian, Marty *(212) 242-1251* 1123 Broadway NY, NY 10010

Booth, Tom Inc *(212) 243-2750* 425 W 23rd St NY, NY 10011

Bouet, Thierry *(212) 219-0707* 153 Mercer St NY, NY 10012

Boyd, Mason *(212) 431-7755* 72 Spring St NY, NY 10012

Brennan, Dan *(212) 925-8333* 568 Broadway NY, NY 10012

Brennan, Eve *(212) 744-0286* 12 E 86th St NY, NY 10028

Brigitte Inc *(212) 243-6811* 160 Fifth Ave NY, NY 10011

Brindle, Carolyn *(212) 534-4177* 203 E 89th St NY, NY 10028

Brody, Sam *(212) 758-0640* 12 E 46th St NY, NY 10017

Brown, Doug *(212) 953-0088* 17 E 45th St NY, NY 10017

Bruck, Nancy *(212) 645-1547* 302 W 12th St NY, NY 10011

Bruml, Kathy *(212) 874-5659* 201 W 77th St NY, NY 10024

Byrnes, Charles *(212) 473-3366* 5 E 19th St NY, NY 10003

c - d

Cadeno, Lucy *(212) 255-9212* 10 W 18th St NY, NY 10011

Cahill, Joe *(212) 751-0529* 135 E 50th St NY, NY 10012

Camera 5 Inc *(212) 989-2004* 6 W 20th St NY, NY 10011

Cammler, Frederic *(212) 757-2676* 1650 Broadway NY, NY 10028

Camp, Woodfin *(212) 481-6900* 116 E 27th St NY, NY 10016

Canter, Theresa *(212) 360-6280* 1675 York Ave NY, NY 10028

Caputo, Elyse *(212) 725-0503* 240 E 27th St NY, NY 10010

Carmel *(212) 925-6216* 69 Mercer St NY, NY 10012

Carp, Stan *(212) 759-8880* 2166 Broadway NY, NY 10024

Casey, Judy ***(212) 255-3252*** **96 Fifth Ave NY, NY 10011**

page 30-33

Casey, Marge *(212) 486-9575* 245 E 63rd St NY, NY 10021

Cedeno, Lucy *(212) 255-9212* 10 W 18th St NY, NY 10011

Celnick, Manny *(212) 420-9326* NY, NY

Chie *(212) 243-2353* 15 E 11th St NY, NY 10003

Chislovsky, Carol *(212) 677-9100* 853 Broadway NY, NY 10003

Chuan, Jason ***(212) 643-0058*** **3 W 30th St NY, NY 10001**

page 56

Cohen, Bruce *(212) 620-7839* 54 W 16th St NY, NY 10011

Cole, Vicki *(212) 431-1212* 134 Reade St NY, NY 10013

Colmer, Brian *(212) 949-2366* NY, NY

Conlon, Jean ***(212) 966-9897*** **461 Broome St NY, NY 10013**

page 129; 142-143

Connolly, Elyse *(212) 598-4473* 21 Gramercy Pk So NY, NY 10003

Cullom, Ellen *(212) 777-1749* 55 E 9th St NY, NY 10003

Daley, Katie ***(212) 410-9319*** **328 E 93rd St NY, NY 10128**

page 18-19

Davis, Gail *(212) 570-0644* 301 E 79th St NY, NY 10021

Davies, Nora ***(212) 628-6657*** **370 E 76th St NY, NY 10021**

page 34-37

Dedell, Jacqueline *(212) 741-2539* 58 W 15th St NY, NY 10011

Delaney, Bill ***(212) 683-8331*** **176 Lexington Ave NY, NY 10016**

page 138-139

Des Verges, Diana *(212) 691-8674* 73 Fifth Ave NY, NY 10003

Devlieger, Mary *(212) 903-4321* 2109 Broadway NY, NY 10023

Dewan, Michael *(212) 927-9458* 250 Cabrini Blvd NY, NY 10033

DiBartolo, Joe *(212) 532-0018* 270 Madison Ave NY, NY 10016

Dictenberg, Robin *(212) 944-2853* 20 W 46th St NY, NY 10036

Dillon, Ellen ***(212) 675-1548*** **NY, NY**

page 24; 152-153

Donaho, Linda *(212) 966-5770* 110 Greene St NY, NY 10012

Dorman, Paul *(212) 826-6737* 419 E 57th St NY, NY 10022

Dorr, Chuck ***(212) 431-5858*** **291 Church St NY, NY 10013**

page 50-51

DuCain, Alex *(212) 772-2840* 111 E 64th St NY, NY 10021

Dunn, Roark *(212) 529-9875* 19 W 8th St NY, NY 10003

e - g

Eagles, Betsy *(212) 582-1501* 162 W 56th St NY, NY 10019

Ekblom, Melissa ***(212) 996-0912*** **NY, NY**

page 28-29

Ellis, Ron *(212) 691-7612* 118 W 27th St NY, NY 10001

Emmerich, Ellen *(212) 477-6413* 145 Fourth Ave NY, NY 10003

Eng, Barbara *(212) 254-8334* 110 E 23rd St NY, NY 10010

Engel, Mary *(212) 580-1051* NY, NY

Englert, Tim *(212) 496-2074* 305 W 84th St NY, NY 10024

Eyre, Susan *(718) 282-5034* 292 Marlboro Rd Brooklyn, NY 11226

Feldman, Robert *(212) 741-7254* 133 W 17th St NY, NY 10011

Fischer, Bob *(212) 755-2131* 135 E 54th St NY, NY 10022

Fishback, Lee *(212) 929-2951* 350 W 21st St NY, NY 10011

Foster, Peter *(212) 593-0793* 870 UN Plaza NY, NY 10017

Fraser, Gaylene *(212) 475-5911* 211 Thompson St NY, NY 10012

Freeman, Susan *(212) 860-8180* 1158 Fifth Ave NY, NY 10029

Friess, Susan *(212) 675-3021* 36 W 20th St NY, NY 10010

Friscia, Sal *(212) 228-4134* 20 W 10th St NY, NY 10011

Furst, Franz *(212) 684-0492* 420 E 55th St NY, NY 10022

Gargagliano, Tony *(212) 661-0850* 216 E 45th St NY, NY 10017

Gaynin, Gail *(212) 255-3040* 241 Central Pk W NY, NY 10024

Gebbia, Doreen *(212) 496-1279* 312 W 88th St NY, NY 10024

Gelb, Elizabeth *(212) 222-1215* 856 West End Ave NY, NY 10025

Gerber, Amy *(212) 206-9194* NY, NY

Giraldi, Tina *(212) 840-8225* 54 W 39th St NY, NY 10018

Goldman, David *(212) 807-6627* 41 Union Sq W NY, NY 10003

Goldman, Howard *(212) 627-2319* 221 W 21st St NY, NY 10011

Goldsmith, Randi *(212) 580-1143* 56 W 84th St NY, NY 10024

Goldstein, Michael L *(212) 874-6933* 107 W 69th St NY, NY 10023

Gomberg, Susan *(212) 473-8747* 145 E 22nd St NY, NY 10010

Goodwin, Phyllis A *(212) 570-6021* 10 E 81st St NY, NY 10028

Gordon, Barbara *(212) 686-3514* 165 E 32nd St NY, NY 10016

Gotham Art Agency *(212) 989-2737* 1123 Broadway NY, NY 10010

Grande, Carla *(212) 966-8263* 50 Prince St NY, NY 10012

Green, Anita ***(212) 674-4788*** **718 Broadway NY, NY 10003**

page 114-115; 148-149

Griffith, Valerie *(212) 675-2089* 10 Sheridan Sq NY, NY 10014

Groom, John *(212) 925-3830* 548 Broadway NY, NY 10012

Gynin, Gail *(212) 255-3040* 241 Central Pk W NY, NY 10024

h - k

Hainy, Barry *(212) 929-4313* 82 Jane St NY, NY 10014

Hajjar, Rene *(212) 777-5361* 220 Park Ave So NY, NY 10003

HALLELUJAH! ARTIST MANAGEMENT

(212) 243-6608 81 Horatio St NY, NY 10014

HANDELMAN, H. LEE *(212) 645-7946* 77 Fifth Ave NY, NY 10011

HANSEN, WENDY *(212) 684-7139* 126 Madison Ave NY, NY 10016

HARE, FRAN *(212) 794-0043* 126 W 23rd St NY, NY 10011

HARMON, ROD *(212) 245-8935* 254 W 51st St NY, NY 10019

HARTNEY, JOEL *(212) 242-8106* 5 W 19th St NY, NY 10011

HEAD, OLIVE *(212) 580-3323* 155 Riverside Dr NY, NY 10024

HENRY, JOHN *(212) 686-6883* 237 E 31st St NY, NY 10016

HERRON, PAT *(212) 683-9039* 80 Madison Ave NY, NY 10016

PAGE 26-27; 42-43; 164-165; 186-189

HEYL, FRAN *(212) 581-6470* 230 Park Ave NY, NY 10017

HILL, JAMES & ASSOCIATES *(212) 302-4646* 1026 Sixth Ave NY, NY 10018

HOEYE, MICHAEL *(212) 362-9546* 120 W 70th St NY, NY 10023

HOLT, RITA *(212) 683-2002* 920 Main St Fords, NJ 08863

HOVDE, NOB *(212) 753-0462* 275 W 96th St NY, NY 10025

PAGE 26-27; 42-43; 186-189

HUREWITZ, GARY *(212) 473-3366* 5 E 19th St NY, NY 10003

HUSAK, JOHN *(212) 463-7025* 236 W 26th St NY, NY 10001

HYDE, TAD & MARINA *(212) 956-3151* 888 Eighth Ave NY, NY 10019

INTERNATIONAL ARTIST MANAGEMENT

(212) 582-1501 162 W 56th St NY, NY 10019

JACOBSEN, VI *(212) 677-3770* 333 Park Ave So NY, NY 10010

JARREAU, JOAN *(212) 691-5903* 34 W 17th St NY, NY 10011

JEDELL, JOAN *(212) 861-7861* 370 E 76th St NY, NY 10021

JOHNSON, KATHERINE *(212) 777-7254* 317 Second Ave NY, NY 10003

KAHN, HARVEY *(212) 752-8490* 50 E 50th St NY, NY 10022

KANE, ODETTE *(212) 807-8730* 119 W 23rd St NY, NY 10011

KAPLAN, HOLLY *(212) 563-2730* 35 W 36th St NY, NY 10018

KAUFMAN, HILLERY *(718) 230-3348* 206 Lincoln Pl Brooklyn, NY 11217

KAUSS, JEAN-GABRIEL *(212) 370-4300* 235 E 40th St NY, NY 10016

KEISERMAN/KANDEL *(212) 691-5860* 160 Fifth Ave NY, NY 10010

KENNEY, JOHN *(212) 279-1515* 251 W 30th St NY, NY 10001

KERSZ, VALERIE *(212) 431-0993* 36 Mott St NY, NY 10003

KESTNER, VG *(212) 535-4144* 427 E 77th St NY, NY 10021

KETCHUM, LAURIE *(212) 481-9592* NY, NY

KIM *(212) 679-5628* 209 E 25th St NY, NY 10010

KLEIN, LES *(212) 255-1963* 104 E 40th St NY, NY 10016

KORMAN, ALLISON *(212) 633-8407* 150 Fifth Ave NY, NY 10011

KORN, ELAINE *(212) 760-0057* 234 Fifth Ave NY, NY 10001

KRAMER & KRAMER *(212) 688-4364* 699 Madison Ave NY, NY 10021

KRAMER, JOAN & ASSOCIATES *(212) 567-5545* 720 Fifth Ave NY, NY 10019

KREIS, URSULA G *(212) 562-8931* 63 Adrian Ave Bronx, NY 10463

KRONGARD, PAULA *(212) 683-1020* 210 Fifth Ave NY, NY 10010

l - m

LAMONT, MARY *(212) 242-1087* 200 W 20th St NY, NY 10011

LANE TALENT INC *(212) 861-7225* 104 Fifth Ave NY, NY 10011

LARKIN, MARY *(212) 308-7744* 308 E 59th St NY, NY 10022

PAGE 116-119

LEE, ALAN *(212) 673-2484* 33 E 22nd St NY, NY 10010

LEE, LIZ *(212) 889-7067* 260 Fifth Ave NY, NY 10001

LEGRAND, JEAN-YVES *(212) 724-5981* 41 W 84th St NY, NY 10024

PAGE 89

LEONE, MINDY *(212) 696-5674* 381 Park Ave So NY, NY 10016

LEONIAN, EDITH *(212) 989-7670* 220 E 23rd St NY, NY 10010

LERMAN, GARY *(212) 683-5777* 113 E 31st St NY, NY 10016

PAGE 64-65; 112

LEVIN, BRUCE *(212) 410-0123* 1691 Third Ave NY, NY 10028

LEWIN, SAMANTHA *(212) 228-5530* 242 E 19th St NY, NY 10003

LGI *(212) 736-4602* 241 W 36th St NY, NY 10018

LONGOBARDI, GERARD *(212) 505-2510* NY, NY

LYNCH, ALAN *(212) 255-6530* 155 Sixth Ave NY, NY 10013

MADRIS, STEPHEN *(212) 744-6668* 445 E 77th St NY, NY 10021

MAIUCCI, MARIE A *(212) 465-8877* 323 W 39th St NY, NY 10018

MANDELL, EILEEN *(212) 860-3148* 61 E 86th St NY, NY 10028

MANN, KEN *(212) 944-2853* 20 W 46th St NY, NY 10036

MAREK & ASSOCIATES INC *(212) 924-6760* 160 Fifth Ave NY, NY 10010

MARLON *(212) 777-5757* 67 E 11th St NY, NY 10003

PAGE 12-13, 15

MARSHALL, EDITH *(212) 877-3921* 40 W 77th St NY, NY 10024

MARTEL, MAUREEN *(212) 972-4747* 17 E 45th St NY, NY 10017

PAGE 82-83

MARX, GALE *(212) 239-4909* NY, NY

MARZENA *(212) 772-2522* NY, NY

PAGE 108-109

MASON, KATHY *(212) 675-3809* 101 W 18th St NY, NY 10011

MAUTNER, JANE *(212) 777-9024* 85 Fourth Ave NY, NY 10003

MAYO, VICKI *(212) 722-7228* 425 E 86th St NY, NY 10028

McKAY, COLEEN *(212) 598-0469* 229 E 5th St NY, NY 10003

MEIXLER, HARRIET *(212) 868-0078* 36 W 37th St NY, NY 10018

PAGE 180

Metz, Bernard *(212) 254-4996* 43 E 19th St NY, NY 10003

Michael, Pamela *(212) 799-8281* 36 Riverside Dr NY, NY 10023

Miller, Susan *(212) 905-8400* 1641 Third Ave NY, NY 10028

Morse, Lauren *(212) 807-1551* 78 Fifth Ave NY, NY 10011

Mosel, Sue *(212) 599-1806* 310 E 46th St NY, NY 10017

Moses, Janice *(212) 779-7929* 155 E 31st St NY, NY 10016

PAGE 44-45; 130-133

Moskowitz, Marion *(212) 719-9879* 342 Madison Ave NY, NY 10173

Moss, Eileen *(212) 980-8061* 333 E 49th St NY, NY 10017

Moss, Susan *(212) 354-8024* 29 W 38th St NY, NY 10018

Murray, Helen *(212) 460-5212* 114 E 13th St NY, NY 10003

Muth, John *(212) 532-3479* 37 W 26th St NY, NY 10010

n - r

Neail, Pamela R *(212) 673-1600* 27 Bleeker St NY, NY 10012

Network Representatives Inc

(212) 529-0404 38 E 23rd St NY, NY 10010

Oesterreicher, Albert

***(212) 643-3100* 488 Seventh Ave NY, NY 10018**

PAGE 57

Ogrudek, Robert *(212) 645-8008* 17 W 17th St NY, NY 10010

Oversee *(212) 219-0707* 153 Mercer St NY, NY 10012

page Associates *(212) 772-0346* 219 E 69th St NY, NY 10021

Palmer-Smith, Glenn *(212) 807-1855* 160 Fifth Ave NY, NY 10010

Pamic, Maja *(212) 302-4646* 1026 Sixth Ave NY, NY 10018

Parvis, Frank *(212) 473-5868* 15 Washington Pl NY, NY 10012

Pasteur, Benjamin *(212) 260-4300* 108 E 16th St NY, NY 10003

Pelaez, Jose *(212) 925-5149* 568 Broadway NY, NY 10012

Perig, Larry *(212) 620-8115* 40 W 17th St NY, NY 10011

Peters, Nancy *(212) 874-7480* 39 W 67th St NY, NY 10023

Petersen, Victoria *(212) 799-7021* 16 W 71st St NY, NY 10023

Picture Group *(212) 688-6330* 344 E 59th St NY,NY 10022

Pinkstaff, Marsha *(212) 246-2300* 222 Central Pk So NY, NY 10019

Priano, Timothy *(212) 686-5277* 200 E 33rd St NY, NY 10016

Puhalski, Ron *(212) 242-2860* 1133 Broadway NY, NY 10010

Pushpin Associates *(212) 674-8080* 215 Park Ave So NY, NY 10003

Quercia, Mat *(212) 477-4491* 78 Irving Pl NY, NY 10003

Radford, Catherine *(212) 683-5777* 113 E 31st St NY, NY 10016

Ray, Maryls *(212) 222-7680* 350 Central Pk W NY, NY 10025

Reese, Kay Associates *(212) 598-4848* 175 Fifth Ave NY, NY 10010

Reid, Pamela *(212) 925-5909* 66 Crosby St NY, NY 10012

Rivelli, Cynthia *(212) 254-0990* 303 Park Ave So NY, NY 10010

Robinson, Madeline *(212) 243-3138* 31 W 21st St NY, NY 10010

Roman, Helen *(212) 874-7074* 140 West End Ave NY, NY 10023

Rosenberg, Arlene *(212) 675-7983* 377 W 11th St NY, NY 10014

Rubin, Adrienne *(212) 628-9513* 416 E 78th St NY, NY 10021

PAGE 14; 66-67

Rudoff, Stan *(212) 679-8780* 271 Madison Ave NY, NY 10016

Russo, Karen *(212) 749-6382* 175 W 92nd St NY, NY 10025

s

Sacramone, Dario *(212) 929-0487* 302 W 12th St NY, NY 10014

PAGE 128

Samuels, Rosemary *(212) 477-3567* 130 W 25th St NY, NY 10001

Sander, Vicki *(212) 683-7835* 155 E 29th St NY, NY 10016

Sartan, Edward *(212) 643-3100* 488 Seventh Ave NY, NY 10018

PAGE 57

Savel, Carin *(212) 799-7318* 332 W 87th St NY, NY 10024

Scharak, Lisa *(212) 371-2159* 401 E 58th St NY, NY 10022

PAGE 154-155

Schecter, Ron *(212) 752-4400* 212 E 49th St NY, NY 10017

Scherr, Dottie *(212) 529-9460* NY, NY

Schiffman, Lisa *(212) 941-1180* 225 Lafayette St NY, NY 10012

Schochat, Kevin R *(212) 243-6229* 221 W 21st St NY, NY 10011

Schon, Herb *(212) 737-2945* 1240 Lexington Ave NY, NY 10028

Schub, Peter & Bear, Robert

(212) 246-0679 37 Beekman Pl NY, NY 10022

Segerstrom, Rebecca *(212) 242-0181* 152 W 26th St NY, NY 10001

Sehven Arts Inc *(212) 532-4571* 135 E 26th St NY, NY 10010

Seyfried, Sarah *(212) 226-4226* 548 Broadway NY, NY 10012

Shamilzadeh, Sol *(212) 532-1977* 1155 Broadway NY, NY 10001

PAGE 97

Sheer, Doug *(212) 732-4216* 29 John St NY, NY 10038

Shepherd, Judith *(212) 242-6554* NY, NY

Siegel, Tema *(212) 696-4680* 461 Park Ave So NY, NY 10016

Simon, Debra *(212) 988-8890* 975 Park Ave NY, NY 10028

Simoneau, Christine *(212) 696-2085* Box 12541 NY, NY 10156

Sims, Jennifer *(212) 860-3005* 1150 Fifth Ave NY, NY 10128

Slocum, Linda *(212) 243-0649* 15 W 24th St NY, NY 10011

Slome, Nancy *(212) 685-8185* 121 Madison Ave NY, NY 10016

Sonneville, Dane *(212) 603-9530* Box 20415 Greeley Stn NY, NY 10001

Source Force *(212) 643-3100* 488 Seventh Ave NY, NY 10018

PAGE 57

Spaeth, Vicki

(718) 520-8632 **70-01 113th St Forest Hills, NY 11375**

PAGE 60-61; 113

Spierman, Shelly *(212) 749-8911* 50 W 96th St NY, NY 10025

Stein, Jonathan *(212) 517-3648* 353 E 77th St NY, NY 10021

Steiner, Susan *(212) 673-4704* 130 E 18th St NY, NY 10003

Stevens, Norma *(212) 427-7235* 1075 Park Ave NY, NY 10028

Stockland, Bill ***(212) 972-4747*** **17 E 45th St NY, NY 10017**

PAGE 82-83

Stogo, Don *(212) 490-1034* 310 E 46th St NY, NY 10017

Stoltzman, Marlon ***(212) 777-5757*** **67 E 11th St NY, NY 10003**

PAGE 12-13; 15

Susse, Ed *(212) 243-1126* 56 W 22nd St NY, NY 10010

t - z

Taborda, Carlos *(212) 734-1903* 344 E 85th St NY, NY 10028

Tannenbaum, Dennis *(212) 279-2838* 286 Fifth Ave NY, NY 10001

Tango *(212) 633-1122* 222 W 23rd St NY, NY 10011

Terzi, Cornelia *(212) 564-7533* 448 E 37th St NY, NY 10018

Thomas, Brenda *(212) 873-7236* 127 W 79th St NY, NY 10024

Tralongo, Katrin *(212) 255-1976* 144 W 27th St NY, NY 10001

Umlas, Barbara ***(212) 534-4008*** **131 E 93rd St NY, NY 10128**

PAGE 52-53; 98-101; 134-135

Valentine, Gloria

(212) 725-1596 **200 E 33rd St NY, NY 10016**

PAGE 145

Van Arnam, Lewis *(212) 541-4787* 154 W 57th St NY, NY 10019

Van Orden, Yvonne *(212) 265-1223* 119 W 57th St NY, NY 10019

Vance, Joy *(212) 219-0808* 80 Varick St NY, NY 10013

Visions & Images *(212) 481-3770* 461 Park Ave So NY, NY 10016

Vitale, Marian ***(212) 683-4225*** **NY, NY**

PAGE 73; 168-169

Von Schreiber, Barbara *(212) 873-6594* 315 Central Park W NY, NY 10025

Wainman, Rick ***(212) 629-6820*** **360 W 36th St NY, NY 10018**

PAGE 120-121

Ward, Wendy *(212) 684-0590* 200 Madison Ave NY, NY 10016

Wasserman, Ted ***(212) 867-5360*** **51 E 42nd St NY, NY 10017**

PAGE 58-59; 136-137

Watson, George ***(212) 645-8616*** **122 W 26th St NY, NY 10001**

PAGE 74-75; 106-107

Wayne, Phillip *(212) 696-5215* 66 Madison NY, NY 10016

Webb, Thomasina *(212) 620-7832* 350 W 24th St NY, NY 10011

Weiner, Mark *(212) 675-6902* 49 W 23rd St NY, NY 10010

Weissberg, Elyse *(212) 406-2566* 299 Pearl St NY, NY 10038

Wheeler, Paul *(212) 564-5430* 145 W 28th St NY, NY 10001

Yellen, Bert Associates *(212) 838-3170* 420 E 54th St NY, NY 10022

Youngs, Maralee *(212) 679-8124* 318 E 39th St NY, NY 10016

Zaccaro, Jim ***(212) 744-4000*** **116 E 78th St NY, NY 10021**

PAGE 10-11

Zanetti, Lucy *(212) 473-4999* 36 E 20th St NY, NY 10003

Zitsman, Cookie *(212) 928-6228* 30 Magaw Pl NY, NY 10033

Zlotnick, Jenny *(212) 431-7680* 14 Prince St NY, NY 10012

STOCK PHOTOGRAPHY

a - o

American Heritage Picture Library

(212) 399-8930 10 Rockefeller Plaza NY, NY 10020

Animals Animals *(212) 982-4442* 65 Bleeker St NY, NY 10012

Archive Pictures *(212) 431-1610* 111 Wooster St NY, NY 10012

Arnold, Peter *(212) 481-1190* 1181 Broadway NY, NY 10001

Art Resource Inc *(212) 505-8700* 65 Bleecker St NY, NY 10012

Berenholtz, Richard ***(212) 223-1302*** **600 W 111th St NY,NY 10025**

PAGE 184-185

Bettmann Archive *(212) 758-0362* 136 E 57th St NY, NY 10022

Black Star *(212) 679-3288* 450 Park Ave So NY, NY 10016

Camera Five Inc *(212) 989-2004* 6 W 20th St NY, NY 10011

Camerique Stock Photography

(212) 685-3870 1181 Broadway NY, NY 10001

Camp, Woodfin Associates *(212) 481-6900* 116 E 27th St NY, NY 10017

Coleman, Bruce Inc *(212) 683-5227* 381 Fifth Ave NY, NY 10016

Comstock ***(212) 353-8600*** **30 Irving Pl NY, NY 10003**

PAGE 194-195

Contact Stock Images *(212) 481-6900* 116 E 27th St NY, NY 10017

Culver Pictures Inc *(212) 645-1672* 150 W 22nd St NY, NY 10011

DeWys, Leo Inc *(212) 689-5580* 1170 Broadway NY, NY 10001

Dot Picture Agency *(212) 684-3441* 50 W 29th St NY, NY 10001

DPI Inc *(212) 627-4060* 19 W 21st St NY, NY 10010

Envision *(212) 243-0415* 220 W 19th St NY, NY 10011

Ewing Galloway *(212) 719-4720* 100 Merrick Rd Rockville Ctr, NY 11570

Focus on Sports *(212) 661-6860* 222 E 46th St NY, NY 10017

Four by Five Inc *(212) 633-0300* 11 W 19th St NY, NY 10011

FPG International

***(212) 777-4210* 251 Park Ave So NY, NY 10010**

page 196

Fundamental Photographs

(212) 473-5770 210 Forsythe St NY, NY 10002

Gamma-Liaison *(212) 888-7272* 150 E 58th St NY, NY 10155

Globe Photos Inc *(212) 689-1340* 275 Seventh Ave NY, NY 10001

Granger Collection, The *(212) 586-0971* 1841 Broadway NY, NY 10023

Image Bank, The *(212) 529-6700* 111 Fifth Ave NY, NY 10003

page 193

Image Resources *(212) 736-2523* 134 W 29th St NY, NY 10001

Index Stock *(212) 929-4644* 126 Fifth Ave NY, NY 10011

International Stock Photos

(212) 696-4666 113 E 31st St NY, NY 10016

Keystone Press Agency Inc *(212) 924-8123* 202 E 42nd St NY, NY 10017

Kramer, Joan *(212) 567-5545* 720 Fifth Ave NY, NY 10019

Life Picture Service *(212) 841-4800* Rm 28-58 Time-Life Bldg NY, NY 10020

Magnum Photos Inc *(212) 966-9200* 72 Spring St NY, NY 10012

Manhattan Views *(212) 255-1477* 41 Union Sq W NY, NY 10003

MediChrome *(212) 679-8480* 232 Madison Ave NY, NY 10016

Memory Shop Inc *(212) 473-2404* 109 E 12th St NY, NY 10003

Monkmeyer Press *(212) 689-2242* 118 E 28th St NY, NY 10016

Omni Photo Communication *(212) 995-0805* 5 E 22nd St NY, NY 10011

p - z

Photo Library Inc *(212) 246-1349* 325 W 45th St NY, NY 10036

Photo Researchers Inc *(212) 758-3420* 60 E 56th St NY, NY 10022

Photo Source *(212) 633-0200* 10 W 26th St NY, NY 10011

Photo World *(212) 777-4214* 251 Park Ave So NY, NY 10010

Photoquest *(212) 929-1927* 175 Fifth Ave NY, NY 10010

Photoreporters *(212) 736-7602* 875 Sixth Ave NY, NY 10001

Phototake *(212) 942-8185* 4523 Broadway NY, NY 10040

Phototeque *(212) 242-6406* 156 Fifth Ave NY, NY 10010

Pictorial Parade *(212) 840-2026* 130 W 42nd St NY, NY 10036

RDR Productions *(212) 586-4432* 351 W 54th St NY, NY 10019

Reference Pictures *(212) 254-0008* 119 Fifth Ave NY, NY 10003

Retna Ltd *(212) 489-1230* 36 W 56th St NY, NY 10019

Reuters Photo Library *(212) 777-6200* 48 E 21st St NY, NY 10010

Roberts, H Armstrong *(212) 685-3870* 1181 Broadway NY, NY 10001

Science Photo Library International

(212) 683-4025 118 E 28th St NY, NY 10016

Shostal Assoc *(212) 686-8850* 145 E 32nd St NY, NY 10016

Sports Illustrated Pictures

(212) 841-3663 Time-Life Bldg NY, NY 10020

Steinhauser, Art Ent *(212) 953-1722* 305 E 40th St NY, NY 10016

Stock Market, The *(212) 684-7878* 1181 Broadway NY, NY 10001

Stock Shop, The *(212) 679-8480* 232 Madison Ave NY, NY 10016

Stockphotos Inc *(212) 686-1196* 373 Park Ave So NY, NY 10016

Sygma Photo News *(212) 765-1820* 225 W 57th St NY, NY 10019

Taurus Photos *(212) 683-4025* 118 E 28th St NY, NY 10016

Telephoto *(212) 406-2440* 8 Thomas St NY, NY 10007

UPI Photo Library *(212) 777-6200* 48 E 21st St NY, NY 10010

Viesti Associates *(212) 734-4890* Box 20424 Cherokee Stn NY, NY 10028

Visions & Images *(212) 627-9040* 127 W 24th St NY, NY 10011

Wheeler Pictures *(212) 564-5430* 145 W 28th St NY, NY 10001

Wide World *(212) 621-1930* 50 Rockefeller Plaza NY, NY 10020

INDEX TO TAB

6

INDEX TO TAB 6

ANIMATION

STOP MOTION

COMPUTER GRAPHICS

ANIMATION DIRECTORS

PAINTBOX ARTISTS

COMP ART/STORY BOARDS

Lucky Charms
Saatchi & Saatchi
DFS/Compton

Pampers/*DMBB*

U.S. Postal Service
Young & Rubicam

Kinder Friends
Ciociola & Co.

New York Telephone
Young & Rubicam

Tampax/*Esty*

Preen 'n Green
Elkman

Cheerios
Saatchi & Saatchi
DFS/Compton

BASF/*Geer, DuBois*

Best Western
James Parry Inc.

Ice Mountain
Waring & LaRosa

In Harmony
Disney Special

THREE GENERATIONS OF ANIMATION.

Mark Zander Productions, Inc.

118 East 25th Street,
New York, NY 10010
(212) 477-3900

Represented by Christopher Zander

KIMMELMAN

MEMBER AICP

ANIMATION

A DIVISION OF KCMP PRODUCTIONS

ORK TELEPHONE—YOUNG & RUBICAM

BURGER KING—N.W. AYER INC.

MULTI-CAT—MONTGOMERY & ASSOC.

CALGON—GREY ADV

KCMP PRODUCTIONS, 50 W. 40TH ST., NEW YORK, NY 10018 (212) 944-7766
PHIL KIMMELMAN, ANIMATION DIRECTOR
CONTACT: JORDAN CALDWELL, DOTTY KIMMELMAN

KCMP PRODUCTIONS LTD
LIVE & ANIMATION

NICKELODEON / MTV NETWORK

TALK ABOUT / ROSSIN, GREENBERG, SERONICK & HILL

RUFFLES / YOUNG & RUBICAM

McDONALD'S / LEO BURNETT

JERRY LIEBERMAN
PRODUCTIONS INC

ANIMATION
76 LAIGHT ST NEW YORK NY 10013
212·431·3452

JERRY LIEBERMAN

PRODUCTIONS INC

ANIMATION

76 LAIGHT ST NEW YORK NY 10013

212·431·3452

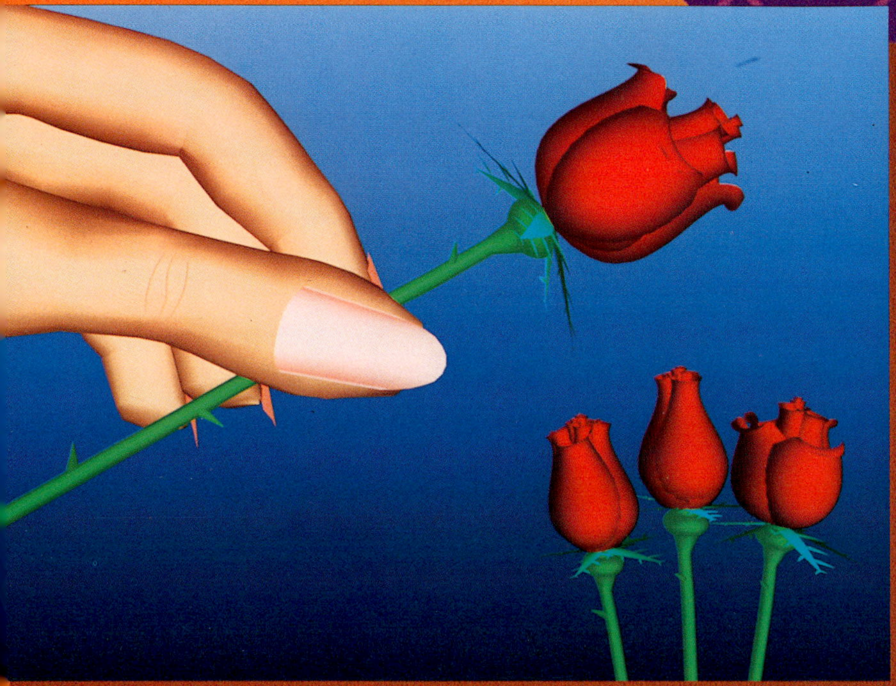

We can lend you a hand . . .

. . . Or design you a character.

(This synthetic persona, made for The Art Institute, works 24 hours a day, mesmerizes the viewers, and presents a "positive attitude").

ENERGY PRODUCTIONS

LOUIE SCHWARTZBERG

2690 BEACHWOOD DRIVE
LOS ANGELES, CALIFORNIA 90068
213 462-3310

NEW YORK,
LOS ANGELES,
JAN ROSS,
213-462-3310

CHICAGO,
RICHARD MIL
312-527-0444

ATLANTA,
MURRAY OKE
404-977-4324

TOKYO,
TEE KUBOKI,
03-232-6628

COMP ART & STORY BOARDS

KEN HAMILTON
ILLUSTRATOR

405 East 56 Street 3E New York, N.Y. 10022 (212) 758-898

• COMP ILLUSTRATION • STORY BOARD

ANIMATION

a - b

ABACAB Productions *(212) 575-3108* 123 W 44th St NY, NY 10001

Alexander Productions *(212) 765-5180* 311 W 43rd St NY, NY 10036

Alfie & Associates *(212) 983-2686* 222 E 44th St NY, NY 10017

Ampersand *(212) 564-9050* 424 W 33st NY, NY 10001

PAGE 1

Animated Productions *(212) 265-2942* 1600 Broadway NY, NY 10019

Animation Services Inc *(212) 333-5656* 221 W 57th St NY, NY 10019

APA Studios *(212) 929-9436* 230 W 10th St NY, NY 10014

Arkay Video Productions, Inc

(201) 725-3003 25 S Main St Manville, NJ 08835

Arron, Jane *(212) 732-1725* 69 Reade St NY, NY 10007

Artbear Pigmation *(914) 353-0192* 64 White Ave S. Nyack, NY 10960

Audio Visual Production

(201) 899-4342 111 Midstreams Pl Brick, NJ 08724

Backle, R.J. Productions *(212) 582-8270* 321 W 44th St NY, NY 10036

Bakst, Edward *(212) 666-2579* 160 W 96th St NY, NY 10025

Ball & Chain Studios *(203) 324-0018* 164 Fairfiled Ave Stamford, CT 06902

Balsmeyer & Everett Inc *(212) 627-3430* 230 W 17th St NY, NY 10011

Bannerman, Isabella *(212) 673-5367* 184 E 7th St NY, NY 10009

Beckerman, Howard Animation

(212) 869-0595 25 W 45th St NY, NY 10036

Big Fun *(212) 226-8303* 304 Mulberry St NY, NY 10012

Bigman Pictures Corp *212) 242-1411* 133 W 19th St NY, NY 10011

PAGE 11

Broadcast Arts *(212) 254-5400* 632 Broadway NY, NY 10012

Broadway Video *(212) 265-7600* 1619 Broadway NY, NY 10019

Bunin, Eleanor Productions *(212) 688-0759* 30 E 60th St NY, NY 10022

Butta, Sal/CVI *(516) 365-4364* 23 Woodland Way Manhasset, NY 11030

Buzzco *(212) 840-0411* 110 W 40th St NY, NY 10018

c - e

Caged Beagle Productions

(914) 939-3999 24 Elizabeth St Port Chester, NY 10573

Canemaker Productions *(212) 874-7462* 120 W 70th St NY, NY 10023

Cel Specialists *(212) 481-0382* 274 Madison Ave NY, NY 10016

Cel-Art Productions *(212) 751-7515* 20 E 49th St NY, NY 10017

Celefx *(212) 689-3300* 444 Park Ave So NY, NY 10016

Cheap Animation *(914) 358-2964* 27 Old Mill Rd W. Nyack, NY 10994

Chelsea Animation *(212) 473-6446* 36 E 23rd St NY, NY 10010

Cohen, Lewis & Co *(212) 420-0303* 36 E 22nd St NY, NY 10010

Colossal Pictures *(212) 633-0022* 160 Fifth Ave NY, NY 10010

Corey, Lee Design Studio *(212) 529-7238* 42 E 23rd St NY, NY 10010

Culhane, Shamus *(212) 873-2042* 325 West End Ave NY, NY 10023

D&R Productions *(212) 370-9113* 516 Fifth Ave NY, NY 10036

D'Andrea Productions *(212) 764-9200* 25 W 45th St NY, NY 10017

Darrer, Tony *(212) 517-8544* 363 E 76th St NY, NY 10021

DMI Productions *(914) 634-5798* 43 Mark Labe New City, NY 10956

Dolphin Productions *(212) 628-5930* Box 23 Harrison, NY 10528

Doros Animation *(212) 627-7220* 156 Fifth Ave NY, NY 10010

EFEX Unlimited Inc *(212) 541-9220* 321 W 44th St NY, NY 10036

Empireeffects *(212) 757-8898* 311 W 43rd St NY, NY 10036

Energy Productions *(212) 505-5260* NY, NY

PAGE 6

EXO Opticals *(212) 840-3222* 28 W 39th St NY, NY 10018

Eyegraphics *(212) 643-8350* 53 W 36th St NY, NY 10018

f - h

F-Stop Studio *(212) 686-2292* 114 E 32nd St NY, NY 10016

Feignbaum & Associates *(212) 246-5099* 508 W 57th St NY, NY 10019

Feldman, Ray Productions *(212) 628-2645* 345 E 81st St NY, NY 10028

Filigree Films Inc *(212) 627-1770* 155 Sixth Ave NY, NY 10013

Film Opticals *(212) 697-4744* 144 E 44th St NY, NY 10017

Film Planning Associates *(212) 989-0611* 44 W 24th St NY, NY 10003

Filmfair *(212) 807-6565* 101 Fifth Ave NY, NY 10003

First Generation Motion Grphcs
(212) 678-7560 496 LaGuardia Pl NY, NY 10012

Flexitoon Studios *(212) 877-2757* 46 W 73rd St NY, NY 10023

Foch, Bill Graphics *(212) 921-9414* 25 W 45th St NY, NY 10036

Friedman, Harold Consortium
(212) 697-0858 420 Lexington Ave NY, NY 10017

Gati Film Effects Inc *(212) 582-9060* 154 W 57th St NY, NY 10019

Giordano, Vincent Productions
(212) 730-1980 **123 W 44th St NY, NY 10036**
PAGE 9

Globus Brothers *(212) 243-1000* 44 W 24th St NY, NY 10010

Goodchild/Solomon *(212) 645-5272* 1123 Broadway NY, NY 10010

Grossman Brothers *(212) 925-1965* 19 Crosby St NY, NY 10013

Henson Associates *(212) 794-2400* 117 E 69th St NY, NY 10021

Hi Test Productions Inc *(212) 505-1061* 738 Broadway NY, NY 10003

HPS/IPS East *(212) 486-6840* 11 E 47th St NY, NY 10017

Hubley Studio *(212) 410-2767* 200 East End Ave NY, NY 10022

i - q

I F Studios *(212) 819-1880* 15 W 38th St NY, NY 10018

Image Network *(212) 877-2517* 645 West End Ave NY, NY 10025

Ink Tank *(212) 869-1630* 2 W 47th St NY, NY 10036

Jannis, Stacy *(212) 831-0781* 150 E 91st St NY, NY 10128

Janos, Franz Productions *(914) 878-9340* RFD #10 Carmel, NY 10512

Kaplan, Jeff *(212) 974-0505* 311 W 43rd St NY, NY 10036

KCMP Productions ***(212) 944-7766*** **50 W 40th St NY, NY 10018**
PAGE 3

Kimmelman Animation ***(212) 944-7766*** **50 W 40th St NY, NY 10018**
PAGE 3

Kurtz & Friends *(212) 989-3535* 1 Union Sq W NY, NY 10003

Liberty Studios *(212) 532-1865* 238 E 26th St NY, NY 10010

Lieberman, Jerry Productions Inc
(212) **431-3452 76 Laight St NY, NY 10013**
PAGE 4

Marshall Films *(212) 255-4120* 222 W 23rd St NY, NY 10011

Metropolis Graphics *(212) 677-0630* 28 E 4th St NY, NY 10003

Mimondo Productions ***(212) 686-9620*** **15 W 26th St NY, NY 10010**
PAGE 11

Modern Power Studio *(718) 366-2754* 238 Troutman St Brooklyn , NY 11217

Mogubgub, Gartrell, Davis *(212) 758-6306* 34 E 58th St NY, NY 10022

New York Animation & Visionworks
(212) 362-6992 200 W 79th St NY, NY 10024

Noyes & Laybourne Enterprises
(212) 406-7377 77 Hudson St NY, NY 10013

Ovation Films *(212) 686-4540* 15 W 26th St NY, NY 10010

Pagnelli, Albert *(212) 719-4105* 21 W 46th St NY, NY 10036

Pan Productions *(718) 237-1945* 223 Water St Brooklyn, NY 11201

Perfect Optical *(212) 473-7010* 112 E 23rd St NY, NY 10010

Perpetual Animation *(212) 989-5353* 841 Broadway NY, NY 10003

Planet Pictures *(212) 477-1032* 66 E 7th St NY, NY 10003

Polestar Films & Assoc Arts
(212) 213-0806 15 W 26th St NY, NY 10010

Prism Film & Tape Ltd *(212) 944-0420* 15 W 38th St NY, NY 10018

Pushpin Group *(212) 674-8080* 215 Park Ave S NY, NY 10003

r - z

R/Greenberg Associates *(212) 239-6767* 350 W 39th St NY, NY 10018

Rankin/Bass Productions *(212) 759-7721* 1 E 53rd St NY, NY 10022

Robinson Productions *(212) 777-8964* 200 E 21st St NY, NY 10010

Rossiter, Deed *(914) 359-8884* 490 Piermont Ave Piermont, NY 10968

Seti Video Communications *(212) 764-7154* 45 W 45th St NY, NY 10036

Shadow Light Productions *(212) 689-7511* 12 W 27th St NY, NY 10001

Staton, Scott Productions
(914) 638-1586 107 N Main New City, NY 10956

Streamline Film Archives *(212) 696-2616* 109 E 29th St NY, NY 10016

Tiani, ALex *(203) 683-3310* 4 Lafayette Ct Greenwich, CT 06830

Vaintrub, Elyse *(718) 636-5391* 11 Sterling Pl Brooklyn, NY 11217

Videart Opticals *(212) 840-2163* 39 W 38th St NY, NY 10018

Videograf *(212) 242-7871* 144 W 27th St NY, NY 10001

Wagner, David *(212) 925-5149* 568 Broadway NY, NY 10012

Wallach Enterprises *(212) 966-1970* 419 Broome St NY, NY 10013

Williams, Brad *(212) 865-0088* 214 Riverside Dr NY, NY 10025

WILLIAMS-FLOOD, DAVID

(201) 420-7475 43 Booraem Ave Jersey City, NJ 07307

WOO ART INTERNATIONAL *(212) 989-7870* 133 W 19th St NY, NY 10011

ZANDER, MARK PRODUCTIONS ***212) 477-3900*** **118 E 25th St NY, NY 10010**

PAGE 2

STOP MOTION

a - o

AERIAL IMAGE VIDEO SERVICES *(212) 279-6026* 875 Sixth Ave NY, NY 10001

AMERICAN FILM ANIMATION *(212) 563-5720* 151 W 28th St NY, NY 10001

ANIMUS FILMS *(212) 391-8716* 2 W 47th St NY, NY 10036

APA STUDIOS *(212) 929-9436* 230 W 10th St NY, NY 10014

ARCADE PICTURES *(212) 242-1411* 133 W 19th St NY, NY 10011

ATLANTIC MOTION PICTURES *(212) 924-6170* 162 W 21st St NY, NY 10011

BALL & CHAIN STUDIOS *(203) 324-0018* 164 Fairfield Ave Stamford, CT 06902

BIGMAN PICTURES CORP

(212) 242-1411 **133 W 19th St NY, NY 10011**

PAGE 11

BROADCAST ARTS *(212) 254-5400* 632 Broadway NY, NY 10012

CEASAR VIDEO GRAPHICS *(212) 684-7673* 137 E 25th St NY, NY 10010

COHEN, LEWIS & CO *(212) 420-0303* 36 E 22nd St NY, NY 10010

COLOSSAL PICTURES *(212) 633-0022* NY, NY

CORBETT, PETER & CO *(212) 989-7892* 17 W 17th St NY, NY 10011

CREATIVE WAYS *(212) 935-0145* 305 E 46th St NY, NY 10017

DOROS ANIMATION *(212) 627-7220* 156 Fifth Ave NY, NY 10010

EIGHTH FRAME CAMERA SVC

(212) 819-0881 45 W 45th St NY, NY 10036

ELECTRIC PICTURE WORKS *(212) 869-2500* 24 W 40th St NY, NY 10018

EMPIRE VIDEO INC *(212) 687-2060* 216 E 45th St NY, NY 10017

F-STOP STUDIO *(212) 686-2292* 114 E 32nd St NY, NY 10016

FANTASTIC ANIMATION MACHINE

(212) 697-2525 12 E 46th St NY, NY 10017

FILMFAIR *(212) 807-6565* 101 Fifth Ave NY, NY 10003

FRANZ, BOB *(201) 384-8039* POB 422 Bergenfield, NJ 07621

FRIEDMAN, HAROLD CONSORTIUM

(212) 697-0858 420 Lexington Ave NY, NY 10017

GATI FILM EFFECTS INC *(212) 582-9060* 154 W 57th St NY, NY 10019

GLOBUS BROTHERS *(212) 243-1008* 44 W 24th St NY, NY 10010

I F STUDIOS *(212) 819-1880* 15 W 38th St NY, NY 10018

JSL VIDEO *(212) 382-3592* 25 W 45th St NY, NY 10036

KCMP Productions *(212) 944-7766* 50 W 40th St NY, NY 10018

PAGE 3

Kimmelman Animation *(212) 944-7766* 50 W 40th St NY, NY 10018

PAGE 3

Liberty Studios *(212) 532-1865* 238 E 26th St NY, NY 10010

Mercury Productions *(212) 869-4073* 7 W 18th St NY, NY 10011

Mimondo Productions *(212) 686-9620* 15 W 26th St NY, NY 10010

PAGE 11

MTI/Compugraph *(212) 355-0510* 885 Second Ave NY, NY 10017

Napoleon Videographics *(212) 279-2000* 460 W 42nd St NY, NY 10036

National Video Industries Inc

(212) 691-1300 15 W 17th St NY, NY 10011

Odyssey Filmakers, Inc *(212) 620-5654* 111 Barrow St NY, NY 10014

Optical House *(212) 869-5840* 25 W 45th St NY, NY 10036

p - z

Post Perfect *(212) 972-3400* 220 E 42nd St NY, NY 10017

R/Greenberg Associates *(212) 239-6767* 350 W 39th St NY, NY 10018

RB/Mavericks Motion Graphics

(212) 382-2424 25 W 45th St NY, NY 10036

Sal Butta/CVI *(516) 365-4364* 23 Woodland Way Manhasset, NY 11030

Sanchez & Co *(212) 391-6735* 15 W 38th St NY, NY 10018

Select Effects *(212) 869-3988* 14 W 45th St NY, NY 10036

Shadow Light Productions Inc

(212) 689-7511 12 W 27th St NY, NY 10001

Stark Studio *(212) 868-5555* 245 W 29th St NY, NY 10001

Technifex *(212) 974-0750* 311 W 43rd St NY, NY 10036

Today Video Inc *(212) 391-1020* 45 W 45th St NY, NY 10036

Totem Film & Tape *(212) 755-4931* RD 12 Crane Rd Carmel, NY 10512

Videart Opticals *(212) 840-2163* 39 W 38th St NY, NY 10018

Videoefx *(212) 541-9220* 321 W 44th St NY, NY 10036

Wallach Enterprises *(212) 966-1970* 419 Broome St NY, NY 10013

Williams-Flood, David

(201) 420-7475 43 Booraem Ave Jersey City, NJ 07307

COMPUTER GRAPHICS

a - c

4-Front Video Design Inc *(212) 944-7055* 225 W 44th St NY, NY 10036

ADM Video Productions

(516) 484-6900 40 Seaview Blvd Port Washington, NY 11050

Alfie & Associates *(212) 983-2686* 222 E 44th St NY, NY 10017

American Video Channels *(212) 765-6324* 321 W 44th St NY, NY 10036

APA Studios *(212) 929-9436* 230 W 10th St NY, NY 10014

Art Machines *(212) 505-6400* 611 Broadway NY, NY 10012

AT & T Post Images

(201) 829-8788 60 Columbia Turnpike Morristown, NJ 07960

Atlantic Motion Pictures *(212) 924-6170* 162 W 21st St NY, NY 10011

Avekta Productions *(212) 686-4550* 164 Madison Ave NY, NY 10016

Bakst, Edward *(212) 666-2579* 160 W 96th St NY, NY 10025

Carob Video *(212) 957-9525* 250 W 57th St NY, NY 10017

Ceasar Video Graphics *(212) 684-7673* 137 E 25th St NY, NY 10010

Celefx *(212) 689-3300* 444 Park Ave So NY, NY 10016

Charisma/Visual Motion *(212) 832-3020* 32 E 57th St NY, NY 10022

Charlex Inc *(212) 719-4600* 2 W 45th St NY, NY 10036

Cohen, Lewis & Co *(212) 420-0303* 36 E 22nd St NY, NY 10010

Computer Graphics Lab

(516) 484-1944 4 Expressway Pl Rosalyn Hghts, NY 11577

Coneptual Graphic Images, Inc

(914) 762-2660 190 N State Rd Briarcliff Manor, NY 10510

Corporation for Art & TV *(212) 787-8258* 45 John St NY, NY 10038

Creative Ways *(212) 935-0145* 305 E 46th St NY, NY 10017

d - i

Darino Films *(212) 228-4024* 222 Park Ave So NY, NY 10003

Data Motion Arts Inc *(212) 382-1155* 56 W 45th St NY, NY 10036

Devlin Video Services *(212) 391-1313* 1501 Broadway NY, NY 10036

DiComo & Agostinelli *(212) 689-8670* 120 E 34th St NY, NY 10016

Digimation *(212) 213-5760* 311 E 85th St NY, NY 10028

Dolphin Productions *(212) 628-5930* Box 23 Harrison, NY 10528

Doros Animation *(212) 627-7220* 156 Fifth Ave NY, NY 10010

Dovetail Group *(212) 316-2452* 127 W 92nd St NY, NY 10025

DT Productions *(718) 788-3328* 488 Fourth Ave Brooklyn, NY 11215

Editel *(212) 867-4600* 222 E 44th St NY, NY 10017

EFX Unlimited Inc *(212) 541-9220* 321 W 44th St NY, NY 10036

Electric Picture Works *(212) 869-2500* 24 W 40th St NY, NY 10018

Fantastic Animation Machine

(212) 697-2525 12 E 46th St NY, NY 10017

Feigenbaum & Assoc *(212) 246-5099* 508 W 57th St NY, NY 10019

Filigree Films Inc *(212) 627-1770* 155 Sixth Ave NY, NY 10013

Filmfair *(212) 807-6565* 101 Fifth Ave NY, NY 10003

Friedman, Harold Consortium

(212) 697-0858 420 Lexington Ave NY, NY 10017

Intelligent Light *(201) 794-7550* 17-01 Pollitt Dr Fairlawn, NJ 07410

International Production Ctr

(212) 582-6530 514 W 57th St NY, NY 10019

j - s

JSL Video *(212) 382-3592* 25 W 45th St NY, NY 10036

Marshall Films *(212) 255-4120* 222 W 23rd St NY, NY 10011

Mercury Productions *(212) 869-4073* 7 W 18th St NY, NY 10011

MTI/Compugraph *(212) 355-0510* 885 Second Ave NY, NY 10017

Musivision Inc *(212) 860-4420* 185 E 85th St NY, NY 10028

Napoleon Videographics *(212) 279-2000* 460 W 42nd St NY, NY 10036

National Video Industries Inc

(212) 691-1300 15 W 17th St NY, NY 10011

New York Animation & Visionworks

(212) 362-6992 200 W 79th St NY, NY 10024

Odyssey Filmmakers Inc *(212) 620-5654* 111 Barrow St NY, NY 10014

Panavideo *(212) 725-2211* 248 E 35th St NY, NY 10016

Post Perfect *(212) 972-3400* 220 E 42nd St NY, NY 10017

Princzko Productions *(212) 683-1300* 9 E 38th St NY, NY 10016

Projection Systems International Inc

(212) 708-0570 219 E 44th St NY, NY 10017

Pyrate Communications *(212) 724-6869* 300 E 42nd St NY, NY 10017

R/Greenberg Associates *(212) 239-6767* 350 W 39th St NY, NY 10018

Rosebush Visions Corp *(212) 398-6600* 25 W 45th St NY, NY 10036

page 5

RVI *(212) 685-4000* 137 E 25th St NY, NY 10010

S/R Video Labs *(201) 224-6676* 77 Rt 5 Edgewater, NJ 07020

Seti Video Communications *(212) 764-7154* 45 W 45th St NY, NY 10036

Shadow Light Productions Inc

212) 689-7511 12 W 27th St NY, NY 10001

SMA Video *(212) 226-7474* 84 Wooster St NY, NY 10012

Sound Concepts *(203) 888-6712* 80 Great Hill Rd Seymour, CT 06483

Synthetic Imagery *(609) 520-9177* 13 Roszel Rd Princeton, NJ 08540

t - z

Teatown Video Inc *(212) 302-0722* 165 W 46th St NY, NY 10036

Telezign/National Video Ctr

(212) 279-2000 460 W 42nd St NY, NY 10036

Transcom Digital *(212) 529-1000* 902 Broadway NY, NY 10010

TVC Graphics *(212) 599-1616* 225 E 43rd St NY, NY 10017

Twin Art *(212) 925-4981* 80 Varick St NY, NY 10013

Unitel Video *(212) 265-3600* 515 W 57th St NY, NY 10019

Vaintrub, Elyse *(718) 636-5391* 11 Sterling Pl Brooklyn, NY 11217

VCA Teletronics *(212) 355-1600* 231 E 55th St NY, NY 10022

Videoefx *(212) 541-9220* 321 W 44th St NY, NY 10036

Videograf *(212) 242-7871* 144 W 27th St NY, NY 10001

VideoWorks *(212) 869-2500* 24 W 40th St NY, NY 10018

Visual Dynamics *(212) 265-3600* 515 W 57th St NY, NY 10019

ANIMATION DIRECTORS

a - b

Aaron, Jane *(212) 732-1725* Jane Aaron

Alexander, Sam *(212) 765-5180* Alexander Productions

Allison, John *(212) 697-0858* Harold Friedman Consortium

Allison, Peter *(212) 697-0858* Harold Friedman Consortium

Apostol, George *(212) 532-1865* Liberty Studios

Armour, Allan A.

(212) 708-0570 Projection Systems International

Augerakis, George *(212) 686-4550* Avekta Productions

Backle, Bob *(212) 582-8270* R J Backle Productions

Bakst, Edward *(212) 666-2579* Edward Bakst

Balsmeyer, Randall *(212) 627-3430* Balsmeyer & Everett Inc

Barham, Thomas *(212) 334-1666* SynthaVision Inc

Basis, Howard *(212) 689-7511* Shadow Light Productions

Baumann, John *(212) 689-3300* Celefx

Becker, Gary *(212) 686-2292* F-Stop Studio

Beckerman, Howard *(212) 869-0595* Beckerman Animation

Beeton, Maija *(212) 957-9525* Carob Video

Berstein, Les *(212) 696-2616* Streamline Film Manufacturing

Blansky, Bob *(212) 582-6530* International Productions Ctr

Blechman, R. O. *(212) 869-1630* The Ink Tank

Boxell, Tim *(212) 633-0022* Colossal Pictures

Brioso, Jerry *(212) 316-2452* Dovetail Group

Brown, Ken *(212) 697-0858* Harold Friedman Consortium

Bruce, David *(212) 532-1865* Liberty Studios

Brunsfeld, Michael *(212) 633-0022* Colossal Pictures

Bunin, Elinor *(212) 688-0759* Elinor Bunin Productions

Butta, Sal *(516) 365-4364* Sal Butta/CVI

c - d

Cafarelli, Vincent J *(212) 840-0411* Buzzco Productions Inc

Canemaker, John *(212) 874-7462* Canemaker Productions

Cardona, Robert *(212) 431-0013* Clearwater Enterprises

Carlee, Jan *(212) 239-6767* R/Greenberg Associates

Chelnik, Marc *(212) 689-7511* Shadow Light Productions

Cherry, Lis *(212) 532-1865* Liberty Studios Inc

Chiarito, Veronica *(212) 944-0420* Prism Film & Tape

Chwast, Seymour *(212) 674-8080* Pushpin Group

Claybrook, Glen *(212) 226-8303* Big Fun

Cochran, George M

(212) 689-9054 George M Cochran Film Prods

Cohen, Lewis *(212) 420-0303* Lewis Cohen & Co Inc

Conn, Peter *(212) 697-0858* Harold Friedman Consortium

Corey, Lee *(212) 529-7238* Corey Design Studio

Corwin, Steven J *(212) 333-3636* Stargate Prods Inc

Cosimo *(212) 633-0022* Giraldi-Suarez Productions

Culhane, Shamus *(212) 873-2042* Shamus Culhane

D'Andrea, Dee *(212) 764-9200* D'Andrea Productions

Danelowitz, Howard

(212) 362-6992 New York Animation & Visionworks

Darino, Ed *(212) 228-4024* Darino Films

Darrer, Tony *(212) 517-8544* Tony Darrer

DaSilva, Ray *(212) 213-6098* Digimation

Davis, Bill *(914) 353-0192* Artbear Pigmation

DeCarlo, Dean *(212) 689-3300* Celefx

Deligter, Richard *(212) 675-5440* Real Productions Inc

Denneen, David *(212) 697-0858* Harold Friedman Consortium

DeWolfe, Gordon *(212) 683-1300* Princzko Productions

Dole, Kevin *(212) 206-6400* Iris Films

Duga, Don *(212) 213-0806* Polestar Films & Assoc Arts

Duga, Irra *(212) 213-0806* Polestar Films & Assoc Srts

e - g

Egan, Patrick *(212) 924-6170* Atlantic Motion Pictures

Eiser, Eric *(212) 924-6170* Atlantic Motion Pictures

Eland, Ted *(212) 382-1155* Data Motion Arts Inc

Elson, Bob *(212) 239-2000* Sheridan Elson Cmmnctns

Evangelides, Doros *(212) 627-7220* Doros Animation

Evelyn, George *(212) 633-0022* Colossal Pictures

Feigenbaum, Bill *(212) 246-5099* Feigenbaum & Associates

Feldman, Ray *(212) 628-2645* Ray Feldman Productions

Finley, Ron *(212) 496-0500* Ron Finley Films

Focht, Bill *(212) 921-9414* Foch Graphics

Frith, Michael *(212) 794-2400* Henson Associates

Fritz, Ronald *(212) 370-9113* D & R Productions

Gati, John *(212) 582-9060* John Gati Film Effects

Gilliam, Terry *(212) 697-0858* Harold Friedman Consortium

Giordano, Vincent

(212) 730-1980 **Vincent Giordano Productions**

PAGE

Glaser, Milton

(212) 697-0858 Harold Friedman Consortium

Goldberg, Syd *(212) 627-1770* Filigree Films Inc

Grau, Jim *(212) 832-3020* Charisma/Visual Motion

Green, B David *(212) 239 6767* R/Greenberg Associates

Greenberg, Richard *(212) 239-6767* R/Greenberg Associates

Griffin, George *(212) 677-0630* Metroplois Graphics

Grillo, Oscar *(212) 714-0090* Power & Light Pctr Co

Grossman, Robert *(212) 925-1965* Grossman Brothers

Guitierez, Gary *(212) 633-0022* Colossal Pictures

h - l

Haring, Julie *(212) 484-6900* ADM Video Productions

Hays, John *(212) 633-0022* Colossal Pictures

Heller, Mark *(212) 696-2616* Streamline Film Manufacturing

Howard, Lee *(212) 929-9436* APA Studios

Hudak, Terry *(203) 888-6712* Sound Concepts

Ivanick, Daniel *(914) 634-5798* DMI Productions

Janos, Fronz *(914) 878-9340* Janos Productions

Johnson, Flip ***(212) 564-9050*** **Ampersand**

PAGE 1

Kahn, Ellen *(212) 925-4981* Twin Art

Kahn, Lynda *(212) 925-4981* Twin Art

Katz, Max *(212) 988-1957* Max Katz Productions

Kessler, Fred *(212) 860-4420* Musivision Inc

Kimmelman, Phil ***(212) 944-7766*** **Kimmelman Animation**

PAGE 3

Kotopoulis, Dino *(212) 944-0420* Prism Film & Tape Ltd

Kriegsman, Michael *(212) 575-3108* ABACAB Productions

Kugel, Candice *(212) 840-0411* Buzzco

Laybourne, Kit *(212) 406-7377* Noyes & Laybourne Enterprises

LeBar, Bob *(212) 697-0858* Harold Friedman Consortium

Lee, Francis *(212) 989-0611* Film Planning Associates

Levi, Charles *(212) 719-4600* Charlex

Levitt, Steve *(212) 697-0858* Harold Friedman Consortium

Lieberman, Jerry *(212) 431-3452* Lieberman Productions Inc

page 4

Linden, Steve *(212) 633-0022* Colossal Pictures

Longauer, Peter *(212) 627-1770* Filigree Films Inc

Lonn, Peter *(212) 697-0858* Harold Friedman Consortium

Looge, Bernard *(212) 697-0858* Harold Friedman Consortium

Lover,Anthony *(212) 532-1865* Liberty Studios Inc

Lucky, Bud *(212) 633-0022* Colossal Pictures

m - q

Mahon, Jim *(212) 794-2400* Henson Associates

Manes, Michael *(212) 989-9267* Mannes Production Group

Margerin, Catherine *(212) 633-0022* Colossal Pictures

Marin, Craig *(212) 877-2757* Flexitoon Studios

Marshall, Richard *(212) 255-4120* Marshall Films

McCabe, Robert *(212) 254-8700* Manhattan Film Works

McGuane, James P *(212) 582-8925* McGuane Studios

Mead, Stephen *(212) 697-2525* Fantastic Animation

Mitton, David *(212) 431-0013* Clearwater Films

Mogubgub, Fred *(212) 758-6306* Mogubgub, Gartrell, Davis

Mrozowski, Robert E *(212) 239-6767* R/Greenberg Associates

Mui, Terry *(212) 627-1770* Filigree Films Inc

Mulcahy, Russell *(212) 213-8363* Opus/MGMM

Napoleon, Marty *(212) 279-2000* Napoleon Videographics

Noisi, Rob *(212) 689-7511* Shadow Light Productions

Noyes, Eli *(212) 406-7377* Noyes & Laybourne

Oakes, Steve *(212) 254-5400* Broadcast Arts

Osborne, Larry *(212) 944-7766* KCMP Productions

page 3

Page, Marcy *(212) 564-9050* Ampersand

page 1

Paladino, Nancy *(212) 869-2500* Electric Picture Works

Paul, Rod *(212) 246-5099* Feigenbaum & Associates

Petricone, Art *(212) 686-4540* Ovation Films

Pilenyi, Janos *(212) 541-9220* EFX Unlimited Inc

Przyluska, Lindia *(212) 633-0022* Colossal Pictures

r - s

Rath, Earl *(212) 879-6200* Jenkins & Co

Rezyka, Mark B *(212) 697-0858* Harold Friedman Consortium

Roberts, Steve *(212) 532-1865* Liberty Studios

Rockley, Ted *(212) 697-0858* Harold Friedman Consortium

Rockmore, Michael *(212) 627-1770* Filigree Films Inc

Rosebush, Judson *(212) 398-6600* Rosebush Visions Corp

page 5

Rosenfeld, Ruthie *(718) 237-1945* Pan Productions

Rosenthal, Peter *(212) 254-5400* Broadcast Arts

Rossiter, Deed *(914) 359-8884* Deed Rossiter

Saz, Michael *(212) 355-0510* MIT/Compugraph

Scagnelli, Janet *(212) 473-6446* Chelsea Animation

Schloff, Alfie *(212) 983-2686* Alfie & Associates

Schon, Jeff *(212) 406-7377* Noyes & Laybourne Enterprises

Schwaid, Victoria *(212) 697-2525* Fantastic Animation

Sellwood, Maureen *212) 564-9050* Ampersand

page 1

Seti, Ray *(212) 764-7154* Seti Video Communications

Sheridan, Bill *(212) 239-2000* Sheridan Elson Cmmnctns

Silvermintz, Hal *(212) 353-9655* Perpetual Animation

Spada, Mark *(212) 691-1300* National Video Industries Inc

Spikol, Allen *(212) 505-6519* Spikol Pictures

St. Pierre, Anne *(212) 684-7673* Ceaser Video Graphics

Staar, David *(212) 254-5400* Broadcast Arts

Stanley, Allan *(212) 628-5930* Dolphin Productions

Steinkamp, Jennifer *(212) 697-2525* Fantastic Animation Mchn

t - z

Taffet, Jill *(212) 697-0858* Harold Friedman Consortium

Takahashu, Drew *(212) 633-0022* Colossal Pictures

Terry, Frank *(212) 807-6565* Filmfair

Thurlbeck, Ken *(212) 924-8000* Mark Ross Films Inc

Tiani, Alex *(212) 683-3310* Alex Tiani

Trattmann, Dee *(212) 213-8363* Opus/MGMM

Tricomi, Edward *(212) 819-1880* I F Studios

Tulchin, Harold M *(212) 986-8270* Tulchin Studios

Vaintrub, Elyse *(718) 636-5391* Elyse Vaintrub

Van Bearle, Susan ***(212) 564- 9050*** **Ampersand**

page 1

Vanderpool, Fred

212) 697-0858 Harold Friedman Consortium

Virgien, Norton ***(212) 477-3900*** **Zander Productions**

page 2

Vivona, Edward *(212) 924-6170* Atlantic Motion Pictures

Wagner, David *(212) 925-5149* David Wagner

Waldman, Stefan *(914) 358-2964* Cheap Animation

Wallach, Peter *(212) 966-1970* Peter Wallach Enterprises

Wedge, Chris *(212) 762-2660* Conceptual Graphic Images

Weil, Alex *(212) 719-4600* Charlex Inc

Weitzman, Moses *(212) 541-9220* EFX Unlimited Inc

Wible, Becky *(212) 689-7511* Shadow Light Productions

Willat, Carl *(212) 633-0022* Colossal Pictures

Williams, Brad *(212) 865-0888* Brad Williams

Williams-Flood, David *(212) 420-7475* David Williams-Flood

Wong, Arnie *(212) 697-0858* Harold Friedman Consortium

Woo, Roger *(212) 989-7870* Woo Art International

Wyatt, Robb *(212) 279-2000* Telezign/Nat'l Video Center

Yeagle, Dean *(914) 939-3999* Caged Beagle Productions

Zander, Jack ***(212) 477-3900*** **Zander Productions**

page 2

Zander, Mark ***(212) 477-3900*** **Zander Productions**

page 2

Zinman, Ralph *(212) 213-8363* Opus/MGMM

PAINTBOX ARTISTS

a - m

Ashman, Penny *(609) 778-1600* NFL Films Video

Baker, Henry *(212) 512-7800* HBO Productions

Belucci, Patti *(212) 512-7800* HBO Productions

Berkner, David *(212) 557-4949* Tapehouse

Butler, Don *(212) 972-3400* Post Perfect

Cabrini, Janice *(212) 972-3400* Post Perfect

Cadorin, Nan *(212) 333-7999* MTV

Cotrupe, Jacki *(212) 935-0145* Creative Ways

DeFlorio, Joe *(212) 575-5082* JSL Video

DeWolfe, Gordon *(212) 683-1300* Princzko Productions

Ehrmann, Linda *(212) 265-8500* Matrix Video

Feldman, Tami *(212) 867-4600* Editel

Finnin, Terri *(212) 687-4000* Manhattan Transfer/Edit

Fox, Brad *(212) 722-1818* MTI/Compugraph

Franklin, Doug *(212) 265-8500* Matrix Video

Garcia, Peter *(212) 869-2500* Electric Picture Works

Graboff, Jon *(212) 725-2211* Panavideo

Haskell, Sharon *(212) 265-7600* Broadway Video

Hill, Robert *(212) 279-2000* Napoleon Videographics

Janos, Fronz *(914) 878-9340* Fronz Janos Productions

Jennings, Dava *(212) 722-1818* MTI/Compugraph

Johnson, Kristen *(212) 719-4600* Charlex

Johnson, Susan *(212) 687-4000* Manhattan Transfer/Edit

Karl, George *(212) 697-2525* The Fantastic Animation Machine

Kijkanjanas, Auchmra

(212) 697-2525 The Fantastic Animation Machine

Kirkpatrick, Robert *(212) 302-2505* Magno Sound and Video

La Scala, John *(212) 741-3733* Longwood Video

Lesser, Tom *(212) 867-4600* Editel

Lew , Janice *(212) 722-1818* MTI/Compugraph

Malaro, Tom *(212) 333-7999* MTV

Minter, Denise *(212) 355-1600* VCA Teletronics

Mocerigo, Roger *(212) 599-1616* TVC Video Inc

O - Z

O'Donnell, Tree *(212) 557-4949* Tapehouse

O'Neill, Eileen

(212) 697-2525 The Fantastic Animation Machine

Ono, Marilyn *(212) 355-1600* VCA Teletronics

Packer, Sharon *(212) 691-1300* National Video

Paladino, Nancy *(212) 869-2500* Electric Picture Works

Paulick, Celeste *(212) 691-1300* National Video

Posch, Michael *(201) 427-7508* Michael Posch

Reznick, Gayle

(212) 677-2525 The Fantastic Animation Machine

Riss, Micha *(212) 599-1616* TVC Video Inc

Ruff, Todd *(212) 265-7600* Broadway Video

Sabatino, Ron *(212) 687-2060* Empire Video

Salladay, Lauri *(212) 944-9090* Windsor Video

Scaparro, Marc *(212) 741-3733* Long Wood Video

SCHWAID, VICTORIA

(212) 697-2525 THE FANTASTIC ANIMATION MACHINE

SCOTT, MICHAEL *(212) 935-0145* CREATIVE WAYS

SEMERAD, JOHN *(212) 719-4600* CHARLEX

SILBERMAN, MIRIAM *(212) 989-9466* REBO ASSOC

SPAIN, RICK *(212) 684-7673* CAESAR VIDEO GRAPHICS

ST. PIERRE, ANNE *(212) 684-7673* CAESAR VIDEO GRAPHICS

WARSHAFSKY, BETH *(212) 869-2500* ELECTRIC PICTURE WORKS

WEISBERG, CALEB *(212) 867-4600* EDITEL

WHITNEY, ADA *(212) 265-7600* BROADWAY VIDEO

WOOD, PAGE *(212) 719-4600* CHARLEX

COMP ART STORY BOARDS

a - d

ART DIRECTOR'S STUDIO *(212) 689-9888* 419 Park Ave So NY, NY 10016

ART FARM *(212) 688-4555* 420 Lexington Ave NY, NY 10170

ART FOR ADVERTISING *(212) 986-9489* 420 Lexington Ave NY, NY 10017

ART STAFF INC *(212) 685-0900* 22 E 40th St NY, NY 10016

BAILER, BRENT *(212) 661-0257* 104 E 40th St NY, NY 10016

BALLARD, WENDY *(212) 410-2259* 332 E 90th St NY, NY 10128

BOLLER, SELIGMAN, ASKINASI *(212) 819-0567* 45 W 45th St NY, NY 10036

BRITT, STEPHEN *(718) 858-1946* 20 Strong Pl Brooklyn, NY 11231

BROWNING, ERNIE *(212) 653-0255* 3395 Reservoir Oval W NY, NY 10467

BUTLER, RITA INC *(212) 888-4140* 123 E 47th St NY, NY 10017

C & R MEDIA PROMOTIONS *(212) 697-4740* 155 E 42nd St NY, NY 10017

CAGED BEAGLE PRODUCTIONS

(914) 939-3999 24 Elizabeth St Pt Chester, NY 10573

CALNAN, JOHN *(212) 909-9123* 909 Third Ave NY, NY 10022

CENSONI, ROBERT *(212) 758-0052* 400 E 59th St NY, NY 10022

COLUMBANI, AL *(212) 473-1070* 155 E 23rd ST NY, NY 10010

COMP 24 *(212) 627-4007* 122 W 27th St NY, NY 10001

COMP ART PLUS *(212) 689-8670* 120 E 34th St NY, NY 10016

CONTINUITY GRAPHIC ASSOCIATES

(212) 869-4170 62 W 45th St NY, NY 10036

CREATIVE FREELANCERS *(212) 398-9540* 62 W 45th St NY, NY 10036

CROCKETT, DAVEY *(212) 517-8329* 17 Leighton Ave Yonkers, NY 10705

CROWELL, JIM *(212) 213-5333* 218 Madison Ave NY, NY 10016

DARRER, TONY *(212) 517-8544* 363 E 76th St NY, NY 10021

DEMARTINO & ASSOCIATES *(212) 764-5591* 25 W 39th St NY, NY 10018

DIAMOND ART STUDIO *(212) 685-6622* 11 E 36th St NY, NY 10016

DUCHI ASSOCIATES *(212) 972-3950* 420 Lexington Ave NY, NY 10017

DVORJAK/GOODSPEED *(212) 475-4580* 165 Lexington Ave NY, NY 10016

e - k

EGAN, BOBBI *(914) 761-8650* 10 Myrtle St White Plains, NY 10606

EYEGRAPHICS *(212) 643-8350* 53 W 36th St NY, NY 10018

FASOLT, NATALIE *(212) 473-5909* 165 Ave A NY, NY 10009

FERRANTI & SCHIUMO *(212) 687-3107* 420 Lexington Ave NY, NY 10017

FOGLE, JAMIE *(718) 624-6862* 483 Henry St Brooklyn, NY 11231

FRANCIS, JUDY *(212) 866-7204* 110 W 96th St NY, NY 10025

FREELANCE SOLUTIONS *(212) 490-3334* 369 Lexington Ave NY, NY 10017

FRITSCH, STEVE *(212) 682-3886* 141 E 44th St NY, NY 10017

GEM STUDIO *(212) 687-3460* 420 Lexington Ave NY, NY 10170

GIOSA, SAL STUDIO *(212) 260-8622* 42 E 23rd ST NY, NY 10010

GREGORI, LEE *(212) 758-1662* 400 E 56th St NY, NY 10022

HAMILTON, KEN *(212) 758-8985* 405 E 56th St NY, NY 10022

PAGE 8

JOSPEH MINDLIN MULVEY *(212) 243-1333* 156 Fifth Ave NY, NY 10011

KING, NANCY *(212) 370-5677* 2 Tudor City Pl NY, NY 10017

KLEB ASSOCIATES *(212) 382-0404* 25 W 45th St NY, NY 10036

KLIROS, THEA *(212) 673-1600* 27 Bleecker St NY, NY 10012

KOMISAROW, RALPH *(212) 873-2231* 300 W 72nd St NY, NY 10023

KUNZ, PETER CO *(914) 687-0400* RD Box 223 High Falls, NY 12440

l - q

LADAS, GEORGE *(212) 673-2208* 157 Prince St NY, NY 10012

LAW, POLLY *(212) 866-3754* 309 W 93rd St NY, NY 10025

LEWIS, DAVID G *(212) 661-0256* 104 E 40th St NY, NY 10016

LICEA, ALFRED *(212) 661-1364* 104 E 40th St NY, NY 10016

LUBBERS, BOB *(212) 688-4555* 420 Lexington Ave NY, NY 10170

MAR-KEN CREATIVE INC *(212) 779-1877* 165 Lexington Ave NY, NY 10016

MARKS, STEVEN STUDIO LTD *(212) 924-7800* 168 Fifth Ave NY, NY 10010

MCCREANOR, MIKE *(212) 927-2138* 80 Haven Ave NY, NY 10032

MCGOVERN, WALT *(212) 661-3131* 132 E 45th St NY, NY 10017

MEYER, FRED *(516) 678-3648* 2632 Sheldon Pl Oceanside, NY 11572

MILLER, NORM ASSOCIATES *(212) 752-4830* 17 E 48th St NY, NY 10017

NAKAI, MICHAEL *(212) 213-5333* 218 Madison Ave NY, NY 10016

NAPOLITIANO, CIRO *(718) 256-6793* 1749 78th St Brooklyn, NY 11214

PAPLARDO, ERIC *(516) 496-3278* Box 281 E Norwich, NY 11732

Parios, Arnold (212) 421-1680 18 E 48th St NY, NY 10017

Postamatic (212) 570-0643 239 E 81st St NY, NY 10028

Pushpin Studios (212) 674-8080 215 Park Ave So NY, NY 10003

r - z

Rada, George (212) 737-4261 1315 Second Ave NY, NY 10021

RC Communications (212) 459-7800 1633 Broadway NY, NY 10019

Redline Illustrations (718) 482-7455 36-34 30th St LIC, NY 11106

RH Graphics (212) 505-5070 251 Park Ave So NY, NY 10010

Robinson Productions (212) 777-8964 200 E 21st St NY, NY 10010

Ross, Debbi (212) 533-9764 137 First Ave NY, NY 10003

Rough Riders (212) 219-1543 55 Mercer St NY, NY 10013

Sacco, Kevin (212) 213-5333 218 Madison Ave NY, NY 10016

Sanford, Steve (212) 254-5862 12 E 22nd St NY, NY 10010

Santa-Donato Studios (212) 921-1550 25 W 39th St NY, NY 10018

Savath, Neva (718) 858-4386 195 Adams St Brooklyn Hghts, NY 11201

Scarmato, Tony Inc (212) 869-8787 16 W 46th St NY, NY 10036

Seti Video Communications (212) 764-7154 45 W 45th St NY, NY 10036

Shields, Ian (203) 853-2307 27 Geneva Rd W Norwalk, CT 06850

Smith, Vernon (212) 515-9476 1137 E 229th Dr N Bronx, NY 10466

Spinks, Frank (212) 661-1363 104 E 40th St NY, NY 10016

Studio 23 (212) 243-7362 6 W 20th St NY, NY 10011

Studio Designs (212) 686-1510 168 Lexington Ave NY, NY 10016

Tavkar, Suhas (212) 682-6367 222 E 46th St NY, NY 10017

Transcom Digital (212) 529-1000 902 Broadway NY, NY 10010

Video Storyboards (212) 689-0207 107 E 31st St NY, NY 10016

Warnock, Shelia (212) 686-9254 320 E 35th St NY, NY 10016

Warriner, John (212) 686-1752 205 E 22nd St NY, NY 10010

Zdinak, Alan (212) 431-4253 Box 1421 NY, NY 10013

INDEX TO TAB 7

FILM VIDEO MUSIC

INDEX TO TAB 7

IMMACULATE CONCEPTION
PETER
CLAYTON
Director
YELLOWBRICK FILMS
(212) 967-2290

TV COMMERCIAL PRODUCTION

a - b

ABACAB Productions *(212) 575-3108* 123 W 44th St NY, NY 10036

Adfilm Producers Inc *(212) 697-9202* 300 E 40th St NY, NY 10016

ADM Video *(516) 484-6900* 40 Seaview Blvd Pt Washington, NY 11050

Ailes Communications *(212) 563-1970* 456 W 43rd St NY, NY 10036

Alton Films *(212) 758-3177* 238 E 61st St NY, NY 10021

American Night *(212) 496-2660* 32 W 76th St NY, NY 10023

Ampersand Productions *(212) 564-9050* 424 W 33rd St NY, NY 10001

Anderson, Robbie *(212) 737-6815* 885 Park Ave NY, NY 10021

Andreozzi/Toback & Co *(212) 477-4200* 118 E 25th St NY, NY 10010

ARC Films *(212) 627-3336* 7 W 18th St NY, NY 10011

Archive Film Productions *(212) 620-3955* 530 W 25th St NY, NY 10001

page 28

Arztco Pictures Inc *(212) 753-1050* 15 E 61st St NY, NY 10021

ASA Film/Video *(212) 741-2329* 191 Seventh Ave NY, NY 10011

Bachner Productions Inc *(212) 673-2946* 360 First Ave NY, NY 10010

Balton Productions *(212) 557-9834* 310 E 46th St NY, NY 10017

Baxter Films *(212) 532-4700* 260 Fifth Ave NY, NY 10001

Bean Productions *(212) 242-8106* 5 W 19th St NY, NY 10011

Beckman Productions *(212) 620-0933* 140 W 16th St NY, NY 10011

Bergman, Lester V *(914) 265-3656* East Mt. Rd So Cold Spring, NY 10516

Berkofsky/Smillie/Barrett
(212) 683-2900 307 E 37th St NY, NY 10016

Berner/Schlamme *(212) 603-0609* 1619 Broadway NY, NY 10019

Bernhard Creative *(212) 752-7455* 655 Madison Ave NY, NY 10021

BFCS *(212) 838-4417* 218 E 50th St NY, NY 10022

Bianchi Films Inc *(212) 505-0670* 141 Fifth Ave NY, NY 10010

Big City Films *(212) 473-3366* 5 E 19th St NY, NY 10003

Birbrower Films *(212) 977-8822* 720 Fifth Ave NY, NY 10019

Boltax Associates *(212) 687-0963* 230 E 44th St NY, NY 10017

Boustany, Paul *(212) 333-7580* 224 W 49th St NY, NY 10019

Brady, Mathew Films *(212) 683-6060* 31 W 27th St NY, NY 10001

Brooks, Alan *(212) 751-6811* 3 Riverview Terrace NY, NY 10022

Bruce, Murray *(212) 627-4500* 31 W 21st St NY, NY 10010

Bunin Productions *(212) 688-0759* 30 E 60th St NY, NY 10022

Burton Productions *(212) 420-1100* 36 E 12th St NY, NY 10003

Buzzco Productions Inc *(212) 840-0411* 110 W 40th St NY, NY 10018

c

Cailor/Resnick *(212) 977-4300* 237 W 54th St NY, NY 10019

Cajun Films *(212) 353-0500* 36 E 20th St NY, NY 10003

Carter Fenske Films *(212) 262-8200* 101 W 57th St NY, NY 10019

CDBIII-Kristy *(212) 244-6187* 400 E 43rd St NY, NY 10036

Chambers & Associates *(212) 243-1134* 135 W 22nd St NY, NY 10011

Charisma/Visual Motion *(212) 832-3020* 32 E 57th St NY, NY 10022

Cherry Mellon Ibbetson *(212) 724-8750* 22 Riverside Dr NY, NY 10023

Cine International *(212) 370-5151* 222 E 44th St NY, NY 10017

Cinematic Directions *(212) 989-3535* 1 Union Sq W NY, NY 10003

Cinepez Pictures *(212) 734-4230* 420 E 81st St NY, NY 10028

Cipoletti, John *(718) 332-8868* 1229 Ave Y Brooklyn, NY 11235

page 27

City Lights Productions *(212) 564-9106* 505 Eighth Ave NY, NY 10018

Coane/Porsche & Quinn *(212) 686-5566* 40 W 27th St NY, NY 10001

Cochran Film *(212) 689-9054* 381 Park Ave S NY, NY 10016

Colossal Pictures *(212) 633-0022* 160 Fifth Ave NY, NY 10010

Communications Plus *(212) 686-9570* 360 Park Ave So NY, NY 10010

Connolly & Co Inc *(212) 206-1332* 155 W 23rd St NY, NY 10003

Cooper & Co *(212) 243-3434* 28 W 25th St NY, NY 10010

Coppos Films *(212) 570-0011* NY, NY

Corbett, Peter & Co *(212) 989-7892* 17 W 17th St NY, NY 10011

Cote Productions *(212) 242-4065* 152 W 25th St NY, NY 10001

Cotts Films Inc *(212) 213-0100* 260 Fifth Ave NY, NY 10001

Creative Media *(212) 995-5080* 304 Park Ave So NY, NY 10010

d - e

D'Elia Uricola & Platt Inc
(212) 889-9778 28 W 27th St NY, NY 10001

Dennis, Guy & Hirsch *(212) 683-6311* 461 Park Ave So NY, NY 10016

deVries Films *(212) 580-2888* 100 Riverside Dr NY, NY 10024

DiComo & Agostinelli *(212) 689-8670* 120 E 34th St NY, NY 10016

Dimension Co *(212) 724-5952* 67 W 83rd St NY, NY 10024

Directing Artists *(212) 759-0700* 236 E 62nd St NY, NY 10021

Directors' Chair/EUE *(212) 867-4030* 222 E 44th St NY, NY 10017

Dorn, Bruce Films *(212) 644-6334* 301 E 48th St NY, NY 10017

Double HH Productions *(212) 687-1312* 300 E 40th St NY, NY 10016

Druck, Mark *(212) 682-5980* 300 E 40th St NY, NY 10016

Duncan & Katz *(212) 460-5545* 21 E 4th St NY, NY 10003

East-West Films *(212) 593-6188* 211 E 51st St NY, NY 10022

Eggers Films *(212) 751-9044* 141 E 55th St NY, NY 10022

Electric Film *(212) 925-3249* 87 Lafayette St NY, NY 10013

Elite Films *(212) 686-0200* 31 E 32nd St NY, NY 10016

Emerald Films *(212) 627-8600* 295 W 4th St NY, NY 10014

Energy Productions *(212) 505-5260* 230 E 15th St NY, NY 10003

Exit Productions *(212) 254-7247* 873 Broadway NY, NY 10003

Eye View Film *(212) 772-3190* 420 E 81st St NY, NY 10028

f - g

Fairbanks Films *(212) 475-5800* 141 Fifth Ave NY, NY 10010

Feldman Films *(212) 371-2330* 252 E 51st St NY, NY 10022

Fernbach Productions *(212) 879-8787* 510 E 74th St NY, NY 10021

Fertik & Co *(212) 877-3468* 251 W 89th St NY, NY 10024

Ficalora *(914) 591-7344* 11 Janet Terrace Irvington, NY 10533

Filigree Films Inc *(212) 627-1770* 155 Sixth Ave NY, NY 10013

Filmfair *(212) 807-6565* 101 Fifth Ave NY, NY 10003

Finley Films *(212) 496-0500* 47 W 73rd St NY, NY 10023

Firehouse Films *(212) 764-1591* 16 W 45th St NY, NY 10036

Flamingo Films *(212) 594-0880* 71 W 35th St NY, NY 10001

Flint Productions *(212) 755-8888* 777 Third Ave NY, NY 10017

Fraker Productions *(212) 752-4422* 919 Third Ave NY, NY 10022

Fred/Alan Inc *(212) 586-6333* 16 W 61st St NY, NY 10023

Friedman Productions

(718) 858-5374 283 Henry St Brooklyn Hghts, NY 11201

Friedman, Harold Consortium

(212) 697-0858 420 Lexington Ave NY, NY 10017

Front Row Films II *(212) 832-1880* 485 Madison NY, NY 10022

Furious Films *(718) 789-7058* 260 Hall St Brooklyn, NY 11205

Garrett & Partners *(212) 307-1350* 224 W 49th St NY, NY 10019

Gibson, Brian *(212) 877-5403* 155 W 68th St NY, NY 10023

Gilson & Aronson Films *(212) 686-5577* 260 Fifth Ave NY, NY 10001

Gindick Productions *(212) 725-2580* 21 E 40th St NY, NY 10016

Giraldi, Frank Studios *(212) 840-8225* 54 W 39th St NY, NY 10018

Giraldi-Suarez *(212) 691-9200* 581 Sixth Ave NY, NY 10011

Glassman, Paulette *(212) 369-3010* 417 E 87th St NY, NY 10128

Gluck Films Inc *(212) 777-2146* 105 E 16th St NY, NY 10003

GMS *(212) 832-2288* 130 E 62nd St NY, NY 10021

Gold, Jay Films *(212) 687-7171* 342 Madison Ave NY, NY 10173

Gomes Loew Inc *(212) 593-9500* 217 E 49th St NY, NY 10017

Goulding-Elliot/Greybar Productions Inc

(212) 867-9014 420 Lexington Ave NY, NY 10170

Griner/Cuesta *(212) 246-7600* 720 Fifth Ave NY, NY 10019

Group One *(212) 983-5350* 51 E 42nd St NY, NY 10017

Grove, Eric Film *(212) 242-7447* 32 W 22nd St NY, NY 10010

h

Hameline, Gerard *(212) 529-8000* 331 Park Ave So NY, NY 10010

Harmony Pictures Inc *(212) 529-1990* 420 E 21st St NY, NY 10010

Harrison Productions *(212) 683-1850* 200 E 36th St NY, NY 10016

Helburn Productions Inc *(212) 683-4980* 161 E 35th St NY, NY 10016

Herman Associates Inc *(718) 706-0913* 215 Park Ave So NY, NY 10016

Herrmann, Eric *(212) 308-5820* 430 E 56th St NY, NY 10022

Hirschenson Productions *(212) 757-7662* 16 W 55th St NY, NY 10019

Hirschfield Productions *(212) 686-9320* 9 E 40th St NY, NY 10016

HISK Productions/NY *(212) 687-4314* 300 E 40th St NY, NY 10016

HKM Productions *(212) 246-9260* 850 Seventh Ave NY, NY 10019

Hodge, David *(212) 245-3623* 935 Eighth Ave NY, NY 10019

Horizon Studios Inc *(212) 725-3840* 217 E 31st St NY, NY 10016

Horn Productions *(212) 794-1300* 435 E 83rd St NY, NY 10028

Horvath Studios *(212) 741-0300* 95 Charles St NY, NY 10014

HPS/IPS East *(212) 486-6840* 11 E 47th St NY, NY 10017

HSI *(212) 627-3600* 7 W 18th St NY, NY 10011

Hudson, Bill & Associates *(212) 679-7199* 30 W 26th St NY, NY 10010

Hunnewell Group *(212) 529-5888* 24 E 23rd St NY, NY 10010

Huss, Michael Inc *(212) 752-7455* 655 Madison Ave NY, NY 10021

i - j

ICM Films *(212) 832-0909* 211 E 51st St NY, NY 10022

Illustra Films Worldwide *(212) 223-4111* 7 E 47th St NY, NY 10017

Image Point *(212) 337-3400* 48 W 25th St NY, NY 10010

Image Realite *(212) 529-3000* 841 Broadway NY, NY 10003

Impact Entertainment Inc

(212) 594-6834 330 W 42nd St NY, NY 10036

Independent Artists *(212) 765-4640* 16 W 56th St NY, NY 10019

Inserts *(212) 244-5757* 252 W 30th St NY, NY 10001

Intergroup Productions *(212) 832-8169* 300 E 59th St NY, NY 10022

International Television Group

(212) 687-3232 300 E 44th St NY, NY 10017

Iris Films *(212) 206-6400* 155 W 23rd St NY, NY 10011

James Productions *(212) 929-7474* c/o CAM 250 First Ave NY, NY 10019

JC Productions Inc *(212) 532-2820* 14 E 39th St NY, NY 10016

Jenkins & Co Films *(212) 879-6200* 510 E 74th St NY, NY 10021

Jenks & Partners *(212) 633-1432* 24 W 25th St NY, NY 10010

Jennie & Co Film Prods *(212) 242-7200* 12 E 12th St NY, NY 10003

Johannes Film *(212) 288-3632* 415 E 85th St NY, NY 10028

Johns & Gorman Films *(212) 677-4600* 305 Second Ave NY, NY 10003

Johnston Films *(212) 683-7500* 140 E 39th St NY, NY 10016

Jones, J. Wesley *(212) 473-4545* 114 E 25th ST NY, NY 10010

JPC Video *(212) 223-0555* 11 E 47th St NY, NY 10017

Jupiter Films *(212) 431-7755* 72 Spring St NY, NY 10012

k - l

Kalamar Productions *(212) 254-8400* 928 Broadway NY, NY 10010

Kasman Productions Inc *(212) 696-1988* 202 E 35th St NY, NY 10016

Katz Associates *(212) 683-8130* 109 E 29th St NY, NY 10016

Katz, Max *(212) 988-1957* 315 E 65th St NY, NY 10021

KCMP Productions *(212) 944-7766* 50 W 40th St NY, NY 10018

Kelly Pictures *(212) 929-6176* Pier 62/23rd St @ 12th Ave NY, NY 10011

Kira/ H Films Inc *(212) 532-1212* 260 Fifth Ave NY, NY 10001

Lacy, N Lee Associates *(212) 633-0303* 230 W 17th St NY, NY 10011

Langley Productions *(212) 581-3930* 536 W 50th St NY, NY 10019

Larkin Productions Inc *(212) 206-8450* 154 W 13th St NY, NY 10011

Lategan, Barry *(212) 228-6850* 502 LaGuardia Pl NY, NY 10012

LCL Productions *(212) 505-9227* 227 E 44th St NY, NY 10017

Leech, Ian & Associates *(212) 751-0022* 140 E 56th St NY, NY 10022

LeFebvre & Associates *(212) 877-5403* 155 W 68th NY, NY 10023

Leodas, Gus Films *(212) 213-4992* 124 E 37th St NY, NY 10016

Levenson *(212) 752-7415* 919 Third Ave NY, NY 10022

Levin Productions *(212) 595-5526* 16A W 88th St NY, NY 10024

Levine, Richard *(212) 925-2020* 594 Broadway NY, NY 10012

Levine, Rick Productions *(212) 734-9600* 59 E 82nd St NY, NY 10028

Levinson Israelson Bell
(212) 472-8888 12 1/2 E 82nd St NY, NY 10028

Libonati, Ed Productions *(212) 582-1660* 353 W 46th St NY, NY 10036

Licata Productions *(212) 645-5050* 31 W 21st St NY, NY 10010

Lipson Film *(212) 505-6800* 58-60 E 13th St NY, NY 10003

Loebel Productions *(203) 798-8754* Precision Rd Danbury, CT 06810

Lovinger/Cohn *(212) 532-3311* 157 E 35th St NY, NY 10016

Luckafilm *(212) 255-2424* 101 Fifth Ave NY, NY 10003

Lucky Films *(212) 645-0700* 322 Eighth Ave NY, NY 10001

Lupano Productions *(212) 463-0300* 151 W 25th St NY, NY 10001

m

Macdonald, Ian *(212) 983-6710* 227 E 44th St NY, NY 10017

MacGuffin Films *(212) 779-8787* 381 Park Ave So NY, NY 10016

Maller-Silverstein *(212) 995-8770* 907 Broadway NY, NY 10010

Manhattan Film/Tape *(212) 254-8700* 907 Broadway NY, NY 10010

Mann, Farhad *(212) 929-7474* c/o CAM 250 First Ave NY, NY 10009

Mannes Group *(212) 989-9267* 10 E 13th St NY, NY 10003

Manno/Schnall *(212) 889-7026* 419 Park Ave So NY, NY 10016

Mansfield Inc *(212) 832-3030* 8 E 48th St NY, NY 10017

Marco, Phil *(212) 929-8082* 104 Fifth Ave NY, NY 10011

Markle & Associates *(212) 246-8642* 630 Ninth Ave NY, NY 10036

Marlis/Seeff *(212) 302-4454* 36 E 20th St NY, NY 10003

Marro, Stephen *(212) 463-0397* 121 W 19th St NY, NY 10011

Marshall Films *(212) 255-4120* 222 W 23rd St NY, NY 10011

Martin, Steve *(212) 953-1825* 141 E 44th St NY, NY 10017

Mason, Bill Pictures *(212) 242-6099* 28 W 25th St NY, NY 10010

Matlin Productions *(212) 247-7741* 515 W 59th St NY, NY 10019

May Day Productions *(212) 684-3555* 115 E 38th St NY, NY 10016

Mayhew Productions *(212) 645-2727* 581 Sixth Ave NY, NY 10011

Mayor's Office of Film *(212) 489-6710* 254 W 54th St NY, NY 10019

Maysles Films *(212) 582-6050* 250 W 54th St NY, NY 10019

McGuane Studio *(212) 582-8925* 36 Horatio St NY, NY 10014

Mendoza, Nick *(212) 935-7113* 141 E 55th St NY, NY 10022

Mercury Productions Inc *(212) 869-4073* 17 W 18th St NY, NY 10011

Meridien Productions *(212) 925-7275* 121 Wooster St NY, NY 10012

Metro 2000 *(212) 764-3570* 15 W 38th St NY, NY 10017

Metro Production Group *(212) 213-3888* 12 W 27th St NY, NY 10001

Michael/Daniel *(212) 777-0121* 101 Fifth Ave NY, NY 10003

Michels, Dennis *(212) 529-5080* 77 Bleecker St NY, NY 10021

Milt Associates Ltd *(212) 751-4141* 60 Sutton Pl So NY, NY 10022

Mirage C.S. Productions *(212) 410-2888* 1675 York Ave NY, NY 10128

Moir Productions *(212) 213-9797* 220 E 23rd St NY, NY 10010

Montage Productions *(212) 571-5877* 254 E 68th St NY, NY 10021

Moore, James Productions *(212) 674-7150* 38 E 19th St NY, NY 10003

MRC Films & Video *(212) 989-1754* 71 W 23rd St NY, NY 10010

Multi Video Group Ltd *(212) 986-1577* 50 E 42nd St NY, NY 10017

MVP Films *(212) 953-1825* 141 E 44th St NY, NY 10017

Myers Films *(212) 685-6888* 49 W 27th St NY, NY 10001

n - p

NBE Productions Ltd *(212) 685-8963* 202 E 35th St NY, NY 10016

New York Animation & Visionworks
(212) 362-6992 200 W 79th St NY, NY 10024

Nicolella & Co (212) 683-5470 381 Park Ave So NY, NY 10016

Noh Hands Productions (212) 674-4833 323 E 18th St NY, NY 10003

Normandy Film Group (212) 684-6192 88 Lexington Ave NY, NY 10016

Odyssey Filmmakers Inc (212) 620-5654 111 Barrow St NY, NY 10014

Onyx Films (212) 769-2153 202 W 81st St NY, NY 10024

Opus/MGMM (212) 929-2900 420 W 24th St NY, NY 10011

Otterson TV Inc (212) 695-6178 251 W 30th St NY, NY 10001

Owen Electric Pictures (212) 924-5570 355 E 86th St NY, NY 10028

Paisley Productions (212) 460-8900 141 Fifth Ave NY, NY 10010

Parineau Films (212) 599-6101 60 E 42nd St NY, NY 10165

Parker, George (212) 971-0011 529 W 42nd St NY, NY 10036

Partners/USA (212) 532-9690 23 W 26th St NY, NY 10010

Pauliny Productions (212) 947-2965 316 Fifth Ave NY, NY 10001

PDR Productions Inc (212) 986-2020 219 E 44th St NY, NY 10017

Perez & Co (212) 477-1080 902 Broadway NY, NY 10010

Petermann Dektor (212) 752-3939 135 E 55th St NY, NY 10022

Petersen Communications
(212) 752-3400 40 E 49th St NY, NY 10017

Petrucelli, Tony Inc (212) 490-9269 300 E 40th St NY, NY 10016

Pfeifer Lopes (212) 832-1177 405 E 57th St NY, NY 10022

Phantasmagoria (212) 586-4890 630 Ninth Ave NY, NY 10036

Picture Vision (212) 995-9797 900 Broadway NY, NY 10003

Pipher/Fox Picures (212) 688-1140 919 Third Ave NY, NY 10022

Pittelli, Patrick (212) 249-8600 801 Madison Ave NY, NY 10021

Porter Productions (212) 529-6363 334 E 22nd St NY, NY 10010

Power & Light (212) 714-0090 35 W 35th St NY, NY 10001

Praxis Film Works Inc (212) 362-2868 140 Riverside Dr NY, NY 10024

Producers East (516) 420-5680 535 Broadhollow Rd NY, NY 11747

Puopolo Productions (212) 725-4830 381 Park Ave So NY, NY 10016

q - r

Quark Video (212) 807-8504 421 Hudson St NY, NY 10014

R/Greenberg (212) 239-6767 350 W 39th St NY, NY 10018

Rain Forest (718) 279-0273 188-12 Northern Blvd Flushing, NY 11358

Randelman, Hal (212) 686-8796 300 E 33rd St NY, NY 10016

Rawi, Schulz (212) 661-1974 80 Park Ave NY, NY 10016

Real Productions Inc (212) 675-5440 530 W 25th St NY, NY 10001

Richman Films (212) 582-9600 322 W 48th St NY, NY 10036

Riso, Adrian (212) 288-6650 166 E 66th St NY, NY 10021

Riverrun Films (212) 645-9070 1133 Broadway NY, NY 10010

RKL Productions (212) 302-0985 56 W 45th St NY, NY 10036

Robbins & Associates (212) 687-8877 121 W 27th St NY, NY 10001

Roberts Productions (212) 883-1030 310 Madison Ave NY, NY 10017

Robins Productions Inc (212) 206-0436 50 W 17th St NY, NY 10011

Ross Productions (212) 986-5122 310 E 46th St NY, NY 10017

Ross, Mark Films Inc (212) 924-8000 48 W 25th St NY, NY 10010

Rossetti Films (212) 505-1160 143 E 19th St NY, NY 10003

Rothberg, Lee (212) 759-0822 3 Dag Hammarskjold Plaza NY, NY 10017

RSA/USA Inc (212) 725-1900 192 Lexington Ave NY, NY 10016

s - t

Sandbank Films
(914) 747-2500 140 Old Saw Mill River Rd Hawthorne, NY 10532

Santandrea Productions (212) 599-1555 34 E 39th St NY, NY 10016

Santiago Inc (212) 529-3494 36 E 12th St NY, NY 10003

Seidman, Barry (212) 255-6666 85 Fifth Ave NY, NY 10003

Sell Pictures Inc (212) 683-9221 210 Fifth Ave NY, NY 10010

September Productions (212) 473-9595 5 E 22nd St NY, NY 10010

Shadow Light (212) 689-7511 12 W 27th St NY, NY 10001

Shelesky/Reynolds (212) 755-5280 316 E 53rd St NY, NY 10022

Sheridan Elson (212) 239-2000 20 W 37th St NY, NY 10018

Shooter's Inc (212) 983-5205 140 E 39th St NY, NY 10016

Shooting Star TV & Film (212) 399-7773 159 W 53rd St NY, NY 10019

Silver, Tony Films Inc (212) 826-6336 242 E 58th St NY, NY 10022

Skoble, Herb & Associates (212) 254-1414 36 E 22nd St NY, NY 10010

Sloan Kasell H/E (212) 819-1717 16 W 46th St NY, NY 10036

Smiling Cat Productions (212) 725-0610 230 E 27th St NY, NY 10016

Smith & Co (212) 818-1888 227 E 44th St NY, NY 10017

Sonnenfeld, Barry (212) 496-6553 Box 1369 Amagansett, NY 11930

Spectrum Associates Inc (212) 563-1680 536 W 29th St NY, NY 10001

Spikol Pictures (212) 505-6519 175 Fifth Ave NY, NY 10010

Spots Films (212) 620-3939 156 Fifth Ave NY, NY 10010

Stargate Productions Inc (212) 333-3636 231 E 55th St NY, NY 10022

Steifel & Co (212) 645-0700 322 Eighth Ave NY, NY 10001

Stone, Marshall (212) 677-0500 106 E 19th St NY, NY 10003

Stone/Mansfield (212) 725-0555 381 Park Ave So NY, NY 10016

Story Piccolo Guliner (212) 529-9090 35 E 21st St NY, NY 10010

Streamline Film (212) 696-2616 109 E 29th St NY, NY 10016

Studio 26 (212) 686-3047 37 W 26th St NY, NY 10010

Sullivan, Ray (212) 628-2645 345 E 81st St NY, NY 10028

Sunlight Pictures (212) 686-5000 322 E 39th St NY, NY 10016

Sussan & Co (212) 533-2200 42 E 23rd St NY, NY 10010

SWA Productions *(212) 661-9580* 144 E 44th St NY, NY 10017

t - z

Take Three Productions *(212) 818-1488* 141 E 44th St NY, NY 10017

Tardio, Neil Productions *(212) 532-3311* 157 E 35th St NY, NY 10016

Teeman/Sleppin *(212) 243-7836* 147 W 26th St NY, NY 10001

Teletechniques Inc *(212) 206-1475* 1 W 19th St NY, NY 10011

They Shoot Films Inc *(212) 685-6070* 251 Fifth Ave NY, NY 10016

Tobin Productions *(212) 724-6869* 300 E 42nd St NY, NY 10017

Triple Vision *(212) 772-0007* 262 E 78th St NY, NY 10021

Tulchin Studios *(212) 986-8270* 240 E 45th St NY, NY 10017

Twin Art *(212) 925-4981* 80 Varick St NY, NY 10013

Ulick Mayo Productions *(212) 473-1600* 141 Fifth Ave NY, NY 10010

UN Productions Inc *(201) 567-5102* 130 Engle St Englewood, NJ 7631

Unangst Productions *(212) 889-4888* 381 Park Ave So NY, NY 10016

US Television *(212) 684-2333* 175 E 62nd St NY, NY 10021

Van Dusen Films *(212) 924-1964* 505 W 23rd St NY, NY 10011

Van Rees & Van Rees *(212) 222-4044* 210 Riverside Dr NY, NY 10025

Verdi & Associated *(212) 888-1829* 400 E 56th St NY, NY 10022

Videograf *(212) 242-7871* 144 W 27th St NY, NY 10001

Virgin Image *(212) 517-4334* 135 E 65th St NY, NY 10021

Vorkapich/Lipson Inc *(212) 505-6800* 58-60 E 13th St NY, NY 10003

Walz, Ken Productions *(212) 826-6010* 219 E 60th St NY, NY 10022

Warner, Robert *(212) 744-7979* 7 E 78th St NY, NY 10021

Wayne, Tony Inc *(212) 683-0733* 300 E 33rd St NY, NY 10016

Webster Productions *(212) 675-3400* 164 W 25th St NY, NY 10001

Welebit Productions *(212) 490-2801* 310 E 44th St NY, NY 10017

Werner Halink *(212) 772-1444* 152 E 74th St NY, NY 10021

Whitman Productions *(212) 750-8788* 160 E 56th St NY, NY 10022

Woll & Associates *(212) 245-3555* 18 W 55th St NY, NY 10019

Working Pictures Corp *(212) 633-0808* 156 Fifth Ave NY, NY 10011

Yellowbrick Films *(212) 967-2290* 330 W 42 St NY, NY 10036

PAGE 2

Young Productions *(212) 787-8954* 118 Riverside Dr NY, NY 10024

Young, Gary *(212) 674-1087* 35 E 20th St NY, NY 10003

Yuhas Productions *(212) 490-2223* 307 E 44th St NY, NY 10017

Zettner, Rick *(212) 490-1034* 310 E 46th St NY, NY 10017

Zoe Productions *(212) 974-0800* 509 Madison Ave NY, NY 10022

TV Commercial Directors

a

Abel, Robert *(212) 620-5654* Odyssey Filmakers

Abrams, Barry *(212) 764-1591* Firehouse Films

Agostinelli, Greg *(212) 689-8670* DiComo & Agostinelli

Akers, Randy *(212) 239-6767* R/Greenberg Associates Inc

Alexander, Larry *(212) 974-0800* Zoe Productions

Alexander, Roger *(212) 765-4640* Independent Artists

Alexander, Sam *(212) 206-6400* Iris Films

Allan, Todd *(212) 627-3600* HSI

Alper, John *(212) 627-8600* Emerald Films

Alpert, Jon *(212) 925-3429* Electric Film

Alton, Bill *(212) 758-3177* Alton Films

Amini, Stephen *(212) 983-5205* Shooter's Productions Inc

Anderson, Clark *(212) 490-1034* Zettner, Rick & Associates

Anderson, Robbie *(212) 737-6815* NY, NY

Andreozzi, Jerry *(212) 477-4200* Andreozzi/Toback & Co

Anneman, John *(212) 620-5654* Odyssey Filmakers

Apoian, Jerry *(212) 832-2288* GMS

Arfman, Phil *(516) 484-6900* ADM Video Productions

Arkin, Alan *(212) 472-8888* Levinson Israelson Bell

Aronson, Josh *(212) 686-5577* Gilson & Aronson Films

Artz, Tony *(212) 753-1050* Artzco Pictures

Ashenhurst, John *(212) 724-8750* Cherry Mellon Ibbetson

Attwell, Bryce *(212) 599-1555* Santandrea Productions

Auerbach, Lillian *(212) 532-3311* Lovinger/Cohn

Avedon, Richard *(212) 206-6400* Iris Films

b

Bachner, Annette *(212) 686-9320* Hirschfield Productions

Baker, Graham *(212) 686-0200* Elite Films

Bal, Walter *(212) 529-3000* Image Realite

Balton, Chris *(212) 557-9834* Balton Productions

Bartkowiak, Andrzej *(212) 505-0670* Bianchi Films Inc

Barton, Bob *(212) 262-8200* Carter Fenske Films

Baxter, Rick *(212) 532-4700* Baxter Films

Bean, John *(212) 242-8106* Bean Productions

Becker, Gean *(212) 832-3030* Mansfield Inc

Beckerman, Arnold *(212) 674-4833* Noh Hands Productions

Bedford, Terry *(212) 242-7200* Jennie & Co

Beineix, Jean-Jaques *(212) 765-4640* Independent Artists

Benson, Peter *(212) 983-5205* Shooter's Productions Inc

Beresford, Jim *(212) 687-8877* Robbins & Associates

Bergman, Lester *(914) 265-3656* Bergman, Lester V

Berkofsky, Mike *(212) 683-2900* Berkofsky/Smillie/Barrett

Berndt, Mark *(212) 529-1990* Harmony Pictures Inc

Bernhard, Alan *(212) 752-7455* Bernhard Creative

Bernstein, Les *(212) 696-2616* Streamline Film

Berris, Ken *(212) 686-0200* Elite Films

Berry, Jeffrey *(212) 687-8877* Robbins & Associates

Bianchi, Ed *(212) 505-0670* Bianchi Films Inc

Bierman, Bob *(212) 686-0200* Elite Films

Bill, Tony *(212) 645-9070* Riverrun Films

Biondo, Robert *(212) 247-7741* Martin Productions

Birbrower, Stew *(212) 977-8822* Birbrower Films

Birnbaum, Harvey *(516) 420-5680* Producers East Media

Black, Richard *(212) 867-4030* EUE/Screen Gems Ltd

Blake, Alan *(212) 242-7200* Jennie & Co Film Productions

Blake, Rebecca *(212) 302-4454* Marlis/Seeff

Blick, John *(212) 683-3311* Dennis, Guy & Hirsch

Bloom III, George *(212) 752-7415* Levenson Productions Ltd

Blum, Chris *(212) 983-5350* Group One

Blume, Howard *(212) 633-0808* Working Pictures Corp

Bollman, Ron *(212) 517-5877* Montage Productions

Boltax, Eric *(212) 687-0963* Boltax Associates

Bonanno, John *(212) 206-6400* Iris Films

Bonner, Lee *(212) 532-3311* Tardio, Neil Productions

Boustany, Paul *(212) 333-7580* Boustany, Paul Productions

Boutonnat, Laurent *(212) 765-4640* Independent Artists

Brady, Matthew *(212) 683-6060* Brady, Matthew Films

Brady, Mike *(212) 633-0303* Lacy, N. Lee/Associates

Brambilla, Marco *(212) 725-1900* RSA/USA Inc

Brooks III, Charles David *(212) 244-6187* CDB III - Kristy

Brooks, Alan *(212) 751-6811* Brooks, Alan Productions

Brooks, Bob *(212) 838-4417* BFCS

Bruce, Murray *(212) 627-4500* Bruce, Murray Productions

Budin, Elbert *(212) 564-9050* Ampersand Productions

Buffman, Ed *(212) 687-8877* Robbins & Associates

Bunche, Peter *(718) 789-7058* Furious Films

Bunin, Elinor *(212) 688-0759* Bunin Productions

Butler, Bill *(212) 752-0500* Petersen Communications

Butler, Michael *(212) 741-3200* Associates Nadel & Butler

C

Cafarelli, Vincent *(212) 840-0411* Buzzco Productions Inc

Cailor, Jerry *(212) 977-4300* Cailor/Resnick

Cammardi, Tom *(212) 686-3047* Studio 26

Campbell, Barbara *(212) 765-4640* Independent Artists

Caporale, Mike *(212) 496-0500* Finley Films

Carlson, Denny *(212) 929-7474* James Productions

Carra, Henry *(212) 582-6050* Maysles Films

Cerutti, Marc *(212) 956-6400* Cerutti Productions

Chalkin, Dennis *(212) 213-4992* Leodas Films

Chambers, Ken *(212) 685-6070* They Shoot Films Inc

Chambers, Richard *(212) 243-1134* Chambers & Associates

Chase, Carlton *(212) 683-2900* Berkofsky/Smillie/Barrett

Chechik, Jeremiah *(212) 679-7199* Hudson, Bill & Associates

Cherry, Peter *(212) 724-8750* Cherry Mellon Ibbetson

Chilvers, Collin *(212) 832-2288* GMS

Churchill, Jack *(212) 779-8787* MacGuffin Films

Cipoletti, John *(718) 332-8868* John Cipoletti Productions

Page 27

Ciupka, Richard *(212) 765-4640* Independent Artists

Clayton, Peter *(212) 967-2290* Yellow brick Films

Page 2

Clemens, Charles *(212) 213-9797* Moir Productions

Coane, Jim *(212) 686-5566* Coane/Porsche & Quinn

Cochran, George *(212) 689-9054* Cochran, George Film

Cohen, Rob *(212) 460-8900* Paisely Productions

Cohen, Robert *(212) 685-6070* They Shoot Films Inc

Cole, Charlie *(212) 741-3200* Associates Nadel & Butler

Collier, Terry *(212) 661-1974* Rawi, Schulz & Co USA Inc

Collins, Christopher Robin *(212) 517-4334* Virgin Image

Conforti, Joe *(212) 532-2820* JC Productions Inc

Connolly, James *(212) 206-1332* Connelly & Co Inc

Cooney, Jeff *(212) 505-9227* LCL Productions

Cooper, Peter *(212) 243-3434* Cooper & Co

Cooper-Bey, Daniel *(212) 213-4992* Leodas Films

Cope, Gil *(212) 532-3311* Lovinger/Cohn

Coppos, Mark *(212) 570-0011* Coppos Films

Corbett, Peter *(212) 989-7892* Corbett, Peter & Co

Corbin, Anton *(212) 633-0303* Lacy, N. Lee/Associates

Cornell, David *(212) 620-3939* Spots Films

Corwin, Steve *(212) 333-3636* Stargate Productions Inc

Cosimo *(212) 691-9200* Giraldi-Suarez

Costello, Shawn *(212) 420-1100* Burton Productions

Cote, Bill *(212) 242-4065* Cote Productions

Cottrell, Julian *(212) 683-2900* Berkofsky/Smillie/Barrett

Cotts, Jerry *(212) 213-0100* Cotts, Jerry Films Inc

Cramer, Ross *(212) 529-8000* Hameline, Gerard Productions

Crippen, Fred *(212) 697-0858* Friedman, Harold Consortium

Cronenwest, Jordan *(212) 645-9070* Riverrun Films

Cruikshank, Sally *(212) 697-0858* Friedman, Harold

Csupo, Gabor *(212) 697-0858* Friedman, Harold Consortium

Cuccinello, Bill *(212) 473-9595* September Productions

Cuesta, Michael *(212) 246-7600* Griner/Cuesta & Associates

Curry, Brian *(201) 567-5102* UN Productions Inc

d

D'Amato, George *(212) 473-1600* Ulick Mayo Productions

D'Elia, Bill *(212) 889-9778* D'Elia Uricola & Platt Inc

Danelowitz, Howard *(212) 362-6992* NY Animation Visionworks

Darby, David *(212) 752-0500* Petersen Communications

Davis, Ken *(212) 725-1900* RSA/USA Inc

Davis, Rod *(212) 529-1990* Harmony Pictures Inc

De Ligter, Richard *(212) 675-5440* Real Productions Inc

Deahl, David *(212) 759-0700* Directing Artists

Dean, Rowan *(212) 724-8750* Cherry Mellon Ibbetson

Del'Orto, Alberto *(212) 777-0121* Michael/Daniel

Demertzis, Ares *(212) 486-6840* HPS/IPS East

Demme, Ken *(212) 867-4030* Director's Chair/EUE

Demshuk, Bob *(212) 213-4992* Leodas Films

Denneen, David *(212) 724-8750* Cherry Mellon Ibbetson

Dennis, Allan *(212) 683-6311* Dennis, Guy & Hirsch

DeSchanel, Caleb *(212) 765-4640* Independent Artists

DeVoto, Joe *(212) 213-4992* Leodas Films

deVries, David *(212) 580-2888* deVries Films

Dexter, Ron *(212) 533-2200* Sussan & Co

Dixon, Geoff *(212) 475-5800* Fairbanks Films

Dole, Kevin *(212) 206-6400* Iris Films

Dollinger, Steve *(212) 529-3000* Image Realite

Dorn, Bruce *(212) 644-6334* Dorn, Bruce Films

Dowad, Bruce *(212) 242-7200* Jennie & Co Film Productions

Dragoti, Stan *(212) 867-4030* EUE/Screen Gems Ltd

Dreyer, David *(212) 533-2200* Sussan & Co

Driscoll, Dan *(212) 473-9595* September Productions

Dubin, Jay *(212) 206-6400* Iris Films

Ducrot, Jerome *(212) 475-5800* Fairbanks Films

e - f

Eberlein, Bob *(212) 867-4030* Director's Chair/EUE

Edwards, Jonathan *(212) 496-2660* American Night

Eggers, Bob *(212) 751-9044* Eggers Films

Ehrhardt, Beau *(212) 213-0800* Corporate Theatre

Eisenberg, Nat *(212) 685-8963* NBE Productions Ltd

Elliot, Bob *(212) 867-9014* Goulding-Elliot/Greybar

Elliot, David *(212) 867-4030* Director's Chair/EUE

Elliot, Mike *(212) 867-4030* Director's Chair/EUE

Elliot, Steve *(212) 867-4030* Director's Chair/EUE

Escobedo, Maria *(718) 279-0273* Rain Forest Films

Ewers, Scott *(212) 983-5350* Group One

Falby, Jed *(212) 645-5050* Licata International Productions

Fash, Mike *(212) 683-8130* Katz Associates

Fengler, John *(212) 684-2333* US Television

Fernbach, Alex *(212) 879-8787* Fernbach Productions

Fertik, Bill *(212) 877-3468* Fertik & Co

Ficalora, Tony *(914) 591-7344* Ficalora Productions

Fleckenstein, John *(212) 472-8888* Levinson Israelson Bell

Flint, Roger *(212) 755-8888* Flint Productions

Forrest, Matt *(212) 929-2900* Opus/MGMM

Fraker, John *(212) 752-4422* Fraker Productions

France, Jeff *(212) 473-3366* Big City Films

Francis, Jon *(212) 645-0700* Stiefel & Co

Fresco, Mike *(212) 529-8000* Hameline, Gerard Productions

Friedman, Marvin *(718) 858-5374* Friedman Productions

Fulford, Len *(212) 838-4117* BFCS

g

Gaffney, Bob *(212) 233-0555* JPC Video

Galfas, Timothy *(212) 529-3000* Image Realite

Gallerini, Andy *(212) 683-7500* Johnston Films

Gartzman, Rudolf *(212) 832-8169* Intergroup Prodcutions

Gast, Leon *(212) 586-4890* Phantasmagoria Productions

Gelbaum, Dennis Jay *(212) 529-3000* Image Realite

Georgevich, Dejan *(212) 633-0808* Working Pictures Corp

Geraldi, Bob *(212) 691-9200* Giraldi-Suarez

Gherardi, Charles *(718) 279-0273* Rain Forest Films

Giacobetti, Francis *(212) 765-4640* Independent Artists

Gibson, Brian *(212) 877-5403* Gibson, Brian Productions

Giddens, Jim *(212) 832-2288* GMS

Ginsberg, Victor *(212) 685-6070* They Shoot Films Inc

Giradli, Frank *(212) 840-8225* Frank Giraldi Studios

Girard, Howard *(212) 206-6400* Iris Films

Glassman, Paulette *(212) 369-3010* Glassman, Paulette

Glaviano, Marco *(212) 889-9778* D'Elia Uricola & Platt Inc

Gluck, Steve *(212) 777-2146* Gluck Films inc

Gold, Peter *(212) 370-5151* Cine International

Goldberg, Syd *(212) 627-1770* Filigree Films Inc

Goldblatt, Stephen *(212) 337-3400* Image Point

Goldschmidt, Peter *(212) 734-4230* Cinepez Pictures

Goldstein, Richard *(212) 582-1660* Libonati, Ed Productions

Gomes, George *(212) 593-9500* Gomes Loew Inc

Goodman, John *(212) 473-9595* September Productions

Gorman, Jeff *(212) 677-4600* Johns & Gorman Films

Goulden Jean Paul *(212) 475-5800* Fairbanks Films

Gouldin, Ray *(212) 867-9014* Gouldin-Elliot/Greybar

Grant, Brian *(212) 929-2900* Opus/MGMM

Grasso, Michael *(212) 683-3311* Dennis, Guy & Hirsch

Grau, Jim Jr. *(212) 832-3020* Charisma/Visual Motion

Green, Allan *(212) 244-5757* Inserts

Greenberg, Burton *(212) 420-1100* Burton Productions

Greenberg, Richard *(212) 239-6767* R/Greenberg

Greenberg, Robbie *(212) 645-9070* Riverrun Films

Griffiths, David *(212) 686-0200* Elite Films

Grillo, Ken *(212) 683-4980* Helburn Productions Inc

Griner, Norman *(212) 246-7600* Griner/Cuesta & Associates

Groshelle, Bill *(212) 697-0858* Friedman, Harold

Grove, Eric *(212) 242-7447* Grove, Eric Film

Grunberg, Laurence *(212) 983-5350* Group One

Guliner, Paul *(212) 529-9090* Story Piccolo Guliner

Guy, Don *(212) 683-3311* Dennis, Guy & Hirsch

h

Haber, Bernie *(212) 697-9202* Adfilm Producers Inc

Hagmann, Stu *(212) 687-4314* Hisk Productions/NY

Halinka, Werner *(212) 772-1444* Halinka, Werner

Hall, Gary *(212) 477-4200* Andreozzi/Toback & Co

Hall, John *(212) 714-0090* Power & Light Picture Co Ltd

Hamburg, Harry *(212) 683-7500* Johnston Films

Hameline, Gerard *(212) 529-8000* Hameline, Gerard

Haney, Dan *(212) 832-2288* GMS

Hanwright, Joseph *(212) 532-1212* Kira/H Films Inc

Harlib, Matt *(212) 697-9202* Adfilm Porducers Inc

Harris, Matthew *(212) 627-3600* HSI

Harrison, Jeanne *(212) 683-1850* Harrison Productions

Hayes, Blair *(212) 751-0022* Leech, Ian & Associates

Heaney, John *(201) 567-5102* UN Productions Inc

Heath, Peter *(212) 832-2288* GMS

Heimann, Richard *(212) 867-4030* Director's Chair/EUE

Heir, Stuart *(212) 477-4200* Andreozzi/Toback & Co

Helburn, William *(212) 683-4980* Helburn Productions Inc

Heller, Mark *(212) 696-2616* Streamline Film

Hello, Scott *(212) 826-6010* Walz, Ken Productions

Hemecker, Ralph *(212) 594-0880* Flamingo Films

Henman, Graham *(212) 246-9260* HKM Productions

Henman, Paul *(212) 255-2424* Luckafilm

Herman, Harvey *(212) 706-0913* Herman, Harvey

Herschelder, Jim *(212) 505-6800* Vorkapich/Lipson Inc

Hertz, Doug *(212) 288-6650* Riso Associates Ltd

Higgens, Tom *(212) 838-4417* BFCS

Hiro *(212) 206-6400* Iris Films

Hirschenson, Bernard *(212) 757-7662* Hirschenson

Hirschfield, Lenny *(212) 686-9320* Hirschfield Productions

Hodge, David *(212) 245-3623* Hodge, David Productions

Hoey, Gordon *(212) 759-0700* Directing Artists

Hogan, David *(212) 246-9260* HKM Productions

Holmes, Martha *(212) 213-4992* Leodas Films

Holtzman, Henry *(212) 627-3600* HSI

Holzemer, Buck *(212) 529-3000* Image Realite

Horn, Steve *(212) 794-1300* Horn Productions

Horsely, Lori *(212) 586-4890* Phantasmagoria Productions

Horvath, James *(212) 741-0300* Horvath & Associates

Howard, Harry *(212) 687-1312* Double HH Productions

Hudson, Bill *(212) 679-7199* Hudson, Bill & Associates

Hulen, Steve (212) 529-9090 Story Piccolo Guliner

Hulme, Bob (212) 777-0121 Michael/Daniel Productions

Huss, Michael (212) 752-7455 Huss, Michael Inc

Hutson, Larry (212) 532-9690 Partners/USA

Hyman, Chuck (212) 725-3840 Horizon Studios Inc

Hyman, Richard (212) 867-4030 Director's Chair/EUE

i - k

Irwin, Patrick (203) 798-8754 Loebel Productions

Israelson, Peter (212) 472-8888 Levinson Israelson Bell

Jackson, David (212) 697-0858 Friedman, Harold

Jacobson, Boyd (212) 929-7474 James Productions

Jankel, Anabel (212) 242-7200 Jennie & Co Film

Javor, Ivan (212) 410-2888 Mirgae C.S. Productions

Jenkins, Andy (212) 879-6200 Jenkins & Co Films

Johannes, Victor (212) 288-3632 Johannes Film

John, Michael (212) 989-9267 Mannes Production Group

Johns, Gary (212) 677-4600 Johns & Gorman Films

Johnston, Jim (212) 683-7500 Johnston Films

Jones, J Wesley (212) 473-4545 Jones, Wesley J Productions

Jones, Jeff (212) 779-8787 MacGuffin Films

Jones, Nick (212) 633-0303 Lacy, N. Lee/Associates

Jordan, Larry (212) 473-9595 September Productions

Kagan, Peter (212) 645-0700 Stiefel & Co

Kahan, Martin (212) 685-6070 They Shoot Films Inc

Kahn, Ellen (212) 925-4981 Twin Art

Kahn, Lynda (212) 925-4981 Twin Art

Kalamar, Tom (212) 254-8400 Kalamar Productions

Kalbfeld, Mark (212) 243-7836 Teeman, Sleepin

Kalsky, Arlene (212) 697-0858 Friedman, Harold

Kanievska, Marek (212) 725-1900 RSA/USA Inc

Karbelnikoff, Michael (212) 246-9260 HKM Productions

Kasman, Mort (212) 696-1988 Kasman Productions Inc

Katz, Max (212) 988-1957 Katz, Max Productions Inc

Katz, Robert (212) 460-5545 Duncan & Katz

Kelinon, Peter (212) 620-5654 Odyssey Filmakers

Kelly, Patrick (212) 929-6176 Kelly Pictures

Kimmel, Adam (212) 477-1080 Perez & Co Inc

Kimmelman, Phil (212) 944-7766 KCMP Productions

Knezvich, Robert (212) 594-6834 Impact Entertainment Inc

Kovacs, Laszlo (212) 627-3336 Arc Films

Kozan, Dan (212) 989-7892 Corbett, Peter & Co

Kriegsman, Michael (212) 575-3108 ABACAB Productions

Krige, Tai (212) 687-8877 Robbins & Associates

Kugel, Candice (212) 840-0411 Buzzco Productions Inc

Kuryla, Henry (212) 627-3336 Arc Films

l

Lacy, Lee (212) 633-0303 Lacy, N. Lee/Associates

Lai, Brian (212) 533-2200 Sussan & Co

Laipis, Gus (212) 706-0913 Herman, Harvey Associates Inc

Lambert, Mary (212) 627-3600 HSI

LaMonte, Lou (212) 687-3232 International Television

Landry, Tim (212) 490-1034 Zettner, Rick & Associates

Langley, David (212) 581-3930 Langley Productions

Larkin, David (212) 594-0880 Flamingo Films

Larkin, John (212) 206-8450 Larkin Productions Inc

Lategan, Barry (212) 228-6850 Lategan, Barry

Lawrence, Alan (212) 620-5654 Odyssey Filmakers

Lawrence, Ray (212) 431-7755 Jupiter Films

Lazarus, Ashley (212) 370-5151 Cine International

Leech, Ian (212) 751-0022 Leech, Ian & Associates

Lefebvre, Katherine (212) 877-5403 LeFebvre, Katherine

Lehman, Richard (212) 302-0985 RKL Productions

Levelle, Peter (212) 765-4640 Independent Artists

Levenson, Bob (212) 752-7415 Levenson Productions Ltd

Levin, Lear (212) 595-5526 Levin Productions

Levine, Richard (212) 925-2020 Levine, Richard Productions

Levine, Rick (212) 734-9600 Levine, Rick Productions

Levinson, Barry (212) 645-9070 Riverrun Films

Levinson, Danny (212) 472-8888 Levinson Israelson Bell

Levinson, Fred (212) 472-8888 Levinson Israelson Bell

Leyser, Ron (212) 473-3366 Big City Films

Leyton, Saul (212) 764-3570 Metro 2000

Libman, Leslie (212) 242-7200 Jennie & Co Film Productions

Libonati, Ed (212) 582-1660 Libonati, Ed Productions

Licata, Ken (212) 645-5050 Licata International

Lieberman, Ron (212) 529-1990 Harmony Pictures Inc

Lindquist, Mark (212) 769-2153 Onyx Films

Loebel, Herb (203) 798-8754 Loebel Productions

Loew, Dick (212) 593-9500 Gomes Loew Inc

Logan, Bruce (212) 751-0022 Leech, Ian & Associates

Logan, Jim *(212) 575-9111* Wade, Roger Productions Inc

Longauer, Peter *(212) 627-1770* Filigree Films Inc

Longo, Robert *(212) 206-6400* Iris Films

Lopes, Rob *(212) 832-1177* Pfeifer Lopes

Lovinger, Jeff *(212) 532-3311* Lovinger/Cohn

Lucka, Klaus *(212) 255-2424* Luckafilm

Lund, Jim *(212) 929-7474* James Productions

Lunn, Roger *(212) 679-7199* Hudson, Bill & Associates

Lupano, Ken *(212) 463-0300* Lupano Productions

Lyne, Adrian *(212) 242-7200* Jennie & Co Film Productions

Lyons, Roger *(212) 627-3600* HSI

m

Maas, Pieter *(212) 475-5800* Fairbanks Films

Macartney, Syd *(212) 633-1432* Jenks & Partners

MacDonald, Ian *(212) 983-6710* MacDonald, Ian Productions

MacKenzie, Ian *(212) 431-7755* Jupiter Films

MacLean, Eduardo *(212) 765-4640* Independent Artists

MacLeod, Stuart *(212) 370-5151* Cine International

Maden, Rick *(212) 661-1974* Rawi, Schulz & Co USA Inc

Madsen, Ken *(212) 832-1177* Pfeifer Lopes

Makin, Harry *(212) 262-8200* Carter Fenske Films

Maller, Jon *(212) 254-8700* Manhattan Film & Tape

Maller, Jonathan *(212) 995-8770* Maller-Silverstein

Mallet, David *(212) 929-2900* Opus/MGMM

Malone, Barbara *(212) 627-1770* Filigree Films Inc

Mangiardi, Maureen *(212) 995-5080* Creative Media Concepts

Mangraviti, Tom *(212) 244-5757* Inserts

Mann, Farhad *(212) 929-7474* Farhad Mann Productions

Mannes, Michael *(212) 989-9267* Mannes Productions Group

Marco, Phil *(212) 929-8082* Marco, Phil

Marhsall, Richard *(212) 255-4120* Marshall Films

Markle, Bill *(212) 246-8642* Markle & Associates

Marles, John *(212) 725-1900* RSA/USA Inc

Marro, Stephen *(212) 463-0397* Marro, Stephen

Marshall, Bill *(212) 533-2200* Sussan & Co

Marshall, Garry *(212) 765-4640* Independent Artists

Marshall, Peter *(212) 254-8700* Manhattan Film & Tape

Martin, Steve *(212) 953-1825* MVP Films

Marx, Richard *(212) 370-5151* Cine International

Mason, Bill *(212) 242-6099* Mason, Bill Pictures

Masters, Quentin *(212) 633-1432* Jenks & Partners

Mastrippolito, Domenic *(212) 687-3414* Hisk Productions/NY

Mayo, Geoffrey *(212) 473-1600* Ulick Mayo Productions

Maysles, Al *(212) 582-6050* Maysles Films

McCarthy, Richard *(212) 645-0700* Stiefel & Co

McGorman, Jim *(212) 473-3366* Big City Films

McGuane, Jim *(212) 582-8925* McGuane Studio

McLaren, Colin *(212) 661-1974* Rawi, Schulz & Co USA Inc

McNamara Michael *(212) 807-6565* Filmfair

McNeil, Dick *(212) 620-3939* Spots Films

Mendoza, Nick *(212) 935-7113* Mendoza, Nick Productions Inc

Meridien, Jacques *(212) 925-7275* Meridien Productions

Meshekoff, Matthew *(212) 633-0303* Lacy, N. Lee/Associates

Metz, Rexford *(212) 764-3570* Metro 2000

Metzner, Jeff *(212) 475-5800* Fairbanks Films

Mevorach, Linda *(212) 206-6400* Iris Films

Miller, Dick *(212) 337-3400* Image Point

Miller, Michael *(212) 517-5877* Montage Productions

Miller, Scott *(212) 832-2288* GMS

Milt, Victor *(212) 751-4141* Milt Associates Ltd

Misiano, Vince *(212) 233-0555* JPC Video

Mitchell, Tony *(212) 929-2900* Opus/MGMM

Moir, Michael *(212) 213-9797* Moir Productions

Montgomery, Patrick *(212) 620-3955* Archive Film page 28

Moon, Sarah *(212) 633-1432* Jenks & Partners

Moore, Larry *(212) 661-1974* Rawi, Schulz & Co USA Inc

Moore, James *(212) 674-7150* Moore, James Productions

Morgan, Patrick *(212) 725-1900* RSA/USA Inc

Morris, Nick *(212) 929-2900* Opus/MGMM

Morrison, Hobby *(212) 777-0121* Michael/Daniel Productions

Morton, Rocky *(212) 242-7200* Jennie & Co Film Productions

Moss, Peter *(212) 679-7199* Hudson, Bill & Associates

Mougin, Claude *(212) 633-1432* Jenks & Partners

Mulcuhy, Russell *(212) 929-2900* Opus/MGMM

Munro, Gordon *(212) 337-3400* Image Point

Murray, Joe *(212) 807-6565* Filmfair

Murray, Phil *(212) 262-8200* Carter Fenske Films

Myers, Barry *(212) 620-3939* Spots Films

Myers, Colleen *(212) 661-1974* Rawi, Schulz & Co USA Inc

Myers, Sid *(212) 685-6888* Myers Films

n - p

Nadel, Bruce *(212) 741-3200* Associates Nadel & Butler

Nicolella, Richard *(212) 683-5470* Nicolella & Co Film

Nolan, Chris *(212) 262-8200* Carter Fenske Films

Norman, Michael *(212) 627-8600* Emerald Films

Noyes, Eli *(212) 807-6565* Filmfair

O Neill, John *(203) 798-8754* Loebel Productions

Oblowitz, Michael *(212) 633-0303* Lacy, N. Lee/Associates

Osborne, Larry *(212) 944-7766* KCMP Productions

Otterson, Bill *(212) 695-6178* Otterson TV Inc

Owen, Michael D *(212) 924-5570* Owen Electric Pictures

Paisley, Jim *(212) 627-3336* Arc Films

Parker, George *(212) 971-0011* Parker, George Productions

Pauliny, Paul *(212) 947-2965* Pauliny, Paul Productions

Pedra, Torres *(212) 686-5000* Sunlight Pictures

Perier, Jean-Marie *(212) 679-7199* Hudson, Bill & Associates

Perks, Bob *(212) 532-9690* Partners/USA

Perweiler, Gary *(212) 254-7247* Exit Productions

Petermann, Fred *(212) 752-3939* Petermann Dektor

Petersen, Bob *(212) 752-0500* Petersen Communications

Petrucelli, Tony *(212) 490-9269* Petrucelli, Tony Inc

Phillips, Ron *(212) 620-5654* Odyssey Filmakers

Piccolo, Jack *(212) 529-9090* Story Piccolo Guliner

Piel, Denis *(212) 431-7755* Jupiter Films

Pitt, George *(212) 563-1680* Spectrum Associates Inc

Pittelli, Patrick *(212) 249-8600* Pittelli, Patrick

Piznarski, Mark *(212) 777-0121* Michael/Daniel Productions

Pope, Gene *(212) 472-8888* Levinson Israelson Bell

Pope, Tim *(212) 517-4334* Virgin Image

Porsche, Bob *(212) 686-5566* Coane/Porsche & Quinn

Portelly, Mike *(212) 929-2900* Opus/MGMM

Porter, Fred *(212) 529-6363* Porter Productions

Poupolo, Lou *(212) 725-4830* Puopolo Productions

q - r

Quinn, Dan *(212) 686-5566* Coane/Porsche & Quinn

Ramsey, Greg *(212) 627-3600* HSI

Randelman, Hal *(212) 686-8796* Randelman, Hal Productions

Rath, Earl *(212) 243-1134* Chambers & Associates

Rathbourn, Ray *(212) 599-1555* Santandrea Productions

Ravon, Jean-Michel *(212) 679-7199* Hudson, Bill & Associates

Rawi, Ousama *(212) 661-1974* Rawi, Schulz & Co USA Inc

Rayner, Joe *(212) 620-5654* Odyssey Filmakers

Reagan, Bob *(212) 620-5654* Odyssey Filmakers

Resnick, Elliot *(212) 977-4300* Cailor/Resnick

Richman, Sheldon *(212) 582-9600* Richman Films

Riso, Adrian *(212) 288-6650* Riso Associates Ltd

Rivas, Ray *(212) 620-5654* Odyssey Filmakers

Roberts, Len *(212) 883-1030* Roberts Productions

Roberts, Randy *(212) 683-2900* Berkofsky/Smillie/Barrett

Robins, Larry *(212) 206-0436* Robins Productions Inc

Robinson, Keith *(212) 586-4890* Phantasmagoria Productions

Ross, Jan *(212) 213-0800* Corporate Theatre

Ross, Mark *(212) 924-8000* Ross, Mark Films Inc

Rossetti, Dominic *(212) 505-1160* Rossetti Films

Rothberg, Lee *(212) 661-9580* SWA Productions

Rubenstein, Michael *(212) 586-4890* Phantasmagoria

Rucker, Dick *(212) 532-9690* Partners/USA

Russell, Patrick *(212) 734-9600* Levine, Rick Productions

s

Sacco, Vittorio *(212) 505-0670* Bianchi Films Inc

Saire, David *(212) 475-5800* Fairbanks Films

Sandbank, Henry *(914) 747-2500* Sandbank, Henry Films

Santandrea, Carmine *(212) 599-1555* Santandrea Productions

Sato, Gary *(212) 570-0011* Coppos Films

Savage, Lee *(212) 697-0858* Friedman, Harold Consortium

Scammell, Peter *(212) 633-0303* Lacy, N. Lee/Associates

Schofield, Stan *(914) 747-2500* Sandbank, Henry Films

Schrom, Michael *(212) 246-7600* Griner/Cuesta & Associates

Schulz, Bob *(212) 661-1974* Rawi, Schulz & Co USA Inc

Schwartz, Bob *(212) 772-3190* Eye View Film Associates Inc

Schwartz, Peter *(212) 353-0500* Cajun Films

Scott, Ridley *(212) 725-1900* RSA/USA Inc

Scott, Tony *(212) 725-1900* RSA/USA Inc

Sebert, John *(212) 262-8200* Carter Fenske Films

Seeff, Norman *(212) 302-4454* Marlis/Seeff

Seidman, Marry *(212) 255-6666* Seidman, Barry Productions

Sell, Jack *(212) 683-9221* Sell Pictures Inc

Seresin, Michael *(212) 838-4117* BFCS

SERJEANT, DESMOND *(212) 724-8750* CHERRY MELLON IBBETSON

SHARP, IVOR *(212) 661-1974* RAWI, SCHULZ & CO USA INC

SHEEHAN, BOBBY *(212) 683-5470* NICOLELLA & CO FILM

SHELESKY, JOE *(212) 755-5280* SHELESKY/REYNOLD PRODUCTIONS

SHERIDAN, WILLIAM *(212) 239-2000* SHERIDAN ELSON COMMUNICATIONS INC

SIEGLER, ROBERT *(212) 684-4250* ACTION PRODUCTIONS INC

SILVER, TONY *(212) 826-6336* SILVER, TONY FILMS INC

SINCLAIR, JOHN *(212) 752-0500* PETERSEN COMMUNICATIONS

SKOBLE, HERB *(212) 254-1414* SKOBLE, HERB & ASSOCIATES

SLEPPIN, STU *(212) 243-7836* TEEMAN, SLEEPIN ENTERPRISES INC

SLOAN, JOHN *(212) 496-0500* FINLEY FILMS

SLOGGETT, RICHARD *(212) 532-3311* LOVINGER/COHN

SMILLIE, PETER *(212) 683-2900* BERKOFSKY/SMILLIE/BARRETT

SMITH, DAVID *(212) 724-8750* CHERRY MELLON IBBETSON

SMITH, GREGORY *(212) 244-5757* INSERTS

SMITH, LEE *(212) 867-4030* DIRECTOR'S CHAIR/EUE

SMITH, LESLIE *(212) 645-9070* RIVERRUN FILMS

SOKOLSKY, MELVIN *(212) 686-5000* SUNLIGHT PICTURES

SOMOROFF, MICHAEL *(212) 645-0700* STIEFEL & CO

SONNENFELD, BARRY *(212) 496-6553* SONNENFELD, BARRY

SONZERO, JIM *(212) 242-7200* JENNIE & CO FILM PRODUCTIONS

SORESEN, DICKSON *(212) 679-7199* HUDSON, BILL & ASSOCIATES

SORKIN, LARRY *(212) 684-2333* US TELEVISION

SPENCER, BERNARD *(212) 529-8000* HAMELINE, GERARD

SPIKOL, ALLEN *(212) 505-6519* SPIKOL PICTURES WORLDWIDE INC

ST. CLOUD, SKY *(212) 633-0303* LACY, N. LEE/ASSOCIATES

STEIGMAN, STEVE *(212) 473-3366* BIG CITY FILMS

STEINBERG, DAVID *(212) 867-4030* DIRECTOR'S CHAIR/EUE

STEINHAUSER, BURT *(212) 879-6200* JENKINS & CO FILMS

STERN, DAVID *(212) 477-4200* ANDREOZZI/TOBACK & CO

STEVENS, MARCUS *(212) 983-5350* GROUP ONE

STIENBERG, DAVID *(212) 867-4030* DIRECTOR'S CHAIR/EUE

STONE, ARNIE *(212) 832-0909* ICM FILMS

STONE, DICK *(212) 725-0555* STONE/MANSFIELD INC

STONE, MARSHALL *(212) 370-1577* STONE, MARSHALL

STORY, MARK *(212) 529-9090* STORY PICCOLO GULINER

STURNER, JOHN *(212) 764-1591* FIREHOUSE FILMS

SUAREZ, SANTIAGO *(212) 529-3494* SANTIAGO INC

SULLIVAN, RAY *(212) 628-2645* SULLIVAN, RAY PRODUCTIONS

SUTTNER, LINTON *(212) 807-6565* FILMFAIR

SWAIM, BOB *(212) 529-3000* IMAGE REALITE

SWEENEY, DON *(212) 244-5757* INSERTS

t

TABAK, MAXINE *(212) 206-6400* IRIS FILMS

TAKAHASI, DREW *(212) 633-0022* COLOSSAL PICTURES

TAKASAKI, KEN *(212) 262-8200* CARTER FENSKE FILMS

TAMMARIELLO *(212) 645-9070* RIVERRUN FILMS

TANNEN, BILL *(212) 867-4030* DIRECTOR'S CHAIR/EUE

TARIDO, NEIL *(212) 532-3311* TARDIO, NEIL PRODUCTIONS

TARLOFSKY, ARLEN *(212) 627-3336* ARC FILMS

TAYLOR, RICHARD *(212) 337-3400* IMAGE POINT

TAYLOR, TERRY *(212) 599-6101* PARINEU FILMS

TEPPER, MAX *(212) 517-5877* MONTAGE PRODUCTIONS

TERRY, FRANK *(212) 807-6565* FILMFAIR

THARP, TWYLA *(212) 206-6400* IRIS FILMS

THOMAS, BRENT *(212) 570-0011* COPPOS FILMS

THOMAS, GLENN *(212) 431-7755* JUPITER FILMS

THORGERSON, STORM *(212) 832-1880* FRONT ROW FILMS II

THORN, DENISE *(212) 929-2900* OPUS/MGMM

THURLBECK, KEN *(212) 517-4334* VIRGIN IMAGE

TIMMER, BILL *(212) 529-1990* HARMONY PICTURES INC

TOBACK, NORMAN *(212) 477-4200* ANDREOZZI/TOBACK & CO

TOBIN, DWIGHT *(212) 724-6864* TOBIN PRODUCTIONS

TOBIN, STEVE *(212) 645-0700* STIEFEL & CO

TORRES, PEDRO *(212) 686-5000* SUNLIGHT PICTURES

TRENNER, MICKEY *(212) 867-4030* DIRECTOR'S CHAIR/EUE

TSUNO, KEIKO *(212) 925-3429* ELECTRIC FILM

TUCCI, TONY *(212) 687-3344* TAKE THREE PRODUCTIONS

TULCHIN, HAL *(212) 685-6070* THEY SHOOT FILMS INC

U - Z

ULICK, MICHAEL *(212) 473-1600* ULICK MAYO PRODUCTIONS

UNANGST, ANDREW *(212) 889-4888* UNANGST PRODUCTIONS

UNTERSEE, CHUCK *(212) 243-1134* CHAMBERS & ASSOCIATES

UTTERBACK, MICHAEL *(212) 679-7199* HUDSON, BILL

VAINTRUB, ELYSE *(212) 696-2616* STREAMLINE FILM

VAN DUSEN, BRUCE *(212) 924-1964* VAN DUSEN FILMS

VAN LINT, DEREK *(212) 532-9690* PARTNERS/USA

VAUGHAN, STEVE *(212) 685-6888* MYERS FILMS

VECCHIARELLA, MICHAEL *(212) 242-8106* BEAN PRODUCTIONS

Village, Park *(212) 683-2900* Berkofsky/Smillie/Barrett

Vorkapich, Ed *(212) 505-6800* Vorkapich/Lipson Inc

Waller, Anthony *(212) 684-6192* Normandy Film Group

Warner, Bob *(212) 744-7979* Warner, Robert Productions

Watkins, Michael *(212) 627-3336* Arc Films

Waxman, Wendy *(212) 685-6070* They Shoot Films Inc

Wayne, Tony *(212) 683-0733* Wayne, Tony Inc

Weber, Bruce *(212) 532-1212* Kira/H Films Inc

Webster, Jay *(212) 675-3400* Webster Productions

Wechter, Paul *(212) 832-1880* Front Row Films II

Weinschenker, Greg *(212) 645-2727* Mayhew Productions

Weintraub, Bruce *(212) 686-3047* Studio 26

Weisman, Joel *(212) 661-9580* SWA Productions

Welebit, Walter *(212) 490-2801* Welebit Productions

Werk, Michael *(212) 620-3939* Spots Films

Werwa, Shelby *(212) 242-7871* Videograf

Wesson, Bernie *(212) 620-3939* Spots Films

Wexler, Haskell *(212) 989-3535* Cinematic Directions

Whitman, Gerald *(212) 750-8788* Whitman Productions

Williams, Larry *(212) 242-7200* Jennie & Co Film Productions

Williams, Tony *(212) 370-5151* Cine International

Wilson, David *(212) 674-4833* Noh Hands Productions

Woll, Yale *(212) 245-3555* Woll & Associates

Woods, Christopher *(212) 475-5800* Fairbanks Films

Woolridge, Marjorie Clarke *(212) 752-7455* Huss, Michael

Young, Barry *(212) 645-9070* Riverrun Films

Young, Dick *(212) 787-8954* Young Productions

Young, Gary *(212) 674-1087* Young, Gary Associates Inc

Young, Ralph *(212) 243-1134* Chambers & Associates

Yuhas, Robert *(212) 490-2223* Yuhas Productions

Zellan, Michael *(212) 599-6101* Parineu Films

Zettner, Rick *(212) 490-1034* Zettner, Rick & Associates

Zieff, Howard *(212) 765-4640* Independent Artists

Zsigmond, Vilmos *(212) 989-3535* Cinematic Directions

Zwart, Jeff *(914) 747-2500* Sandbank, Henry Films

CORPORATE FILM/VIDEO

a - b

1776 Productions *(212) 736-1776* 511 W 54th St NY, NY 10019

29th St Video Inc *(212) 594-7530* 339 W 29th St NY, NY 10001

ABACAB Productions *(212) 575-3108* 123 W 44th St NY, NY 10019

Action Productions *(212) 684-4250* 14 E 39th St NY, NY 10016

Adfilm Producers Inc *(212) 697-9202* 300 E 40th St NY, NY 10016

Aegis Productions *(212) 684-0810* 114 E 39th St NY, NY 10016

Albi, Dom Associates *(212) 799-2202* 251 W 92nd St NY, NY 10025

All-Star *(212) 645-8529* 156 Fifth Ave NY, NY 10010

Apollo *(212) 489-8433* 619 W 54th St NY, NY 10019

Arkay Video *(201) 725-3003* 25 S Main St Manville, NJ 08835

Arrow Communications *(212) 677-2500* 121 E 24th St NY, NY 10010

Arztco Pictures Inc *(212) 753-1050* 15 E 61st St NY, NY 10021

ASA Film *(212) 741-2329* 191 Seventh Ave NY, NY 10011

Audio Visual *(201) 899-4342* 111 Midstreams Pl Brick, NJ 08724

B Video *(212) 489-0721* 333 W 52nd St NY, NY 10019

Balton Productions *(212) 557-9834* 310 E 46th St NY, NY 10017

Beckman, Michael *(212) 620-0933* 140 W 16th St NY, NY 10011

Biles, Kevin Design *(212) 206-1717* 5 E 16th St NY, NY 10003

Boltax Associates *(212) 687-0963* 230 E 44th St NY, NY 10017

Brainstorm *(212) 686-1580* 220 E 23rd St NY, NY 10010

Brett Productions Inc *(212) 876-2515* 1641 Third AVe NY, NY 10128

Broad Street Productions *(212) 480-8031* 50 Broad St NY, NY 10004

Budget Entertainment
(718) 490-2496 1396 Coney Island Ave Brooklyn, NY 11230

Burton Productions *(212) 420-1100* 36 E 12th St NY, NY 10003

c - d

Cailor/Resnick *(212) 977-4300* 237 W 54th St NY, NY 10019

Camera Control *(212) 505-9227* 227 E 44th St NY, NY 10017

Caribiner Inc *(212) 541-5300* 16 W 61st St NY, NY 10023

Cerutti Productions *(212) 956-6400* 720 Fifth Ave NY, NY 10019

Cinema Arts *(212) 246-2860* 333 W 52nd St NY, NY 10019

Cinemaker Inc *(212) 595-7327* 1974 Broadway NY, NY 10023

Cipoletti, John *(718) 332-8868* 1229 Ave Y Brooklyn, NY 11235
PAGE 27

Circle Project *(212) 807-1096* 230 W 13th St NY, NY 10011

Coane, Porsche & Quinn *(212) 686-5566* 40 W 27th St NY, NY 10001

Coleman Productions *(212) 947-0937* 330 W 42nd St NY, NY 10036

Concepts Unlimited *(212) 246-9612* 315 W 57th St NY, NY 10019

Connors Productions *(212) 807-0966* 242 W 27th St NY, NY 10001

Corporate Theatre *(212) 213-0800* 15 W 26th St NY, NY 10010

Cortez/Seidner Inc *(212) 753-6600* 227 E 56th St NY, NY 10022

Cote Productions (212) 242-4065 152 W 25th St NY, NY 10001

Craven Film Corp (212) 463-7190 5 W 19th St NY, NY 10011

Creative Media Concepts (212) 995-5080 304 Park Ave So NY, NY 10010

Critical Image Ltd (212) 594-2586 4 W 37th St NY, NY 10018

Cutting Edge (212) 799-2174 115 W 88th St NY, NY 10024

DeVries Films (212) 580-2888 100 Riverside Dr NY, NY 10024

Dimension Co (212) 724-5952 67 W 83rd St NY, NY 10024

Dimension Productions Inc (212) 725-3840 217 E 31st St NY, NY 10016

Dokumenta (212) 246-3699 322 W 57th St NY, NY 10019

Donath Communications (212) 289-4134 401 E 88th St NY, NY 10128

Double HH Productions (212) 687-1312 300 E 40th St NY, NY 10016

Druck, Mark Productions (212) 682-5980 300 E 40th St NY, NY 10016

Duncan & Katz (212) 460-5545 21 E 4th St NY, NY 10003

e - g

East West Films (212) 593-6188 211 E 51st St NY, NY 10022

Effective Communications Arts
(212) 333-5656 221 W 57th St NY, NY 10019

Electric Film (212) 925-3429 87 Lafayette St NY, NY 10013

Exploration Inc (212) 370-9191 304 E 45th St NY, NY 10017

Eye View Film (212) 772-3190 420 E 81st St NY, NY 10028

Famavision (718) 273-1780 2750 Richmond Terrace Staten Isl, NY 10303

Fast Forward (914) 684-0555 30 Virginia Rd White Plains, NY 10603

Feldman Small Associates (212) 505-8888 623 Broadway NY, NY 10012

Film Friends (212) 929-7728 16 E 17th St NY, NY 10011

Fiorentino, Imero (212) 246-0600 44 W 63rd St NY, NY 10023

Fireside Entertainment (212) 769-1950 1 Lincoln Pl NY, NY 10023

Fischer Films (718) 852-2643 28 Verandah Pl Brooklyn, NY 11201

Flamingo Films (212) 594-0880 71 W 35th St NY, NY 10001

Foothill Productions (212) 877-0973 70 W 83rd St NY, NY 10024

Fraker Productions (212) 752-4422 919 Third Ave NY, NY 10022

Frame Accurate (212) 977-9100 601 W 50th St NY, NY 10019

Fred/Alan Inc (212) 586-6333 16 W 61st St NY, NY 10023

Friedman, Marvin (718) 858-5374 283 Henry St Brooklyn, NY 11201

Furious Films (718) 789-7058 260 Hall St Brooklyn, NY 11205

Fusion Media (212) 529-4100 611 Broadway NY, NY 10012

Garland Coporate (212) 481-3838 381 Park Ave So NY, NY 10016

Gindick Productions (212) 725-2580 21 E 40th St NY, NY 10016

Giraldi, Frank Studios (212) 840-8225 34 W 39th St NY, NY 10018

Gittelman Film Associates (212) 889-9140 112 E 36th St NY, NY 10016

Global Concepts (203) 227-7555 70 Birch Hill Rd Weston, CT 06883

GLYN/NET Inc (212) 560-6980 356 W 58th St NY, NY 10019

Gold Productions (212) 759-8785 300 E 51st St NY, NY 10022

Gold, Steve (212) 463-7660 156 Fifth Ave NY, NY 10010

Goodchild/Solomon (212) 645-5272 1123 Broadway NY, NY 10010

Gorilla Films (212) 840-3938 165 W 47th St NY, NY 10036

Goulding-Elliot/Greybar Productions Inc
(212) 867-9014 420 Lexington Ave NY, NY 10170

Graphic Media (201) 540-1597 373 Rte 46 West Fairfield, NJ 07006

Greenwood Productions (212) 265-7060 347 W 55th St NY, NY 10019

Gries Cinema (718) 544-6637 150-62 Jewel Ave Flushing, NY 11367

h - k

Halcyon Days Production (212) 686-8744 102 E 30th St NY, NY 10016

Hans Film Productions (212) 382-1280 25 W 38th St NY, NY 10018

Harrison Productions (212) 683-1850 200 E 36th St NY, NY 10016

Hav-Cam Inc (212) 749-3673 752 West End Ave NY, NY 10025

Hirschenson Productions (212) 757-7662 16 W 55th St NY, NY 10019

Hirschfield Productions Inc (212) 686-9320 9 E 40th St NY, NY 10016

Hodge, David Productions (212) 245-3623 935 Eighth Ave NY, NY 10019

Horizon Studio Inc (212) 725-3840 217 E 31st St NY, NY 10016

Hunnewell Productions (212) 529-5888 24 E 23rd St NY, NY 10010

ICM Films (212) 832-0909 211 E 51st St NY, NY 10022

Image Zone (212) 924-8804 19 W 21st St NY, NY 10010

Impact Entertainment Inc (212) 594-6834 330 W 42nd St NY, NY 10036

In Focus Productions (212) 371-3338 123 E 54th St NY, NY 10022

Independent Visions (212) 255-4047 220 W 19th St NY, NY 10011

Intergroup Productions (212) 832-8169 300 E 59th St NY, NY 10022

International Media (201) 756-4060 718 Sherman Ave Plainfield, NJ 07060

Jalbert Productions (516) 351-5878 7 Bouton Rd Lloyd Harbor, NY 11743

Jones, Lee (201) 489-3229 150 Overlook Ave Hackensack, NJ 07601

JPC Video (212) 223-0555 11 E 47th St NY, NY 10017

Kalamar Productions (212) 254-8400 928 Broadway NY, NY 10010

Katz Associates (212) 683-8130 109 E 29th St NY, NY 10016

Katz, Max Productions Inc (212) 988-1957 315 E 65th St NY, NY 10021

Keating & Duffy (212) 695-3126 1220 Broadway NY, NY 10001

Killiam Shows Archives (212) 679-8230 6 E 39th St NY, NY 10016

l - m

Lachman, Wayne (212) 861-0366 111 E 65th St NY, NY 10021

Lancit Media (212) 977-9100 601 W 50th St NY, NY 10019

Lane Pictures (212) 840-6355 35 W 45th St NY, NY 10036

Lanin, Howard Productions *(212) 752-0960* 59 E 54th St NY, NY 10022

Leland Co, The *(212) 633-0100* 121 W 27th St NY, NY 10001

Leodas & Arbusto *(212) 213-4992* 124 E 37th St NY, NY 10016

Levenson Productions Ltd *(212) 752-7415* 919 Third Ave NY, NY 10022

Levine & Associates *(212) 683-7177* 31 E 28th St NY, NY 10016

Libonati, Ed Productions *(212) 582-1660* 353 W 46th St NY, NY 10036

Licata International *(212) 645-5050* 31 W 21st St NY, NY 10010

Lindberg Productions *(212) 719-2060* 49 W 46th St NY, NY 10036

Lipson Film Associates *(212) 505-6800* 58-60 E 13th St NY, NY 10003

LNS Productions *(718) 698-3001* 527 Third Ave NY, NY 10016

Loebel Productions *(203) 798-8754* Precision Rd Danbury , CT 06810

Lorcott Productions Inc *(212) 744-4465* 255 W 26th St NY, NY 10001

Lupano Productions *(212) 463-0300* 151 W 25th St NY, NY 10001

Macaluso, Susan *(718) 426-8606* 37-55 77th St Jackson Hghts, NY 11372

Manhattan Film/ Tape *(212) 254-8700* 907 Broadway NY, NY 10010

Mansfield Inc *(212) 832-3030* 8 E 48th St NY, NY 10017

Markle & Associates *(212) 246-8642* 630 Ninth Ave NY, NY 10036

Marro, Stephen *(212) 463-0397* 121 W 19th St NY, NY 10011

Martin, Bill Productions *(212) 645-9550* 110 W 17th St NY, NY 10011

Martin, Steve Productions *(212) 953-1825* 141 E 44th St NY, NY 10017

Matlin Productions *(212) 247-7741* 515 W 59th St NY, NY 10019

Maysles Films *(212) 582-6050* 250 W 54th St NY, NY 10019

Mazin-Wyckoff Productions *(212) 475-4366* 36 E 12th St NY, NY 10003

McGaune Studio *(212) 582-8925* 36 Horatio St NY, NY 10014

Media Arts *(212) 865-8156* 925 West End Ave NY, NY 10025

Meridien Productions *(212) 925-7275* 121 Wooster St NY, NY 10012

Metro 2000 *(212) 764-3570* 15 W 38th St NY, NY 10017

MG Productions *(212) 688-1455* 26 E 64th St NY, NY 10022

Michels, Dennis Associates *(212) 529-5080* 77 Bleecker St NY, NY 10021

Mirage, C.S. Productions *(212) 410-2888* 1675 York Ave NY, NY 10128

Morton, Jack Productions *(212) 758-8400* 830 Third Ave NY, NY 10022

MRC Films & Video *(212) 989-1754* 71 W 23rd St NY, NY 10010

Muppet Meeting Films *(212) 794-2400* 117 E 69th St NY, NY 10021

NBE Productions Ltd *(212) 685-8963* 202 E 35th St NY, NY 10016

New Media Service *(212) 674-1300* 49 E 21st St NY, NY 10010

Noh Hands Productions *(212) 674-4833* 323 E 18th St NY, NY 10003

Normandy Film Group *(212) 684-6192* 88 Lexington Ave NY, NY 10016

o - r

Onyx Films *(212) 769-2153* 202 W 81st St NY, NY 10024

Owen Electric Pictures *(212) 924-5570* 355 E 86th St NY, NY 10028

Pariseau/Edwards *(212) 633-0600* 236 W 26th St NY, NY 10001

Pauliny Productions *(212) 947-2965* 316 Fifth Ave NY, NY 10001

PCS Film Productions *(212) 697-2765* 12 E 46th St NY, NY 10017

PDR Prodcutions *(212) 986-2020* 219 E 44th St NY, NY 10017

Petersen Communications *(212) 752-0500* 40 E 49th St NY, NY 10017

Pfeffer Film *(718) 268-1818* 138-04 76th Ave Kew Gardens Hills, NY 11367

Producers East *(516) 420-5680* 535 Broadhollow Rd Melville, NY 11747

Production Place *(212) 661-8893* 307 E 44th St NY, NY 10017

Professional Video *(212) 683-3615* 115 E 34th St NY, NY 10016

Prometheus Productions *(212) 677-2140* 110 E 23rd St NY, NY 10010

Puopolo Productions *(212) 725-4830* 381 Park AVe So NY, NY 10016

R/Greenberg, Associates *(212) 239-6767* 350 W 39th St NY, NY 10018

Rain Forest Films *(718) 279-0273* 188-12 Northern Blvd Flushing, NY 11358

Rapid Deployment Films *(212) 608-6005* 46 Ann St NY, NY 10038

Riso, Adrian Associates Ltd *(212) 288-6650* 166 E 66th St NY, NY 10021

RKL Productions *(212) 302-0985* 56 W 45th St NY, NY 10036

Roberts Productions *(212) 883-1030* 310 Madison Ave NY, NY 10017

Ross Productions *(212) 986-5122* 310 E 46th St NY, NY 10017

s

Santandrea Productions *(212) 599-1555* 34 E 39th St NY, NY 10016

Satellite *(914) 576-2554* 38 Centre Ave New Rochelle, NY 10801

Scene East Productions *(212) 226-6525* 153 Mercer St NY, NY 10012

Seagull Productions *(212) 989-1631* 42 W 12th St NY, NY 10011

Sell Pictures Inc *(212) 683-9221* 210 Fifth Ave NY, NY 10010

September Productions *(212) 473-9595* 5 E 22nd St NY, NY 10010

Sheridan Elson *(212) 239-2000* 20 W 37th St NY, NY 10018

Shooter's Productions Inc *(212) 983-5205* 140 E 39th St NY, NY 10016

Shooting Star TV & Film *(212) 399-7773* 159 W 53rd St NY, NY 10019

Silver, Tony Films Inc *(212) 826-6336* 242 E 58th St NY, NY 10022

Silvermine Films *(212) 582-4056* 315 W 57th St NY, NY 10019

Sloan Kasell H/E *(212) 819-1717* 16 W 46th St NY, NY 10036

SMA Video *(212) 226-7474* 84 Wooster St NY, NY 10012

Smiling Cat Productions *(212) 725-0610* 230 E 27th St NY, NY 10016

Smith & Co *(212) 818-1888* 227 E 44th St NY, NY 10017

Snow, Phoebe *(212) 481-8001* 37 W 26th St NY, NY 10010

Spalla Video Productions *(212) 765-4646* 301 W 45th St NY, NY 10036

Spectrum Associates Inc *(212) 563-1680* 536 W 29th St NY, NY 10001

Spikol Pictures *(212) 505-6519* 175 Fifth Ave NY, NY 10010

Stone, Richard *(212) 725-0555* 381 Park Ave So NY, NY 10016

Stone/Mansfield *(212) 725-0555* 381 Park Ave So NY, NY 10016

t - z

TAKE THREE PRODUCTIONS *(212) 687-3344* 141 E 44th St NY, NY 10017

TALAN, LEN & ASSOCIATES *(212) 868-1694* 484 W 43rd St NY, NY 10036

TEEMAN/SLEPPIN *(212) 243-7836* 147 W 26th St NY, NY 10001

TELETECHNIQUES INC *(212) 206-1475* 1 W 19th St NY, NY 10011

TELETIME VIDEO *(212) 288-1765* 117 Cutter Mill Rd Great Neck, NY 11021

TOBIN PRODUCTIONS *(212) 724-6869* 300 E 42nd St NY, NY 10017

TRIDENT COMMUNICATION *(212) 243-4412* 48 W 21st St NY, NY 10010

UN PRODUCTIONS INC *(201) 567-5102* 130 Engle St Englewood, NJ 07631

US TELEVISION *(212) 684-2333* 175 E 62nd St NY, NY 10021

VERDI & ASSOCIATES *(212) 888-1829* 400 E 56th St NY, NY 10022

VIDEO PLANNING *(212) 582-5066* 325 W 56th St NY, NY 10019

VIDEOGRAF *(212) 242-7871* 144 W 27th St NY, NY 10001

VIDEOWARE CORPORATION *(212) 399-3811* 727 Eleventh Ave NY, NY 10019

VORKAPICH/LIPSON INC *(212) 505-6800* 58-60 E 13th St NY, NY 10003

WADE, ROGER *(212) 575-9111* 15 W 44th St NY, NY 10036

WALZ, KEN PRODUCTIONS INC *(212) 826-6010* 219 E 60th St NY, NY 10022

WARNER, ROBERT PRODUCTIONS *(212) 744-7979* 7 E 78th St NY, NY 10021

WASHINGTON PLACE *(212) 929-4730* 108 Washington Pl NY, NY 10014

WELEBIT PRODUCTIONS *(212) 490-2801* 310 E 44th St NY, NY 10017

WHITMAN PRODUCTIONS *(212) 750-8788* 160 E 56th St NY, NY 10022

WILLIAM/GERARD *(212) 265-8800* 888 Seventh Ave NY, NY 10019

WOLL & ASSOCIATES *(212) 245-3555* 18 W 55th St NY, NY 10019

WORKING PICTURES *(212) 633-0808* 156 Fifth Ave NY, NY 10011

YOUNG, DICK PRODUCTIONS *(212) 787-8954* 118 Riverside Dr NY, NY 10024

YOUNG, GARY ASSOCIATES INC
(212) 674-1087 35 E 20th St NY, NY 10003

Z-CO ENTERPRISES *(212) 410-0882* 355 E 86th St NY, NY 10028

ZACKS & PERRIER *(212) 463-7300* 96 Morton St NY, NY 10014

FILM REPS

a - z

ALETA *(212) 410-4367* 224 E 95th St NY, NY 10128

BLOCK FILM GROUP *(212) 989-3535* 1 Union Sq W NY, NY 10003

BOOT PRODUCTIONS *(212) 688-1140* 919 Third Ave NY, NY 10022

CLAIRE, PATRICIA ASSOCIATES *(212) 633-0022* 160 Fifth Ave NY, NY 10010

COLEMAN, WENDY *(212) 505-5260* 230 E 15th St NY, NY 10003

COMMERICAL ARTISTS *(212) 353-1103* 156 Fifth Ave NY, NY 10011

COVINGTON, BROOKE *(212) 645-9070* 1133 Broadway NY, NY 10010

DIRECTING ARTISTS *(212) 759-0700* 236 E 62nd St NY, NY 10021

DUBIN, MORTY *(212) 206-6400* 155 W 23rd St NY, NY 10011

HAYES & CO *(212) 755-8888* 777 Third Ave NY, NY 10017

ICED TEA PRODUCTIONS *(212) 557-8185* 307 E 37th St NY, NY 10016

INDEPENDENT ARTISTS *(212) 765-4640* 16 W 56th St NY, NY 10019

JACOBS, NANCY *(212) 650-0388* 1274 First Ave NY, NY 10021

LANDES, DEBORAH *(212) 751-9044* 141 E 55th St NY, NY 10022

NAITONE, JOHN *(212) 644-6334* 301 E 48th St NY, NY 10017

PIPHER/FOX PICTURES *(212) 688-1140* 919 Third Ave NY, NY 10022

SHOOTING STARS *(212) 888-8999* 9 E 47th St NY, NY 10017

SILBERMAN PRODUCTIONS *(212) 787-2787* 137 W 74th St NY, NY 10023

SOIREF, BARBARA *(212) 517-5877* 254 E 68th St NY, NY 10021

STOGO, DON *(212) 490-1034* 310 E 46th St NY, NY 10017

STOLTZ & PARTNERS *(212) 744-5333* 502 LaGuardia NY, NY 10012

TRIPLE VISION *(212) 772-0007* 262 E 78th St NY, NY 10021

TURNER, LAURIE *(212) 246-9260* 850 Seventh Ave NY, NY 10019

VANDERMEER, MARK *(212) 929-7474* 250 First Ave NY, NY 10019

WARREN, ANN & ASSOCIATES *(212) 877-5403* 155 W 68th St NY, NY 10023

ZACCARO, JIM & ASSOCIATES *(212) 744-4000* 116 E 78th St NY, NY 10021

DIRECTOR OF PHOTOGRAPHY REPS

a - z

CHERIFF, STACY *(212) 243-0419* 445 W 23rd St NY, NY 10011

CINEMACRAFT *(212) 475-3410* 1 University Pl NY, NY 10003

DATTNER & ASSOCIATES *(212) 684-7529* 10 Waterside Pl NY, NY 10010

FRIEDMAN, JILL *(212) 722-3322* 65 E 96th St NY, NY 10128

GERSH AGENCY *(212) 977-1818* 130 W 42nd St NY, NY 10036

RICHARD REPS *(212) 966-8410* 225 Lafayette NY, NY 10012

OFF LINE

a - b

29TH STREET VIDEO INC *(212) 594-7530* 339 W 29th St NY, NY 10001

A CUT ABOVE EDITORIAL *(212) 661-4949* 17 E 45th St NY, NY 10017

ADM VIDEO *(516) 484-6900* 40 Seaview Blvd Port Washington, NY 11050

ADWAR VIDEO CORP *(516) 785-1200* 2370 Merrick Rd Bellmore, NY 11710

Alba/Editorial ***(212) 967-7345*** **330 W 42nd St NY, NY 10036**

PAGE 19

Altschuler & Co *(212) 790-4813* 1180 Sixth Ave NY, NY 10036

American Video Channels Inc *(212) 765-6324* 321 W 44th St NY, NY 10036

Animated Video *(212) 265-2942* 1600 Broadway NY, NY 10019

ANS International Video *(212) 736-1007* 396 Fifth Ave NY, NY 10018

Apollo & Assoc Production *(212) 489-8433* 619 W 54th St NY, NY 10019

Aquarius Transfer Ltd *(212) 581-0123* 12 E 46th St NY, NY 10017

Araness Communications *(212) 582-6246* 244 W 49th St NY, NY 10019

Arkay Video *(201) 725-3003* 25 S Main St Manville, NJ 08835

Artel Video Inc *(212) 315-5665* 1600 Broadway NY, NY 10019

August Films *(212) 582-7025* 321 W 44th St NY, NY 10036

Backstreet Edit *(212) 684-5001* 49 W 27th St NY, NY 10001

BC Video Productions *(212) 242-4065* 152 W 25th St NY, NY 10001

Bert's Place *(212) 682-5891* 141 E 44th St NY, NY 10017

BNS Video Service *(212) 223-0909* 527 W 36th St NY, NY 10018

c

C & C Visual Ltd *(212) 684-3830* 225 W 44th St NY, NY 10036

Caesar Video Graphics *(212) 684-7673* 137 E 25th St NY, NY 10010

Carob Video *(212) 957-9525* 250 W 57th St NY, NY 10019

Carob Video South *(212) 925-3440* 8 Beach St NY, NY 10013

Centerlight Television *(212) 929-4745* 245 W 19th St NY, NY 10011

Charles, Michael *(212) 953-2490* 6 E 45th St NY, NY 10017

Chung Group, The *(212) 832-0530* 11 E 47th St NY, NY 10017

Cine Metric Inc *(212) 532-4140* 290 Madison Ave NY, NY 10017

Cine Tape Inc *(212) 355-0700* 241 E 51st St NY, NY 10022

Cine-Vid *(212) 704-4000* 25 W 45th St NY, NY 10036

Cinema Arts Associates Inc *(212) 246-2860* 333 W 52nd St NY, NY 10019

City Lights Productions *(212) 564-9106* 505 Eighth Ave NY, NY 10018

Color Leasing Studios *(212) 662-2655* 330 Route 46 E Fairfield, NJ 07006

Com/Tech Communication *(212) 826-2935* 770 Lexington Ave NY, NY 10021

Connors Productions *(212) 807-0966* 242 W 27th St NY, NY 10001

Creative Services *(212) 573-9269* 708 Third Ave NY, NY 10017

Creative Ways *(212) 935-0145* 305 E 46th St NY, NY 10017

Crescent Cutters Inc *(212) 687-2802* 304 E 45th St NY, NY 10017

Crew Cuts *(212) 371-4545* 9 E 47th St NY, NY 10017

Cutting Edge Editorial *(212) 599-4233* 420 Lexington Ave NY, NY 10017

d - e

DC Video *(212) 431-1646* 270 Lafayette St NY, NY 10012

Dee's, David Even-Time *(212) 764-4700* 62 W 45th St NY, NY 10036

DeKart Video *(212) 219-9240* 133 Chrystie St NY, NY 10002

Dell, Jeff Film Service *(212) 371-7915* 241 E 51st St NY, NY 10022

Devlin Video Services *(212) 391-1313* 1501 Broadway NY, NY 10036

DJM Films and Tape *(212) 687-0111* 4 E 46th St NY, NY 10017

Du Art Video *(212) 757-3681* 245 W 55th St NY, NY 10019

DWJ Associates Inc *(212) 684-4000* 295 Madison Ave NY, NY 10017

East End *(212) 489-1865* 513 W 54th St NY, NY 10019

Editing Concepts *(212) 980-3340* 214 E 50th St NY, NY 10022

Editing House, The *(212) 286-0666* 304 E 45th St NY, NY 10017

Editing Machine *(212) 757-5420* 630 Ninth Ave NY, NY 10036

Editor's Hideaway *(212) 661-3850* 219 E 44th St NY, NY 10017

Editors *(212) 317-0862* 220 E 48th St NY, NY 10017

Editors Corner *(212) 535-8668* 415 E 71st St NY, NY 10021

Editors Film Service ***(212) 371-0862*** 220 E 48th St NY, NY 10017

PAGE 25

Editors Gas Video Inc *(212) 832-6690* 16 E 48th St NY, NY 10017

Electric Film *(212) 925-3429* 87 Lafayette St NY, NY 10013

Electronic Arts Intermix *(212) 473-6822* 10 Waverly Pl NY, NY 10003

Electronic Cutting Room *(212) 334-8464* 200 W 51st St NY, NY 10019

Encore Teleproductions *(203) 268-7487* 600 Main St Monroe, CT 06468

Ettinger Video *(212) 226-8489* 4 White St NY, NY 10013

f - k

Famavision *(718) 273-1780* 2750 Richmond Terrace Staten Isl, NY 10303

Film-Rite Inc *(212) 575-6801* 1185 Sixth Ave NY, NY 10036

Film/Video Arts *(212) 673-9361* 817 Broadway NY, NY 10003

Filmbillders *(212) 683-4004* 10 E 40th St NY, NY 10016

Filmpower *(212) 286-0666* 304 E 45th St NY, NY 10017

Finamore, Doanld P *(212) 582-5265* 619 W 54th St NY, NY 10019

First Edition/Composite Films *(212) 838-3044* 5 E 47th St NY, NY 10017

Frame Accurate *(212) 977-9100* 601 W 50th St NY, NY 10019

Framerunner *(212) 874-1730* 1995 Broadway NY, NY 10023

G.B.S. Video *(212) 463-8863* 44 W 24th St NY, NY 10010

Goodchild/Solomon *(212) 645-5272* 1123 Broadway NY, NY 10010

Grenadier Productions *(212) 687-2638* 141 E 44th St NY, NY 10017

Ground Control Video *(212) 683-5455* 49 W 27th St NY, NY 10001

Harvey's Place *(212) 688-5510* 919 Third Ave NY, NY 10022

Hayes Film Editing *(212) 683-5080* 9 E 40th St NY, NY 10016

Horn/Eisenberg *(212) 391-8166* 16 W 46th St NY, NY 10036

Hudson Editorial *(212) 840-3860* 25 W 43rd St NY, NY 10036

Intercontinental Televideo Inc

(212) 719-0202 29 W 38th St NY, NY 10018

International Video *(212) 730-1411* 1501 Broadway NY, NY 10036

Invision Productions *(201) 414-8833* 360 Glenwood Ave E Orange, NJ 07017

J & D Laboratories *(212) 691-5613* 12 W 21st St NY, NY 10010

Jones & Associates *(212) 753-9015* 248 E 48th St NY, NY 10017

JPC Video *(212) 223-0555* 11 E 47th St NY, NY 10017

Jubin, Robert Ltd *(212) 319-4747* 11 E 47th St NY, NY 10017

Jupiter Editorial Services *(212) 460-5600* 201 E 16th St NY, NY 10003

KCC Audio/Video *(212) 228-3063* 31 Bond St NY, NY 10012

Koko-Baz Inc *(212) 627-3803* 28 W 25th St NY, NY 10010

Kopel Films *(212) 757-4742* 930 9th Ave NY, NY 10036

KTV Consultants *(212) 223-0520* 226 E 54th St NY, NY 10022

l - n

L & D Film/Video *(212) 315-0410* 630 Ninth Ave NY, NY 10036

Language & Motion *(212) 489-1865* 513 W 54th St NY, NY 10019

Longwood Video *(212) 741-3733* 32 W 22nd St NY, NY 10010

LRP Video *(212) 759-0822* 3 Dag Hammarskjold Plaza NY, NY 10017

Mabli, Richard *(212) 686-3047* 37 W 26th St NY, NY 10010

Magno Sound & Video Inc *(212) 302-2505* 729 Seventh Ave NY, NY 10019

Mandelbaum, Len *(212) 362-6973* 165 West End Ave NY, NY 10023

Manhattan Video *(212) 683-6565* 12 W 27th St NY, NY 10001

Markle & Associates *(212) 246-8642* 630 Ninth Ave NY, NY 10036

Matrix Video *(212) 265-8500* 727 Eleventh Ave NY, NY 10019

Maysles Films *(212) 582-6050* 250 W 54th St NY, NY 10019

Mazin-Wyckoff *(212) 475-4366* 36 E 12th St NY, NY 10003

Messina Editorial *(212) 481-3456* 18 E 41st St NY, NY 10017

Morty's Film Services *(212) 696-5040* 10 E 40th St NY, NY 10016

MRC Films & Video *(212) 989-1754* 71 W 23rd St NY, NY 10010

MS Editorial *(212) 333-7590* 200 W 57th St NY, NY 10019

MTI/Compugraph Inc *(212) 355-0510* 885 Second Ave NY, NY 10017

Multi Video Group Ltd *(212) 986-1577* 50 E 42nd St NY, NY 10017

MVP Martin *(212) 283-5237* 458 W 144th St NY, NY 10031

Myrik, Ron Productions *(212) 685-0726* 34 E 29th St NY, NY 10016

National Video Industries Inc *(212) 691-1300* 15 W 17th St NY, NY 10011

NBC Telesales *(212) 664-4754* 30 Rockefeller Plaza NY, NY 10112

NEP Productions *(212) 382-1100* 56 W 45th St NY, NY 10036

New Atlantic Productions *(212) 967-1690* 330 W 42nd St NY, NY 10036

NJN Productions *(201) 648-3928* 980 Broad St Newark, NJ 7102

Northeast Video Inc *(212) 661-8830* 420 Lexington Ave NY, NY 10017

Northstar Video *(212) 337-3200* 581 Sixth Ave NY, NY 10011

o - s

Oasis Film & Tape *(212) 983-3131* 141 E 44th St NY, NY 10017

Off-Line Video *(212) 695-7417* 251 W 30th St NY, NY 10001

On Track Video *(212) 645-2040* 124 W 24th St NY, NY 10011

Otterson TV Inc *(212) 695-6178* 251 W 30th St NY, NY 10001

Palace Production Ctr *(203) 853-1740* 29 N Main St S Norwalk, CT 06854

Palestrini Editing *(212) 752-3348* 477 Madison Ave NY, NY 10022

Panavideo *(212) 725-2211* 248 E 35th St NY, NY 10016

PAT Film & Video Services *(212) 247-0900* 630 Ninth Ave NY, NY 10036

Pelco Editorial *(212) 319-3348* 757 Third Ave NY, NY 10017

PEM Inc *(516) 420-5680* 535 Broadhollow Rd Melville, NY 11747

Phantasmagoria *(212) 586-4890* 630 Ninth Ave NY, NY 10036

Photosonic Editing Inc *(212) 599-4233* 420 Lexington NY, NY 10017

Picsonic Productions *(212) 575-1910* 25 W 45th St NY, NY 10036

Pineyro Film & Video Services *(212) 627-0707* 19 W 21st St NY, NY 10010

Post Time Ltd *(212) 661-2727* 219 E 44th St NY, NY 10017

Power Post Production Inc *(212) 840-3860* 25 W 43rd St NY, NY 10036

PrimaLux Video *(212) 206-1402* 30 W 26th St NY, NY 10010

Princzko Productions *(212) 683-1300* 9 E 38th St NY, NY 10016

Quark Video *(212) 807-8504* 421 Hudson St NY, NY 10014

R.G. Video *(212) 997-1464* 21 W 46th St NY, NY 10036

Rafik *(212) 475-7884* 814 Broadway NY, NY 10003

Rainbow Network *(516) 328-6710* 35 N. Tyson Ave Floral Pk, NY 11001

Rebo Associates *(212) 989-9466* 530 W 25th St NY, NY 10001

Rosebud Productions *(212) 983-3131* 141 E 44th St NY, NY 10017

Rosenberg Video Services *(212) 744-1111* 308 E 79th St NY, NY 10021

Ross-Gaffney Inc *(212) 719-2744* 21 W 46th St NY, NY 10036

RVI *(212) 685-4000* 137 E 25th St NY, NY 10010

S G Video *(212) 972-2280* 211 E 43rd St NY, NY 10017

S/R Video Labs *(201) 224-6676* 77 Rt 5 Edgewater, NJ 07020

Salamandra Images *(212) 779-0707* 6 E 39th St NY, NY 10016

Silver, Tony Films Inc *(212) 826-6336* 242 E 58th St NY, NY 10022

Sound Concepts *(203) 888-6712* 80 Great Hill Rd Seymour , CT 06483

Spalla Video Productions *(212) 765-4646* 301 W 45th St NY, NY 10036

Splice Is Nice *(212) 599-1711* 141 E 44th St NY, NY 10017

Stone Cutters *(212) 421-9404* 422 Madison Ave NY, NY 10017

Studio 7 *(212) 977-7700* 1697 Broadway NY, NY 10019

Synapse Telecommunications *(212) 370-9191* 304 E 45th St NY, NY 10017

Synchrofilm Services *(212) 719-2966* 72 W 45th St NY, NY 10036

Synesthetics *(212) 431-4112* 58 Walker St NY, NY 10013

t - z

Take Three Productions *(212) 687-3344* 141 E 44th St NY, NY 10017

Tapehouse *(212) 557-4949* 216 E 45th St NY, NY 10017

Tapestry Productions *(212) 677-6007* 924 Broadway NY, NY 10010

Teatown Video Inc *(212) 302-0722* 165 W 46th St NY, NY 10036

Technisphere Corp *(212) 777-5100* 29 E 19th St NY, NY 10003

Telstar Editing *(212) 730-1000* 29 W 38th St NY, NY 10018

Traiman Associates Inc *(212) 889-3400* 160 Madison Ave NY, NY 10016

Transcom Digital *(212) 529-1000* 902 Broadway NY, NY 10010

Transvideo Broadcast *(212) 265-4141* 506 West 57th St NY, NY 10019

Tulchin Studios/Directors *(212) 986-8270* 240 E 45th St NY, NY 10017

TVC Video Inc *(212) 599-1616* 225 E 43rd St NY, NY 10017

UN Productions Inc *(201) 567-5102* 130 Engle St Englewood, NJ 07631

Unitel Video Inc *(212) 265-3600* 515 W 57th St NY, NY 10019

Uptown Edit *(212) 580-2075* 21 W 86th St NY, NY 10024

Valkhn Film & Video ***(212) 586-1603*** 1600 Broadway NY, NY 10019

PAGE 21

VCA Teletronics *(212) 355-1600* 231 E 55th St NY, NY 10022

Video 35 *(212) 864-1408* 254 W 98th St NY, NY 10025

Video Center of NJ *(201) 935-0900* 228 Park Ave E Rutherford, NJ 07073

Video Deal Productions *(212) 645-3790* 5 W 20th St NY, NY 10011

Video Team Inc *(212) 629-8010* 522 W 36th St NY, NY 10018

Videogenix of NY *(212) 925-0445* 503-511 Broadway NY, NY 10012

Videolife Productions *(212) 620-0146* 17 W 20th St NY, NY 10011

Videotime International *(212) 477-6011* 41 E 7th St NY, NY 10003

Vidlo Video *(212) 475-4140* 40 E 21st St NY, NY 10010

Wachter Editorials *(212) 399-7770* 159 W 53rd St NY, NY 10019

Wechsler Group *(212) 787-8699* 185 West End Ave NY, NY 10023

West, J Inc *(212) 685-2863* 114 E 32nd St NY, NY 10016

Westbrook Film Svc *(212) 254-9561* 118 E 25th St NY, NY 10010

Wiliams, Billy Editing *(212) 753-8250* 231 E 51st St NY, NY 10022

World Cinevision *(212) 265-4587* 321 W 44th St NY, NY 10036

ON LINE

a - c

29th Street Video Inc *(212) 594-7530* 339 W 29th St NY, NY 10001

ADM Video *(516) 484-6900* 40 Seaview Blvd Port Washington, NY 11050

Aerial Image Video Services *(212) 279-6026* 875 Sixth Ave NY, NY 10001

All Mobile Video *(212) 757-8919* 630 Ninth Ave NY, NY 10036

American Video Channels *(212) 765-6324* 321 W 44th St NY, NY 10036

Animated Video *(212) 265-2942* 1600 Broadway NY, NY 10019

ANS Internatonal Video *(212) 736-1007* 396 Fifth Ave NY, NY 10018

Artel Video *(212) 315-5665* 1600 BRoadway NY, NY 10019

AT & T Post *(201) 829-8788* 60 Columbia Trnpk Morristown, NJ 07960

August Films *(212) 582-7025* 321 W 44th St NY, NY 10036

C & C Visual Ltd *(212) 684-3830* 225 W 44th St NY, NY 10036

Carob Video *(212) 957-9525* 250 W 57th St NY, NY 10019

Carob Video South *(212) 925-3440* 8 Beach St NY, NY 10013

Ceasar Video Graphics *(212) 684-7673* 137 E 25th St NY, NY 10010

Centerlight Television *(212) 929-4745* 245 W 19th St NY, NY 10011

Chung Group, The *(212) 832-0530* 11 E 47th St NY, NY 10017

Cine Tape *(212) 355-0700* 241 E 51st St NY, NY 10022

Cine-Vid Post Production *(212) 704-4000* 25 W 45th St NY, NY 10036

City Lights Productions *(212) 564-9106* 505 8th Ave NY, NY 10018

Color Leasing Studios *(212) 662-2655* 330 Route 46 E Fairfield, NJ 07006

Com/Tech *(212) 826-2935* 770 Lexington Ave NY, NY 10021

Communications Plus *(212) 686-9570* 360 Park Ave So NY, NY 10010

Creative Services *(212) 573-9269* 708 Third Ave NY, NY 10017

Creative Ways *(212) 935-0145* 305 E 46th St NY, NY 10017

CVS Inc *(212) 684-7114* 137 E 25th St NY, NY 10010

d - j

DeKart Video *(212) 219-9240* 133 Chrystie St NY, NY 10002

Dell, Jeff Film Service *(212) 371-7915* 241 E 51st St NY, NY 10022

Devlin Video Services *(212) 391-1313* 1501 Broadway NY, NY 10036

Du Art Video *(212) 757-3681* 245 W 55th St NY, NY 10019

Editing House, The *(212) 286-0666* 304 E 45th St NY, NY 10017

Editor's Hideaway *(212) 661-3850* 219 E 44th St NY, NY 10017

Electric Film *(212) 925-3429* 87 Lafayette St NY, Ny 10013

Electronic Cutting Room *(212) 334-8464* 200 W 51st St NY, NY 10019

Empire Video Inc *(212) 687-2060* 216 E 45th St NY, NY 10017

Encore Teleproductions *(203) 268-7487* 600 Main St Monroe, CT 06468

Ettinger Video *(212) 226-8489* 4 White St NY, NY 10013

Famavision *(718) 273-1780* 2750 Richmond Terrace Staten Isl, NY 10303

Filmbillders *(212) 683-4004* 10 E 40th St NY, NY 10016

First Edition/Composite Films *(212) 838-3044* 5 E 47th St NY, NY 10017

Framerunner *(212) 874-1730* 1995 Broadway NY, NY 10023

G.B.S. Video *(212) 463-8863* 44 W 24th St NY, NY 10010

HD TV Enterprises Inc *(212) 874-4524* 228 W 71st St NY, NY 10023

Horn/Eisenberg *(212) 391-8166* 16 W 46th St NY, NY 10036

Image Mix *(212) 752-3010* 305 E 46th St NY, NY 10017

International Production Ctr

(212) 582-6530 514 W 57th St NY, NY 10019

J & D Laboratories *(212) 691-5613* 12 W 21st St NY, NY 10010

k - o

KCC Audio/Video *(212) 228-3063* 31 Bond St NY, NY 10012

KTV Consultants *(212) 223-0520* 226 E 54th St NY, NY 10022

Liberty Studios *(212) 532-1865* 238 E 26th St NY, NY 10010

Longwood Video Inc *(212) 741-3733* 32 W 22nd St NY, NY 10010

LRP Video *(212) 759-0822* 3 Dag Hammarskjold Pl NY, NY 10017

Magno Sound & Video Inc *(212) 302-2505* 729 Seventh Ave NY, NY 10019

Manhattan Transfer *(212) 687-4000* 545 Fifth Ave NY, NY 10017

Matrix Video *(212) 265-8500* 727 Eleventh Ave NY, NY 10019

Modern Telecommunications Inc

(212) 355-0510 885 Second Ave NY, NY 10017

Multi Video Group Ltd *(212) 986-1577* 50 E 42nd St NY, NY 10017

MVP Martin *(212) 283-5237* 458 W 144th St NY, NY 10031

Myrvik, Ron Productions *(212) 685-0726* 34 E 29th St NY, NY 10016

National Video Industries Inc *(212) 691-1300* 15 W 17th St NY, NY 10011

NBC Telesales *(212) 664-4754* 30 Rockefeller Plaza NY, NY 10112

NEP Productions *(212) 382-1100* 56 W 45th St NY, NY 10036

Nexus Productions *(212) 679-2180* 10 E 40th St NY, NY 10016

NJN Productions *(201) 648-3928* 980 Broad St Newark, NJ 07102

Northeast Video Inc *(212) 661-8830* 420 Lexington Ave NY, NY 10017

Northstar Video *(212) 337-3200* 581 Sixth Ave NY, NY 10011

On Track Video *(212) 645-2040* 124 W 24th St NY, NY 10011

Otterson TV Inc *(212) 695-6178* 251 W 30th St NY, NY 10001

p - s

Palace Production *(203) 853-1740* 29 N Main St S Norwalk, CT 06854

Palestrini Editing *(212) 752-3348* 477 Madison Ave NY, NY 10022

Panavideo *(212) 725-2211* 248 E 35th St NY, NY 10016

PEM Inc *(516) 420-5680* 535 Broadhollow Rd Melville, NY 11747

Picsonic Productions *(212) 575-1910* 25 W 45th St NY, NY 10036

Post Perfect *(212) 972-3400* 220 E 42nd St NY, NY 10017

PrimaLux Video *(212) 206-1402* 30 W 26th St NY, NY 10010

Princzko Productions *(212) 683-1300* 9 E 38th St NY, NY 10016

Quark Video *(212) 807-8504* 421 Hudson St NY, NY 10014

R.G. Video *(212) 997-1464* 21 W 46th St NY, NY 10036

Rainbow Network *(516) 328-6710* 35 N Tyson Ave Floral Pk, NY 11001

Rebo Associates *(212) 989-9466* 530 W 25th St NY, NY 10001

Rosenberg Video Service *(212) 744-1111* 308 E 79th St NY, NY 10021

Ross-Gaffney Inc *(212) 719-2744* 21 W 46th St NY, NY 10036

Rutt Video *(212) 685-4000* 137 E 25th St NY, NY 10010

Sound Concepts *(203) 888-6712* 80 Great Hill Rd Seymour , CT 06483

Splice Is Nice *(212) 599-1711* 141 E 44th St NY, NY 10017

Stone Cutters *(212) 421-9404* 422 Madison Ave NY, NY 10017

Studio 7 *(212) 977-7700* 1697 Broadway NY, NY 10019

Stylianou Productions Inc *(212) 687-5708* 301 Madison Ave NY, NY 10017

Synapse Telecommunications *(212) 370-9191* 304 E 45th St NY, NY 10017

Synchrofilm Services *(212) 719-2966* 72 W 45th St NY, NY 10036

t - z

Tapehouse *(212) 557-4949* 216 E 45th St NY, NY 10017

Tapestry Productions *(212) 677-6007* 924 Broadway NY, NY 10010

Teatown Video Inc *(212) 302-0722* 165 W 46th St NY, NY 10036

Technisphere Corp *(212) 777-5100* 29 E 19th St NY, NY 10003

Telstar Editing *(212) 730-1000* 29 W 38th St NY, NY 10018

Today Video Inc *(212) 391-1020* 45 W 45th St NY, NY 10036

Traiman Associates Inc *(212) 889-3400* 160 Madison NY, NY 10016

Transcom Digital *(212) 529-1000* 902 Broadway NY, NY 10010

Transvideo Broadcast *(212) 265-4141* 506 W 57th St NY, NY 10019

Trident Communication *(212) 243-4412* 48 W 21st St NY, NY 10010

Tulchin Studios Directors *(212) 986-8270* 240 E 45th St NY, NY 10017

TVC Video *(212) 599-1616* 225 E 43rd St NY, NY 10017

UN Productions Inc *(201) 567-5102* 130 Engle St Englewood, NJ 07631

Unitel Video Inc *(212) 265-3600* 515 W 57th St NY, NY 10019

VCA Teletronics *(212) 355-1600* 231 E 55th St NY, NY 10022

PAGE 1

Video Center of NJ *(201) 935-0900* 228 Park Ave E Rutherford, NJ 07073

Video Team Inc *(212) 629-8010* 522 W 36th St NY, NY 10018

Videogenix *(212) 925-0445* 503-511 Broadway NY, NY 10012

West, J Inc *(212) 685-2863* 114 E 32nd St NY, NY 10016

FILM EDITORS

a - e

A Cut Above Editorial Inc *(212) 661-4949* 17 E 45th St NY, NY 10017

Ani-Live Film Service *(212) 983-1918* 222 E 46th St NY, NY 10017

Apollo & Assoc Production *(212) 489-8433* 619 W 54th St NY, NY 10019

Araness Communications Inc *(212) 582-6246* 244 W 49th St NY, NY 10019

Backstreet Edit *(212) 684-5001* 49 W 27th St NY, NY 10001

Bender Editorial *(212) 867-1515* 27 E 39th St NY, NY 10016

Bert's Place *(212) 682-5891* 141 E 44th St NY, NY 10017

Canarick's Co Ltd *(212) 972-1015* 50 E 42nd St NY, NY 10017

Charles, Michael *(212) 953-2490* 6 E 45th St NY, NY 10017

Cine Tape Inc *(212) 355-0070* 241 E 51st St NY, NY 10022

City Lights Productions *(212) 564-9106* 505 Eighth Ave NY, NY 10018

Creative Visual *(201) 585-1847* 2175 LeMoine Ave Ft. Lee, NJ 07024

Crescent Cutters Inc *(212) 687-2802* 304 E 45th St NY, NY 10017

Crew Cuts *(212) 371-4545* 9 E 47th St NY, NY 10017

Cutting Edge Editorial *(212) 599-4233* 420 Lexington Ave NY, NY 10017

Dee's, David Even-Time *(212) 764-4700* 62 W 45th St NY, NY 10036

Deitch, Edward Inc *(212) 245-3395* 300 W 55th St NY, NY 10019

Dell, Jeff Film Service *(212) 371-7915* 241 E 51st St NY, NY 10022

DJM Films *(212) 687-0111* 4 E 46th St NY, NY 10017

East End *(212) 489-1865* 513 W 54th St NY, NY 10019

Editing Concepts *(212) 980-3340* 214 E 50th St NY, NY 10022

Editing House, the *(212) 286-0666* 304 E 45th St NY, NY 10017

Editing Machine *(212) 757-5420* 630 Ninth Ave NY, NY 10036

Editors Corner *(212) 535-8668* 415 E 71st St NY, NY 10021

Editors Film Service *(212) 371-0862* 220 E 48th St NY, NY 10017

PAGE 25

Editors Gas Video Inc *(212) 832-6690* 16 E 48th St NY, NY 10017

f - l

Feldman Films *(212) 371-2330* 252 E 51st St NY, NY 10022

Film-Rite *(212) 575-6801* 1185 Sixth Ave NY, NY 10036

Filmpower *(212) 286-0666* 304 E 45th St NY, NY 10017

Finamore, Donald P *(212) 582-5265* 619 W 54th St NY, NY 10019

Fine Cut Post Production *(212) 869-8198* 16 W 45th St NY, NY 10036

First Edition/Composite Films *(212) 838-3044* 5 E 47th St NY, NY 10017

Gold, Jay Films Inc *(212) 687-7171* 342 Madison Ave NY, NY 10173

Grenadier Productions *(212) 687-2638* 141 E 44th St NY, NY 10017

Ground Control Video *(212) 683-5455* 49 W 27th St NY, NY 10001

Grove, Eric Film *(212) 242-7447* 32 W 22nd St NY, NY 10010

Harvey's Place *(212) 688-5510* 919 Third Ave NY, NY 10022

Hayes Film Editing *(212) 683-5080* 9 E 40th St NY, NY 10016

Horn/Eisenberg *(212) 391-8166* 16 W 46th St NY, NY 10036

Hudson Editorial *(212) 840-3860* 25 W 43rd St NY, NY 10036

Invision Productions *(201) 414-8833* 360 Glenwood Ave E Orange, NJ 07017

JPC Video *(212) 223-0555* 11 E 47th St NY, NY 10017

Jubin Ltd *(212) 319-4747* 11 E 47th St NY, NY 10017

L & D Film/Video *(212) 315-0410* 630 Ninth Ave NY, NY 10036

Landa, Saul Inc *(212) 877-5553* 35 W 87th St NY, NY 10024

Language & Motion *(212) 489-1865* 513 W 54th St NY, NY 10019

LFR Editorial Inc *(212) 682-5950* 20 E 46th St NY, NY 10017

LM Communications *(212) 283-2509* 60 Hamilton Terrace NY, NY 10031

m - q

Mabli, Richard *(212) 686-3047* 37 W 26th St NY, NY 10010

Manahattan Transfer *(212) 687-4000* 545 Fifth Ave NY, NY 10017

Mandelbaum, Len *(212) 362-6973* 165 West End Ave NY, NY 10023

Messina Editorial *(212) 481-3456* 18 E 41st St NY, NY 10017

Morty's Film Services *(212) 696-5040* 10 E 40th St NY, NY 10016

MRC Films & Video *(212) 989-1754* 71 W 23rd St NY, NY 10010

MS Editorial *(212) 333-7590* 200 W 57th St NY, NY 10019

Multi Video Group Ltd *(212) 986-1577* 50 E 42nd St NY, NY 10017

Myrvik, Ron Productions *(212) 685-0726* 34 E 29th St NY, NY 10016

Negative Matchers Inc *(212) 354-4180* 45 W 45th St NY, NY 10036

Oasis Film & Tape *(212) 983-3131* 141 E 44th St NY, NY 10017

Palestrini Editing *(212) 752-3348* 477 Madison Ave NY, NY 10022

PAT Video/Film Services *(212) 247-0900* 630 Ninth Ave NY, NY 10036

PDR Productions Inc *(212) 986-2020* 219 E 44th St NY, NY 10017

Pelco Editorial *(212) 319-3348* 757 Thrid Ave NY, NY 10017

PEM Inc *(516) 420-5680* 535 Broadhollow Rd Melville, NY 11747

Phantasmagoria *(212) 586-4890* 630 Ninth Ave NY, NY 10036

Photosonic Editing Inc *(212) 599-4233* 420 Lexington Ave NY, NY 10017

Pineyro Film & Video Services *(212) 627-0707* 19 W 21st St NY, NY 10010

Power Post Production Inc *(212) 840-3860* 25 W 43rd St NY, NY 10036

r - z

Reflections XXII *(212) 247-5370* 263 W 54th St NY, NY 10019

Rich Enterprises Corp *(212) 685-0040* 15 W 26th St NY, NY 10010

Rosebud Productions *(212) 983-3131* 141 E 44th St NY, NY 10017

Ross-Gaffney Inc *(212) 719-2744* 21 W 46th St NY, NY 10036

S G Video *(212) 972-2280* 211 E 43rd St NY, NY 10017

Salamandra Images *(212) 779-0707* 6 E 39th St NY, NY 10016

Sandpiper Editorial Service *(212) 921-1570* 50 W 40th St NY, NY 10018

Schultz Inc *(212) 972-2579* 211 E 43rd St NY, NY 10017

Silver, Tony Films Inc *(212) 826-6336* 242 E 58th St NY, NY 10022

Sommerschield, Bengt *(212) 686-3149* 333 E 30th St NY, NY 10016

Sound Concepts *(203) 888-6712* 80 Great Hill Rd Seymour, CT 06483

Spalla Video Productions *(212) 765-4646* 301 W 45th St NY, NY 10036

Spectrum Associates Inc *(212) 563-1680* 536 W 29th St NY, NY 10001

Splice Is Nice *(212) 599-1711* 141 E 44th St NY, NY 10017

Startmark *(212) 371-7915* 241 E 51st St NY, NY 10022

Stone Cutters *(212) 421-9404* 422 Madison Ave NY, NY 10017

Stylianou Productions Inc *(212) 687-5708* 301 Madison Ave NY, NY 10017

Synapse Telecommunications *(212) 370-9191* 304 E 45th St NY, NY 10017

Synchrofilm Services *(212) 719-2966* 72 W 45th St NY, NY 10036

Take 5 Editorial Service *(212) 759-7404* 681 Lexington Ave NY, NY 10022

Take Three Productions *(212) 687-3344* 141 E 44th St NY, NY 10017

Traiman Associates Inc *(212) 889-3400* 160 Madison Ave NY, NY 10016

Valkhn Film & Video *(212) 586-1603* 1600 Broadway NY, NY 10019

PAGE 21

Wachter Editorials *(212) 319-7770* 159 W 53rd St NY, NY 10019

Wechsler Group *(212) 787-8699* 185 West End Ave NY, NY 10023

Westbrook Film Service *(212) 254-9561* 118 E 25th St NY, NY 10010

Williams, Billy Editing *(212) 753-8250* 231 E 51st St NY, NY 10022

World Cinevision *(212) 265-4587* 321 W 44th St NY, NY 10036

DUPLICATIONS

a - i

ADM Video *(516) 484-6900* 40 Seaview Blvd Pt Washington, NY 11050

Aerial Image Video Services *(212) 279-6026* 875 Sixth Ave NY, NY 10001

All Mobile Video Inc *(212) 757-8919* 630 Ninth Ave NY, NY 10036

American TV Video *(212) 688-6222* 248 E 48th St NY, NY 10017

American Video Channels *(212) 765-6324* 321 W 44th St NY, NY 10036

Animated Video *(212) 265-2942* 1600 Broadway NY, NY 10019

ANS International Video *(212) 736-1007* 396 Fifth Ave NY, NY 10018

Aquarius Transfer *(212) 581-0123* 12 E 46th St NY, NY 10017

Audio Plus Video *(201) 767-3800* 240 Pegasus Ave Northvale, NJ 07647

C & C Visual *(212) 869-4900* 225 W 44th St NY, NY 10036

Carob Video South *(212) 925-3440* 8 Beach St NY, NY 10013

Centerlight Television *(212) 929-4745* 245 W 19th St NY, NY 10011

Cine Magnetics Video *(212) 542-0700* 50 W 40th St NY, NY 10018

Cine-Vid Post Production *(212) 704-4000* 25 W 45th St NY, NY 10036

Cutting Edge Editorial *(212) 599-4233* 420 Lexington Ave NY, NY 10017

CVS Inc *(212) 684-7114* 137 E 25th St NY, NY 10010

Devlin Video Servcies *(212) 391-1313* 1501 Broadway NY, NY 10036

DJM Films Inc *(212) 687-0111* 4 E 46th St NY, NY 10017

Editing Concepts Prints, Inc *(212) 697-9630* 216 E 45th St NY, NY 10017

GLOBE VIDEO SERVICES INC *(212) 695-6868* 286 Fifth Ave NY, NY 10001

IIIDB VIDEO SPECIALISTS *(212) 677-6856* 121 E 24th St NY, NY 10010

IMAGE MIX *(212) 752-3010* 305 E 46th St NY, NY 10017

INTERCONTINENTAL *(212) 719-0202* 29 W 38th St NY, NY 10018

INTERNATIONAL VIDEO *(212) 730-1411* 1501 Broadway NY, NY 10036

j - q

J & D LABORATORIES *(212) 691-5613* 12 W 21st St NY, NY 10010

JONES & ASSOCIATES *(212) 753-9015* 248 E 48th St NY, NY 10017

JSL VIDEO SERVICES INC *(212) 575-5082* 25 W 45th St NY, NY 10036

LANDYVISION *(212) 734-1402* 400 E 83rd St NY, NY 10028

MAGNO SOUND & VIDEO INC *(212) 302-2505* 729 Seventh Ave NY, NY 10019

MEDIATECH EAST *(212) 463-8300* 216 W 18th St NY, NY 10011

MGS VIDEO SERVICES *(212) 765-4500* 619 W 54th St NY, NY 10019

MOONLIGHT *(212) 245-6630* 1600 Broadway NY, NY 10019

MTI/COMPUGRAPH *(212) 355-0510* 885 Second Ave NY, NY 10017

MULTI-VIDEO GROUP LTD *(212) 986-1577* 50 E 42nd St NY, NY 10017

MVP MARTIN *(212) 283-5237* 458 W 144th St NY, NY 10031

NATIONAL VIDEO CENTER *(212) 279-2000* 460 W 42nd St NY, NY 10036

NORTHEAST VIDEO INC *(212) 661-8830* 420 Lexington Ave NY, NY 10017

ON TRACK VIDEO *(212) 645-2040* 124 W 24th St NY, NY 10011

PANAVIDEO *(212) 725-2211* 248 E 35th St NY, NY 10016

PDR PRODUCTIONS INC *(212) 986-2020* 219 E 44th St NY, NY 10017

PELCO PRINTS INC *(212) 319-3348* 757 Third Ave NY, NY 10017

PICSONIC PRODUCTIONS *(212) 575-1910* 25 W 45th St NY, NY 10036

QUARK VIDEO *(212) 807-8504* 421 Hudson St NY, NY 10014

R G VIDEO *(212) 719-2744* 21 W 46th St NY, NY 10036

RAFIK *(212) 475-7884* 814 Broadway NY, NY 10003

REBO ASSOCIATES *(212) 989-9466* 530 W 25th St NY, NY 10001

REILLY VIDEO *(212) 463-0058* 508 W 26th St NY, NY 10001

RVI/RUTT VIDEO INC *(212) 685-4000* 137 E 25th St NY, NY 10010

s - z

SYNAPSE TELECOMMS INC *(212) 370-9191* 304 E 45th St NY, NY 10017

SYNCROFILM SERVICES INC *(212) 719-2966* 72 W 45th ST NY, NY 10036

TELETECHNIQUES INC *(212) 206-1475* 1 W 19th St NY, NY 10011

TFI *(212) 708-0500* 619 W 54th St NY, NY 10019

TODAY VIDEO INC *(212) 391-1020* 45 W 45th St NY, NY 10036

TRANSVIDEO BROADCAST *(212) 265-4141* 506 W 57th St NY, NY 10019

TV-R/MASTERCOLOR *(212) 541-4030* 333 W 52nd St NY, NY 10019

TVC VIDEO *(212) 599-1616* 225 E 43rd St NY, NY 10017

TYLIE JONES/EAST *(212) 753-9015* 248 E 48th St NY, NY 10017

UN PRODUCTIONS INC *(201) 567-5102* 130 Engle St Englewood, NJ 07631

UNITEL VIDEO *(212) 265-3600* 515 W 57th St NY, NY 10019

VCA TELETRONICS *(212) 355-1600* 231 E 55th St NY, NY 10022

PAGE 1

VIDEO CASSETTE TRANSFERS *(212) 575-8433* 1501 Broadway NY, NY 10036

VIDEO CENTRAL INC *(212) 947-6960* 225 W 36th St NY, NY 10018

VIDEO DUB INC *(212) 757-3300* 423 W 55th St NY, NY 10019

VIDEOPLUS *(201) 892-7400* 1131 Bay Ave Point Pleasant, NJ 08742

VIDEOWORKS INC *(212) 869-2500* 24 W 40th St NY, NY 10018

PAGE 29

WINDSOR VIDEO *(212) 944-9090* 8 W 38th St NY, NY 10018

WINKLER VIDEO ASSOCIATES *(212) 753-9300* 248 E 48th St NY, NY 10017

TRANSFERS

a - z

ADM VIDEO *(516) 484-6900* 40 Seaview Blvd Pt Washington, NY 11050

ALL CHANNELS VIDEO INC *(212) 247-3428* 630 Ninth Ave NY, NY 10036

AMERICAN TV VIDEO *(212) 688-6222* 248 E 48th St NY, NY 10017

AMERICAN VIDEO CHANNELS *(212) 765-6324* 321 W 44th St NY, NY 10036

AQUARIUS TRANSFER LTD *(212) 581-0123* 12 E 46th St NY, NY 10017

AUDIO PLUS VIDEO *(201) 767-3800* 240 Pegasus Ave Northvale, NJ 07647

CINE MAGNETICS VIDEO *(212) 542-0700* 50 W 40th St NY, NY 10018

CINE-VID *(212) 704-4000* 25 W 45th St NY, NY 10036

DEVLIN VIDEO SERVICES *(212) 391-1313* 1501 Broadway NY, NY 10036

EDITEL *(212) 867-4600* 222 E 44th St NY, NY 10017

IMAGE MIX *(212) 752-3010* 305 E 46th St NY, NY 10017

INTERCONTINENTAL *(212) 719-0202* 29 W 38th St NY, NY 10018

JSL VIDEO SERVICES INC *(212) 575-5082* 25 W 45th St NY, NY 10036

LANDYVISION *(212) 734-1402* 400 E 83rd St NY, NY 10028

LRP VIDEO *(212) 759-0822* 3 Dag Hammarskjold PL NY, NY 10017

MAGNO SOUND & VIDEO INC *(212) 302-2505* 729 Seventh Ave NY, NY 10019

MANHATTAN TRANSFER/EDIT INC *(212) 687-4000* 545 Fifth Ave NY, NY 10017

MOONLIGHT *(212) 245-6630* 1600 Broadway NY, NY 10019

MTI/COMPUGRAPH *(212) 355-0510* 885 Second Ave NY, NY 10017

NATIONAL VIDEO CENTER *(212) 279-2000* 460 W 42nd St NY, NY 10036

ON TRACK VIDEO *(212) 645-2040* 124 W 24th St NY, NY 10011

OTTERSON TV INC *(212) 695-6178* 251 W 30th St NY, NY 10001

PICSONIC *(212) 575-1910* 25 W 45th St NY, NY 10036

POSITIVE TRANSFER LTD *(212) 888-2722* 605 Fifth Ave NY, NY 10017

Quark Video *(212) 807-8504* 421 Hudson St NY, NY 10014

R.G. Video *(212) 719-2744* 21 W 46th St NY, NY 10036

Rebo Associates *(212) 989-9466* 530 W 25th St NY, NY 10001

Spectrum Light Productions *(212) 477-0346* 208 E 21st St NY, NY 10010

Synapse Telecomms, Inc *(212) 370-9191* 304 E 45th St NY, NY 10017

Tapehouse *(212) 557-4949* 216 E 45th St NY, NY 10017

Tapestry Productions *(212) 677-6007* 924 Broadway NY, NY 10010

TFI *(212) 708-0500* 619 W 54th St NY, NY 10019

Today Video Inc *(212) 391-1020* 45 W 45th St NY, NY 10036

TV-R/Mastercolor Transfer *(212) 541-4030* 333 W 52nd St NY, NY 10019

TVC Video *(212) 599-1616* 225 E 43rd St NY, NY 10017

VCA Teletronics *(212) 355-1600* 231 E 55th St NY, NY 10022

PAGE 1

Video Dub Inc *(212) 757-3300* 423 W 55th St NY, NY 10019

Videoefx *(212) 541-9220* 321 W 44th St NY, NY 10036

Videotime International *(212) 477-6011* 41 E 7th St NY, NY 10003

VideoWorks Inc *(212) 869-2500* 24 W 40th St NY, NY 10018

PAGE 29

Windsor Video *(212) 944-9090* 8 W 38th St NY, NY 10018

SPFX FILM
a - z

Actors Make-up Studio *(212) 719-3772* 165 W 47th St NY, NY 10036

Alfie & Associates *(212) 983-2686* 222 E 44th St NY, NY 10017

American Film Animation *(212) 563-5720* 151 W 28th St NY, NY 10001

APA Studios *(212) 929-9436* 230 W 10th St NY, NY 10014

Associates & Ferren *(516) 537-7800* Wainscott NW Rd Wainscott, NY 11975

Balsmeyer & Everett *(212) 627-3430* 230 W 17th St NY, NY 10011

Broadcast Arts Inc *(212) 254-5400* 632 Broadway NY, NY 10012

Brooklyn Model Works
(718) 834-1944 60 Washington Ave Brooklyn, NY 11205

Charlex *(212) 719-4600* 2 W 45th St NY, NY 10036

Cimmelli *(914) 356-2232* 120 No Pascack Rd Spring Valley, NY 10977

Cipoletti, John *(718) 332-8868* 1229 Ave Y Brooklyn, NY 11235

PAGE 27

Cynosure Films *(212) 245-1648* 630 Ninth Ave NY, NY 10036

D'Andrea Productions Inc *(212) 593-0077* 20 E 49th St NY, NY 10017

DeFilippo, Dom Studio Inc *(212) 986-5444* 215 E 37th St NY, NY 10016

Doros Animations Studio Inc *(212) 627-7220* 156 Fifth Ave NY, NY 10010

Editel/New York *(212) 867-4600* 222 E 44th St NY, NY 10017

EFEX Specialists *(718) 937-2417* 35-39 37th St LIC, NY 11101

EFX Unlimited Inc *(212) 541-9220* 321 W 44th St NY, NY 10036

Empireffects *(212) 757-8898* 311 W 43rd St NY, NY 10036

EXO Graphics *(212) 840-3222* 28 W 39th St NY, NY 10018

Fantastic Animation *(212) 697-2525* 12 E 46th St NY, NY 10017

Film Opticals *(212) 697-4744* 144 E 44th St NY, NY 10017

Franz, Bob *(201) 384-8039* Box 422 Bergenfield, NJ 07621

Gati, John Film Effects Inc
(212) 582-9060 154 W 57th St NY, NY 10019

Globus Brothers Stages *(212) 243-1000* 44 W 24th St NY, NY 10010

Greenberg, R Associates Inc *(212) 239-6767* 350 W 39th St NY, NY 10018

Grossman Brothers *(212) 925-1965* 19 Crosby St NY, NY 10013

Holographic Laserland *(212) 686-9397* 240 E 26th St NY, NY 10010

JPC Visuals *(212) 223-0555* 11 E 47th St NY, NY 10017

Maniatis, Michael *(212) 620-0398* 48 W 22nd St NY, NY 10010

Rossiter & Co *(914) 359-8884* 490 Piermont St Piermont, NY 10968

Select Effects *(212) 869-3988* 14 W 45th St NY, NY 10036

Wallach Enterprises *(212) 966-1970* 419 Broome St NY, NY 10013

Zeller International *(212) 627-7676* Main St Box Z Downsville, NY 13755

STOCK FOOTAGE

a - z

ALDEN FILMS *(201) 462-3522* Stage Coach Rd Freehold, NJ 07728

AMERICAN MUSEUM NATURAL HISTORY

(212) 769-5421 CPW & 79th St NY, NY 10024

ARCHIVE FILM PRODUCTIONS ***(212) 620-3955*** 530 W 25th ST NY, NY 10001

PAGE 28

BNS VIDEO SERVICE *(212) 223-0909* 527 W 36th St NY, NY 10018

BROADCAST NEWS SERVICE *(212) 223-0909* 527 W 36th St NY, NY 10018

CBS *(212) 975-2834* 524 W 57th St NY, NY 10019

CHERTOK ASSOCIATES *(212) 874-0797* 185 West End Ave NY, NY 10023

COE FILM ASSOCIATES *(212) 831-5355* 65 E 96th St NY, NY 10128

DARINO FILMS/THE LIBRARY OF SPECIAL EFFECTS

(212) 228-4024 222 Park Ave So NY, NY 10003

ENERGY PRODUCTIONS *(212) 505-5260* 230 E 15th St NY, NY 10003

FILM SEARCH *(212) 532-0600* 232 Madison Ave NY, NY 10016

FILMS INC *(914) 667-0800* 35 South West St Mt. Vernon, NY 10550

HALCYON DAYS PRODUCTIONS *(212) 686-8744* 102 E 30th St NY, NY 10016

HEARST METROTONE NEWS *(212) 682-7690* 235 E 45th St NY, NY 10017

IMAGEWAYS *(212) 265-1287* 440 W 47th St NY, NY 10036

INTERNATIONAL MEDIA *(201) 756-4060* 718 Sherman Ave Plainfield, NJ 07060

IVY FILMS *(212) 382-0111* 165 W 46th St NY, NY 10036

JALBERT PRODUCTIONS *(516) 351-5878* 7 Bonton Rd Lloyd Harbor, NY 11743

KILLIAM SHOWS ARCHIVES *(212) 679-8230* 6 E 39th St NY, NY 10016

MAJOR LEAGUE BASEBALL PRODUCTIONS

(212) 921-8100 1212 Sixth Ave NY, NY 10036

MOVIETONE NEWS *(212) 408-8450* 460 W 54th St NY, NY 10019

NATIONAL HOCKEY LEAGUE SERVICES

(212) 921-8100 1212 Sixth Ave NY, NY 10036

NBC VIDEO NEWS *(212) 664-4444* 30 Rockefeller Plaza NY, NY 10012

NEWSREEL ACCESS SYSTEMS *(212) 826-2800* 150 E 58th St NY, NY 10155

NFL FILMS *(609) 778-1600* 330 Fellowship Rd Mt. Laurel, NJ 08054

PAN AM FILM LIBRARY *(212) 354-4180* 10 Prince Lane Westbury, NY 11590

PETRIFIED FILMS *(212) 242-5461* 430 W 14th St NY, NY 10014

PRELINGER ASSOCIATES *(212) 255-8866* 430 W 14th St NY, NY 10014

RICHTER, ROBERT *(212) 947-1395* 330 W 42nd St NY, NY 10036

SECOND LINE SEARCH *(212) 594-5544* 330 W 42nd St NY, NY 10036

SHERMAN GRINBERG *(212) 765-5170* 630 Ninth Ave NY, NY 10036

SPALLA, RICK *(212) 765-4646* 301 W 45th St NY, NY 10036

STREAMLINE FILM ARCHIVES *(212) 696-2616* 109 E 29th St NY, NY 10016

TIMESTEPS PRODUCTIONS *(201) 669-1930* 2 Glenside Dr W. Orange, NJ 07052

TRANSWORLD *(212) 254-0586* 2 Lexington Ave NY, NY 10010

UNIT ONE FILM PRODUCTIONS *(212) 865-6201* 540 W 114th St NY, NY 10025

VISNEWS INTERNATIONAL USA *(212) 698-4500* 630 Fifth Ave NY, NY 10111

WORLD WIDE TELEVISION NEWS *(212) 265-4520* 31 W 44th St NY, NY 10035

VIDEO FACILITIES

a - l

29TH ST VIDEO *(212) 594-7530* 339 W 29th St NY, NY 10001

ACTION PRODUCTIONS INC *(212) 684-4250* 14 E 39th St NY, NY 10016

ADM VIDEO *(516) 484-6900* 40 Seaview Blvd Pt Washington, NY 11050

ALL MOBILE VIDEO *(212) 757-8919* 630 Ninth Ave NY, NY 10036

AMERICAN VIDEO CHANNELS *(212) 765-6324* 321 W 44th St NY, NY 10036

BC VIDEO PRODUCTIONS *(212) 242-4065* 152 W 25th St NY, NY 10001

BROADWAY VIDEO *(212) 265-7600* 1619 Broadway NY, NY 10019

CAROB VIDEO *(212) 957-9525* 250 W 57th St NY, NY 10019

CAROB VIDEO SOUTH *(212) 925-3440* 8 Beach St NY, NY 10013

CBS Inc (212) 975-2234 524 W 57th St NY, NY 10019

Cine Studio Inc (212) 581-1916 241 W 54th St NY, NY 10019

Cine-Vid Post Production (212) 704-4000 25 W 45th St NY, NY 10036

Color Leasing Studios (212) 662-2655 330 Route 46 E Fairfield, NJ 07006

Communications Plus Video (212) 686-9570 360 Park Ave So NY, NY 10010

Creative Ways (212) 935-0145 305 E 46th St NY, NY 10017

CVS Inc (212) 684-7114 137 E 25th St NY, NY 10010

Du Art Video (212) 757-3681 245 W 55th St NY, NY 10019

Editel (212) 867-4600 222 E 44th St NY, NY 10017

Encore Teleproductions (203) 268-7487 600 Main St Monroe, CT 06468

Famavision (718) 273-1780 2750 Richmond Terrace Staten Isl, NY 10303

Fox Television (212) 246-4300 333 W 52nd St NY, NY 10019

Hav-Cam Inc (212) 749-3673 752 West End Ave NY, NY 10025

HBO Studio Productions (212) 512-7800 120A E 23rd St NY, NY 10010

Image Mix (212) 752-3010 305 E 46th St NY, NY 10017

Intercontinental (212) 719-0202 29 W 38th St NY, NY 10018

International Productions Center (212) 582-6530 514 W 57th St NY, NY 10019

Jubin, Robert Ltd (212) 319-4747 11 E 47th St NY, NY 10017

KCC Audio/Video (212) 228-3063 31 Bond St NY, NY 10012

Liberty Studios (212) 532-1865 238 E 26th St NY, NY 10010

Longwood Video (212) 741-3733 32 W 22nd St NY, NY 10010

LRP Video (212) 759-0822 3 Dag Hammarskjold Pl NY, NY 10017

m - z

Magno Sound & Video Inc (212) 302-2505 729 Seventh Ave NY, NY 10019

Manhattan Video (212) 683-6565 12 W 27th St NY, NY 10001

MTI/Compugraph (212) 355-0510 885 Second Ave NY, NY 10017

MVP Martin (212) 283-5237 458 W 144th St NY, NY 10031

National Video (212) 279-2000 460 W 42nd St NY, NY 10036

National Video Industries Inc (212) 691-1300 15 W 17th St NY, NY 10011

NBC Telesales (212) 664-4754 30 Rockefeller Pl NY, NY 10112

NEP Productions (212) 382-1100 56 W 45th St NY, NY 10036

NJN Productions (201) 648-3928 980 Broad St Newark, NJ 07102

Northstar Video (212) 337-3200 581 Sixth Ave NY, NY 10011

Panavideo (212) 725-2211 248 E 35th St NY, NY 10016

Post Perfect (212) 972-3400 220 E 42nd St NY, NY 10017

Princzko Productions (212) 683-1300 9 E 38th St NY, NY 10016

Producers East (516) 420-5680 535 Broadhollow Rd Melville, NY 11747

Quark Video (212) 807-5804 421 Hudson St NY, NY 10014

Rebo Associates (212) 989-9466 530 W 25th St NY, NY 10001

Rosenberg Video Services (212) 744-1111 308 E 79th St NY, NY 10021

Santandrea Productions (212) 599-1555 34 E 39th St NY, NY 10016

Silvercup Studios (718) 784-3390 45-25 21st St LIC, NY 11101

Studio 57 (212) 765-8183 1392 Sixth Ave NY, NY 10019

Studio 7 (212) 997-7700 1697 Broadway NY, NY 10019

Synapse Telecommunications (212) 370-9191 304 E 45th St NY, NY 10017

Sync Sound (212) 246-5580 450 W 56th St NY, NY 10019

Telstar Video (212) 689-1040 206 E 29th St NY, NY 10016

Today Video Inc (212) 391-1020 45 W 45th St NY, NY 10036

Transvideo (212) 265-4141 506 W 57th St NY, NY 10019

TVC Video Inc (212) 599-1616 225 E 43rd St NY, NY 10017

UN Productions Inc (201) 567-5102 130 Engle St Englewood, NJ 07631

Unitel Video Inc (212) 265-3600 515 W 57th St NY, NY 10019

VCA Teletronics (212) 355-1600 231 E 55th St NY, NY 10022

PAGE 1

Video Center of NJ (201) 935-0900 228 Park Ave E Rutherford, NJ 07073

Videolife Productions (212) 620-0146 17 W 20th St NY, NY 10011

VideoWorks Inc (212) 869-2500 24 W 40th St NY, NY 10018

PAGE 29

Windsor Video (212) 944-9090 8 W 38th St NY, NY 10018

WNET/Net Telecon (212) 560-2068 356 W 58th St NY, NY 10019

VIDEO PRODUCERS

a - d

1776 Productions (212) 736-1776 511 W 54th St NY, NY 10019

29th Street Video Inc (212) 594-7530 339 W 29th St NY, NY 10001

ACT Productions (212) 353-2900 24 E 21st St NY, NY 10010

Action Productions (212) 684-4250 14 E 39th St NY, NY 10016

ADM Video (516) 484-6900 40 Seaview Blvd Pt Washington, NY 11050

Advance Communications Intl (212) 691-5080 20 W 23rd St NY, NY 10010

Ailes Communications (212) 563-1970 456 W 43rd St NY, NY 10036

Altshuler & Co (212) 790-4813 1180 Sixth Ave NY, NY 10036

American Montage (212) 645-3791 5 W 20th St NY, NY 10011

Apollo & Assoc (212) 489-8433 619 W 54th St NY, NY 10019

ARC Films (212) 627-3336 7 W 18th St NY, NY 10011

Arkay Video (201) 725-3003 25 S Main St Manville, NJ 08835

B Video (212) 489-0721 333 W 52nd St NY, NY 10019

Baxter Films (212) 532-4700 260 Fifth Ave NY, NY 10001

BC Video Productions (212) 242-4065 152 W 25th St NY, NY 10001

Beckman Productions (212) 620-0933 140 W 16th St NY, NY 10011

Berner/Schlamme (212) 603-0609 1619 Broadway NY, NY 10019

BNS Video Service (212) 223-0909 527 W 36th St NY, NY 10018

Boltax Associates (212) 687-0963 230 E 44th St NY, NY 10017

Broadcast Arts (212) 254-5400 632 Broadway NY, NY 10012

Bunin Productions (212) 688-0759 30 E 60th St NY, NY 10022

Burton Productions (212) 420-1100 36 E 12th St NY, NY 10003

Caesar Video Graphics (212) 684-7673 137 E 25th St NY, NY 10010

Cailor/Resnick (212) 977-4300 237 W 54th St NY, NY 10019

Canarick's Co Ltd (212) 972-1015 50 E 42nd St NY, NY 10017

Carob Video (212) 957-9525 250 W 57th St NY, NY 10107

Charlex (212) 719-4600 2 W 45th St NY, NY 10036

Cinemakers Inc (212) 595-7327 1974 Broadway NY, NY 10023

City Lights Productions (212) 564-9106 505 8th Ave NY, NY 10018

Coane, Porsche & Quinn (212) 686-5566 40 W 27th St NY, NY 10001

Com/Tech Communication (212) 826-2935 770 Lexington Ave NY, NY 10021

Connors Productions (212) 807-0966 242 W 27th St NY, NY 10001

CVS Inc (212) 684-7114 137 E 25th St NY, NY 10010

DC Video (212) 431-1646 270 Lafayette NY, NY 10012

DeFilippo Studio Inc (212) 986-5444 215 E 37th St NY, NY 10016

DeKart Video (212) 219-9240 133 Chrystie St NY, NY 10002

Dimension Co (212) 724-5952 67 W 83rd St NY, NY 10024

Duncan & Katz (212) 460-5545 21 E 4th St NY, NY 10003

DWJ Associates Inc (212) 684-4000 295 Madison Ave NY, NY 10017

e - o

East-West Films (212) 593-6188 211 E 51st St NY, NY 10022

Editing Machine (212) 757-5420 630 Ninth Ave NY, NY 10036

Electric Film (212) 925-3529 87 Lafayette St NY, NY 10013

Electric Picture Works (212) 869-2500 24 W 40th St NY, NY 10018

Even-Time Ltd (212) 764-4700 62 W 45th St NY, NY 10036

Eye View Film Associates Inc (212) 772-3190 420 E 81st St NY, NY 10028

Famavision (718) 273-1780 2750 Richmond Terrace Staten Isl, NY 10303

Fast Forward (914) 684-0555 30 Virginia Rd White Plains, NY 10603

Fertik & Co (212) 877-3468 251 W 89th St NY, NY 10024

Field Productions (212) 477-9016 16 E 23rd St NY, NY 10010

Fischer Films (718) 852-2643 28 Verandah Pl Brooklyn, NY 11201

Fox Television (212) 246-4300 333 W 52nd St NY, NY 10019

Furious Films (212) 254-5508 57 E 11th St NY, NY 10003

G.B.S. Video (212) 463-8863 44 W 24th St NY, NY 10010

Globus Brothers (212) 243-1008 44 W 24th St NY, NY 10010

GLYN/NET Inc (212) 560-6980 356 W 58th St NY, NY 10019

Harrison Productions (212) 683-1850 200 E 36th St NY, NY 10016

Hav-Cam Inc (212) 749-3673 752 West End Ave NY, NY 10025

Horvath (212) 741-0300 95 Charles St NY, NY 10014

Hunnewell Group (212) 529-5888 24 E 23rd St NY, NY 10010

Intergroup Productions (212) 832-8169 300 E 59th St NY, NY 10022

Isaac Productions (212) 431-6160 180 Duane St NY, NY 10013

JC Productions Inc (212) 532-2820 14 E 39th St NY, NY 10016

JPC Video (212) 223-0555 11 E 47th St NY, NY 10017

Kingfish Video Productions (212) 925-8448 524 Broadway NY, NY 10012

Koko-Baz Inc (212) 627-3803 28 W 25th St NY, NY 10010

Levine, Richard Productions (212) 925-2020 594 Broadway NY, NY 10012

LM Communications (212) 283-2509 60 Hamilton Terrace NY, NY 10031

Lorcott Productions Inc (212) 744-4465 255 W 26th St NY, NY 10001

Manhattan Media (212) 769-1324 16 W 69th St NY, NY 10023

Mannes Production Group (212) 989-9267 10 E 31st St NY, NY 10003

Marshall Stone/Stone Paul Productions
(212) 677-0500 106 E 19th St NY, NY 10003

Matrix Video (212) 265-8500 727 Eleventh Ave NY, NY 10019

May Day Productions (212) 684-3555 115 E 38th St NY, NY 10016

Mercury Productions (212) 869-4073 7 W 18th St NY, NY 10011

Metro 2000 (212) 764-3570 15 W 38th St NY, NY 10017

MRC Films & Video (212) 989-1754 71 W 23rd St NY, NY 10010

Multi Video Group Ltd (212) 986-1577 50 E 42nd St NY, NY 10017

Myrvik, Ron Productions (212) 685-0726 34 E 29th St NY, NY 10016

NBC Telesales (212) 664-4754 30 Rockefeller Pl NY, NY 10112

NEP Productions (212) 382-1100 56 W 45th St NY, NY 10036

New Atlantic Productions (212) 967-1690 330 W 42nd St NY, NY 10036

On Track Video (212) 645-2040 124 W 24th St NY, NY 10011

p - z

Palace Productions (203) 853-1740 29 N Main St S Norwalk, CT 06854

Petrucelli, Tony Inc (212) 490-9269 300 E 40th St NY, NY 10016

Phoenix Communications (212) 921-8100 1212 Sixth Ave NY, NY 10036

Praxis Media (203) 853-1740 29 N Main St S. Norwalk, CT 06854

Producers East (516) 420-5680 535 Broadhollow Rd Melville, NY 11747

Professional Video (212) 683-3615 115 E 34th St NY, NY 10016

Prometheus Productions (212) 677-2140 110 E 23rd St NY, NY 10010

Randelman, Hal Productions (212) 686-8796 300 E 33rd St NY, NY 10016

Rebo Associates (212) 989-9466 530 W 25th St NY, NY 10001

Rosen, Peter Productions Inc (212) 535-8927 9 E 78th St NY, NY 10021

Sandbank Films (914) 747-2500 140 Old Saw Mill River Hawthorne, NY 10532

Santandrea Productions (212) 599-1555 34 E 39th St NY, NY 10016

Seti Video Communications (212) 764-7154 45 W 45th St NY, NY 10036

Sheridan-Elson (212) 239-2000 20 W 37th St NY, NY 10018

Shooting Star TV & Film (212) 399-7773 159 W 53rd St NY, NY 10019

SMA Video (212) 226-7474 84 Wooster St NY, NY 10012

Spectrum Associates Inc (212) 563-1680 536 W 29th St NY, NY 10001

Stiefel & Co (212) 645-0700 322 Eighth Ave NY, NY 10001

Stone, Richard (212) 725-0555 381 Park Ave So NY, NY 10016

Stone/Mansfield (212) 725-0555 381 Park Ave So NY, NY 10016

Studio 7 (212) 977-7700 1697 Broadway NY, NY 10019

Take Three Productions (212) 687-3344 141 E 44th St NY, NY 10017

Tapestry Productions (212) 677-6007 924 Broadway NY, NY 10010

Teletime Video (212) 288-1765 117 Cutter Mill Rd Great Neck, NY 11201

Transcom Digital (212) 529-1000 902 Broadway NY, NY 10010

Trident Communication (212) 243-4412 48 W 21st St NY, NY 10010

Tulchin Studios (212) 986-8270 240 E 45th St NY, NY 10017

UN Productions Inc (201) 567-5102 130 Engel St Englewood, NJ 07631

US Television (212) 684-2333 175 E 62nd St NY, NY 10021

Video Deal Productions (212) 645-3790 5 W 20th St NY, NY 10011

Video Marketplace (212) 736-1007 396 Fifth Ave NY, NY 10018

Video Planning (212) 582-5066 325 W 56th St NY, NY 10019

Video Team Inc (212) 629-8010 522 W 36th St NY, NY 10018

Videograf (212) 242-7871 144 W 27th St NY, NY 10001

Videography Productions Inc (212) 570-6888 353 E 76th St NY, NY 10021

Videolife Productions (212) 620-0146 17 W 20th St NY, NY 10011

Videoware Corporation (212) 399-3811 727 Eleventh Ave NY, NY 10019

Videowave (212) 971-6030 20 W 37th St NY, NY 10018

Vidlo Video Productions (212) 475-4140 40 E 21st St NY, NY 10011

PAGE 31

Visual Perspectives (212) 678-7555 298 Fifth Ave NY, NY 10018

Wallach Enterprises (212) 966-1970 419 Broome St NY, NY 10013

Washington Place (212) 929-4730 108 Washington Pl NY, NY 10014

Werwa Enterprises (212) 929-4456 144 W 27th St NY, NY 10001

WNET/Net Telecon (212) 560-2068 356 W 58th St NY, NY 10019

World Wide (212) 362-4440 1995 Broadway NY, NY 10023

Young, Gary Associates Inc (212) 674-1087 35 E 20th St NY, NY 10003

Zacks & Perrier (212) 463 7300 96 Morton St NY, NY 10014

Zodiac Video (212) 532-6016 12 W 27th St NY, NY 10001

MULTI MEDIA

a - l

Advance Commuications (212) 691-5080 20 W 32rd St NY, NY 10010

Albi, Dom Associates (212) 799-2202 251 W 92nd St NY, NY 10025

Audio Visual (201) 899-4342 111 Midstreams Pl Brick, NJ 08724

Biles, Kevin Design (212) 206-1717 5 E 16th St NY, NY 10003

Brainstorm Productions Inc (212) 686-1580 220 E 23rd St NY, NY 10010

C & K Studios (212) 997-1760 701 Seventh Ave NY, NY 10036

Caribiner Inc (212) 541-5300 16 W 61st St NY, NY 10023

Cine International (212) 370-5151 222 E 44th St NY, NY 10017

Concepts Unlimited (212) 246-9612 315 W 57th St NY, NY 10019

Contempo Communications (212) 247-4444 1841 Broadway NY, NY 10023

Corporate Theatre (212) 213-0800 15 W 26th St NY, NY 10010

Cortez/Seidner Inc (212) 753-6600 227 E 56th St NY, NY 10022

Critical Image Ltd (212) 594-2586 4 W 37th St NY, NY 10018

Dale Cameragraphics (212) 696-9440 12 W 27th St NY, NY 10001

Des Pro Studio (212) 243-5373 133 W 21st St NY, NY 10011

Ditterline, Edward (212) 489-8989 254 W 51st St NY, NY 10019

Essential Slide Services (212) 986-4250 222 E 44th St NY, NY 10017

Exploration Inc (212) 370-9191 304 E 45th St NY, NY 10017

Faye Productions *(212) 246-0430* 325 W 45th St NY, NY 10036

Fiorentino, Imero Associates *(212) 246-0600* 44 W 63rd St NY, NY 10023

Gindick Productions *(212) 725-2580* 21 E 40th St NY, NY 10016

Giraldi, Frank Studios *(212) 840-8225* 34 W 39th St NY, NY 10018

Graphic Media *(201) 540-1597* 373 Rte 46 W Fairfield, NJ 07006

Greenwood Productions *(212) 265-7060* 347 W 55th St NY, NY 10019

Hoschander, Emanuel *(212) 686-8580* 213 E 38th St NY, NY 10016

Icon Communications *(212) 688-5155* 717 Lexington Ave NY, NY 10022

Image Zone *(212) 924-8804* 19 W 21st St NY, NY 10010

Infinite Image *(212) 679-3631* 419 Park Ave So NY, NY 10016

Keeble Cavaco Duka *(212) 315-3052* 853 Seventh Ave NY, NY 10019

Kenwood Creative *(212) 563-3337* 115 W 31st St NY, NY 10001

Kruger & Assoc *(212) 571-0617* 9 Murray St NY, NY 10007

Lancit Media *(212) 977-9100* 601 W 50th St NY, NY 10019

Levine & Assoc *(212) 683-7177* 31 E 28th St NY, NY 10016

London Multimedia *(212) 213-4522* 381 Fifth Ave NY, NY 10016

Lovett & Assoc *(212) 627-1885* 87 Fifth Ave NY, NY 10003

m - z

Maple Communications *(212) 944-6337* 1156 Sixth Ave NY, NY 10036

Martin Audi's Visual Corp *(212) 541-5900* 423 W 55th St NY, NY 10019

Martin Productions *(212) 645-9550* 110 W 17th St NY, NY 10011

Mazin-Wyckoff *(212) 475-4360* 36 E 12th St NY, NY 10003

Meeting Environment *(212) 677-3500* 9 E 19th St NY, NY 10003

Morton Productions *(212) 758-8400* 830 Third Ave NY, NY 10022

New Media Service *(212) 674-1300* 49 E 21st St NY, NY 10010

Prometheus Productions *(212) 677-2140* 110 E 23rd St NY, NY 10010

Roger Wade Productions *(212) 575-9111* 15 W 44th St NY, NY 10036

Ross Productions *(212) 986-5122* 310 E 46th St NY, NY 10017

Salisbury & Salisbury *(212) 575-0770* 15 W 45th St NY, NY 10036

Santandrea Productions *(212) 599-1555* 34 E 39th St NY, NY 10016

Saxton Communication*(212) 867-2210* 124 E 40th St NY, NY 10016

Sell Pictures *(212) 683-9221* 210 Fifth Ave NY, NY 10010

Shaw Associates *(212) 757-3988* 525 W 52nd St NY, NY 10019

Snow, Phoebe T Productions *(212) 481-8001* 37 W 26th St NY, NY 10010

Teletechniques Inc *(212) 206-1475* 1 W 19th St NY, NY 10011

Tony Paris Associates *(212) 686-6150* 137 E 25th St NY, NY 10010

Trident Communications *(212) 243-4412* 48 W 21st St NY, NY 10010

Vision Associates Inc *(212) 935-1830* 665 Fifth Ave NY, NY 10022

Washington Place *(212) 929-4730* 108 Washington Pl NY, NY 10014

William/Gerard *(212) 265-8800* 888 Seventh Ave NY, NY 10019

Windsor Video *(212) 944-9090* 8 W 38th St NY, NY 10018

Zabarkes Productions *(212) 736-7750* 335 W 38th St NY, NY 10018

Zacks & Perrier *(212) 463-7300* 96 Morton St NY, NY 10014

MUSIC PRODUCERS

a - b

Airborne Productions *(212) 861-2035* 300 E 71st St NY, NY 10021

AJR Music Productions Inc *(212) 724-5658* 302 W 87th St NY, NY 10024

Alexander, John Eric *(212) 929-1114* 111 W 24th St NY, NY 10011

Allen Associates Inc *(212) 826-9889* 15 W 44th St NY, NY 10036

Alta Vista Music *(212) 349-8095* 77 Warren St NY, NY 10007

Alters Inc *(212) 757-8300* 301 W 53rd St NY, NY 10019

Amphion Music *(212) 744-8813* 352 E 86th St NY, NY 10028

Andriello, Tabby Music *(212) 594-1810* 19 W 34th St NY, NY 10001

Anthill Music *(212) 355-1600* 231 E 55th St NY, NY 10022

Anthony, Tom Music *(212) 391-1500* 151 W 46th St NY, NY 10036

APM *(212) 977-5680* 888 Seventh Ave NY, NY 10106

Applebaum Music *(212) 765-2669* 330 W 58th St NY, NY 10019

Applegate/Schwartz *(212) 242-6819* 158 W 23rd St NY, NY 10011

Aquarius Music Productions *(212) 581-0123* 12 E 46th St NY, NY 10017

Archangel Music *(212) 580-7768* 200 W 79th St NY, NY 10024

Aries Sound International *(212) 838-4940* 245 E 63rd St NY, NY 10021

Asch Music Production *(212) 288-9798* 308 E 80th St NY, NY 10021

Ascher, Emile *(800) 328-8637* 145 E 49th St NY, NY 10017

Audio Directors *(212) 924-5850* 325 W 19th St NY, NY 10011

Behrke & Grant Music *(212) 873-0298* 390 West End Ave NY, NY 10024

Benderoth, Steve *(212) 586-2474* 350 W 55th St NY, NY 10019

Big Time Productions Inc

(212) 724-4637 100 Riverside Dr NY, NY 10024

Bingham Music *(212) 787-5400* POB 474 No Salem, NY 10560

PAGE 33

Black Productions *(212) 865-5933* 895 West End Ave NY, NY 10025

Bloody Mary Music Ltd *(212) 877-1488* 121 W 72nd St NY, NY 10023

Braunstein Music Inc *(212) 736-0067* 484 W 43rd St NY, NY 10036

Brickman Arrangement *(212) 418-0706* 210 Fifth Ave NY, NY 10010

Brock Musik Inc *(212) 972-5599* 370 Lexington Ave NY, NY 10017

Brywell Productions *(212) 877-3995* 50 W 77th St NY, NY 10024

Buffalo Productions *(212) 418-0406* 128 E 56th St NY, NY 10022

c - d

Canick Productions *(212) 389-9409* Midtown Sta Box 180 NY, NY 11222

Carroll, Michael Music *(212) 807-8852* 240 E 55th St NY, NY 10022

Centra Productions *(212) 496-0234* 260 W 71st St NY, NY 10023

Chapin's Music Works *(212) 333-7799* 1650 Broadway NY, NY 10019

Chesky Productions Inc *(212) 586-7799* 300 W 53rd St NY, NY 10019

Ciani Musica Inc *(212) 777-7755* 30 E 23rd St NY, NY 10010

Cibley, Philip *(212) 986-2219* 138 E 38th St NY, NY 10016

Colby, John Music *(212) 222-6780* 527 W 110th St NY, NY 10025

Contempo Communications *(212) 247-4444* 1841 Broadway NY, NY 10023

Corelli Jacobs Recording Inc *(212) 382-0220* 25 W 45th St NY, NY 10036

Cowan, Victor *(212) 751-5733* 531 Moriches Rd St James, NY 11780

CP Sound *(212) 532-5528* 200 Madison Ave NY, NY 10016

Crushing Enterprises Inc *(212) 265-0741* 157 W 57th St NY, NY 10019

Crystal & Co *(212) 580-7142* 38 W 69th St NY, NY 10023

Curtiss Music Concept *(212) 582-1667* 1650 Broadway NY, NY 10019

Custer, Arthur *(212) 255-1000* 1133 Broadway NY, NY 10010

Dansicker, Michael Music *(212) 362-0680* 471 West End Ave NY, NY 10029

Daum, Glen *(212) 719-5349* 110 W 40th St NY, NY 10018

Del Gatto Pearl Music *(212) 877-4837* 201 W 77th St NY, NY 10024

DMA Productions *(718) 961-9583* POB 1302 Rockefeller Ctr Stn NY, NY 10185

DSM Producers *(212) 245-0006* 161 W 54th St NY, NY 10019

e - g

East-West Music *(212) 262-9170* 77 E 12th St NY, NY 10003

Easy Writer Music Inc *(212) 758-6555* 433 E 51st St NY, NY 10022

Eaton, Roy Music Inc *(212) 980-9046* 595 Main St Roosevlt Islnd, NY 10044

Eisenberg, Ron Productions *(212) 242-3900* 527 W 110th St NY, NY 10025

Electro Nova Studios *(212) 687-5838* 342 Madison Ave NY, NY 10017

Elias Associates Inc *(212) 807-6151* 6 W 20th St NY, NY 10011

Elsmere Music *(914) 234-9201* Empire Bldg Box 185 Bedford, NY 10506

En Espanol/Music Market *(212) 759-5490* 320 E 57th St NY, NY 10022

Fair Film Scoring *(212) 966-2852* 268 Elizabeth St NY, NY 10012

Fontana, Joe *(212) 529-6655* 611 Broadway NY, NY 10012

Freedman Productions *(212) 925-8534* 474 Greenwich NY, NY 10013

Friedman Production *(212) 734-1975* 150 E 72nd St NY, NY 10021

Full House Productions Inc *(212) 645-2228* 150 Fifth Ave NY, NY 10011

Gagnon Productions *(212) 496-9245* 240 W 73rd St NY, NY 10023

Garisto, Louis Associates *(212) 929-1673* 400 E 56th St NY, NY 10022

Gavin Productions Inc *(212) 751-6020* 127 E 28th St NY, NY 10016

Gerardi Music *(212) 874-6436* 160 W 73rd St NY, NY 10023

Gesben Productions Inc *(212) 679-6437* 235 E 25th St NY, NY 10010

GNU Music Inc *(212) 889-3781* 112 Lexington Ave NY, NY 10016

Goodman, Tommy Ent Inc *(212) 489-1641* 101 W 57th St NY, NY 10019

Graham, Ed Productions *(212) 986-9775* 200 Park Ave NY, NY 10166

Grobman, Bernard *(212) 598-4757* 635 E 14th St NY, NY 10019

Gusman Ent Inc *(212) 787-5254* 300 Central Park West NY, NY 10024

h - j

Ham, Al *(203) 929-6395* 90 Soundview Ave Huntington, CT 06484

Haries, Philips Production *(212) 684-4664* 8 W 76th St NY, NY 10023

Hayes, Kevin Music *(212) 684-4664* 8 W 76th St NY, NY 10023

HEA Productions Inc *(212) 758-4120* 219 E 49th St NY, NY 10017

Hest Productions *(212) 601-4151* 1650 Broadway NY, NY 10019

Hill Music Inc *(212) 683-2273* 116 E 37th St NY, NY 10016

Hippogriff Productions *(212) 481-9877* 246 Fifth Ave NY, NY 10001

Hit Factory *(212) 664-1000* 237 W 54th St NY, NY 10019

HLC *(213) 464-6333* 6528 Sunset Blvd Hollywood, CA 90028

HMS Two Music Ltd *(212) 580-1920* 46 W 85th St NY, NY 10024

Hoffman Music *(212) 724-4818* 205 W 79th St NY, NY 10024

Hook-Line & Singer *(212) 247-7272* 315 W 57th St NY, NY 10019

Horowitz Music *(212) 661-6880* 301 Madison Ave NY, NY 10017

Hot Spots Music *(212) 316-2183* 314 W 94th St NY, NY 10025

Hummingbird Productions *(212) 265-6161* 1756 Broadway NY, NY 10019

Hwang, Jason Music *(212) 529-9494* 328 E 6th St NY, NY 10003

Iris *(212) 245-3059* 340 W 57th St NY, NY 10019

It's the Gling Inc *(212) 925-1342* 519 Broome St NY, NY 10013

Jana Productions *(212) 697-4415* 750 Third Ave NY, NY 10017

January, Bob *(212) 360-6628* 1705 First Ave NY, NY 10128

Jewell Production *(212) 362-0516* 2020 Broadway NY, NY 10023

Jingle Belle Inc *(212) 239-0751* 484 W 43rd St NY, NY 10036

Joyce-Rae Productions *(212) 580-3116* 305 W 86th St NY, NY 10024

JPM Productions *(212) 473-2212* 167 Bleecker St NY, NY 10012

Jump Productions *(212) 355-6959* 245 E 57th St NY, NY 10022

k - m

Kalehoff, Edd Productions *(212) 924-1885* 111 W 24th St NY, NY 10011

Kamen Audio *(212) 575-4660* 701 Seventh Ave NY, NY 10036

Kaplan High Impact *(718) 436-9025* 81 Ocean Parkway Brooklyn, NY 11218

Karp Music Inc *(212) 840-3285* 260 W 39th St NY, NY 10018

Katz, Marc Alexander *(212) 769-4836* 2350 Broadway NY, NY 10024

Kinder & Bryant *(212) 724-6800* 41 W 73rd St NY, NY 10023

Lamm, Jamie Music *(212) 580-1797* 250 W 85th St NY, NY 10024

Lavsky Music *(212) 697-9800* 16 E 42nd St NY, NY 10017

Leiderman, BJ Music *(212) 255-2360* 248 W 21st St NY, NY 10011

Leshaw, Howard *(212) 982-8419* 210 Thompson St NY, NY 10012

Levitt Enterprises *(212) 944-9672* 15 W 44th St NY, NY 10036

Loeb, Steve Music *(212) 226-4293* 112 Greene St NY, NY 10012

Look & Co *(212) 627-3500* 170 Fifth Ave NY, NY 10010

Lovenotes Music Inc *(212) 219-1603* 349 E 49th St NY, NY 10017

Lucas, David Associates *(212) 581-3970* 320 W 46th St NY, NY 10036

M&I Recording Enterprises *(212) 582-0210* 630 Ninth Ave NY, NY 10036

Macrose Music *(212) 206-1323* 353 W 19th St NY, NY 10011

Magic Venture Studios *(212) 645-4748* 111 W 24th St NY, NY 10011

Maiden Lane Music *(212) 866-8993* 2700 Broadway NY, NY 10025

Mandel, Mike *(212) 868-0345* 400 W 43rd St NY, NY 10036

Maximum Sequential *(212) 226-1030* 476 Broadway NY, NY 10013

McBrien Productions Inc *(212) 758-0505* 141 E 56th St NY, NY 10022

Mega Music Corp *(212) 838-3212* 345 E 62nd St NY, NY 10021

Messina Music Inc *(212) 541-6677* 420 W 45th St NY, NY 10036

Metropolis Music *(212) 246-8420* 1650 Broadway NY, NY 10019

Miller, Jessie Original Music *(212) 724-6467* 145 W 71st St NY, NY 10023

Monterey Music *(212) 935-9697* 160 E 48th St NY, NY 10017

Morrow, Charles Associates *(212) 529-4550* 611 Broadway NY, NY 10012

Murtaugh Music *(516) 333-8699* 2000 Lilac Drive Wesstbury, NY 11590

Musicvisions Inc *(212) 308-1251* 220 E 63rd St NY, NY 10021

My Kind Of Music Co *(212) 686-3746* 137 E 38th St NY, NY 10016

MZH & F Inc *(212) 575-5180* 2 W 45th St NY, NY 10036

n - r

Nash, Bob Music *(914) 354-0179* 9 Hidden Valley Dr Suffern, NY 10901

New York Audio *(212) 243-6826* 140 W 22nd St NY, NY 10011

Newfound Music *(212) 929-3037* 250 W 57th St NY, NY 10019

No Soap Productions *(212) 581-5572* 161 W 54th St NY, NY 10019

North Forty Productions Inc *(212) 751-8300* 252 E 51st St NY, NY 10022

Not Just Jingles *(212) 246-6468* 1650 Broadway NY, NY 10036

Nutmeg Music *(212) 921-8005* 45 W 45th St NY, NY 10036

O'Farrill Music Ltd *(212) 799-3297* 574 West End Ave NY, NY 10024

Oasis Music Inc *(212) 481-6464* 15 W 26th St NY, NY 10010

Panorama Music Works *(203) 323-7022* 455 Hope St Stamford, CT 06906

Perfect Sound *(212) 315-5854* 1697 Broadway NY, NY 10019

Petersen Music Inc *(212) 477-6124* 205 E 16th St NY, NY 10003

Philhofer Music *(212) 633-0022* 1601 W 22nd St Minneapolis, MN 55405

Philips, Anne Production *(212) 580-2349* 170 West End Ave NY, NY 10023

Pinder Lane *(212) 489-0880* 159 W 53rd St NY, NY 10019

Pisces Music Inc *(212) 682-1860* 12 E 46th St NY, NY 10017

Plotkin/JMP *(914) 232-3458* POB 660 Goldens Bridge, NY 10526

PMC International *(212) 541-4620* 250 W 49th St NY, NY 10019

Power, Robert *(212) 288-7694* 203 E 74th St NY, NY 10021

Pucci, Germana *(212) 777-4323* 810 Broadway NY, NY 10003

Quinn Associates Inc *(212) 582-7566* 309 W 57th St NY, NY 10019

Radio Band of America *(212) 687-4800* 1350 Sixth Ave NY, NY 10019

Radio Kings *(212) 772-7055* 211 W 56th St NY, NY 10019

Raw Cream Music Inc *(212) 226-7230* 10 Hubert St NY, NY 10013

Reel to Reel Recording *(212) 889-1557* 303 Fifth Ave NY, NY 10016

Rhodes Music Ltd *(212) 245-5045* POB 1550 Radio City Stat NY, NY 10101

Rice, Todd Music Service *(212) 489-2321* 211 W 58th St NY, NY 10019

Rivellino Music *(914) 769-5734* 5 Palmer Lane Thornwood, NY 10594

Rocky Road *(212) 873-9481* 142 West End Ave NY, NY 10023

s

SA Productions Inc *(212) 765-2669* 330 W 58th St NY, NY 10019

Sanders, Rich Music *(212) 398-1458* 130 W 42nd St NY, NY 10036

Schurtz, Carl Music *(212) 737-3069* 401 E 82nd St NY, NY 10028

Schwartz Recording Inc *(212) 687-4180* 420 Lexington Ave NY, NY 10170

Score Productions Inc *(212) 751-2510* 254 E 49th St NY, NY 10017

Scores Unlimited *(718) 624-2571* 16 Dean St Brooklyn, NY 11201

Scott-Textor *(212) 333-3621* 449 W 50th St NY, NY 10019

Sebesky Productions *(212) 582-2960* 101 W 57th St NY, NY 10019

See Spot Run *(212) 874-5047* 66 W 85th St NY, NY 10024

Shelton Leigh Palmer & Co *(212) 714-1710* 19 W 36th St NY, NY 10018

Sicurella, Joe/Aversa, Frank *(212) 398-1211* 62 W 45th St NY, NY 10036

Sidray Enterprises *(212) 535-5339* 799 Park Ave NY, NY 10021

Silvestri Stone & Higgins Inc *(212) 213-8184* 207 E 30th St NY, NY 10016

Singer & Co *(212) 662-5987* 752 West End Ave NY, NY 10025

Slope Sounds *(718) 783-7299* 809 Union St Brooklyn, NY 11215

Small Productions *(212) 873-8026* 322 W 48th St NY, NY 10036

Smith Music *(212) 254-0321* 632 Broadway NY, NY 10012

Smythe & Company *(212) 645-1166* 16 W 19th St NY, NY 10011

Sokolov, Elliot Music *(212) 874-0122* 30 W 88th St NY, NY 10024

Sound Design by Zantay *(212) 288-7370* 236 E 75th St NY, NY 10021

Sound For Images *(212) 228-4091* 59 W 10th St NY, NY 10011

Sound Suite *(212) 246-0314* 534 W 50th St NY, NY 10019

Soundtrack/NY *(212) 420-6010* 25 E 21st St NY, NY 10010

Splash Productions Inc *(212) 695-3665* 123 W 28th St NY, NY 10001

Stevens Photo Retouching *(212) 628-6484* 353 E 77th St NY, NY 10021

Strauss, Bill *(212) 929-5960* 135 W 14th St NY, NY 10011

Sun Group *(212) 255-1000* 1133 Broadway NY, NY 10010

Sunday Productions Inc *(212) 246-2000* 888 Eighth Ave NY, NY 10019

Sutcilffe Music Inc *(212) 420-9292* 41 Fifth Ave NY, NY 10003

t - z

TAJ *(212) 355-0030* 304 E 55th St NY, NY 10024

Tallman Music Productions *(212) 688-5120* 919 Third Ave NY, NY 10022

TNG Earthling Inc *(212) 799-4181* 110 W 86th St NY, NY 10024

Transfermation Studios *(212) 687-6500* 17 E 45th St NY, NY 10017

TRF Prod Music Libraries *(212) 753-3234* 40 E 49th St NY, NY 10017

Twinstar Music *(212) 362-8100* 1995 Broadway NY, NY 10023

Ulfik Productions *(212) 704-0888* 130 W 42nd St NY, NY 10036

Urbont Associates *(212) 799-0641* 330 W 72nd St NY, NY 10023

Venture Sound *(201) 359-5110* 121 Meadowbrook Dr Somerville, NJ 08878

Waldo, Terry Enterprises *(212) 362-5922* 335 W 88th St NY, NY 10024

Warner/Levinson Corp *(212) 496-7575* 1995 Broadway NY, NY 10023

Weber & Soden Assoc *(212) 684-1385* 164 Madison Ave NY, NY 10016

Weinberg, Fred *(212) 349-6644* 16 Dundee Rd Stamford, CT 06903

Wheeler, Harold *(212) 586-6780* 230 W 55th St NY, NY 10019

Wheelerbeck Music Inc *(212) 627-1950* 12 W 21st St NY, NY 10010

Wilber Music Inc *(212) 949-1190* 48 E 43rd St NY, NY 10017

Wild Spot Productions *(212) 826-0810* 57 W 57th St NY, NY 10019

Woloshin Inc *(212) 684-7222* 95 Madison Ave NY, NY 10016

Write Sound Music *(212) 724-3082* 142 West End Ave NY, NY 10023

Zager, Michael *(212) 977-7244* 220 Central Park So NY, NY 10019

Zuback, Frank *(212) 956-5550* 250 W 57th St NY, NY 10019

Music Libraries & Sound FX

a - z

APM *(212) 977-5680* 888 Seventh Ave NY, NY 10106

Aquarius Music Production *(212) 581-0123* 12 E 46th St NY, NY 10017

Ar-Vee Sound Services Inc *(212) 459-9588* 630 Ninth Ave NY, NY 10036

Ascher, Emile *(800) 328-8637* 145 E 49th St NY, NY 10017

Audio Directors *(212) 924-5850* 325 W 19th St NY, NY 10011

Berliner, Ralph *(212) 873-6390* 35 W 90th St NY, NY 10024

CBS Special Products *(212) 975-5073* 51 W 52nd St NY, NY 10019

Ciani/Musica Inc *(212) 777-7755* 30 E 23rd St NY, NY 10010

Cibley, Philip *(212) 986-2219* 138 E 38th St NY, NY 10016

Corelli Jacobs Recording Inc *(212) 382-0220* 25 W 45th St NY, NY 10036

DeWolfe Music Library *(212) 382-0220* 25 W 45th St NY, NY 10036

DSM Producers *(212) 245-0006* 161 W 54th St NY, NY 10019

Electro Nova Studios *(212) 687-5838* 342 Madison Ave NY, NY 10017

Hi Test Productions Inc *(212) 505-1061* 738 Broadway NY, NY 10003

Hit Factory *(212) 664-1000* 237 W 54th St NY, NY 10019

Lavsky Music *(212) 697-9800* 16 E 42nd St NY, NY 10017

Media Sound *(212) 765-4700* 311 W 57th St NY, NY 10019

Metropolis Music *(212) 246-8420* 1650 Broadway NY, NY 10019

Music & Sound *(201) 560-8444* 711 East Main St Bridgewater, NJ 08807

NFL Films *(800) 257-5853* 330 Fellowship Rd Mt. Laurel, NJ 08054

Norman Kasow *(212) 279-2000* 460 W 42nd St NY, NY 10036

Omnimusic *(516) 883-0121* 52 Main St Port Washington, NY 11050

Pathe Pictures *(212) 247-4767* 161 W 54th St NY, NY 10019

Picture Scores Inc *(212) 869-5885* 42 W 38th St NY, NY 10018

Pisces Music Inc *(212) 682-1860* 12 E 46th St NY, NY 10017

Power Play Studios *(718) 729-1780* 38-12 30th St LIC, NY 11101

PPX Enterprises Inc *(212) 247-6010* 300 W 55th St NY, NY 10019

Score Productions Inc (212) 751-2510 254 E 49th St NY, NY 10017

Servisound Inc (212) 921-0555 35 W 45th St NY, NY 10036

Shelton Leigh Palmer & Co (212) 714-1710 19 W 36th St NY, NY 10018

Sound One Corp (212) 765-4757 1619 Broadway NY, NY 10019

Sound Patrol (212) 213-6666 6 E 39th St NY, NY 10017

Sound Shop (212) 757-5700 321 W 44th St NY, NY 10036

Soundhound Inc (212) 575-8664 45 W 45th St NY, NY 10036

Sounds Alive Inc (212) 953-1677 600 Third Ave NY, NY 10016

Southern Music Library (212) 265-3910 1740 Broadway NY, NY 10019

Stock Rock (212) 473-1883 111 Third Ave NY, NY 10003

Studio C (212) 986-2219 POB 767 Murray Hill St NY, NY 10156

Sync Sound Inc (212) 246-5580 450 W 56th St NY, NY 10019

TNG/Earthling Inc (212) 799-4181 110 W 86th St NY, NY 10024

Transfermation Studios (212) 687-6500 17 E 45th St NY, NY 10017

TRF Producers (212) 753-3234 40 E 49th St NY, NY 10017

Ulfik Productions (212) 704-0888 130 W 42nd St NY, NY 10036

Valentino, Thomas J. Inc (212) 869-5210 151 W 46th St NY, NY 10036

Voices (212) 935-9820 16 E 48th St NY, NY 10017

RECORDING STUDIOS

a - k

A & R Recording Inc (212) 397-0300 322 W 48th St NY, NY 10036

A&J Recording Studios Inc (212) 724-5658 302 W 87th St NY, NY 10024

Anthill Music (212) 355-1600 231 E 55th St NY, NY 10022

Aquarius Transfer Ltd (212) 581-0123 12 E 46th St NY, NY 10017

Ar-Vee Sound Services Inc (212) 459-9588 630 Ninth Ave NY, NY 10036

ATC Research Inc (212) 757-2305 360 W 55th St NY, NY 10019

Audio Department Inc (212) 586-3503 119 W 57th St NY, NY 10019

Automated Sound Studios (212) 869-8520 1500 Broadway NY, NY 10036

Bee Vee Sound Inc (212) 949-9170 211 E 43rd St NY, NY 10017

Berliner, Ralph (212) 873-6390 35 W 90th St NY, NY 10024

Charles Recording Inc (212) 819-0920 130 W 42nd St NY, NY 10036

Chelsea Sound (212) 869-4440 130 W 42nd St NY, NY 10036

Cinema/Sound Ltd (212) 799-4800 311 W 75th St NY, NY 10023

Cinequip Inc (212) 308-5100 241 E 51st St NY, NY 10022

City Lights Productions (212) 564-9106 505 Eighth Ave NY, NY 10018

Clack Inc Sound Studio (212) 575-5566 56 W 45th St NY, NY 10036

Clinton Recording (212) 246-2444 653 Tenth Ave NY, NY 10036

Counterpoint Recording (212) 398-9550 723 Seventh Ave NY, NY 10019

CP Sound (212) 532-5528 200 Madison Ave NY, NY 10016

Cue Recording Studios (212) 921-9221 1156 Sixth Ave NY, NY 10036

DB Sound Studios (212) 764-6000 25 W 45th St NY, NY 10036

Delta Recording Corp (212) 840-1350 16 W 46th St NY, NY 10036

Dimensional Sound Inc (212) 247-6010 301 W 54th St NY, NY 10019

Du Art Film Labs Inc (212) 757-4580 245 W 55th St NY, NY 10019

East Side Film & Video (212) 867-0730 216 E 45th St NY, NY 10017

Eastside Film & Video Inc (212) 867-0730 216 E 45th St NY, NY 10017

Electric Lady Studios (212) 677-4700 52 W 8th St NY, NY 10011

Electro Nova Studios (212) 687-5838 342 Madison Ave NY, NY 10017

Full House Productions Inc (212) 645-2228 150 Fifth Ave NY, NY 10011

Giant Sound (212) 247-1160 1776 Broadway NY, NY 10019

Greene Street Recording Inc (212) 226-4278 112 Greene St NY, NY 10012

Greyrock Studio (914) 967-6515 478 Grace Church St NY, NY 10573

Hi Test Productions (212) 505-1061 738 Broadway NY, NY 10003

Hip Pocket Studios (212) 255-5313 37 W 20th St NY, NY 10011

Ibero-American Productions (212) 245-7826 630 Ninth Ave NY, NY 10036

III DB Sound Specialists Inc (212) 677-6856 121 E 24th St NY, NY 10010

Intergalactic Music Inc (212) 333-3306 353 W 48th St NY, NY 10036

Irwin, Chuck (212) 633-1875 1133 Broadway NY, NY 10010

Kalehoff Productions (212) 924-1885 111 W 24th St NY, NY 10011

Kamen Audio Productions (212) 575-4660 701 Seventh Ave NY, NY 10036

KCC Audio/Video (212) 228-3063 31 Bond St NY, NY 10012

Kornfeld, Dan (212) 685-6633 271 Madison Ave NY, NY 10016

l - s

Lavsky's Music House (212) 697-9800 16 E 42nd St NY, NY 10017

Lifecycle (212) 244-6714 15 Washington Pl White Plains, NY 10603

M&I Recording Enterprises (212) 582-0210 630 Ninth Ave NY, NY 10036

Magno Empire Sound (212) 302-2505 18 W 45th St NY, NY 10038

Magno II (212) 757-8855 1600 Broadway NY, NY 10019

Magno Penthouse (212) 757-8855 1540 Broadway NY, NY 10036

Malen (212) 921-7878 2 W 45th St NY, NY 10036

Manhattan Center Studios (212) 279-7740 311 W 34th St NY, NY 10001

Manhattan Recording (212) 929-5960 135 W 14th St NY, NY 10011

Master Sound Astoria (718) 786-3400 34-12 36th St Astoria, NY 11106

Media Sound (212) 765-4700 311 W 57th St NY, NY 10019

Metropolis Music Ltd (212) 246-8420 1650 Broadway NY, NY 10019

Mix Place Inc, The (212) 759-8311 663 Fifth Ave NY, NY 10022

Music & Sound (201) 560-8444 711 East Main St Bridgewater, NJ 08807

MZH & F (212) 594-2600 12 W 37th St NY, NY 10018

National Video Ctr *(212) 279-2000* 460 W 42nd St NY, NY 10036

Navesync Sound *(212) 246-0100* 513 W 54th St NY, NY 10019

NEP Productions Inc *(212) 382-1100* 56 W 45th St NY, NY 10036

New York Sound/Onomatopoeia

(212) 869-3540 72 W. 45th St NY, NY 10036

Nola Recording Studios Inc *(212) 586-0040* 111 W 57th St NY, NY 10019

Nutmeg Recording *(212) 921-8005* 45 W 45th St NY, NY 10036

Omni Audio Products *(212) 869-3990* 580 Eighth Ave NY, NY 10018

On Track Sound *(212) 755-6092* 60 Sutton Pl So NY, NY 10022

Penny Lane Studios *(212) 687-4800* 1350 Sixth Ave NY, NY 10019

Perfect Sound Studio *(212) 315-5852* 1697 Broadway NY, NY 10019

Pisces Music Inc *(212) 682-1860* 12 E 46th St NY, NY 10017

Platinum Island *(212) 473-9497* 676 Broadway NY, NY 10012

Power Play Studios *(718) 729-1780* 38-12 30th St LIC, NY 11101

Quadrasonic Recording *(212) 730-1035* 723 Seventh Ave NY, NY 10019

RCA Recording Studios *(212) 930-4062* 1133 Sixth Ave NY, NY 10036

Reel to Reel Recording *(212) 889-1557* 303 Fifth Ave NY, NY 10016

Ross-Gaffney Inc *(212) 719-2744* 21 W 46th St NY, NY 10036

Sadler Recording Studios *(212) 684-0960* 118 E 28th St NY, NY 10016

Schwartz Recording Inc *(212) 687-4180* 420 Lexington Ave NY, NY 10170

Schwartz Recording Studios *(212) 687-4180* 420 Lexington NY, NY 10170

Sear Sound *(212) 582-5380* 235 W 46th St NY, NY 10036

Secret Sound Studio *(212) 691-7674* 147 W 24th St NY, NY 10011

Servisound Inc *(212) 921-0555* 35 W 45th St NY, NY 10036

Sigma Sound Studios Inc *(212) 582-5055* 1697 Broadway NY, NY 10019

Skyline Studios Inc *(212) 594-7484* 36 W 37th St NY, NY 10018

Sound Heights *(718) 237-0250* 124 Montague St Brooklyn Hghts, NY 11201

Sound Ideas/Recording *(212) 869-2666* 151 W 46th St NY, NY 10036

Sound One Corp *(212) 765-4757* 1619 Broadway NY, NY 10019

Sound Patrol *(212) 213-6666* 6 East 39th St NY, NY 10016

Sound Shop *(212) 757-5700* 321 W 44th St NY, NY 10036

Soundhound Inc *(212) 575-8664* 45 W 45th St NY, NY 10036

Soundtek *(212) 489-0806* 1780 Broadway NY, NY 10019

Sun Group *(212) 255-1000* 1133 Broadway NY, NY 10010

Sunset Productions *(212) 832-8020* 226 E 54th St NY, NY 10022

Superdupe Creations Inc *(212) 683-6854* 295 Madison Ave NY, NY 10017

Sync Sound Inc *(212) 246-5580* 450 W 56th St NY, NY 10019

t - z

Tape Tracks Ltd *(212) 575-9673* 56 W 45th St NY, NY 10036

Titra *(212) 757-7129* 1600 Broadway NY, NY 10019

TNG/Earthling Inc *(212) 799-4181* 110 W 86th St NY, NY 10024

Track Transfers Inc *(212) 730-1635* 45 W 45th St NY, NY 10036

Trackworks Recording *(212) 921-7878* 2 W 45th St NY, NY 10036

Trans/Audio Inc *(212) 265-6225* 254 W 54th St NY, NY 10019

Transcom Digital *(212) 529-1000* 902 Broadway NY, NY 10010

Transfermation Studios *(212) 687-6500* 17 E 45th St NY, NY 10017

United Recording Labs *(212) 751-4660* 681 Fifth Ave NY, NY 10022

Uptown Chelsea Sound *(212) 869-4440* 130 W 42nd St NY, NY 10036

V&W Sound Transfers Inc *(212) 757-5221* 630 Ninth Ave NY, NY 10036

Valentino, Thomas J Inc *(212) 869-5210* 151 W 46th St NY, NY 10036

Voiceplus *(212) 966-2121* 177 E 87th St NY, NY 10128

Warehouse Recording *(212) 265-6060* 320 W 46th St NY, NY 10036

Westrax Recording Ltd *(212) 947-0533* 484 W 43rd St NY, NY 10036

SOUND STAGES

a - m

34th Street Stage *(212) 889-9388* 235 E 34th St NY, NY 10016

3G Stages Inc *(212) 247-3130* 236 W 61st St NY, NY 10023

A.C.T. Video Productions *(212) 255-7111* 27 W 20th St NY, NY 10011

Atelier Fourth Street Studio *(212) 243-3550* 295 W 4th St NY, NY 10014

ATV *(212) 925-7373* 11 Mercer St NY, NY 10013

Boken II *(212) 924-0438* 111 Leroy St NY, NY 10014

Boken Inc *(212) 581-5507* 513 W 54th St NY, NY 10019

Breitrose-Seltzer Stages *(212) 807-0664* 383 W 12th St NY, NY 10014

Broadcast Arts Inc *(212) 254-5400* 632 Broadway NY, NY 10012

Broadway Studios *(718) 274-9121* 25-09 Broadway Astoria, NY 11106

Camera Mart Stages *(212) 757-6977* 460 W 54th St NY, NY 10019

CBS Operations *(212) 975-2318* 524 W 57th St NY, NY 10019

Center Stage *(212) 355-1600* 503 W 33rd St NY, NY 10036

Cine Studio *(212) 581-1916* 241 W 54th St NY, NY 10019

Communications Plus *(212) 686-9570* 360 Park Ave So NY, NY 10010

Dance Gallery *(212) 685-5972* 242 E 14th St NY, NY 10003

DeFilippo, Dom Studio, Inc *(212) 986-5444* 215 E 37th St NY, NY 10016

Devlin Productions Inc *(212) 582-5572* 150 W 55th St NY, NY 10019

DSI/Veritas Studios *(212) 581-2050* 527 W 45th St NY, NY 10036

Empire Stages of New York *(718) 392-4747* 50-20 25th St LIC, NY 11101

Farkas Films Inc *(212) 679-8212* 385 Third Ave NY, NY 10016

Flying Tiger Communications *(212) 929-1156* 155 W 18th St NY, NY 10011

Globus Brothers Studio *(212) 243-1000* 44 W 24th St NY, NY 10010

Group W Cable Inc *(212) 304-3000* 5120 Broadway NY, NY 10034

HBO Studio Productions *(212) 512-7800* 120A E 23rd St NY, NY 10010

Horvath Studios *(212) 714-0300* 95 Charles St NY, NY 10014

Ibero-American Productions

(212) 245-7826 630 Ninth Ave NY, NY 10036

Image Mix Inc *(212) 752-3010* 305 E 46th St NY, NY 10017

International Productions Center

(212) 582-6530 514 W 57th St NY, NY 10019

Jay-Gee Stages *(212) 695-0100* 641 W 59th St NY, NY 10019

Kaufman Astoria Studio *(718) 392-5600* 34-12 36th St Astoria, NY 11106

Little House, Astoria *(718) 726-3231* 11-44 31st Ave LIC, NY 11106

LRP Video *(212) 759-0822* 3 Dag Hammarskjold Plaza NY, NY 10017

Magno Sound & Video *(212) 757-8855* 212 W 48th St NY, NY 10036

Manhattan Bridge *(212) 288-3883* 156 Tillary St Brooklyn Hghts, NY 11201

Manhattan Transfer/Edit Inc

(212) 687-4000 545 Fifth Ave NY, NY 10017

Manhattan Video *(212) 683-6565* 12 W 27th St NY, NY 10001

Master Sound Astoria *(718) 786-3400* 34-12 36th St Astoria, NY 11106

Matrix Video *(212) 265-8500* 727 Eleventh Ave NY, NY 10019

Midtown Studio *(212) 564-9405* 35 W 31st St NY, NY 10001

Ministage *(212) 697-8388* 304 E 45th St NY, NY 10017

Mother Sound Stages *(212) 529-5097* 210 E 5th St NY, NY 10003

Movie Mobile/Riverview Studios

(718) 545-7200 30-15 Vernon Blvd Astoria, NY 11102

MTI Television City *(212) 722-1818* 1443 Park Ave NY, NY 10029

MTI/Compugraph *(212) 355-0510* 885 Second Ave NY, NY 10017

n - z

National Video Ctr *(212) 279-2000* 460 W 42nd St NY, NY 10036

National Video Industries *(212) 691-1300* 15 W 17th St NY, NY 10011

NBC Telesales *(212) 664-4754* 30 Rockefeller Plaza NY, NY 10112

Ninety Fifth St. Studio *(212) 831-1231* 206 E 95th St NY, NY 10028

North Star Video *(212) 996-9666* 423 E 90th St NY, NY 10028

NY Productions Center *(212) 867-4030* 222 E 44th St NY, NY 10017

Our Studios *(212) 529-1111* 622 Broadway NY, NY 10012

Overland Stage *(212) 581-4469* 511 W 54th St NY, NY 10019

Panvideo *(212) 725-2211* 248 E 35th St NY, NY 10016

Phoenix Stage Ltd *(212) 581-7670* 537 W 59th St NY, NY 10019

Primalux Video *(212) 206-1402* 30 W 26th St NY, NY 10010

Production Center *(212) 675-2211* 221 W 26th St NY, NY 10001

Rathe Productions *(212) 242-9000* 555 W 23rd St NY, NY 10011

Rebo Associates *(212) 989-9466* 530 W 25th St NY, NY 10001

Reeves Teletape *(212) 573-8600* 708 Third Ave NY, NY 10017

Riverview Studio *(718) 545-7200* 30-15 Vernon Blvd Astoria, NY 11102

Shinbone Alley Stage *(212) 420-8463* 680 Broadway NY, NY 10012

Silvercup Studios, Inc *(718) 784-3390* 42-25 21st St LIC, NY 11101

Soho Video *(212) 473-6947* 116 W Houston St NY, NY 10012

Specialty Space Corp *(212) 947-0808* 450 W 31st St NY, NY 10001

Studio 39 *(212) 685-1771* 144 E 39th St NY, NY 10016

Teletechniques Inc *(212) 580-9551* 1 W 19th St NY, NY 10011

Telstar Video *(212) 689-1040* 206 E 29th St NY, NY 10016

Times Square Studios *(212) 704-9700* 1481 Broadway NY, NY 10036

Today Video *(212) 391-1020* 45 W 45th St NY, NY 10036

Trans Video *(212) 265-4141* 506 W 57th St NY, NY 10019

Tulchin Studios *(212) 986-8270* 240 E 45th St NY, NY 10017

TVC Video *(212) 599-1616* 225 E 43rd St NY, NY 10017

Unitel Video Services Inc *(212) 265-3600* 515 W 57th ST NY, NY 10019

Veritas Studios *(212) 581-2050* 527 W 45th St NY, NY 10036

Wallach, Peter *(212) 966-1970* 419 Broome St NY, NY 10013

Windsor Total Video *(212) 725-8080* 565 Fifth Ave NY, NY 10017

LIGHTING & GRIP

a - g

Balcar Tekno *(212) 889-5080* 15 E 30th St NY, NY 10016

Barbizon Electric Co Inc *(212) 586-1620* 426 W 55th St NY, NY 10019

Big Apple Lights Corp *(212) 226-0925* 533 Canal St NY, NY 10013

Boken Inc *(212) 581-5507* 513 W 54th St NY, NY 10019

Camera Mart *(212) 757-6977* 456 W 55th St NY, NY 10019

Camera Service Center Inc *(212) 757-0906* 625 W 54th St NY, NY 10019

CECO International Corp *(212) 206-8280* 440 W 15th St NY, NY 10011

Cestare, Thomas Inc *(516) 742-5550* 188 Herricks Rd Mineola, NY 11501

Cine 60 Inc *(212) 586-8782* 630 Ninth Ave NY, NY 10036

Erik Lighting *(212) 901-3100* 4077 Park Ave NY, NY 10457

Feature Systems Inc *(212) 736-0447* 512 W 36th St NY, NY 10018

Ferco *(212) 245-4800* 707 11th Ave NY, NY 10019

Filmtrucks Inc *(212) 243-1500* Pier 40 No River NY, NY 10014

Fiorentino Imero Assoc Inc *(212) 246-0600* 44 W 63rd St NY, NY 10023

GDR Equipment *(212) 247-3130* 236 W 61st St NY, NY 10023

General Camera Corp *(212) 594-8700* 540 W 36th St NY, NY 10018

Goblin Market *(718) 447-7157* 52 St. Marks Pl Staten Isl, NY 10301

Godard *(212) 620-0480* 11 W 20th St NY, NY 10011

h - z

Hotlights *(212) 645-5295* 133 W 19th St NY, NY 10011

Kruger & Assoc *(212) 571-0617* 9 Murray St NY, NY 10007

Lee Lighting America Ltd *(212) 691-1910* 534 W 25th St NY, NY 10001

LEGS/Manhattan Inc *(212) 807-6644* Pier 62 Hudson River NY, NY 10011

Liberty Lighting Ltd *(212) 627-9455* 236 W 27th St NY, NY 10001

Lowel Light Manufacturing *(212) 947-0950* 475 10th Ave NY, NY 10018

LTM Corp Of America *(212) 243-9288* 437 W 16th St NY, NY 10011

Matthews *(212) 691-4720* 236 W 26th St NY, NY 10011

Movie Lites *(212) 989-2318* 460 W 24th St NY, NY 10011

New York Flash Rental *(212) 353-0600* 704 Broadway NY, NY 10003

New York Lighting *(718) 963-2644* 975 Grand St Brooklyn, NY 11211

Photo-Tekniques/City Lights
(212) 219-9444 568 Browadway NY, NY 10012

Production Arts Lighting *(212) 489-0312* 636 Eleventh Ave NY, NY 10036

Sparks, R.D. Ltd *(212) 633-1969* 16 Jane St NY, NY 10014

Teletechniques Inc *(212) 206-1475* 1 W 19th St NY, NY 10011

Temmer Lighting/Grip *(212) 206-1475* 1 W 19th St NY, NY 10011

Visual Services *(212) 580-9551* 1 W 19th St NY, NY 10011

Xeno Lights *(212) 766-0786* 1 Hudson St NY, NY 10013

Ziplights *(212) 737-7907* 885 Park Ave NY, NY 10021

CAMERAS & ACCESSORIES

a - z

A/T Scharff Rentals *(212) 582-4400* 599 Eleventh Ave NY, NY 10036

Adcom Communications *(212) 265-1760* 555 W 57th St NY, NY 10019

All Mobile Video *(212) 757-8919* 630 Ninth Ave NY, NY 10036

ARC Video *(212) 629-0009* 511 W 33rd St NY, NY 10001

Astoria Studios *(718) 392-5600* 34-12 36th St Astoria, NY 11106

Broadcast Video *(212) 541-5390* 333 W 52nd St NY, NY 10019

C & F Equipment *(718) 636-9560* 195 Fourth Ave Brooklyn, NY 11217

Camera Mart Inc *(212) 757-6977* 456 W 55th St NY, NY 10019

Camera Service Center Inc *(212) 757-0906* 625 W 54th St NY, NY 10019

Ceco International Corp *(212) 206-8280* 440 W 15th St NY, NY 10011

Cine 60 Inc *(212) 206-8782* 630 Ninth Ave NY, NY 10036

Cinergy Communications *(212) 582-2900* 321 W 44th St NY, NY 10036

Electric Film *(212) 925-3429* 87 Lafayette St NY, NY 10013

Famavision *(718) 273-1780* 2750 Richmond Terrace Staten Isl, NY 10303

Feature Systems Inc *(212) 736-0447* 512 W 36th St NY, NY 10018

FERCO Inc *(212) 245-4800* 707 Eleventh Ave NY, NY 10019

Filmtrucks Inc *(212) 243-1500* Pier 40 North River NY, NY 10014

Flying Tiger Communication *(212) 929-1156* 155 W 18th St NY, NY 10011

G & R Video Inc *(212) 564-7260* 522 W. 36th St NY, NY 10018

General Camera Corp *(212) 594-8700* 540 W 36th St NY, NY 10018

Laumic Co *(212) 889-3300* 306 E 39th St NY, NY 10016

Lee Lighting America Ltd *(121) 691-1910* 534 W 25th St NY, NY 10001

LEGS/Manhattan *(212) 807-6644* Pier 62 @ 23rd St NY, NY 10011

Miller Associates Ltd *(212) 741-8011* 48 W 21st St NY, NY 10010

MPCS Video Industries Inc *(212) 586-3690* 514 W 57th St NY, NY 10019

New York Flash Rental *(212) 741-1165* 48 W 21st St NY, NY 10011

Paris Film *(718) 740-2020* 213-23 99th Ave Queens Village, NY 11429

Pro Camera & Lighting Rentals
(212) 695-1330 511 W 33rd St NY, NY 10001

Rapid Deployment Films *(212) 608-6005* 46 Ann St NY, NY 10038

Reliance Audio Visual Corp *(212) 586-5000* 623 W 51st St NY, NY 10019

Roessel CPT *(718) 424-1600* 48-20 70th St Woodside, NY 11377

Ross-Gaffney Inc *(212) 719-2744* 21 W 46th St NY, NY 10036

Schneider Corp *(516) 496-8500* 400 Crossways Park Dr Woodbury, NY 11797

Select Audio Visual *(212) 598-9800* 902 Broadway NY, NY 10010

Spera Corp *(212) 629-0009* 511 W 33rd St NY, NY 10001

Staging Techniques *(212) 736-5727* 342 W 40th St NY, NY 10018

Super 16/35 Studio *(718) 857-3274* POBox 69 Forest Hills, NY 11375

Technisphere Corporation *(212) 777-5100* 29 E 19th St NY, NY 10003

Technological Cinevideo Svc *(212) 247-6517* 630 Ninth Ave NY, NY 10036

Teletechniques *(212) 206-1475* 1 W 19th St NY, NY 10011

Video 35 *(212) 864-1408* 201 W 94th St NY, NY 10025

Video Central *(212) 947-6960* 225 W 36th St NY, NY 10018

Video Poeple Rentals *(201) 891-3372* 166 Front St Secaucus, NJ 07094

Visual Service *(212) 580-9551* 40 W 72nd St NY, NY 10036

INDEX TO TAB 8

INDEX TO TAB 8

Monique Pillard, President

CLORINDA
HAIR AND
Make up
718-767-2080
718-353-5473
NABET MEMBER
REVL
LOUIS FERA
GIVENC
ADOL
UNGA
VOGUE ADVERTISI
FASHION OF THE TIM
COSMOPOLIT
ITALY: DONNA, AMI
Photo: Marco Glavi
Hand Painting: Jim A

CASEY:

PHOTOGRAPHERS

TORKIL GUDNASON
CALLIOPE
CHRISTOPHER MICAUD
RICHARD CORMAN
ANDREW MACPHERSON
MARTIN BRADING
RICHARD BAILEY

MAKE-UP

MARK HAYLES
MARIA DE SCHNEIDER
GLENNA FRANKLIN

HAIR

HOWARD FUGLER
GREY ZISSER
TROY HALTERMAN

HAIR & MAKE-UP

ROB VAN DORSSEN
JAMES REDA
JUDITH O'CONNOR

ILLUSTRATION

KONSTANTIN

JUDY CASEY INC. • NINETY SIX FIFTH AVENUE • NEW YORK • NEW YORK • 10011 • 212-255-3252

MODELS

a - l

AMERICAN MODEL MANAGEMENT

(212) 759-0570 444 Madison Ave NY, NY 10022

AVENUE MODELS *(212) 533-9877* 35 East 21st St NY, NY 10010

BARBIZON AGENCY *(212) 239-1110* 15 Penn Plaza NY, NY 10001

BETHANN MODELS *(212) 925-2153* 36 Northmore NY, NY 10013

BIG BEAUTIES/LITTLE WOMEN

(212) 685-1270 159 Madison Ave NY, NY 10016

BOOKERS INC *(212) 645-9706* 39 West 19th St NY, NY 10011

BOULEVARD MODEL *(212) 473-1900* 35 E 21st St NY, NY 10010

CLICK MODEL MANAGEMENT

(212) 315-2200 881 Seventh Ave NY, NY 10019

CONOVER MODELS & TALENT INTL

(212) 772-3593 370 East 76th St NY, NY 10021

DEL MARCO, GRACE *(212) 629-6404* 350 Fifth Ave NY, NY 10118

ELITE MODEL MANAGEMENT

(212) 529-9700 **111 East 22nd St NY, NY 10010**

PAGE 1

ELITE RUNWAY INC *(212) 686-5600* 149 Madison Ave NY, NY 10016

EXPRESSIONS *(212) 557-4460* 310 Madison Ave NY, NY 10017

FACES *(212) 661-1515* 567 Third Ave NY, NY 10016

FORD MODELS *(212) 753-6500* 344 East 59th St NY, NY 10022

FORD'S CHILDREN *(212) 688-8628* 344 East 59th St NY, NY 10022

FOSTER-FELL *(212) 334-1324* 80 Varick St NY, NY 10013

FUNNYFACE *(212) 752-6090* 440 East 62nd St NY, NY 10021

GEORGE, MARGO MODEL AGENCY

(914) 294-8144 159 W. Main St Goshen, NY 10924

HV MODELS *(212) 751-3005* 18 East 53rd St NY, NY 10022

ICE REPRESENTS *(212) 925-4888* 250 Lafayette St NY, NY 10002

IMG MODELS *(212) 755-1414* 150 East 58th St NY, NY 10155

JOHNSTON MODEL AGENCY

(203) 622-1137 32 Field Point Rd Greenwich, CT 06830

JORDAN, JOE MODEL MANAGEMENT

(212) 463-8455 156 Fifth Ave NY, NY 10010

KENCY MODEL AGENCY

(212) 254-5005 40 East 23rd St NY, NY 10010

KRONICK & KELLY & LAUREN LTD

(212) 684-5223 220 Fifth Ave NY, NY 10001

L'IMAGE *(212) 477-2100* 35 E 21st St NY, NY 10010

m - z

MANNEQUIN INC *(212) 755-1456* 150 East 58th St NY, NY 10155

MANNER MODELS *(212) 475-5001* 874 Broadway NY, NY 10001

MCDERMOTT, MARGE ENTERPRISES

(212) 889-1583 216 East 39th St NY, NY 10016

MCDONALD - RICHARDS *(212) 627-3100* 156 Fifth Ave NY, NY 10010

MILLER MODEL & TALENT MANAGEMENT

(212) 696-5555 550 Third Ave NY, NY 100016

MODELS/TALENT INTERNATIONAL

(212) 302-8450 1457 Broadway NY, NY 10036

MOSTLY MODELS *(212) 213-0116* 164 Madison Ave NY, NY 10016

MYSTIQUE MODEL MANAGEMENT INC

(212) 228-7807 141 Fifth Ave NY, NY 10010

NAME *(212) 334-0101* 75 Varick St NY, NY 10013

OUR AGENCY *(212) 982-5626* 112 East 23rd St NY, NY 10010

PAULINE'S *(212) 750-8383* 444 Madison Ave NY, NY 10022

PERKINS MODELS *(212) 582-9511* 1697 Broadway NY, NY 10019

PETITE MODEL MANAGEMENT

(212) 759-9304 123 East 54th St NY, NY 10022

PIX TALENT *(212) 246-1379* 1697 Broadway NY, NY 10019

PLUS MODEL MANAGEMENT *(212) 997-1785* 49 West 37th St NY, NY 10018

PRESTIGE MODELS, INC *(201) 891-8600* 291 Franklin Ave Wyckoff, NJ 7481

RASCALS UNLIMITED *(212) 517-6500* 135 East 65th St NY, NY 10021

ROGERS & LERMAN *(212) 889-8233* 37 East 28th St NY, NY 10016

ROOS, GILLA LTD. *(212) 758-5480* 555 Madison Ave NY, NY 10022

RYAN, CHARLES V. ENTERPRISES

(212) 245-2225 200 West 57th St NY, NY 10019

SCHULLER TALENT/ NY KIDS *(212) 532-6005* 276 Fifth Ave NY, NY 10001

SELECT *(212) 725-5444* 381 Park Ave South NY, NY 10016

SLIQUE MODEL MANAGEMENT

(212) 213-0119 164 Madison Ave NY, NY 10016

STARS MODEL MANAGEMENT *(212) 988-1400* 360 East 65th St NY, NY 10021

TOTALOOK *(718) 816-1532* 10 Bay Street Landing Staten Island, NY 10301

TRACY'S KIDS, LTD. *(212) 925-2200* 270 Lafayette St NY, NY 10012

VAN DER VEER PEOPLE INC *(212) 688-2880* 401 East 57th St NY, NY 10022

WEE-WILLY'S *(212) 779-0351* 9 East 37th St NY, NY 10016

WILHELMINA MODELS *(212) 532-7141* 9 East 37th St NY, NY 10016

ZOLI MANAGEMENT *(212) 752-4943* 146 East 56th St NY, NY 10022

ZOOM *(212) 481-3000* 12 East 33rd St NY, NY 10016

HAIR & MAKE-UP

a - c

AARON, MARY *(212) 627-4304* 380 W 12th St NY, NY 10014

ABRAMS, RON *(212) 580-0705* NY, NY

ALFIERI, LEANNE NEWTON *(212) 206-0737* 108 W 18th St NY, NY 10011

ALLINGTON, RAY *(212) 925-8333* 568 Broadway NY, NY 10012

ALSONDO, MICHAEL *(212) 586-6300* NY, NY

ALVAREZ, BOUSHELLE *(212) 861-7225* 444 E 82nd St NY, NY 10028

ANDERSEN, MATTU *(212) 941-1180* 225 Lafayette St NY, NY 10012

ANGELL, JEFF *(212) 929-4636* 70A Greenwich Ave NY, NY 10011

ART & COMMERCE *(212) 206-0737* 108 W 18th St NY, NY 10011

ATHA, STEVE *(212) 239-7206* 344 W 38th St NY, NY 10018

B, BILLY *(212) 206-0737* 108 W 18th St NY, NY 10011

BANTRY, BRYAN *(212) 245-0200* 105 W 55th St NY, NY 10019

BARBELLA, NEIL *(718) 238-3402* 9281 Shore Rd Brooklyn, NY 11209

BARUCH, LIZ *(212) 752-8174* 245 E 58th St NY, NY 10022

BAZ, BARRY *(212) 308-4022* 146 E 56th St NY, NY 10022

BECKER, PHILIPPE *(212) 686-5277* 200 E 33rd St NY, NY 10016

PAGE 3

BELTRANDI, NANCY *(212) 529-0404* 38 E 23rd St NY, NY 10010

BERNAL, RORY *(212) 243-6811* 160 Fifth Ave NY, NY 10010

BOCAS, SANDRA *(212) 242-1086* 435 W 23rd St NY, NY 10011

BOOKER, COLIN *(212) 245-0200* 105 W 55th St NY, NY 10019

BOWDEN, PATRICIA *(212) 925-8333* 568 Broadway NY, NY 10012

BRENNAN, DAN *(212) 925-8333* 568 Broadway NY, NY 10012

BRIGITTE INC *(212) 243-6811* 160 Fifth Ave NY, NY 10010

BROWN, PATRICIA *(212) 308-4022* 146 E 56th St NY, NY 10022

BRUSOCK, JIM *(212) 838-3170* 420 E 54th St NY, NY 10022

BUCKLEY, MAREL *(212) 353-0060* 172 East 4th St NY, NY 10009

CASEY, JUDY *(212) 255-3252* 96 Fifth Ave NY, NY 10011

PAGE 5

CAYDEM, ALEXIS *(212) 688-4364* 699 Madison Ave NY, NY 10021

CLORINDA *(718) 767-2080* 147-11 16th Rd Whitestone, NY 11357

PAGE 2

COHEN, NANCY *(212) 861-7225* 444 E 82nd St NY, NY 10028

COLE, LORIN *(212) 674-8871* NY, NY

COLE, VICKI *(212) 431-1212* 134 Reade St NY, NY 10013

COSTELLI, RALPH *(212) 688-4364* 699 Madison Ave NY, NY 10021

CRAWFORD, JIM *(201) 963-0764*

CREATIVE WORKFORCE *(212) 645-4885* 675 Hudson St NY, NY 10014

CROFTON, PADDY *(212) 582-1501* 162 W 56th St NY, NY 10019

d - i

D'APICE, MICHAEL *(212) 410-9319* 328 E 93rd St NY, NY 10128

DALEY, KATIE *(212) 410-9319* 328 E 93rd St NY, NY 10128

DESIMONE, JOSEPH *(212) 924-3766* 234 W 13th St NY, NY 10011

DEVEGA, LEONARDO *(212) 582-1501* 162 W 56th St NY, NY 10019

DI ZEBBA, GABRIELE *(212) 431-1212* 134 Reade St NY, NY 10013

DICARLO, JOHN *(212) 243-6608* 81 Horatio St NY, NY 10014

DIPRIMA, JOANNE *(212) 532-4571* 135 E 26th St NY, NY 10010

DUCAIN, ALEX *(212) 772-2840* 111 E 64th St NY, NY 10021

EDUARDO *(212) 529-0404* 38 E 23rd St NY, NY 10010

ELKIND, PAULETTE *(212) 315-3088* NY, NY

EMMACK, LEE *(212) 861-7225* 444 E 82nd St NY, NY 10028

ENGELMAN, DEBORAH *(212) 242-1086* 435 W 23rd St NY, NY 10011

ESPOSITO, PEGGY *(212) 877-7345* NY, NY

EVANS, KRIS *(212) 686-5277* 200 E 33rd St NY, NY 1001

PAGE 3

FARMAN, BARBARA *(212) 924-6760* 160 Fifth Ave NY, NY 10010

FORBES, ALLAN *(212) 308-4022* 146 E 56th St NY, NY 10022

FRIED, ELIZABETH *(212) 242-9347* 255 W 23rd ST NY, NY 10011

FRIEDMAN, BRENT *(212) 674-8871* NY, NY

GALE, GARY *(212) 683-4514* 240 E 27th St NY, NY 10016

GALJOUR, CHRIS *(212) 941-1180* 225 Lafayette St NY, NY 10012

GARCIA *(212) 889-3028* NY, NY

GEIGER, PAM *(212) 245-0200* 105 W 55th St NY, NY 10019

GILLETTE, RICK *(212) 925-8333* 568 Broadway NY, NY 10012

GIORGIO *(212) 925-8333* 568 Broadway NY, NY 10012

GRANN, SUSANNE *(212) 532-4571* 135 E 26th St NY, NY 10010

GREEN, GARETH *(212) 925-8333* 568 Broadway NY, NY 10012

GREGORY, DONNA *(212) 431-1212* 134 Reade St NY, NY 10013

GREINER, GREG *(212) 529-6646* NY, NY

GRUNDY, AL *(212) 582-1501* 162 W 56th St NY, NY 10019

GURSTRE, ANGELICA *(212) 532-4571* 135 E 26th St NY, NY 10010

HALLELUJAH! ARTIST MANAGEMENT
(212) 243-6608 81 Horatio St NY, NY 10014

HEITZNER, ILISE *(212) 752-8174* 245 E 58th St NY, NY 10022

HMS BOOKINGS *(212) 929-4636* 70A Greenwich Ave NY, NY 10011

HOFMAN, GINGER *(212) 645-4885* 675 Hudson St NY, NY 10014

HOUSER, SUSAN *(212) 752-8174* 245 E 58th St NY, NY 10022

HOWARD, CHARLES *(212) 889-3028* NY, NY

HUCKABAY, CARL *(212) 752-8174* 245 E 58th St NY, NY 10022

ILNSEHER, FRANCOIS *(212) 245-0200* 105 W 55th St NY, NY 10019

INTERNATIONAL ARTIST MANAGEMENT

(212) 582-1501 162 W 56th St NY, NY 10019

j - q

JACOBSON, DAWN *(212) 925-8333* 568 Broadway NY, NY 10012

JONES, JEFF *(212) 929-4636* 70A Greenwich Ave NY, NY 10011

JONES, STEVEN *(212) 431-1212* 134 Reade St NY, NY 10013

KAUSS, JEAN GABRIEL *(212) 370-4300* 235 E 40th St NY, NY 10016

KELLER, BRUCE CLYDE *(212) 532-4571* 135 E 26th St NY, NY 10010

KING, SHAKA *(212) 410-9319* 328 E 93rd St NY, NY 10128

KNIGHT, WILLIAM *(212) 674-8871* NY, NY

KRAMER & KRAMER *(212) 688-4364* 699 Madison Ave NY, NY 10021

KRAMER, STAN *(212) 861-7225* 444 E 82nd St NY, NY 10028

LACOURTE, ROBERT *(212) 532-4571* 135 E 26th St NY, NY 10010

LANE, JUDY *(212) 861-7225* 444 E 82nd St NY, NY 10028

LEONARD, DAVID *(212) 683-4514* 240 E 27th St NY, NY 10016

LEWIS, PASCAL *(212) 431-1212* 134 Reade St NY, NY 10013

LEWIS, RON *(212) 925-8333* 568 Broadway NY, NY 10012

LINDSEY, MARK *(212) 353-0060* 172 East 4th St NY, NY 10009

LONGOBARDI, GERARD *(212) 505-2510* NY, NY

LYNCH, SIBBY *(212) 242-1086* 435 W 23rd St NY, NY 10011

MACAULAY, HELENE *(212) 924-6760* 160 Fifth Ave NY, NY 10010

MACHADA, MARIA *(212) 861-7225* 444 E 82nd St NY, NY 10028

MADLIN, MARIE *(212) 370-4300* 235 E 40th St NY, NY 10016

MANN, MARTHA *(212) 431-6252* NY, NY

MAREK *(212) 924-6760* 160 Fifth Ave NY, NY 10010

MARIN, RICARDO *(212) 683-4514* 240 E 27th St NY, NY 10016

MARTIN, JENNIFER *(212) 582-1501* 162 W 56th St NY, NY 10019

MARLON ***(212) 777-5757*** **67 E 11th St NY, NY 10003**

PAGE 4

MCMAHON, JANINE *(212) 645-4885* 675 Hudson St NY, NY 10014

MILENA *(212) 929-4636* 70A Greenwich Ave NY, NY 10011

MINASSIAN, AMIE *(718) 446-8048* 62-75 Austin St Rego Pk, NY 11374

MITANI, AKIRA *(212) 308-4022* 146 E 56th St NY, NY 10022

NARVAEZ, ROBIN *(212) 371-6378* 360 E 55th St NY, NY 10022

NETWORK REPRESENTATIVES INC

(212) 529-0404 38 E 23rd St NY, NY 10010

OGDEN, RITA *(212) 620-3023* 200 W 15th St NY, NY 10011

PEREZ, JAMES *(212) 683-4514* 240 E 27th St NY, NY 10016

PHILIPS, DANIEL *(212) 925-8333* 568 Broadway NY, NY 10012

PIETRO, STEPHAN *(212) 674-8871* NY, NY

PITTMAN, JANE *(212) 582-1501* 162 W 56th St NY, NY 10019

POLLUTRO, JODY *(212) 533-3995* 145 E 16th St NY, NY 10003

PRIANO, TIMOTHY ***(212) 686-5277*** **200 E 33rd St NY, NY 10016**

PAGE 3

r - z

REDA, JAMES ***(212) 255-3252*** **96 Fifth Ave NY, NY 10011**

PAGE 5

REILEY, STEVE *(212) 929-4636* 70A Greenwich Ave NY, NY 10011

ROGERS, WENDY *(212) 861-7225* 444 E 82nd St NY, NY 10028

ROSENAST, ERICA *(212) 645-4885* 675 Hudson St NY, NY 10014

RULON, KENT *(212) 752-8174* 245 E 58th St NY, NY 10022

RUTLEDGE, JOHN *(212) 674-8871* NY, NY

SANDERS, MICHELLE *(212) 532-4571* 135 E 26th St NY, NY 10010

SANSONE, BARBARA *(212) 431-1212* 134 Reade St NY, NY 10013

SAVIN, MARIE MADELEINE *(212) 206-0737* 108 W 18th St NY, NY 10011

SCHIFFMAN, LISA *(212) 941-1180* 225 Lafayette St NY, NY 10012

SEHVEN ARTS INC *(212) 532-4571* 135 E 26th St NY, NY 10010

SEHVEN, AUGUST *(212) 532-4571* 135 E 26th St NY, NY 10010

SEPHTON, MARK *(212) 242-1086* 435 W 23rd St NY, NY 10011

SIMON *(212) 529-0404* 38 E 23rd St NY, NY 10010

SNOW, ROBERT *(212) 688-4364* 699 Madison Ave NY, NY 10021

SONDERA, TRACEY *(212) 582-1501* 162 W 56th St NY, NY 10019

SUGA *(212) 421-4400* 115 E 57th St NY, NY 10022

TAKOS, JAMES *(212) 925-8333* 568 Broadway NY, NY 10012

TAMBLYN, THOM *(212) 683-4514* 240 E 27th St NY, NY 10016

TANG, MICHELLE *(212) 532-4571* 135 E 26th St NY, NY 10010

TOMOKO *(212) 924-6760* 160 Fifth Ave NY, NY 10010

VAN DORSSEN, ROB ***(212) 255-3252*** **96 Fifth Ave NY, NY 10011**

PAGE 5

VANO, ROBERT *(212) 924-6760* 160 Fifth Ave NY, NY 10010

VON SOLOS, AARON *(212) 982-8493* NY, NY

VON WIJNBERGE, HARIE *(212) 308-4022* 146 E 56th St NY, NY 10022

WALTERS, PRUDENCE *(212) 752-8174* 245 E 58th St NY, NY 10022

WARREN, JEWEL *(212) 505-0166* NY, NY

WEIS, JAMES THEADFORD *(212) 674-8871* NY, NY

WESTMORELAND, BILL *(212) 206-0737* 108 W 18th St NY, NY 10011

Wong, Lorraine *(212) 532-4571* 135 E 26th St NY, NY 10010

Wright, Jon *(212) 532-4571* 135 E 26th St NY, NY 10010

Wylder, Scott *(212) 645-4885* 675 Hudson St NY, NY 10014

Yellen Associates *(212) 838-3170* 420 E 54th St NY, NY 10022

Yoshi *(212) 924-6760* 160 Fifth Ave NY, NY 10010

Zanya *(212) 674-8871* NY, NY

Zoli Illusions *(212) 308-4022* 146 E 56th St NY, NY 10022

HAIR

a - g

Aleman, Michelle *(212) 245-0200* 105 W 55th St NY, NY 10019

Art & Commerce *(212) 206-0737* 108 W 18th St NY, NY 10011

Bantry, Bryan *(212) 245-0200* 105 W 55th St NY, NY 10019

Barry, Mitch *(212) 925-8552* 82 Greene St NY, NY 10011

Baruch, Liz *(212) 752-8174* 245 E 58th St NY, NY 10022

Basile *(212) 532-4571* 135 E 26th St NY, NY 10010

Beaumont, Bruce-Libre *(212) 370-4300* 235 E 40th St NY, NY 10016

Bets *(212) 941-1180* 225 Lafayette St NY, NY 10012

Bowden, Trevor *(212) 925-8552* 82 Greene St NY, NY 10011

Brennan, Dan *(212) 925-8333* 568 Broadway NY, NY 10012

Buckley, Marel *(212) 353-0600* 172 East 4th St NY, NY 10009

Capozzoli, Ron *(212) 732-5379* 40 Harrison St NY, NY 10013

Carino *(212) 941-1180* 225 Lafayette St NY, NY 10012

Casey, Judy *(212) 255-3252* 96 Fifth Ave NY, NY 10011

PAGE 5

Christiaan *(212) 246-1919* NY, NY

Cofano, Madeleine *(212) 925-5909* 66 Crosby St NY, NY 10012

Cohen, Gad *(212) 924-6760* 160 Fifth Ave NY, NY 10010

Cohen, Sasha *(212) 370-4300* 235 E 40th St NY, NY 10016

Cohl *(212) 245-0200* 105 W 55th St NY, NY 10019

Cole, Vicki *(212) 431-1212* 134 Reade St NY, NY 10013

Coleman, Ian *(212) 674-8871* NY, NY

Comacho, Raymond *(212) 925-8552* 82 Greene St NY, NY 10011

Dal Corso, Joseph *(212) 741-2276* NY, NY

Danino *(212) 242-6387* NY, NY

DeMay, Anthony *(212) 752-8174* 245 E 58th St NY, NY 10022

Dessange, Bruno *(212) 245-0200* 105 W 55th St NY, NY 10019

Downs, Christopher *(212) 686-5277* 200 E 33rd St NY, NY 10016

PAGE 3

Downs, Timothy *(212) 353-0060* 172 East 4th St NY, NY 10009

Ezel *(212) 431-1212* 134 Reade St NY, NY 10013

Fekkai, Frederic *(212) 838-3170* 420 E 54th St NY, NY 10022

Foster, Terry *(212) 889-7067* 260 Fifth Ave NY, NY 10001

Fugler, Howard *(212) 255-3252* 96 Fifth Ave NY, NY 10011

PAGE 5

Gabriel, Eric *(212) 242-6387* NY, NY

Garren *(212) 686-5277* 200 E 33rd St NY, NY 10016

PAGE 3

Gilbert, Odile *(212) 245-0200* 105 W 55th St NY, NY 10019

Groves, Rodney *(212) 206-0737* 108 W 18th St NY, NY 10011

h - n

Halterman, Troy *(212) 255-3252* 96 Fifth Ave NY, NY 10011

PAGE 5

Hamid *(212) 242-1086* 435 W 23rd St NY, NY 10011

Hammond, Danny *(212) 353-0060* 172 East 4th St NY, NY 10009

Hilliard, Alex *(212) 245-0200* 105 W 55th St NY, NY 10019

Hopson, Maury *(212) 460-5212* 114 E 13th St NY, NY 10009

International Artist Management
(212) 582-1501 162 W 56th St NY, NY 10019

Julien *(212) 206-0737* 108 W 18th St NY, NY 10011

Kauss, Jean Gabriel *(212) 370-4300* 235 E 40th St NY, NY 10016

Keo, Richard *(212) 206-0737* 108 W 18th St NY, NY 10011

King, Harry *(212) 760-0057* 234 Fifth Ave NY, NY 10001

King, Lindie *(212) 688-4364* 699 Madison Ave NY, NY 10021

Kinigson, David *(212) 431-1212* 134 Reade St NY, NY 10013

Knight, William *(212) 674-8871* NY, NY

Knoll, Stephen *(212) 688-4364* 699 Madison Ave NY, NY 10021

Korn, Elaine *(212) 760-0057* 234 Fifth Ave NY, NY 10001

Kramer & Kramer *(212) 688-4364* 699 Madison Ave NY, NY 10021

Lee, Liz Inc *(212) 889-7067* 260 Fifth Ave NY, NY 10001

Lempiere, Stephane *(212) 924-6760* 160 Fifth Ave NY, NY 10010

LeSalon, Bruno *(212) 925-8333* 568 Broadway NY, NY 10012

Lopez, Michael *(212) 308-4022* 146 E 56th St NY, NY 10022

Losi *(212) 242-6387* NY, NY

Lucha, Tony *(212) 941-1180* 225 Lafayette St NY, NY 10012

Lynch, Sibby *(212) 242-1086* 435 W 23rd St NY, NY 10011

Maligne, Didier *(212) 245-0200* 105 W 55th St NY, NY 10019

Malone, Ian *(212) 431-1212* 134 Reade St NY, NY 10013

Mancuso, Kevin *(212) 242-6387* NY, NY

Marek *(212) 924-6760* 160 Fifth Ave NY, NY 10010

Marianna *(212) 246-1919* NY, NY

Marlon *(212) 777-5757* 67 E 11th St NY, NY 10003

PAGE 4

Martin, Rodney *(212) 245-0200* 105 W 55th St NY, NY 10019

Matsuo, Shunji *(212) 838-3170* 420 E 54th St NY, NY 10022

Mazzei, Michael *(212) 924-6760* 160 Fifth Ave NY, NY 10010

McAulay, Tony *(212) 620-0284* NY, NY

McKiver, Thomas *(212) 219-0707* 153 Mercer St NY, NY 10012

McKnight, Sam *(212) 245-0200* 105 W 55th St NY, NY 10019

Mikula, Donald *(212) 245-0200* 105 W 55th St NY, NY 10019

Murray, Helen *(212) 460-5212* 114 E 13th St NY, NY 10003

O - Z

Omar *(212) 242-6387* NY, NY

Oribe *(212) 242-6387* NY, NY

Oversee *(212) 219-0707* 153 Mercer St NY, NY 10012

Pattison, Anne *(718) 783-0277* 277 Washington Ave Brooklyn, NY 11205

Pinnell, Max *(212) 431-1212* 134 Reade St NY, NY 10013

Pipino, Marc *(212) 245-0200* 105 W 55th St NY, NY 10019

Pipino, Ric *(212) 245-0200* 105 W 55th St NY, NY 10019

Priano, Thom *(212) 686-5277* 200 E 33rd St NY, NY 10016

PAGE 3

Priano, Timothy *(212) 686-5277* 200 E 33rd St NY, NY 10016

PAGE 3

Ramsay, Dawn *(212) 431-1212* 134 Reade St NY, NY 10013

Recine, Bob *(212) 925-5909* 66 Crosby St NY, NY 10012

Reid, Pamela *(212) 925-5909* 66 Crosby St NY, NY 10012

Rocky *(212) 582-1501* 162 W 56th St NY, NY 10019

Sahag, John *(212) 371-4777* 18 E 53rd St NY, NY 10022

Sava, Gabriel *(212) 688-4364* 699 Madison Ave NY, NY 10021

Savic, Peter *(212) 206-0737* 108 W 18th St NY, NY 10011

Schiffman, Lisa *(212) 941-1180* 225 Lafayette St NY, NY 10012

Schramm, Emily *(212) 620-0284* NY, NY

Sehven Arts Inc *(212) 532-4571* 135 E 26th St NY, NY 10010

Spazzoli, Maxie *(212) 777-5757* 67 E 11th St NY, NY 10003

PAGE 4

Spellman, Daniel *(516) 791-3246* 33 Cambridge St Valley Stream, NY 11581

Spezzacatena, Bob *(212) 759-7985* NY, NY

Stam, Ronnie *(212) 219-0707* 153 Mercer St NY, NY 10012

Tammaro, Michael *(212) 925-8333* 568 Broadway NY, NY 10012

Tricomi, Edward *(212) 924-6760* 160 Fifth Ave NY, NY 10010

Vigorelli, Gabrieli *(212) 924-6760* 160 Fifth Ave NY, NY 10010

Vincent *(212) 431-1212* 134 Reade St NY, NY 10012

Virginie *(212) 582-1501* 162 W 56th St NY, NY 10019

Warn, Kerry *(212) 925-8552* 82 Greene St NY, NY 10011

Watson, Elizabeth *(212) 925-8552* 82 Greene St NY, NY 10011

Whyte, Alan *(212) 925-8333* 568 Broadway NY, NY 10012

Wong, Sam *(212) 532-4571* 135 E 26th St NY, NY 10010

Woodley, Jeffrey *(212) 582-1501* 162 W 56th St NY, NY 10019

Yacomine, Paul *(212) 925-8333* 568 Broadway NY, NY 10012

Yamasa *(212) 924-6760* 160 Fifth Ave NY, NY 10010

Yellen Associates *(212) 838-3170* 420 E 54th St NY, NY 10022

Zisser, Grey *(212) 255-3252* 96 Fifth Ave NY, NY 10011

PAGE 5

Zoli Illusions *(212) 308-4022* 146 E 56th St NY, NY 10022

MAKE-UP

a - f

Adams, Richard *(212) 308-4022* 146 E 56th St NY, NY 10022

Alberto, Carlo *(212) 243-6811* 160 Fifth Ave NY, NY 10010

Anastacia *(212) 431-9214* NY, NY

Andersen, Brigette Reiss *(212) 925-5909* 66 Crosby St NY, NY 10012

Andersson, Helen *(212) 645-4885* 675 Hudson St NY, NY 10014

Ando, Hiromi *(212) 924-6760* 160 Fifth Ave NY, NY 10010

Ariella *(212) 889-7067* 260 Fifth Ave NY, NY 10001

Art & Commerce *(212) 206-0737* 108 W 18th St NY, NY 10011

Aucoin, Kevin *(212) 460-5212* 114 E 13th St NY, NY 10009

Avery, Margaret *(212) 838-3170* 420 E 54th St NY, NY 10022

Axmen, Audrey *(212) 532-4571* 135 E 26th St NY, NY 10010

Bantry, Brian *(212) 245-0200* 105 W 55th St NY, NY 10019

Barnes, Byron *(212) 683-4514* 240 E 27th St NY, NY 10016

Bernardi, Renato *(212) 431-1212* 134 Reade St NY, NY 10013

Blanco, Daniel *(212) 686-5277* 200 E 33rd St NY, NY 10016

PAGE 3

Brennan, Dan *(212) 925-8333* 568 Broadway NY, NY 10012

Brigitte Inc *(212) 243-6811* 160 Fifth Ave NY, NY 10010

Brown, Bobbi *(212) 925-8333* 568 Broadway NY, NY 10012

Brumberger Studio *(212) 840-7179* 233 W 42nd St NY, NY 10036

Cantello, Linda *(212) 245-0200* 105 W 55th St NY, NY 10019

Casey, Judy *(212) 255-3252* 96 Fifth Ave NY, NY 10011

PAGE 5

Cooper, Fran *(212) 925-8552* 82 Greene St NY, NY 10011

Cole, Vicki *(212) 431-1212* 134 Reade St NY, NY 10013

Creative Workforce *(212) 645-4885* 675 Hudson St NY, NY 10014

De Schneider, Maria *(212) 255-3252* 96 Fifth Ave NY, NY 10011

PAGE 5

Donahue, Kate *(212) 683-4514* 240 E 27th St NY, NY 10016

Dunn, Wesley *(212) 686-5277* 200 E 33rd St NY, NY 10016

PAGE 3

Fass, Adele *(212) 674-8871* NY, NY

Franklin, Glenna *(212) 255-3252* 96 Fifth Ave NY, NY 10011

PAGE 5

g - m

Gadson, Craig *(212) 838-3170* 420 E 54th St NY, NY 10022

Giana *(212) 688-4364* 699 Madison Ave NY, NY 10021

Gillian, B.J. *(212) 777-5757* 67 E 11th St NY, NY 10003

PAGE 4

Gray, Tracey *(212) 431-1212* 134 Reade St NY, NY 10013

Greenwell, Mary *(212) 245-0200* 105 W 55th St NY, NY 10019

Guillemot, Marine *(212) 925-8333* 568 Broadway NY, NY 10012

Hallelujah! Artist Management

(212) 243-6608 81 Horatio St NY, NY 10014

Haney, Kevin *(914) 949-5598* 28 Lind Ave White Plains, NY 10605

Hayles, Mark *(212) 255-3252* 96 Fifth Ave NY, NY 10011

PAGE 5

HMS Bookings *(212) 929-4636* 70A Greenwich Ave NY, NY 10011

International Artist Management

(212) 582-1501 162 W 56th St NY, NY 10019

Iphergan, Rose *(212) 370-4300* 235 E 40th St NY, NY 10016

Jenrette, Pamela *(212) 673-4748* 300 Mercer St NY, NY 10003

Joseph, Cindy *(212) 925-8333* 568 Broadway NY, NY 10012

Kashuk, Sonia *(212) 924-6760* 160 Fifth Ave NY, NY 10010

Kauss, Jean Gabriel *(212) 370-4300* 235 E 40th St NY, NY 10016

Knight, William *(212) 674-8871* NY, NY

Korn, Elaine *(212) 760-0057* 234 Fifth Ave NY, NY 10001

Kramer & Kramer *(212) 688-4364* 699 Madison Ave NY, NY 10021

Laden, Bob *(718) 229-0638* 25-55 Bell Blvd Bayside, NY 11360

Lafontaine, Marie-Josee *(212) 924-6760* 160 Fifth Ave NY, NY 10010

Lane, Judy *(212) 861-7225* 444 E 82nd St NY, NY 10028

Lear, Connie *(212) 861-7225* 444 E 82nd St NY, NY 10028

Lee, Liz *(212) 889-7067* 260 Fifth Ave NY, NY 10001

Lefton, Jackie *(212) 370-4300* 235 E 40th St NY, NY 10016

Levy, Sophie *(212) 245-0200* 105 W 55th St NY, NY 10019

Linter, Sandy *(212) 925-8552* 82 Greene St NY, NY 10011

Lopez, Leslie *(212) 925-8552* 82 Greene St NY, NY 10011

Lynch, Sibby *(212) 242-1086* 435 W 23rd St NY, NY 10011

Maddie, Mike *(718) 712-1665* 148-73 Huxley St Rosedale, NY 11422

Maller, Bonnie *(212) 245-0200* 105 W 55th St NY, NY 10019

Marais, Stephane *(212) 206-0737* 108 W 18th St NY, NY 10011

Marek *(212) 924-6760* 160 Fifth Ave NY, NY 10010

Marin, Carlos *(212) 243-6608* 81 Horatio St NY, NY 10014

Marlon *(212) 777-5757* 67 E 11th St NY, NY 10003

PAGE 4

Marziali, Glenn *(212) 460-5212* 114 E 13th St NY, NY 10003

Mason, Linda *(212) 941-0459* NY, NY

Massarelli, Wayne *(212) 929-4636* 70A Greenwich Ave NY, NY 10011

Masters, Mariella Smith *(212) 245-0200* 105 W 55th St NY, NY 10019

Matsuura, John *(212) 431-1212* 134 Reade St NY, NY 10013

McDevitt, Joe *(212) 688-4364* 699 Madison Ave NY, NY 10021

Mercier, Laura *(212) 925-5909* 66 Crosby St NY, NY 10012

Metz, Timothy *(212) 206-0737* 108 W 18th St NY, NY 10011

Michael, Liz *(212) 206-0737* 108 W 18th St NY, NY 10011

Mills, Joey *(212) 760-0057* 234 Fifth Ave NY, NY 10001

Mulholland, Moyra *(212) 777-5757* 67 E 11th St NY, NY 10003

PAGE 4

Murray, Helen *(212) 460-5212* 114 E 13th St NY, NY 10003

n - z

Nahmias, Mark *(212) 941-1180* 225 Lafayette St NY, NY 10012

Nars, Francis *(212) 431-9214* NY, NY

Network Representatives Inc

(212) 529-0404 38 E 23rd St NY, NY 10010

Nottingham, Nadiya *(212) 686-5277* 200 E 33rd St NY, NY 10016

PAGE 3

Oakley, Sara *(212) 749-5912* 270 Riverside Dr NY, NY 10025

Paoletti, Andrea *(212) 924-6760* 160 Fifth Ave NY, NY 10010

Pemberton, Teresa *(212) 777-5757* 67 E 11th St NY, NY 10003

PAGE 4

Poussard, Patrick *(212) 308-4022* 146 E 56th St NY, NY 10022

Priano, Timothy *(212) 686-5277* 200 E 33rd St NY, NY 10016

PAGE 3

Quesada, Ricki *(212) 431-1212* 134 Reade St NY, NY 10013

Reid, Pamela *(212) 925-5909* 66 Crosby St NY, NY 10012

Rex *(212) 760-0057* 234 Fifth Ave NY, NY 10001

Richardson, John *(212) 861-7225* 444 E 82nd St NY, NY 10028

Rodman, Letha *(212) 838-3170* 420 E 54th St NY, NY 10022

Rosely *(212) 582-1501* 162 W 56th St NY, NY 10019

Rumiko *(212) 925-8333* 568 Broadway NY, NY 10012

Schaefer, Mark *(212) 370-4300* 235 E 40th St NY, NY 10016

Schall, Nancy *(212) 529-0404* 38 E 23rd St NY, NY 10010

Schiffman, Lisa *(212) 941-1180* 225 Lafayette St NY, NY 10012

Sehven Arts Inc *(212) 532-4571* 135 E 26th St NY, NY 10010

Sephton, Mark *(212) 242-1086* 435 W 23rd St NY, NY 10011

Siegel, Lea *(212) 529-0404* 38 E 23rd St NY, NY 10010

Special Make-Up Effects Studio

(914) 693-2752 68 Colonial Ave Dobbs Ferry, NY 10522

Stacia, Ana *(212) 431-9214* NY, NY

Strettell, Jo *(212) 206-0737* 108 W 18th St NY, NY 10011

Tamblyn, Thom *(212) 683-4514* 240 E 27th St NY, NY 10016

Velasco, Danny *(212) 431-1212* 134 Reade St NY, NY 10013

Voyski, Michel *(212) 925-8552* 82 Greene St NY, NY 10011

Watson, Elizabeth *(212) 925-8552* 82 Greene St NY, NY 10011

Wells, Reggie *(212) 308-4022* 146 E 56th St NY, NY 10022

Yellen Associates *(212) 838-3170* 420 E 54th St NY, NY 10022

Zoli Illusions *(212) 308-4022* 146 E 56th St NY, NY 10022

STYLISTS

a - f

Abbamonte, Mary *(212) 249-9397* 17 E 64th St NY, NY 10021

Abbate, Marie *(212) 243-6811* 160 Fifth Ave NY, NY 10010

Albright, Irene *(212) 752-8174* 245 E 58th St NY, NY 10022

Allyson, Dana *(212) 752-8174* 245 E 58th St NY, NY 10022

Amadori, Scott *(212) 308-4022* 146 E 56th St NY, NY 10022

Arnett, Angie *(718) 932-3832* Brooklyn, NY

Art & Commerce *(212) 206-0737* 108 W 18th St NY, NY 10011

Bafaro, Johanna *(212) 966-6464* 5 White St NY, NY 10013

Baker, Martha *(212) 517-9060* 1630 York Ave NY, NY 10028

Baruch, Liz *(212) 752-8174* 245 E 58th St NY, NY 10022

Berman, Benicia *(212) 737-9627* 399 E 72nd St NY, NY 10021

Braxton, Jocelyn *(212) 308-4022* 146 E 56th St NY, NY 10022

Briggs, Eddie *(212) 529-0404* 38 E 23rd St NY, NY 10010

Brigitte Inc *(212) 243-6811* 160 Fifth Ave NY, NY 10010

C & C Productions *(212) 472-3700* 445 E 80th St NY, NY 10021

Celle, Christine *(212) 431-1212* 134 Reade St NY, NY 10013

Chin, Fay *(212) 219-8770* 67 Vestry St NY, NY 10013

Cohen, Susan *(212) 755-3157* NY, NY

Cole, Vicki *(212) 431-1212* 134 Reade St NY, NY 10013

Creative Workforce *(212) 645-4885* 675 Hudson St NY, NY 10014

Cronin, Terri *(212) 529-0404* 38 E 23rd St NY, NY 10010

Daner, Carol *(212) 243-8152* 200 W 20th St NY, NY 10011

David, Jan *(212) 431-1212* 134 Reade St NY, NY 10013

Davidson/Frank Photo Stylists

(212) 799-2651 209 W 86th St NY, NY 10024

Dehornois, Jacques *(212) 370-4300* 235 E 40th St NY, NY 10016

Derene, Leslie *(212) 532-4571* 135 E 26th St NY, NY 10010

Deutsch, Lisbeth *(212) 255-0079* 184 W 4th St NY, NY 10014

Donofrio, Marc *(212) 532-4571* 135 E 26th St NY, NY 10010

Duplan, Mande *(212) 925-5909* 66 Crosby St NY, NY 10012

Eng, Chris *(212) 477-8786* 545 E 14th St NY, NY 10009

Feirstein, Joyce *(212) 472-3753* 445 E 80th St NY, NY 10021

Ferguson, Laura *(212) 529-0404* 38 E 23rd St NY, NY 10010

Fox, Paula *(212) 529-0404* 38 E 23rd St NY, NY 10010

Fradkin, Mindy *(212) 243-0202* 313 W 75th St NY, NY 10023

g - o

Gerry, Catherine *(212) 769-4355* 309 W 90th St NY, NY 10024

Goday, Dale *(212) 254-4062* 55 E 11th St NY, NY 10003

Goldenberg, Lisa *(212) 532-4571* 135 E 26th St NY, NY 10010

Goldman, Pamela *(212) 532-4571* 135 E 26th St NY, NY 10010

Goldstein, Lori *(212) 206-0737* 108 W 18th St NY, NY 10011

Gong, Julie *(718) 237-2350* Brooklyn, NY

Goodkind, Elisa *(212) 752-8174* 245 E 58th St NY, NY 10022

Gunn, Georgia *(212) 924-6760* 160 Fifth Ave NY, NY 10010

Haddock, Sherry *(212) 532-4571* 135 E 26th St NY, NY 10010

Hallelujah! Artist Management

(212) 243-6608 81 Horatio St NY, NY 10014

Harrington, Kate *(212) 777-5757* 67 E 11th St NY, NY 10003

PAGE 4

Hochberg, Netti *(212) 758-8711* NY, NY

Hyde, Beverly *(212) 529-0404* 38 E 23rd St NY, NY 10010

Ingrid *(212) 243-6811* 160 Fifth Ave NY, NY 10010

Johnson, Beth *(212) 532-4571* 135 E 26th St NY, NY 10010

Kauss, Jean Gabriel *(212) 370-4300* 235 E 40th St NY, NY 10016

Kay, Judy *(212) 807-0664* 83 Old Well Rd Purchase, NY 10577

Kimmel, Lily *(212) 431-1212* 134 Reade St NY, NY 10013

Klein, Mary Ellen *(212) 683-6351* NY, NY

Kleinman, Judith *(212) 529-0404* 38 E 23rd St NY, NY 10010

Kurs, Pat *(212) 758-4523* 865 First Ave NY, NY 10017

LaPierre, Joanne *(212) 529-0404* 38 E 23rd St NY, NY 10010

Lauglin, Bill *(212) 529-0404* 38 E 23rd St NY, NY 10010

Levy, Curtis *(212) 752-8174* 245 E 58th St NY, NY 10022

Llewelyn *(212) 532-4571* 135 E 26th St NY, NY 10010

Magidson, Peggy *(212) 912-1410* NY, NY

Mahoney, Claire *(212) 529-0404* 38 E 23rd St NY, NY 10010

Marek *(212) 924-6760* 160 Fifth Ave NY, NY 10010

Markbein, Eliette *(212) 666-1068* 235 W 102nd St NY, NY 10025

Marlon ***(212) 777-5757*** **67 E 11th St NY, NY 10003**

PAGE 4

Mokus & Co *(212) 619-8130* 146 Duane St NY, NY 10013

Network Representatives

(212) 529-0404 38 E 23rd St NY, NY 10010

Newman, Cindy *(201) 224-3736*

O'Brien, Teresa *(212) 308-4022* 146 E 56th St NY, NY 10022

Obe, Takeshi *(212) 941-1180* 225 Lafayette St NY, NY 10012

Odette *(212) 735-5776* NY, NY

Orefice, Jeanette

(718) 802-1396 82 Schermerhorn Brooklyn Hghts, NY 11201

Oversee *(212) 219-0707* 153 Mercer St NY, NY 10012

p - z

Phillips, Ranirianne *(212) 645-4885* 675 Hudson St NY, NY 10014

Pietra, Michele *(212) 598-4991* 150 Thompson St NY, NY 10012

Promisel, Shelley *(212) 475-7602* 2 Fifth Ave NY, NY 10011

Radov, Fern *(212) 529-0404* 38 E 23rd St NY, NY 10010

Reid, Pamela *(212) 925-5909* 66 Crosby St NY, NY 10012

Ritchie, Eva *(212) 925-9427* 492 Broome St NY, NY 10013

Roth, Ana *(212) 645-4885* 675 Hudson St NY, NY 10014

Sabatier, Sylvie *(212) 370-4300* 235 E 40th St NY, NY 10016

Safir, Lisa *(212) 752-8174* 245 E 58th St NY, NY 10022

Sampson, Linda *(212) 925-6821* 431 W Broadway NY, NY 10012

Santiago *(212) 308-4022* 146 E 56th St NY, NY 10022

Schevorton, Linda *(212) 691-0881* 150 Ninth Ave NY, NY 10011

Schiffman, Lisa *(212) 941-1180* 225 Lafayette St NY, NY 10012

Schulman, Susan Barr *(212) 308-4022* 146 E 56th St NY, NY 10022

Sehven Arts *(212) 532-4571* 135 E 26th St NY, NY 10010

Sheffy, Nina A ***(212) 662-0709*** **838 West End Ave NY, NY 10025**

PAGE 13

Sidor, Susan *(212) 243-6608* 81 Horatio St NY, NY 10014

Slote, Ina *(212) 679-4584* 7 Park Ave NY, NY 10016

Smith, Rose *(212) 758-8711* 400 E 56th St NY, NY 10022

Sokolec, Jerri *(212) 308-4022* 146 E 56th St NY, NY 10022

Sommers, Pam *(718) 875-9721* 136 Amity St Brooklyn, NY 11201

Sprudin, Magdalen *(212) 924-6760* 160 Fifth Ave NY, NY 10010

Stevens, Charles *(212) 529-0404* 38 E 23rd St NY, NY 10010

Strambio, Nicoletta *(212) 431-1212* 134 Reade St NY, NY 10013

Strongin, Randy *(212) 242-1715* 210 W 21st St NY, NY 10011

Sullivan, Dee *(212) 532-4571* 135 E 26th St NY, NY 10010

Tiagi *(212) 308-4022* 146 E 56th St NY, NY 10022

Turk, Barbara *(212) 941-1180* 225 Lafayette St NY, NY 10012

Van Thiet, Muriel Phan

(212) 206-0737 108 W 18th St NY, NY 10011

Warkov, Aaron *(212) 529-0404* 38 E 23rd St NY, NY 10010

Watson, Lorye *(212) 245-6688* 420 W 46th St NY, NY 10036

Welslow, Mikel *(212) 930-2420* 595 West End Ave NY, NY 10024

Wexler, Marilyn *(212) 580-9556* 58 W 68th St NY, NY 10023

WHITAKER, ROSS *(212) 529-0404* 38 E 23rd St NY, NY 10010

WHITE, ALEXANDER *(212) 308-4022* 146 E 56th St NY, NY 10022

WOLF, BRANA *(212) 219-0707* 153 Mercer St NY, NY 10012

ZOLI ILLUSIONS *(212) 308-4022* 146 E 56th St NY, NY 10022

FOOD STYLISTS

a - z

BATTIFARANO, A.J. *(212) 877-7138* 230 W 76th St NY, NY 10023

BENNER, DYNE *(212) 688-7571* 311 E 60th St NY, NY 10022

BRODER, ANN *(516) 368-2454* 30 Beacon Lane E. Northport, NY 11731

BUCKNER, JACQUELINE *(212) 737-5746* 509 E 81st St NY, NY 10028

BURNSTEIN, SIDNEY *(212) 582-1501* 162 W 56th St NY, NY 10019

CANNON, SUKY *(516) 351-1390* 50 Shore Dr Huntington, NY 11743

CANTOR, LYNN *(914) 623-9471* 6 Danville Ct W Nyack, NY 10994

COOKE, VICKIE EMERSON *(212) 674-5547* 380 Lafayette St NY, NY 10003

CRONK, ALICE *(201) 327-2982* 10 Mohigan Way Mahwah, NJ 07430

DEVILLEMEUVE, KATHY

(516) 595-2710 5 Whispering Ct Dix Hills, NY 11746

FARRAN, PHILIP *(212) 758-3254* 340 E 52nd St NY, NY 10022

GELBES, CAROL *(212) 580-3485* 545 West End Ave NY, NY 10024

GODAY, DALE *(212) 254-4062* 55 E 11th St NY, NY 10003

HARRINGTON, SUSIE *(212) 581-6470* 90 Colin St Yonkers, NY 10701

HODGDON, MARILINDA *(212) 735-6583* 225 E 95th St NY, NY 10128

INTERNATIONAL ARTIST MANAGEMENT

(212) 582-1501 162 W 56th St NY, NY 10019

JAFFE, CHERYLE *(212) 861-7728* 200 E 82nd St NY, NY 10028

LANGAN, MARIANNE

(201) 327-2666 536 W Saddle River Upper Saddle River, NJ 07458

MESHEJIAN, ZABEL *(212) 242-2459* 125 Washington Pl NY, NY 10014

PRICE, MARET *(914) 779-8546* 7 Gramaton Ct Bronxville, NY 10708

PRITCHARD, RUSSELL *(212) 967-4201* 308 W 40th St NY, NY 10018

ROSENBLATT, RICKI *(212) 206-8383* 77 Perry St NY, NY 10014

SHERN, STEPHEN *(212) 807-8765* 165 W 23rd St NY, NY 10011

SINCLAIR, JOANNA *(212) 255-3895* 304 W 11th St NY, NY 10014

SWENSON, ANDREA *(212) 228-6504* NY, NY

TALBOTT, POLLY *(212) 686-2493* 300 E 33rd St NY, NY 10016

TEMPLE, KAREN *(212) 924-7870* 337 W 21st St NY, NY 10011

WEINRIB, HELGA *(212) 628-9509* 880 Lexington Ave NY, NY 10021

WINTERS, PATRICIA *(212) 249-6337* 215 E 68th St NY, NY 10021

ZEKAUSKAS, ANN *(212) 879-7909* 21 W 89th St NY, NY 10024

CASTING

a - e

ACTORS UNLIMITED CASTING SVC

(212) 489-9520 353 W 54th St NY, NY 10019

ASSOCIATED CASTING GROUP *(212) 725-0014* 300 E 44th St NY, NY 10017

BCI/GOLDLOVE, SEROW & SINDLINGER

(212) 627-7300 151 W 25th St NY, NY 10001

BRINKER, JANE CASTING *(212) 924-3322* 51 W 16th St NY, NY 10011

BROWN, DEBORAH *(212) 581-0404* 250 W 57th St NY, NY 10017

BURTON, KATE CASTING *(212) 929-0948* 39 W 19th St NY, NY 10011

C & C PRODCUTIONS UNLIMITED

(212) 472-3700 445 E 80th St NY, NY 10021

CAST AWAY! CASTING SVC *(960) 755-0960* 14 Sutton Pl So NY, NY 10022

CENTRAL CASTING OF NY *(212) 582-4933* 200 W 54th St NY, NY 10019

CERNIELLO, MARIA ASSOCIATES *(212) 889-8199* NY, NY

COMPLETE CASTING *(212) 382-3835* 240 W 44th St NY, NY 10036

CONTEMPORARY CASTING LTD

(212) 838-1818 41 E 57th St NY, NY 10022

CRAMER, ISABELLE CASTING *(212) 586-8400* 641 W 59th St NY, NY 10019

CTP CASTING *(212) 696-1100* 22 W 27th St NY, NY 10001

PAGE 15

DELMONTE, MERRY L CASTING

(212) 279-2000 460 W 42nd St NY, NY 10036

DESETA, DONNA CASTING *(212) 239-0988* 424 W 33rd St NY, NY 10001

f - q

FACES AND PLACES *(212) 924-1022* 124 W 24th St NY, NY 10011

FAY, SILVIA CASTING *(212) 889-2626* 71 Park Ave NY, NY 10016

FREMONT, MAUREEN CASTING

(212) 678-7209 641 W 59NY, NY 10019

GOLDEN CASTING *(212) 496-0146* 133 W 72nd St NY, NY 10023

GRECO, MARIA & ASSOC CASTING

(212) 231-5500 1261 Broadway NY, NY 10001

HENDERSON, JUDY & ASSOC CASTING

(212) 877-0225 330 W 89th St NY, NY 10024

HERMAN & LIPSON CASTING *(212) 807-7706* 24 W 25th St NY, NY 10010

HOWARD, STUART ASSOC CASTING

(212) 477-2323 215 Park Ave So NY, NY 10003

Hyde Hamlet Casting *(212) 730-1842* 165 W 46th St NY, NY 10036

Jacobs, Judith Casting *(212) 744-3758* 336 E 81st St NY, NY 10028

Kelly & Case Casting *(212) 463-8630* 155 W 13th St NY, NY 10011

Kressel, Lynn Casting *(212) 581-6990* 111 W 57th St NY, NY 10019

McCorkle Casting Ltd *(212) 840-0992* 264 W 40th St NY, NY 10018

Moroe/Olsen & Assoc Inc

(212) 243-0078 Box 1266 Old Chelsea Sta NY, NY 10011

Our Agency *(212) 982-5626* 112 E 23rd St NY, NY 10010

Pasciuto, Joanne Casting *(212) 944-6420* 1457 Broadway NY, NY 10036

People Finders *(212) 265-3221* 1775 Broadway NY, NY 10019

Pepino, Mike Casting *(212) 431-3323* 270 Lafayette St NY, NY 10012

Puckett, Irma Casting *(212) 645-0030* 39 W 19th St NY, NY 10011

r - z

Reed & Melsky Casting *(212) 505-5000* 928 Broadway NY, NY 10010

Reed/Sweeney/Reed Casting

(212) 265-8541 1780 Broadway NY, NY 10019

Richmond/Mussenden Casting

(212) 473-7155 141 Fifth Ave NY, NY 10010

Roberts, Toni *(212) 627-2250* 150 Fifth Ave NY, NY 10011

Roscoe, Mike Casting *(212) 725-0014* 153 E 37th St NY, NY 10016

Sala, Margaret Celebrity Casting

(212) 628-4343 240 E 76th St NY, NY 10021

Seff, Sherie Casting *(212) 947-7408* 322 W 57th St NY, NY 10019

Sender, Shirley Casting *(212) 924-1055* 92 Horatio St NY, NY 10014

Shapiro, Barbara Casting

(212) 582-8228 111 W 57th St NY, NY 10019

Todd, Joy Casting *(212) 239-4469* 2 W 32nd St NY, NY 10001

Urell Casting *(212) 582-0132* 641 W 59th St NY, NY 10019

Weber, Joy Casting *(212) 245-5220* 250 W 57th St NY, NY 10019

Williams, Bill Casting *(212) 255-0500* 119 W 25th St NY, NY 10001

Wollin, Marji Camner Casting

212) 472-2528 233 E 69th St NY, NY 10021

Zeiner, Jeffrey *(212) 245-1237* 451 W 43rd St NY, NY 10036

TALENT PAYMENT

a - z

Bon Bon Producitons Ltd

(212) 489-7666 888 Seventh Ave NY, NY 10019

Broadcast Business Consultants

(212) 687-3525 41 E 42nd St NY, NY 10017

Broadcast Traffic & Residuals

(212) 682-5200 666 Third Ave NY, NY 10017

Cinema Payments Inc *(212) 757-5131* 1560 Broadway NY, NY 10036

Complete Casting *(212) 382-3835* 240 W 44th St NY, NY 10036

Consultants for Talent Payment / CTP Casting

(212) 696-1100 22 W 27th St NY, NY 10001

PAGE 15

Paychex Inc *(212) 581-7600* 250 W 57th St NY, NY 10107

Production Payments Inc *(212) 741-7777* 79 Fifth Ave NY, NY 10003

Tra-Flix *(212) 645-4700* 12 W 21st St NY, NY 10010

INDEX TO TAB

9

LABS RETOUCHERS PRINTING

9

INDEX TO TAB 9

LABS

RETOUCHERS

ELECTRONIC IMAGING

PRINTERS

TYPOGRAPHERS

COLOR SEPARATORS

ENGRAVERS

LAMINATORS

EMBOSSERS

SIGNAGE & NEON

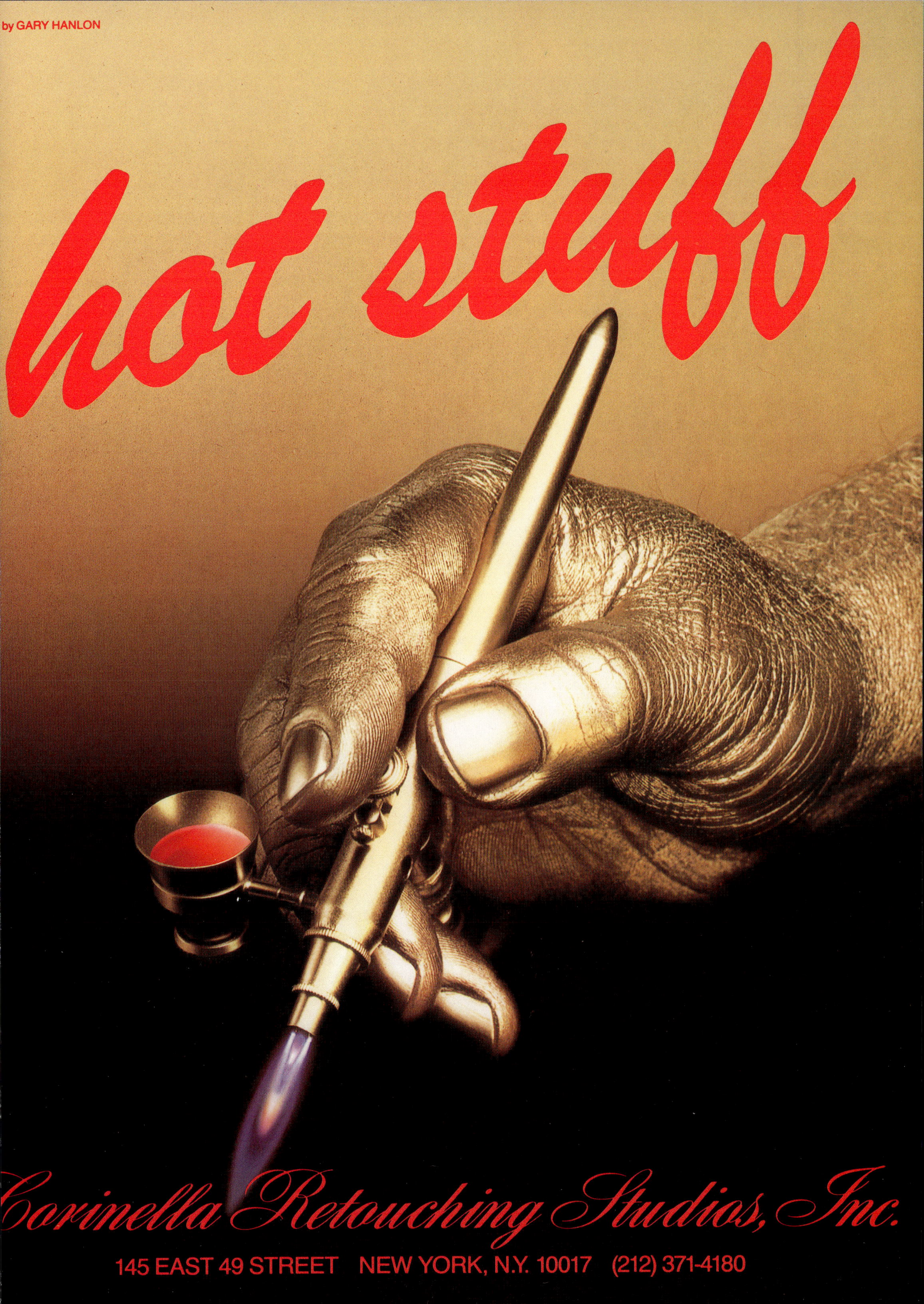
by GARY HANLON
hot stuff
Corinella Retouching Studios, Inc.
145 EAST 49 STREET NEW YORK, N.Y. 10017 (212) 371-4180

Morris Lane ©

photo
exchange, inc.

1 west 20th street
new york city 10011
212-675-6582

Morris Lane ©

FOTOS INCOLORLTD

156 5TH AVENUE
NEW YORK CITY 10010
(212) 691-8360

Designer: Lori Taube

Morris Lane ©

The unseen hand of the perfectionist...

Geoff Spear © 1988/ Designer Fragrance Division / Cosmair

...this is the retoucher's art. Flawless images...the only purpose of the perfectionists at Colorscope. Experienced professionals combine the finest retouching tradition with state-of-the-art electronic retouching and digital camera services, to create a most unique studio. This is why the Colorscope client list includes:

Saatchi & Saatchi
Chiat/Day inc. Advertising
Anne Klein/Anne Klein II
Chesebrough/Pond's Inc.
L'Oreal Cosmetic and Fragrance Division/ Cosmair, Inc.
Estée Lauder, Inc.

COLORSCOPE

2 1 2 . 2 1 3 . 3 4 2 2

Photographed by Sante D'Orazio
Courtesy of Bloomingdale's

LABS

a - c

ADS-N Color Lab *(212) 675-4981* 20 W 22nd St NY, NY 10011

Advance Color Labs *(212) 807-0446*—50 West 17th St NY, NY 10011

Alchemy Color Ltd *(212) 997-1944*—125 W 45th St NY, NY 10036

Apco Apeda/Rik Shaw *(212) 586-5755*—525 West 52nd St NY, NY 10019

Aurora Color Lab *(212) 952-7222* 594 Broadway NY, NY 10012

Authenticolor Inc *(212) 867-7905* 227 East 45th St NY, NY 10017

Baboo Color Lab *(212) 807-1574* 37 West 20th St NY, NY 10011

Bay Custom Labs *(212) 807-7979* 37 W 20th St NY, NY 10011

Ben-Ness Lab *(212) 674-0511* 50 East 13th St NY, NY 10003

Beninati Custom Labs *(212) 869-5149* 42 W 38th St NY, NY 10019

Box 1 Photographic *(212) 239-0283* 112 W 31st St NY, NY 10001

Central Color *(914) 681-0218* One Prospect Ave White Plains, NY 10607

Chroma Copy *(212) 399-2420* 423 West 55th St NY, NY 10019

Chromedome Inc *(212) 695-3961* 13 W 36th St NY, NY 10018

Chromeworks *(212) 529-4440* 323 Park Ave So NY, NY 10010

Clone A Chrome *(212) 206-1644* 15 W 20th St NY, NY 10011

Color By Pergament ***(212) 213-8310*** **38 East 30th St NY, NY 10016**

PAGE 8

Color Masters Inc ***(212) 889-7464*** **143 E 27th St NY, NY 10016**

PAGE 10

Color Maxim *(212) 725-8787* 22 W 27th St NY, NY 10001

Color Perfect *(212) 777-1210* 200 Park Ave So NY, NY 10003

Color Unlimited *(212) 463-9095* 126 W 22nd St NY, NY 10011

Color West Labs *(212) 362-0094* 73 W 82nd St NY, NY 10024

Color Wheel Inc *(212) 697-2434* 227 E 45th St NY, NY 10017

Colorite Film Processing *(212) 532-2116* 115 E 31st St NY, NY 10016

ColorVision *(212) 221-7040* 29 W 38th St NY, NY 10018

Cosmic Sound Delight *(212) 688-8686* 225 E 43rd St NY, NY 10017

Cousins Color Lab *(212) 691-9696* 19 W 19 St. NY, NY 10011

Creative Color Inc *(212) 764-3077* 40 E 49th St NY, NY 10017

Crown/Colorama Labs ***(212) 279-1950*** **440 Ninth Ave NY, NY 10001**

PAGE 12

d - i

Darkroom Inc *(212) 687-8920* 222 E 46th St NY, NY 10017

Dimension Color Labs Inc *(212) 354-5918* 1040 Sixth Ave NY, NY 10018

Duggal Color Projects *(212) 242-7000* 9 W 20th St NY, NY 10011

EDSTAN STUDIO WEST *(212) 489-1190* 321 W 44th St NY, NY 10036

EAD COLOR: EVANS, AVEDISIAN, DISTEFANO

(212) 869-9870 29 W 38th St NY, NY 10018

PAGE 9

FINLEY PHOTOGRAPHICS *(212) 986-7920* 405 Lexington Ave NY, NY 10174

FINLEY PHOTOGRAPHICS *(212) 725-1110* 152 Madison Ave NY, NY 10016

FINLEY PHOTOGRAPHICS *(212) 751-3932* 509 Madison Ave NY, NY 10022

FINLEY PHOTOGRAPHICS *(212) 382-0791* 64 W 48th St NY, NY 10036

FINLEY PHOTOGRAPHICS *(212) 986-6151* 750 Third Ave NY, NY 10017

FINLEY PHOTOGRAPHICS *(212) 752-6336* 850 Third Ave NY, NY 10022

FOTO-STYLE *(212) 242-0706* 5 W 20th St NY, NY 10011

FOUR COLOR PHOTO LAB *(212) 889-3399* 10 E 39th St NY, NY 10016

FRENCHY'S COLOR LAB *(212) 889-7787* 10 E 38th St NY, NY 10016

GADS COLOR *(212) 629-6955* 135 W 41st St NY, NY 10036

GW COLOR LAB INC *(212) 677-3800* 36 E 23rd St NY, NY 10010

H&S COLOR LAB *(212) 221-0685* 260 W 39th St NY, NY 10018

H-Y PHOTO SERVICES *(212) 371-3018* 16 E 52nd St NY, NY 10017

HONG COLOR *(212) 924-2080* 666 Sixth Ave NY, NY 10010

HOROWITZ, KEN PHOTO SERVICES

(212) 505-7031 22 E 21st St NY, NY 10010

PAGE 8

Image Masters Color Lab *(212) 243-2301* 59 W 19th St NY, NY 10011

Image Photographic Lab *(212) 867-4747* 507 Fifth Ave NY, NY 10017

In Color Ltd *(212) 691-8360* 156 Fifth Ave NY, NY 10010

PAGE 2

j - m

J.M.W. Studio *(212) 645-0022* 25 Union Sq. West NY, NY 10003

Jellybean Photographic *(212) 679-4888* 99 Madison Ave NY, NY 10016

K & L *(212) 661-5600* 222 E 44th St NY, NY 10017

L & I Color Lab *(212) 206-7733* 34 W 17th St NY, NY 10011

Lafayette Color *(212) 925-9565* 238 Lafayette St NY, NY 10012

Larson Color Corp *(212) 674-0610* 123 Fifth Ave NY, NY 10003

Laumont *(212) 245-2113* 333 W 52nd St NY, NY 10019

Lawrence Color Systems *(212) 944-7039* 250 W 40th St NY, NY 10018

Leiberman, Ken Labs Inc *(212) 633-0500* 118 W 22nd St NY, NY 10011

PAGE 9

Light Photo *(212) 777-4910* 900 Broadway NY, NY 10003

Loy-Taubman Inc *(212) 685-6871* 34 E 30th St NY, NY 10016

Mann & Greene *(212) 481-6868* 320 E 39th St NY, NY 10016

Martin-Arnold *(212) 675-7270* 150 Fifth Ave NY, NY 10011

Maxi-Color *(212) 645-8828* 56 W 22nd St NY, NY 10010

Mayer, Kurt Color Lab *(212) 532-3738* 1170 Broadway NY, NY 10001

McCurdy & Cardinale *(212) 695-5140* 65 W 36th St NY, NY 10018

Memory Keeper *(212) 691-9047* 147 W 14th St NY, NY 10011

Miller Associates *(212) 752-4830* 17 E 48th St NY, NY 10017

Modernage *(212) 752-3993* 239 E 53rd St NY, NY 10022

Modernage *(212) 227-4767* 150 Fulton St NY, NY 10030

Modernage *(212) 997-1800* 1150 Sixth Ave NY, NY 10036

Moser, Klaus T. Ltd *(212) 475-0038* 127 E 15th St NY, NY 10003

My Lab Inc *(212) 255-3771* 40 W 24th St NY, NY 10010

PAGE 10

My Own Color Lab *(212) 391-8638* 45 W 45th St NY, NY 10036

n - r

NE Photo Service *(212) 563-1646* 358 Seventh Ave NY, NY 10001

New York Film Works *(212) 475-5700* 928 Broadway NY, NY 10010

Newman Photographics *(212) 505-1840* 400 Lafayette St NY, NY 10003

Ornaal Color Corp *(212) 675-3850* 24 W 25th St NY, NY 10010

Photographic Color *(718) 786-4770* 10-36 47th Rd LIC, NY 11101

Photographics Unlimited *(212) 255-9678* 17 W 17th St NY, NY 10011

Photorama *(212) 354-5280* 239 W 39th St NY, NY 10018

PHOTOWORKS INC *(212) 807-7990* 119 W 23rd St NY, NY 10011

PICTURE PERFECT INC *(212) 255-3822* 636 Sixth Ave NY, NY 10011

PORTOFOTO *(212) 226-9788* 596 Broadway NY, NY 10012

QUALITY COLOR LAB *(212) 753-2200* 305 E 46th St NY, NY 10017

RAFFI CUSTOM PHOTO LAB *(212) 719-2929* 21 W 46th St NY, NY 10036

RAINBOW GRAPHICS *(212) 869-3232* 49 W 45th St NY, NY 10036

RASULO GRAPHIC SERVICES *(212) 686-2861* 36 E 31st St NY, NY 10016

REITER-DULBERG LABS INC *(212) 582-6871* 250 W 54th St NY, NY 10019

REPLICHROME *(212) 929-0409* 41 Union Sq W NY, NY 10003

REPRODUCTION COLOR SPECIALISTS
(212) 683-0833 9 E 38th St NY, NY 10016

ROGERS COLOR LAB CORP *(212) 683-6400* 165 Madison Ave NY, NY 10016

S - Z

S&S COLOR *(212) 398-1570* 250 W 40th St NY, NY 10018

SANG COLOR INC *(212) 594-4205* 19 W 34th St NY, NY 10001

SCHNEIDER/ERDMAN INC *(212) 777-0649* 32 Cooper Sq NY, NY 10003

SCOPE ASSOCIATES *(212) 243-0032* 56 W 22nd St NY, NY 10010
PAGE 11

SHOWBRAN PRO PHOTO *(212) 868-5888* 1347 Broadway NY, NY 10018

SILVERSMITHS B&W *(212) 645-9422* 141 W 20th St NY, NY 10011

SMP GRAPHIC SERVICES CENTER
(212) 254-2282 26 E 22nd St NY, NY 10010

SPECTRA PHOTO EAST *(212) 529-3636* 293 E 10th St NY, NY 10009

SPECTRA PHOTO INC *(212) 989-0626* 77 Christopher St NY, NY 10014

SPECTRA PHOTO INC *(212) 533-1860* 510 Laguardia Pl NY, NY 10012

STEWART COLOR LAB *(212) 868-1440* 563 11th St NY, NY 10036

STUDIO CHROME LAB INC *(212) 989-6767* 36 W 25th St NY, NY 10001

STUDIO X CORP *(212) 989-9233* 20 W 20th St NY, NY 10011

SUPERIOR FOTOTECH *(212) 246-5110* 432 W 45th St NY, NY 10036

TARTARO PHOTO SERVICES *(212) 683-6100* 37 W 26th St NY, NY 10010

TONY COLOR LAB INC *(212) 807-7988* 120 W 20th St NY, NY 10011

TRP Slavin Color Service
(212) 674-5700 920 Broadway NY, NY 10010

Ulitmate Image *(212) 683-4838* 443 Park Ave So NY, NY 10016

Universal Photo *(212) 924-2500* 5 E 17th St NY, NY 10001

US Color Lab *(212) 254-7200* 65 Bleecker St NY, NY 10012

Van Chromes Inc *(212) 302-5700* 21 W 46th St NY, NY 10036

Vidachrome *(212) 279-0880* 260 W 35th St NY, NY 10001

Ward, Jack Color Inc *(212) 725-5200* 220 E 23rd St NY, NY 10010

Waro Custom Photo Lab *(212) 391-4117* 37 W 39th St NY, NY 10018

Way Color Inc *(212) 921-2335* 15 W 39th St NY, NY 10014

Zoref Color Labs Inc *(212) 686-3040* 10 E 39th St NY, NY 10016
PAGE 11

Retouchers
a - f

Anselmo Studio *(212) 753-1606* 211 E 51st St NY, NY 10022

Appel, Albert *(212) 989-6585* 27 W 20th St NY, NY 10011

AT&S Retouching *(212) 986-0977* 230 E 44th St NY, NY 10012

Aurora Retouching *(212) 255-0620* 10 W 19th St NY, NY 10011

Belart Associates *(212) 753-2625* 515 Madison Ave NY, NY 10022

Bell-Taitt, Carolyn *(212) 645-9466* 1123 Broadway NY, NY 10010

Bellis, Dave Studio *(212) 753-3740* 155 E 55th St NY, NY 10022

Benjamin, Bernard *(212) 722-7773* 1763 Second Ave NY, NY 10128

Berger, Jack *(212) 245-5705* 41 W 53rd St NY, NY 10019

Bishop Studio Inc. *(212) 889-3525* 236 E 36th St NY, NY 10016

Blae, Ken Retouching *(212) 869-3488* 1501 Broadway NY, NY 10036

Bonaventura Studio *(212) 687-9208* 307 E 44th St NY, NY 10017

Cacchione & Sheehan *(212) 929-3636* 61 W 23rd St NY, NY 10011

Carlson & Forino Studios *(212) 697-7044* 230 E 44th St NY, NY 10017

Cavalluzzo, Dan *(212) 921-5954* 49 W 45th St NY, NY 10036

Chromeworks *(212) 529-4440* 323 Park Ave So NY, NY 10010

Color Masters Inc *(212) 889-7464* 143 E 27th St NY,NY 10016
PAGE 10

Color Design Inc *(212) 255-8103* 10 W 19th St NY, NY 10011

Color-Maxim Inc *(212) 725-8787* 22 W 27th St NY, NY 10001

Colorscope *(212) 213-3422* 138 E 34th St NY, NY 10016
PAGE 3

Cooke, Catherine *(212) 980-8420* 160 E 48th St NY, NY 10017

Corinella Retouching *(212) 371-4180* 145 E 49th St NY, NY 10017
PAGE 1

Cortese/Musikar *(212) 627-8400* 153 W 27th St NY, NY 10001

Crapanzano, Joseph *(212) 983-4299* 230 E 44th St NY, NY 10017

Crowell, Joyce Studio *(212) 683-3055* 333 E 30th St NY, NY 10016

Crown/Colorama Labs
***(212) 279-1950* 370 W 35th St NY, NY 10001**
PAGE 12

Diamond Art Studios *(212) 685-6622* 11 E 36th St NY, NY 10016

Diamond, Richard *(212) 697-4720* 50 E 42nd St NY, NY 10017

Diana Studio *(212) 757-0445* 301 W 53rd St NY, NY 10019

DiPietro-Turiel *(212) 752-2260* 210 E 47th St NY, NY 10017

Duggal Color Projects *(212) 242-7000* 9 W 20th St NY, NY 10011

EAD Color: Evans, Avedisian, Distefano
***(212) 869-9870* 29 W 38TH ST NY, NY 10018**
PAGE 9

Ecay, Thom *(212) 840-6277* 49 W 45th St NY, NY 10036

Egelston *212) 213-9095* 333 Fifth Ave NY, NY 10016

Faber, Janet *(212) 734-4750* 346 E 81st St NY, NY 10028

Faddi Studios *(212) 689-9595* 435 Fifth Ave NY, NY 10016

Fodale Studios *(212) 755-0150* 247 E 50th St NY, NY 10022

Frommer, Eric *(212) 944-8241* 25 W 39th St NY, NY 10018

g - r

Gayde Associates *(212) 421-4088* 515 Madison Ave NY, NY 10022

Gilbert Studio *(212) 255-7805* 127 W 24th St NY, NY 10011

Graphic Systems Inc *(212) 242-8787* 33 W 17th St NY, NY 10011

Gray, George *(212) 989-1707* 236 W 26th St NY, NY 10001

Greller, Fred Associates *(212) 535-6240* 325 E 64th St NY, NY 10021

Grubb, Lou Retouching *(212) 873-2561* 155 Riverside Dr NY, NY 10024

Jaeger Retouching *(212) 840-6278* 49 W 45th St NY, NY 11735

K-G Studio *(212) 840-7930* 16 W 46th St NY, NY 10036

Kastle & Kastle Studio Inc *(212) 679-2860* 10 E 39th St NY, NY 10016

Katz, Baruch Studio *(212) 947-8074* 252 W 37th St NY, NY 10018

Katz, David Studio *(212) 889-5038* 6 E 39th St NY, NY 10016

Leiberman, Ken Labs Inc *(212) 633-0500* 118 W 22nd St NY NY 10011

PAGE 9

Leitstein, Harold *(212) 752-8490* 50 E 50th St NY, NY 10022

Lukon Art Service *(212) 575-0474* 56 W 45th St NY, NY 10036

Mandl, Bela Retoucher *(212) 355-0478* 325 E 57th St NY, NY 10022

Marshall Studios *(212) 944-7771* 2 W 45th St NY, NY 10036

Martin, Tulio G *(212) 245-6489* 234 W 56th St NY, NY 10019

Mayer, Kurt *(212) 532-3738* 1170 Broadway NY, NY 10001

McWilliams/Wellbeck *(212) 725-0050* 141 E 25th St NY, NY 10016

PAGE 4-5

Medina Studios *(212) 867-3113* 141 E 44th St NY, NY 10017

Mendes, A.V. *(212) 869-2819* 49 W 45th St NY, NY 10036

Modernage Custom Photo Labs

(212) 997-1800 1150 Sixth Ave NY, NY 10036

Modernage *(212) 752-3993* 239 E 53rd St NY, NY 10022

Modernage *(212) 227-4767* 150 Fulton St NY, NY 10030

Musilli *(212) 753-5477* 210 E 47th St NY, NY 10022

My Lab Inc *(212) 255-3771* 40 W 24th St NY, NY 10010

PAGE 10

Norkin, Scott *(212) 905-8571* 353 E 77th St NY, NY 10021

North Light Studio *(212) 563-7325* 39 W 32nd St NY, NY 10001

Paccione Inc *(212) 755-0965* 150 E 56th St NY, NY 10022

Palevitz Retouching *(212) 684-6026* 333 E 30th St NY, NY 10016

Photo Retouching by Mrln Hwkrg

(212) 206-1342 56 W 22nd St NY, NY 10010

Pinto, Frank Studios *(212) 758-1833* 349 E 49th St NY, NY 10017

Precision Chromes *(212) 575-0120* 32 W 38th St NY, NY 10018

Prussack Studios *(212) 755-2470* 155 E 55th St NY, NY 10022

Pucci, Germana *(212) 777-4323* 810 Broadway NY, NY 10003

R&V Studio *(212) 944-9590* 323 W 39th St NY, NY 10018

Ram Retouching *(212) 532-1148* 152 E 35th St NY, NY 10016

Reiter Dulberg Labs Inc *(212) 582-6871* 250 W 54th St NY, NY 10019

Retouchers Gallery *(212) 697-6544* 160 E 38th St NY, NY 10016

Retouching Graphics Inc *(212) 838-1867* 321 E 54th St NY, NY 10022

Retouching Inc *(212) 867-7905* 227 E 45th St NY, NY 10017

Rivera & Schiff Associates *(212) 695-8546* 39 W 32nd St NY, NY 10001

Ruhl Retouching *(212) 838-4808* 324 E 50th St NY, NY 10022

s - z

San Photo-Art Services *(212) 594-0850* 165 W 29th St NY, NY 10001

Scott Associates, Diane *(212) 355-4616* 339 E 58th St NY, NY 10022

Sharkey Studio *(212) 265-1036* 301 W 53rd St NY, NY 10019

Smith, Maureen *(212) 580-9428* 2025 Broadway NY, NY 10023

Spano/Roccanova *(212) 840-7450* 16 W 46th St NY, NY 10036

Spector Studios *(212) 594-5766* 47 W 34th St NY, NY 10001

Spectrum *(212) 687-3359* 230 F 44th St NY, NY 10017

Stanley, Joseph *(212) 246-1258* 211 W 58th St NY, NY 10019

Stevens Photo Retouching *(212) 628-6484* 353 E 77th St NY, NY 10021

Studio Casas *(212) 941-0846* 131 Mercer St NY, NY 10012

Tanksley Studios Inc *(212) 752-1150* 210 E 47th St NY, NY 10017

The Retouchables *(212) 867-4225* 104 E 40th St NY, NY 10016

Touchstone Retouching *(212) 935-1997* 50 E 50th St NY, NY 10022

PAGE 6-7

Trio Studio *(212) 752-4875* 18 E 48th St NY, NY 10017

Truglio Associates *(212) 563-7130* 165 W 29th St NY, NY 10001

Turiel, David *(212) 752-2260* 210 E 47th St NY, NY 10017

Ultra Retouching Studios *(212) 935-9182* 324 E 50th St NY, NY 10022

Venezia, Don *(212) 644-2883* 515 Madison Ave NY, NY 10017

Ward, Jack Color Inc *(212) 725-5200* 220 E 23rd St NY, NY 10010

Way Color Inc *(212) 687-5610* 420 Lexington Ave NY, NY 10017

Winter, Jerry Retouching *(212) 490-0876* 333 E 45th St NY, NY 10017

Wishney Associates *(212) 242-2223* 33 W 17th St NY, NY 10011

Wolsk, Bernard Inc *(212) 818-9024* 20 E 46th St NY, NY 10017

Wood, Joan *(212) 627-8494* 156 Fifth Ave NY, NY 10011

Zazula, Hy *(212) 819-0444* 2 W 46th St NY, NY 10036

Zoref Color Labs Inc *(212) 686-3040* 10 E 39th St NY, NY 10016

ELECTRONIC IMAGING

a - z

COLORSCOPE ***(212) 213-3422*** **138 E 34th St NY, NY 10016**

PAGE 3

CREATIVE LITHOGRAPHY *(212) 691-9930* 263 Ninth Ave NY, NY 10001

DUGGAL COLOR PROJECTS *(212) 242-7000* 9 W 20th St NY, NY 10011

FRENCHY'S COLOR LAB *(212) 889-7787* 10 E 38th St NY, NY 10016

GS IMAGING SERVICES *(201) 933-8585* 1 Kero Rd Carlstadt, NJ 07072

KORDET GRAPHICS *(212) 627-4111* 50 W 23rd St NY, NY 10010

MASTER EAGLE *(212) 924-8277* 40 W 25th St NY, NY 10001

POTOMAC GRAPHIC *(212) 924-4880* 508 W 26th St NY, NY 10001

SPANO/ROCCANOVA *(212) 840-7450* 16 W 46th St NY, NY 10036

WARD, JACK COLOR INC *(212) 725-5200* 220 E 23rd St NY, NY 10010

ZAZULA, HY *(212) 819-0444* 2 W 46th St NY, NY 10036

PRINTERS

a - d

36 EAST 30TH ST GROUP *(212) 686-8200* 36 E 30th St NY, NY 10016

A & H LITHO *(212) 925-5593* 481 Washington St NY, NY 10013

ACE OFFSET SERVICE *(212) 431-5222* 200 Hudson St NY, NY 10013

ADAMS GROUP INC *(212) 255-4900* 225 Varick St NY, NY 10013

ADLON PRESS *(212) 929-8675* 37 W 20th St NY, NY 10011

ADVANCE PRINTING CO *(212) 924-8940* 345 Hudson St NY, NY 10014

ADVERTISING AGENCIES SVC CO *(212) 687-0590* 216 E 45th St NY, NY 10017

ALEXOGRAPHIC PRESS *(212) 243-0146* 225 Varick St NY, NY 10014

ALTAG PRESS INC *(212) 402-0044* 960962 Washington Ave Bronx, NY 10456

AMERICAN BANK NOTE CO
(914) 353-3320 300 Corporate Dr Blauvelt, NY 10913

AMSEL LITHO CORP *(212) 620-0400* 200 Varick St NY, NY 10014

ARCATA GRAPHICS *(212) 827-2700* 1185 Sixth Ave NY, NY 10036

ART GRAPHICS LITHO CORP *(212) 695-7430* 1328 Broadway NY, NY 10001

ART-PRO GRAPHICS *(212) 473-4100* 47 E 19th St NY, NY 10003

ARW PRODUCTIONS *(212) 889-5085* 404 Park Ave So NY, NY 10016

ASSOCIATED OFFSET CO *(212) 924-6415* 54 W 21st St NY, NY 10010

ASTORIA PRESS INC *(212) 255-6768* 435 Hudson St NY, NY 10014

ATWATER PRESS INC *(212) 675-2710* 207 W 25th St NY, NY 10001

BAT LITHO PUBLISHING CORP *(212) 431-3366* 480 Canal St NY, NY 10013

BAYBERRY PRINTING & LITHO
(212) 966-2217 148 Lafayette St NY, NY 10013

BEACON PRESS *(212) 691-5050* 225 Varick St NY, NY 10014

BEACON PRINTING CO *(212) 924-1000* 304 Hudson St NY, NY 10013

BRAD PRINTING & LITHO CORP
(212) 315-4844 250 W 57th St NY, NY 10107

BRIDGE LITHOGRAPHIC CO *(212) 989-1160* 160 Varick St NY, NY 10013

BROSE OFFSET & LITHO CO *(212) 989-2650* 345 Hudson St NY, NY 10014

BURTON COLOR LITHOGRAPH CO
(212) 226-7757 250 W Broadway NY, NY 10013

CALTONE LITHOGRAPHERS INC *(212) 594-2424* 406 W 31st St NY, NY 10001

CAMBRIDGE PRESS *(212) 254-9571* 47 E 19th St NY, NY 10003

CAPITOL LITHOGRAPHERS INC *(212) 924-6300* 233 Spring St NY, NY 10013

CARILLON LITHOGRAPHING CORP
(212) 254-5840 37 E 18th St NY, NY 10003

CAROL PRINTING CORP *(212) 243-5858* 275 Seventh Ave NY, NY 10001

CASE-HOYT PRINTING *(212)489-1991* 810 Seventh Ave NY, NY 10019

CIRCLE PRESS *(212) 925-9915* 480 Canal St NY, NY 10013

COLOR LITHOGRAPHERS INC *(212) 255-3200* 225 Varick St NY, NY 10014

COLORCRAFT OFFSET INC *(212) 243-2100* 250 Hudson St NY, NY 10013

CONTINENTAL LITHO CORP *(212) 246-2830* 1600 Broadway NY, NY 10019

COPY SHOP *(212) 924-2700* 636 11th St NY, NY 10036

CRAFTON GRAPHIC CO *(212) 736-3143* 229 W 28th St NY, NY 10001

CRAFTSMAN COLOR LITHO *(212) 675-8200* 40 W 25th St NY, NY 10010

CREATIVE LITHOGRAPHIC CONSULTANTS
(212) 481-9252 230 Fifth Ave NY, NY 10001

CREATIVE LITHOGRAPHY *(212) 691-9930* 263 Ninth Ave NY, NY 10001

CREST COLOR LITHO CORP *(212) 929-4332* 180 Varick St NY, NY 10014

CURTIS PRINTING *(212) 685-0670* 114 E 32nd St NY, NY 10016

CUSTOM OFFSET INC *(212) 243-4804* 180 Varick St NY, NY 10013

d - k

DESIGN PRESS *(212) 675-2747* 119 W 23rd St NY, NY 10011

D.F. WHITE INC *(212) 243-3000* 54 W 21st St NY, NY 10010

DIRECT PRESS MODERN LITHO
(516) 271-7000 386 Oakwood Rd Huntington Sta, NY 11746

DONNELLEY & SONS *(212) 490-9500* 100 Park Ave NY, NY 10017

DNP (AMERICA), INC. *(212) 686-1919* 2 Park Ave NY, NY 10016

EMPIRE COLOR LITHOGRAPHERS
(212) 924-7866 200 Varick St NY, NY 10013

ENTERPRISE PRESS INC *(212) 741-2111* 627 Greenwich St NY, NY 10014

EXCEL PRINTING CO *(212) 741-1098* 54 W 21st St NY, NY 10010

FACULTY PRESS *(718) 851-6666* 1449 37th St Brooklyn, NY 11218

Fenn & Fenn Lithographers *(212) 925-4800* 75 Varick St NY, NY 10013

Four Seasons Litho *(516) 349-3222* 7 Fairchild Ct Plainview, NY 11803

Froelich-Greene Color Press Inc

(212) 285-0549 21 Dwight Pl Fairfield, NJ 07006

Gem Art Assoc *(212) 691-9180* 345 Hudson St NY, NY 10014

Georgian Press Inc *(212) 924-4820* 175 Varick St NY, NY 10014

Griffith Inc, Dexter *(212) 243-8400* 448 W 16th St NY, NY 10011

Guaranteed Printing *(212) 929-2410* 216 W 18th St NY, NY 10011

Hampshire Press Inc *(212) 242-4647* 54 W 21st St NY, NY 10010

Hanover Litho *(212) 989-1710* 131 Varick St NY, NY 10013

Hanover Lithographing Inc *(212) 765-2190* 645 W 44th St NY, NY 10036

Harvest Printing Co *(212) 967-9494* 229 W 28th St NY, NY 10001

Head Printing Co Inc *(212) 431-4960* 250 W Broadway NY, NY 10013

Herst Litho *(212) 245-4666* 620 12th Ave NY, NY 10036

Hopp Press Inc *(212) 279-1800* 460 W 34th St NY, NY 10001

Howard Press Inc *(212) 675-5260* 20 W 22nd St NY, NY 10010

Hudson Printing Co Inc *(212) 966-5400* 200 Hudson St NY, NY 10013

Jeremy Printing Corp *(212) 966-2223* 200 Hudson St NY, NY 10013

Karr Graphics Corp *(212) 645-6000* 233 Spring St NY, NY 10013

Kenner Printing Co Inc *(212) 807-8800* 418 W 25th St NY, NY 10001

Keystone Envelope Corp *(718) 237-4800* 35 York St Brooklyn, NY 11201

Kim Lithographing Corp *(212) 989-1250* 158 W 27th St NY, NY 10001

KLN Publishing Services Inc *(212) 686-8200* 36 E 30th St NY, NY 10016

Kordett Graphics *(212) 627-4111* 50 W 23rd St NY, NY 10010

Krueger Co *(212) 661-4242* 485 5th Ave NY, NY 10017

Kubes, Victor O *(212) 989-5464* 207 W 25th St NY, NY 10001

l - o

LaSalle Litho Corp *(212) 597-7300* 815 Hctnsn Rv Pkwy Bronx, NY 10465

Latham Process *(212) 966-4500* 200 Hudson St NY, NY 10013

Lawford Press Inc *(212) 239-8500* 129 W 29th St NY, NY 10001

Lawrence Lithographers Ltd

(212) 489-1210 545 W 45th St NY, NY 10036

Lebanon Valley Offset Co *(212) 764-3760* 40 W 40th St NY, NY 10018

Leebo Printing Co *(212) 989-8444* 207 W 25th St NY, NY 10001

Lerman Graphics *(212) 925-6400* 480 Canal St NY, NY 10013

Levine Brothers *(212) 929-8956* 111 Eighth Ave NY, NY 10011

Lind Brothers *(212) 924-9280* 111 Eighth Ave NY, NY 10011

Litho Art Inc *(212) 242-7650* 175 Varick St NY, NY 10014

Litho Plus Inc *(212) 989-6800* 5-17 48th Ave LIC, NY 11101

Lynn Art Offset Corp *(212) 675-7065* 333 Hudson St NY, NY 10013

M R Printing *(212) 889-3430* 9 E 38th St NY, NY 10016

Mail & Express Printing Co *(212) 255-4900* 225 Varick St NY, NY 10013

Mansfield Press Inc *(212) 265-5411* 620 Twelfth Ave NY, NY 10036

Master Eagle Photoengraving

(212) 924-8277 40 W 25th St NY, NY 10010

Medallion Assoc Ltd *(212) 929-9130* 37 W 20th St NY, NY 10011

Midtown Litho *(212) 564-1966* 406 W 31st St NY, NY 10001

Mill River Press *(718) 875-5832* 116 Nassau St Brooklyn, NY 11201

Miller & Son Inc *(212) 255-7284* 20 W 22nd St NY, NY 10010

Milo Press *(212) 686-2682* 141 E 25th St NY, NY 10010

Mirror Graphics *(212) 924-1056* 150 Varick St NY, NY 10013

MJ Offset Corp *(212) 242-8655* 115 W 27th St NY, NY 10001

Moffa Press Inc *(718) 482-0044* 44-02 Eleventh St LIC, NY 11101

Mohican Press Inc *(212) 929-4040* 54 W 21st St NY, NY 10010

Mondadori/NY *(212) 505-7900* 740 Broadway NY, NY 10003

National Reprographics Inc

(212) 736-5674 110 W 32nd St NY, NY 10016

Neff Lithographing Co *(212) 255-4690* 233 Spring St NY, NY 10013

Ness Lithography *(212) 563-0300* 233 Spring St NY, NY 10013

New York City Press Inc *(212) 924-7107* 207 W 25th St NY, NY 10001

Newport Graphics *(212) 925-5500* 80 Varick St NY, NY 10013

p - z

Pace Press Inc *(212) 246-8100* 636 Eleventh Ave NY, NY 10036

Pan American Lithographing Crp

(212) 989-7250 175 Varick St NY, NY 10014

Park Ave Copy Center *(212) 684-1300* 45 E 30th St NY, NY 10016

Penco Graphics Inc *(212) 675-3360* 150 Varick St NY, NY 10013

Perni Color Process Corp *(212) 242-4660* 170 Varick St NY,, NY 10013

Phoenix Color *(212) 936-7300* 47-07 30th Pl LIC, NY 11101

Photo Comp Press *(212) 675-0606* 410 West St NY, NY 10014

Pizzi *(212) 986-1658* 141 E 44th St NY, NY 10036

Polychrome Lithography Co Inc

(212) 980-9700 845 Third Ave NY, NY 10022

Potomac Graphic *(212) 924-4880* 508 W 26th St NY, NY 10001

Prestone Printing Corp Inc

(212) 695-6441 450 Seventh Ave NY, NY 10123

Print Out Press *(212) 989-3232* 135 W 27th St NY, NY 10001

Promotion Photo *(212) 645-1450* 41 Union Sq W NY, NY 10003

Promotion Service *(212) 925-4428* 100 Sixth Ave NY, NY 10013

Raleigh Lithograph Corp *(212) 966-1880* 100 Sixth Ave NY, NY 10013

Ramapo Litho Corp *(212) 564-1877* 225 Varick St NY, NY 10014

Rapoport Printing Corp *(212) 226-5501* 195 Hudson St NY, NY 10013

Roselin Litho Service *(212) 677-1900* 33 E 21st St NY, NY 10010

Saxon Graphics *(212) 714-1500* 575 Eighth Ave NY, NY 10018

Scott, S.D. Printing Co Inc *(212) 226-7100* 145 Hudson St NY, NY 10013

Seaboard Lithograph Corp *(212) 475-3481* 37 E 18th St NY, NY 10003

Shea, John *(212) 431-8856* 195 Hudson St NY, NY 10013

Shear & Son *(212) 925-2842* 200 Hudson St NY, NY 10013

Skilkraft *(212) 925-6400* 480 Canal St NY, NY 10013

Sterling Regal Inc *(212) 213-5440* 141 E 25th St NY, NY 10010

Sterling Roman Press Inc *(212) 226-1800* 75 Varick St NY, NY 10013

Tabard Press Corp *(212) 924-6260* 345 Hudson St NY, NY 10014

Tanagraphics *(212) 255-6876* 263 Ninth Ave NY, NY 10001

Toppan Printing *(212) 489-7740* 680 Fifth Ave NY, NY 10019

Typeshop Inc, The *(212) 354-8181* 45 W 45th St NY, NY 10036

United Lithographing Corp *(718) 786-8100* 47-47 32nd Pl LIC, NY 11101

Walbern Press Inc *(212) 564-0444* 406 W 31 NY, NY 10001

Walkerprint *(212) 431-1121* 285 W Broadway NY, NY 10013

Waterman Lithographers *(212) 924-2300* 115 W 27th St NY, NY 10001

West Side Printing & Litho Co *(212) 925-6400* 480 Canal St NY, NY 10013

Westmore Litho Printing Co *(212) 477-4631* 333 Hudson St NY, NY 10013

Woodbury & Co *(212) 683-0851* 485 Fifth Ave NY, NY 10017

Yorkshire/Southland Printing *(212) 242-4934* 180 Varick St NY, NY 10013

Zarett Graphics Corp *(212) 529-7500* 135 Fifth Ave NY, NY 10010

TYPOGRAPHERS a - k

219 Type Inc *(212) 219-TYPE* 143 Franklin St NY, NY 10013

36 East 30th St Group *(212) 686-8200* 36 E 30th St NY, NY 10016

Ad Agencies Headliners *(212) 697-4820* 216 E 45th St NY, NY 10017

Adroit Graphic Composition *(212) 243-1929* 537 Greenwich St NY, NY 10013

Advertising Agecnies Svc Co *(212) 687-0590* 216 E 45th St NY, NY 10017

Allied Typographers *(212) 246-6940* 49 E 21st St NY, NY 10010

Alphatype Corp *(212) 594-3970* 20 E 46th St NY, NY 10017

Antiquated Typographers Ltd *(212) 695-2404* 406 W 31st St NY, NY 10001

Art-Pro Graphics *(212) 473-4100* 47 E 19th St NY, NY 10003

Barkley & Surrey *(212) 766-9431* 110 Greenwich St NY, NY 10006

Baumwell, M.J. Typography *(212) 687-8840* 216 E 45th St NY, NY 10013

Black Ink Typographers *(212) 819-0045* 165 W 46th St NY, NY 10036

Boro Typographers *(212) 475-7850* 49 E 21st St NY, NY 10010

Bridge Graphics *(212) 732-2350* 29 John St NY, NY 10038

Capitol-Crosby Typographers *(212) 966-5750* 130 Crosby St NY, NY 10012

Cardinal Type Service Inc *(212) 489-1717* 545 W 45th St NY, NY 10036

Carnase Typography *(212) 674-1185* 303 Park Ave So NY, NY 10010

Characters Typographic Services *(212) 947-0900* 5 W 36th St NY, NY 10018

Commercial Typographers *(212) 243-7503* 122 W 26th St NY, NY 10001

Compmasters *(212) 924-1729* 34 W 15th St NY, NY 10011

Compo-Set Typographers *(212) 431-4515* 200 Hudson St NY, NY 10013

Concord Typographic Svc Inc *(212) 889-2293* 212 Fifth Ave NY, NY 10010

Copy Shop *(212) 924-2700* 636 11th Ave NY, NY 10036

Creative Media *(212) 593-1621* 969 First Ave NY, NY 10022

Cromwell Type-Ad Svc Inc *(212) 695-6362* 406 W 31st St NY, NY 10001

CT & Photogenic Graphics Inc *(212) 675-7500* 27 W 24th St NY, NY 10010

CTC *(212) 594-3434* 5 W 36th St NY, NY 10018

Dawn Typography Services *(212) 807-7224* 134 W 26th St NY, NY 10001

Empire Typographers *(212) 254-8822* 300 Park Ave So NY, NY 10010

Fact Typographers Inc *(212) 221-1565* 29 W 38th St NY, NY 10018

Fine Art Typographers *(212) 398-9640* 25 W 39th St NY, NY 10018

Fine Composition *(212) 243-3380* 635 Sixth Ave NY, NY 10011

Franklin Typographers Inc *(212) 736-4707* 225 W 39th St NY, NY 10018

Gerard Assoc Photo Type Inc *(212) 691-4960* 163 W 23rd St NY, NY 10011

Graphic Word *(212) 924-1111* 80 Eighth Ave NY, NY 10011

Hartog Phototype Inc *(212) 689-7141* 1261 Broadway NY, NY 10001

Henricks, Charles *(212) 925-1572* 75 Varick St NY, NY 10013

ICR Graphics Inc *(212) 564-1385* 254 W 31st St NY, NY 10001

Karr Graphics Corp *(212) 645-6000* 233 Spring St NY, NY 10013

Komel Productions Inc *(212) 682-3498* 219 E 44th St NY, NY 10017

Koppel & Son Co Inc *(212) 279-5400* 406 W 31st St NY, NY 10001

l - z

Latent Lettering Co (212) 221-0055 29 W 38th St NY, NY 10018

Lincoln Typographers Inc (212) 769-0606 100 W 67th St NY, NY 10023

Line & Tone (212) 921-8333 246 W 38th St NY, NY 10018

LLyod & Germain Typographics

(212) 686-8181 10 W 38th St NY, NY 10016

M&M Typographers Inc (212) 243-4645 155 W 19th St NY, NY 10011

Madison Type (212) 889-9840 232 Madison Ave NY, NY 10016

Malin Typographers Inc (212) 966-4214 270 Lafayette St NY, NY 10012

Microcomputer Publishing Center

(212) 463-8585 4 W 20th St NY, NY 10011

Ortiz Typographic Co (212) 947-3848 260 W 29th St NY, NY 10001

Pastore De Pamphilis Rampone

(212) 477-3300 303 Park Ave So NY, NY 10010

Photo Lettering Inc (212) 490-2345 216 E 45th St NY, NY 10017

Photographic Lettering (212) 687-6575 6 E 39th St NY, NY 10016

Potomac Graphics (212) 924-4880 508 W 26th St NY, NY 10001

Prieston Photo Engraving (212) 243-5335 124 W 24th St NY, NY 10011

Primor Typographers Inc (212) 269-7916 85 Washington St NY, NY 10006

Print & Design Inc (212) 243-0191 119 W 23rd St NY, NY 10011

Prototype (212) 807-8797 119 W 23rd St NY, NY 10011

Royal Composing Room Inc

(212) 254-1177 902 Broadway NY, NY 10010

Saxon Graphics (212) 714-1500 575 Eighth Ave NY, NY 10018

Scott, Harrison Graphics (212) 255-9251 54 W 21st St NY, NY 10010

SR Linotypers Inc (212) 925=5190 270 Lafayette NY, NY 10012

Starkey Corp (212) 925-1572 75 Varick St NY, NY 10013

Swift Typographers Inc (212) 925-3680 75 Varick St NY, NY 10013

TGA Communications (212) 807-7788 18 E 16th St NY, NY 10003

Tone Graphics Inc (212) 675-8900 27 W 24th St NY, NY 10010

True To Type Inc (212) 475-6438 175 5th Ave NY, NY 10010

Typeshop Inc, The (212) 354-8181 45 W 45th St NY, NY 10036

Typographic Images Inc (212) 645-6100 216 W 18th St NY, NY 10011

TypoGraphic Innovations (212) 764-6464 246 W 38th St NY, NY 10018

Typographics Plus Inc (212) 869-8440 16 W 46th St NY, NY 10036

Ultracomp Typographers (212) 689-3420 381 Park Ave So NY, NY 10016

US Lithograph Typographers

(212) 673-3210 853 Broadway NY, NY 10003

V & M Graphics (212) 219-3370 481 Washington St NY, NY 10013

Vulcan Typography Co (212) 557-4990 216 E 45th St NY, NY 10017

Wizard Graphics (212) 686-8200 36 E 30th St NY, NY 10016

World Typeface Center Inc

(212) 473-5510 303 Park Ave So NY, NY 10010

Zimmering & Zinn (212) 989-3151 50 W 23rd St NY, NY 10010

COLOR SEPARATIONS

a - m

Aardvark Computer Color

(212) 691-3000 135 W 27th St NY, NY 10001

Accent on Color

(516) 222-0020 750 Zeckendorf Blvd Garden City, NY 11530

Belvedere Graphic Arts (212) 967-7778 253 W 35th St NY, NY 10001

Bengal Graphics Inc (212) 924-1762 175 Varick St NY, NY 10014

Brunel, Jean (212) 219-1780 143 Franklin St NY, NY 10013

Cama Reproductions (212) 633-1830 127 W 25th St NY, NY 10001

Color Lithographers Inc (212) 255-3200 225 Varick St NY, NY 10014

Color Machine Inc (212) 279-6700 141 W 28th St NY, NY 10001

Colorscripts Plus (212) 752-0902 509 Madison Ave NY, NY 10022

Colotone (212) 557-5564 35 E 38th St NY, NY 10016

Computerized Quality Sprtn Inc

(212) 925-0554 145 Hudson St NY, NY 10013

Craftsman Color Lithographers

(212) 675-8200 40 W 25th St NY, NY 10001

Film Reproductions In Print

(212) 255-6722 155 Sixth Ave NY, NY 10013

Fine Arts Reproduction Co

(212) 226-1607 132 Lafayette St NY, NY 10013

FP Color Separations Inc (212) 661-5570 1 E 44th St NY, NY 10017

Graphic Sales Inc (212) 972-2445 60 E 42nd St NY, NY 10017

Graphiti Lithographic Plate

(212) 473-3700 902 Broadway NY, NY 10010

Kwik International Color Ltd

(212) 929-3800 111 Eighth Ave NY, NY 10014

Lammon Company (212) 505-9100 10 E 21st St NY, NY 10010

Manda Graphics Inc (212) 986-0380 216 W 18th St NY, NY 10011

n - w

New York Color Center (212) 764-8640 1211 Sixth Ave NY, NY 10036

Newport Graphics *(212) 925-5500* 80 Varick St NY, NY 10013

Noral Color Corp *(212) 582-6150* 211 W 56th St NY, NY 10019

Offset Separations Corp *(212) 354-5540* 15 W 39th St NY, NY 10018

Pictorial Powers Inc *(212) 840-6460* 151 W 40th St NY, NY 10018

Pioneer Moss Reproductions Inc
(212) 947-1550 460 W 34th St NY, NY 10001

Potomac Graphic Industries Inc
(212) 924-4880 508 W 26th St NY, NY 10001

Prima-Color Inc *(212) 302-5925* 1501 Broadway NY, NY 10036

Queens Group New York Inc
(212) 757-9410 150 W 58th St NY, NY 10019

Reilly New York Graphics *(212) 463-0058* 508 W 26th St NY, NY 10001

Reprocolor USA Ltd *(212) 353-8410* 117 E 24th St NY, NY 10010

Restivo Graphics Inc *(212) 967-7857* 253 W 35th St NY, NY 10001

Sheer Film & Plate Svc *(212) 627-9225* 233 Spring St NY, NY 10013

Spectra II Separations Inc *(212) 255-1110* 225 Varick St NY, NY 10014

Spectrum Colour Repro *(212) 691-7373* 119 W 23rd St NY, NY 10011

Sterling Regal Inc *(212) 213-5440* 141 E 25th St NY, NY 10010

Stuart Color Graphics *(212) 564-7788* 406 W 31st St NY, NY 10016

Tandem Associates & Color *(212) 675-0444* 38 W 21st St NY, NY 10011

Tru Color *(212) 213-8220* 200 Madison Ave NY, NY 10016

Westphal Inc *(212) 477-7500* 740 Broadway NY, NY 10003

ENGRAVERS

a - z

Brunel, Jean *(212) 219-1780* 143 Franklin St NY, NY 10013

Cardinal Photo Engraving *(212) 242-2051* 131 Varick St NY, NY 10013

Citation Photo Engraving *(212) 242-1662* 147 W 22nd St NY, NY 10011

Esquire Photo Engraving Co Inc
(212) 929-4527 4 W 22nd St NY, NY 10010

Gramercy Lane Photo Engrv
(212) 691-9898 114 W 26th St NY, NY 10001

Horan Engraving Co *(212) 689-8585* 44 W 28th St NY, NY 10001

Karr Graphics Corp *(212) 645-6000* 233 Spring St NY, NY 10013

Mercury Photo Engravers Corp
(212) 489-1855 244 W 49th St NY, NY 10019

Pioneer Moss Reproductions Inc
(212) 947-1550 460 W 34th St NY, NY 10001

Prieston Photo-Engraving *(212) 243-5335* 124 W 24th St NY, NY 10011

Simmons-Beal *(212) 971-4000* 350 W 31st St NY, NY 10001

Universal *(212) 691-7676* 150 W 22nd St NY, NY 10010

Verilen Reproductions *(212) 971-4000* 350 W 31st St NY, NY 10001

Walker-Prismatic Engraving Co
(212) 689-5353 141 E 25th St NY, NY 10010

Woodbury & Co *(212) 683-0851* 485 Fifth Ave NY, NY 10017

LAMINATORS

a - z

Dennis Laminating Inc *(212) 239-8450* 143 W 30th St NY, NY 10001

Erizan Inc *(212) 247-4646* 423 W 55th St NY, NY 10019

Idesco Corp *(212) 889-2530* 37 W 26th St NY, NY 10010

Lamimount Processing Inc *(212) 593-3447* 150 E 58th St NY, NY 10155

Laminae Laminating Ltd *(212) 682-5138* 100 E 42nd St NY, NY 10017

Laminall Plastics Co *(718) 786-6480* 11-42 46th Rd LIC, NY 11101

Laminology *(212) 206-9242* 1 1/2 W 20th St NY, NY 10011

Malcolm & Hayes *(212) 682-1316* 694 Third Ave NY, NY 10017

Modern Laminating Service *(212) 682-5045* 698 Third Ave NY, NY 10017

Morgan Laminating *(212) 242-5010* 150 W 22nd St NY, NY 10017

EMBOSSERS

a - z

Arkadia Label Corp *(212) 243-7133* 126 W 22nd St NY, NY 10011

Bergazyn & Son Inc *(212) 243-3850* 627 Greenwich St NY, NY 10014

Beyer Gerd Inc *(212) 302-9059* 265 W 40th St NY, NY 10018

Card Processing Inc *(718) 768-1855* 147 41st St Brooklyn, NY 11232

Fischer-Partelow Inc *(212) 244-5660* 438 W 37th St NY, NY 10018

Freedman Cut-Outs Inc *(212) 243-4700* 444 W 17th St NY, NY 10011

Freedman Die Cutters Inc *(212) 929-7000* 85 Tenth Ave NY, NY 10011

Gailer, John Inc *(212) 243-5662* 137 Varick St NY, NY 10013

Hollis Press Inc *(212) 617-0400* 890 Garrison Ave Bronx, NY 10474

Ornamental Embossings Inc *(212) 226-2388* 247 Centre St NY, NY 10013

Perfect Gold Stamping *(212) 226-2351* 107 Grand St NY, NY 10013

Service Die Cutting Co *(212) 255-1740* 304 Hudson St NY, NY 10013

Staff Die Cutting Co Inc *(212) 675-4097* 542 W 22nd St NY, NY 10011

Sterling Mounting & Finishing
(212) 736-8305 406 W 31st St NY, NY 10001

VARIETY GOLD STAMPING CO

(212) 912-1809 29 Sheer Plaza Plainview, NY 11803

WELSH COLD STAMPERS INC *(212) 505-9200* 139-141 Ludlow St NY, NY 10022

SIGNAGE & NEON

a - z

ACTIVE SIGNS *(212) 564-9696* 122 W 29th St NY, NY 10001

ALPHA ENGRAVING CO *(212) 247-5266* 888 Eighth Ave NY, NY 10019

ARTISTIC NEON BY GASPER

(718) 821-1550 75-49 61st St Glendale, NY 11385

ARTKRAFT STRAUSS SIGN CORP

(212) 265-5155 830 Twelfth Ave NY, NY 10019

BIG APPLE SIGN CORP *(212) 575-0706* 247 W 35th St NY, NY 10001

CITI SIGNWRITERS INC *(212) 772-0726* 31 W 46th St NY, NY 10036

DE-SIGN LETTERS *(212) 673-6211* 15 W 18th St NY, NY 10003

DURA ARCHITECTURAL SIGNAGE

(718) 706-6400 48-15 32nd Pl LIC, NY 11101

FORREST SIGN CO *(212) 319-0100* 949 Second Ave NY, NY 10022

JEWELITE SIGNS & LETTERS *(212) 683-4474* 154 Reade St NY, NY 10013

LET THERE BE NEON *(212) 226-4883* 38 White St NY, NY 10013

MANHATTAN NEON SIGN CORP

(212) 714-0430 335 W 38th St NY, NY 10018

MECURY-NEON SIGNS *(212) 219-0542* 69 E 116th St NY, NY 10002

MIDTOWN NEON SIGN CORP *(212) 736-3838* 550 W 30th St NY, NY 10001

MITTEN LETTERS *(212) 741-1000* 85 Fifth Ave NY, NY 10003

NEON CITY *(212) 255-8278* 539 Sixth Ave NY, NY 10011

NEON DESIGN ASSOC *(212) 431-8162* 484 Broadway NY, NY 10013

NEON ILLUMINATED *(212) 678-4456* 66 W 109th St NY, NY 10024

REGENT SIGNS *(212) 982-6622* 58 Second Ave NY, NY 10003

SAY IT IN NEON *(212) 691-7977* 434 Hudson St NY, NY 10014

SIGN DESIGN *(212) 744-0042* 317 E 75th St NY, NY 10021

SPECIALTY SIGNS CO INC *(212) 243-8521* 54 W 21st St NY, NY 10010

INDEX TO TAB 10

LOCATION & STUDIO SUPPORT SERVICES

10

INDEX TO TAB 10

LOCATION & STUDIO RENTAL

LOCATION SERVICES

PHOTO SUPPLY

ART SUPPLY

BACKDROPS

SET CONSTRUCTION

MODEL MAKING SPFX

PROPS

ANTIQUE AND FURNITURE

FLORISTS

ANIMALS

COSTUMERS

ACRYLICS

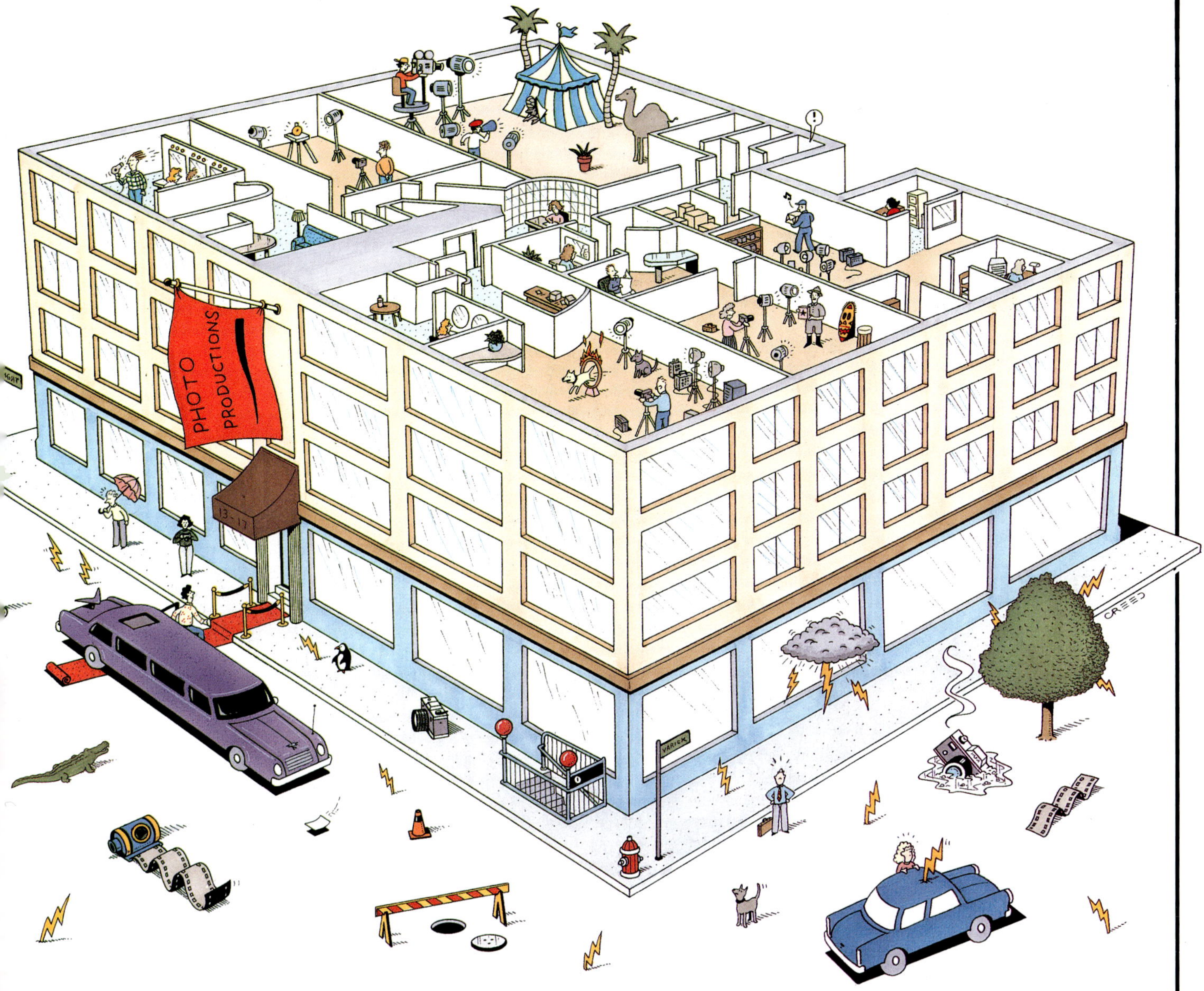
PHOTO PRODUCTIONS
13-17
VARICK
CREED

LOCATION & STUDIO RENTAL

a - o

20/20 PHOTOGRAPHER'S PLACE *(212) 675-2020* 20 W 20th St NY, NY 10011

2B STUDIO *(212) 679-5537* 1200 Broadway NY, NY 10001

APOLLO STUDIOS *(212) 477-0800* 704 Broadway NY, NY 10003

BIG SKY STUDIO *(212) 239-0999* 450 W 31st St NY, NY 10001

CAMEO STUDIO BY ZAC *(212) 645-9494* 34 Renwick St NY, NY 10013

PAGE 4

CODALIGHT RENTAL STUDIO *(212) 206-9333* 151 W 19th St NY, NY 10011

COLUMNS, THE *(212) 941-8133* 584 Broadway NY, NY 10012

CONTACT STUDIOS *(212) 354-6400* 165 W 47th St NY, NY 10036

DAKOTA STUDIO *(212) 691-2197* 78 Fifth Ave NY, NY 10011

DANIEL AUBRY *(212) 598-4191* 365 First Ave NY, NY 10010

DUGGAL COLOR PROJECTS *(212) 242-7000* 9 W 29th St NY, NY 10011

FALCON-PRODUCTIONS STUDIOS *(212) 594-8204* 6 W 32nd St NY, NY 10001

GANSEVOORT STUDIO *(212) 691-2847* 53 Gansevoort St NY, NY 10014

GIRL SCOUT LOCATIONS

(516) 883-8409 1 Hillside Ave Port Washington, NY 11050

Hugh Bell Studio *(212) 260-2260* 873 Broadway NY, NY 10003

Ihara Studio *(212) 219-9363* 568 Broadway NY, NY 10012

Knole *(516) 626-2841* 174 Post Rd Westbury, NY 11568

Lighthouse *(212) 929-9001* 76 Ninth Ave NY, NY 10011

Lodge Location, The *(201) 727-4900* 24 Sunset Lake Rd Blairstown, NJ 07825

Masterview *(212) 629-6330* 450 W 31st St NY, NY 10001

PAGE 3

McLoughlin Studio *(212) 206-8209* 148 W 24th St NY, NY 10011

MW Productions Inc Studio *(212) 675-5932* 126 Fifth Ave NY, NY 10011

Nabe Studio *(212) 807-6024* 153 W 27th St NY, NY 10001

N Y Flash/Daylight Studio *(212) 929-3232* 704 Broadway NY, NY 10003

Silva-Cone Studios *(212) 279-0900* 260 W 36th St NY, NY 10018

Soho Entertainment *(212) 226-4576* 80 Varick St NY, NY 10013

Studio 35 *(212) 925-1117* 52 White St NY, NY 10013

Studio 705 *(212) 925-7334* 568 Broadway NY, NY 10012

Studio C *(212) 564-0606* 145 W 28th St NY, NY 10001

Tabu Studio *(212) 947-0808* 450 W 31st St NY, NY 10001

Tekno *(212) 889-5080* 15 E 30th St NY, NY 10016

Trinity Studio *(212) 483-9493* 44 Trinity Pl NY, NY 10006

Wallach Enterprises *(212) 966-1970* 419 Broome St NY, NY 10013

Wave Hill *(212) 549-3200* 675 W 252nd St Bronx, NY 10471

Yellowdot *(212) 5 32-4010* 47 E 34th St NY, NY 10016

p - z

PDN Studio *(212) 677-8418* 49 E 21st St NY, NY 10010

Penthouse A *(212) 714-0076* 25 W 31st St NY, NY 10001

Perfect Space, A *(212) 941-0262* Box 1669 NY, NY 10013

Photo Productions Services

(212) 226-1100 **13-17 Laight St NY, NY 10013**

PAGE 1

Photo Tekniques/City Lights

(212) 219-9444 568 Broadway NY, NY 10012

Professional Photo Supply

(212) 924-1200 **141 W 20th St NY, NY 10011**

PAGE 6

Puck Film Studios *(212) 925-7766* 295 Lafayette St NY, NY 10012

PAGE 3

Riverview Loft Studio *(212) 947-0808* 21 Mill Hill Rd Woodstock, NY 12498

Rotem Studio *(212) 947-9455* 259 W 30th St NY, NY 10001

Schnoodle Studios *(212) 431-7788* 54 Bleecker St NY, NY 10012

LOCATION SERVICES

a - k

Abramowitz & Vine *(201) 509-8080* 35 Norman Rd Upper Montclair, NJ 07043

ALSAM *(212) 548-4467* POB 1767 Murray Hill St NY, NY 10156

Amram, Jeff *(212) 677-4081* NY, NY

Ayoub, Jimmy *(212) 598-4467* 132 E 16th St NY, NY 10003

Belle Forma Locations Ltd

(914) 834-5554 32 Vine Rd Larchmont, NY 10538

Brok, Trell *(212) 288-6120* NY, NY

C & C Productions *(212) 472-3700* 445 E 80th St NY, NY 10021

Cacciatore, John *(212) 247-5678* NY, NY

Camarada, George *(212) 431-7256* NY, NY

Chemtob, Robert *(212) 222-4081* NY, NY

Clough, Alan *(212) 645-0742* NY, NY

Duyrea, Randall *(718) 622-2239* Brooklyn, NY

Fincher, Les *(212) 475-3258* 902 Broadway NY, NY 10011

Fitzgerald, David *(212) 864-1152* NY, NY

Franzreb, John *(718) 273-7828* 52 Park View Pl Staten Isl, NY 10310

Giardini, Bob *(212) 431-3192* NY, NY

Great Locations *(212) 691-1761* 136 Waverly Pl NY, NY 10014

Henkel, Steve *(516) 536-3720* NY , NY

Hinden, Elizabeth *(212) 734-0765* NY, NY

Holaday, Tom *(212) 663-5522* NY, NY

Karan, Josh *(212) 923-1680* NY, NY

Knee, Steve *(212) 734-0605* NY, NY

Kuttner, Larry *(201) 569-5889* 350 Lafayette St Creskill, NJ 07626

l - z

Leach, Ed Inc *(212) 691-3450* 160 Fifth Ave NY, NY 10011

Location NY *(914) 634-3988* 32 Mark Lane New City, NY 10956

Locations Inc *(212) 481-9111* 445 Fifth Ave NY, NY 10016

PAGE 5

Locations Unlimited *(212) 741-3048* 277 W 10th St NY, NY 10014

Location USA *(212) 807-5506* 204 W 20th St NY, NY 10011

Luck, Owen *(212) 924-5451* NY, NY

Marks, Arthur *(212) 685-2761* 140 E 40th St NY, NY 10016

Mayor's Office for Film & TV

(212) 489-6710 254 W 54th St NY, NY 10019

Miller, Charles *(212) 222-1802* NY, NY

Mauriello, Joseph *(212) 242-6644* 1 World Trade Ctr NY, NY 10047

Nassau Cnty Film Commission

(516) 535-4160 1550 Franklin Ave Mineola, NY 11501

NJ Transit Special Operations

(201) 468-8559 1160 Raymond Blvd Newark, NJ 07102

Norwood, John Jr *(212) 473-7195* NY, NY

NY ST Gov's Office Mtn Pct & TV

(212) 309-0540 230 Park Ave NY, NY 10169

Randall, Monica Locations

(516) 921-7438 Box 75 Oyster Bay, NY 11771

Reichman, Michael *(718) 282-3454* Brooklyn, NY

Ren Rose Locations Ltd

(201) 992-4264 4 Sandalwood Dr Livingston, NJ0 7039

Robbins, Judie Locations ***(212) 633-6440*** **1133 Broadway NY, NY 10010**

PAGE 5

Sapolis, Gary *(914) 666-0180* NY, NY

Seiler, Frank *(212) 989-7072* NY, NY

Shimm, Mark *(212) 874-5047* NY, NY

Shore, Ira & Rita *(212) 505-2725* 510 E 20th St NY, NY 10009

Suffolk Cnty Mtn Pct & TV

(516) 360-4800 Veterans Mem Hwy Hauppauge, NY 11788

Suryea, Randall *(718) 622-2239* NY, NY

Waller, Mitch *(212) 517-5880* NY, NY

Weisberg, Steve *(718) 768-6082* NY, NY

Wild Locations *(212) 391-6647* 1375 Broadway NY, NY 10018

Wolfson, Paula *(212) 741-3048* 277 W 10th St NY, NY 10014

PHOTO SUPPLY

a - l

47th St Photo *(212) 398-1410* 67 W 47th St NY, NY 10036

47th St Photo *(212) 260-4410* 35 E 18th St NY, NY 10003

AAA Camera Exchange *(212) 242-5800* 43 Seventh Ave NY, NY 10011

Adorama *(212) 741-0052* 42 W 18th St NY, NY 10011

Advance Camera *(212) 944-1410* 15 W 46th St NY, NY 10036

Alkit Pro Camera *(212) 674-1515* 222 Park Ave So NY, NY 10003

Alkit Pro Camera *(212) 832-2101* 866 Third Ave NY, NY 10017

Arkin Medo Inc *(212) 685-1969* 30 E 33rd St NY, NY 10016

B & H Photo *(212) 206-1010* 119 W 17th St NY, NY 10011

Balcar-Tekno Lighting Systems

(212) 889-5080 15 E 30th St NY, NY 10016

Ben-Ness Photo *(212) 255-4270* 114 University Pl NY, NY 10003

Bi-Rite Camera *(212) 685-2130* 15 E 30th St NY, NY 10016

Cambridge Camera Exchange

(212) 675-8600 45 Seventh Ave NY, NY 10011

Camera Barn *(212) 867-9280* 341 Madison Ave NY, NY 10016

Camera Barn *(212) 233-3080* 198 Broadway NY, NY 10038

Camera Barn *(212) 947-3510* 1272 Broadway NY, NY 10001

CECO International Corp *(212) 206-8280* 440 W 15th St NY, NY 10010

Doi Camera Place *(212) 661-0876* 342 Madison Ave NY, NY 10173

Executive Photo *(212) 947-5290* 120 W 31st St NY, NY 10001

FERCO *(212) 245-4800* 707 Eleventh Ave NY, NY 10019

Flash Clinic *(212) 673-4030* 9 E 19th St NY, NY 10003

Foto Care Ltd *(212) 741-2990* 170 Fifth Ave NY, NY 10010

Foto-Cell *(212) 924-7474* 49 W 23rd St NY, NY 10010

Garden Camera *(212) 868-1420* 145 W 30th St NY, NY 10001

Ghitelman, Gil Cameras *(212) 924-3020* 166 Fifth Ave NY, NY 10010

Godard *(212) 620-0480* 11 W 20th St NY, NY 10011

Grand Central Camera

(212) 986-2270 420 Lexington Ave NY, NY 10019

Hansen, Ken Photo *(212) 777-5900* 920 Broadway NY, NY 10010

Hirsch Photo Ltd *(212) 557-1150* 699 Third Ave NY, NY 10017

Hotlights *(212) 645-5295* 133 W 19th St NY, NY 10011

Jaybee Photo *(212) 420-9797* 133 Fifth Ave NY, NY 10003

K & M Camera *(212) 532-1106* 377 E 23rd St NY, NY 10010

Lee Lighting America Ltd *(212) 691-1910* 534 W 25th St NY, NY 10001

LEGS/Manhattan *(212) 807-6644* Pier 62 @23rd St NY, NY 10011

Lens & Repro Equip Corp

(212) 675-1900 **33 W 17th St NY, NY 10011**

PAGE 7

Lexington Camera Stores *(212) 758-0345* 642 Lexington Ave NY, NY 10022

Lowel Light Manufacturing *(212) 947-0950* 475 10th Ave NY, NY 10018

m - z

MATTHEWS *(212) 691-4720* 236 W 26th St NY, NY 10011

MERIT PHOTO SHOP *(212) 730-7430* 550 Eighth Ave NY, NY 10018

META PHOTO SUPPLY *(212) 725-0962* 244 Madison Ave NY, NY 10016

NEW YORK CAMERA *(212) 695-0697* 131 W 35th St NY, NY 10001

NEW YORK FLASH RENTAL *(212) 353-0600* 704 Broadway NY, NY 10003

OLDEN CAMERA *(212) 725-1234* 1265 Broadway NY, NY 10001

PHOTO EXCHANGE *(212) 675-6583* 1 W 20th St NY, NY 10011

PAGE 2, TAB 9

PHOTO MARKETPLACE *(212) 989-8500* 11 W 20th St NY, NY 10011

PHOTO-TEKNIQUES/CITY LIGHTS *(212) 219-9444* 568 Broadway NY, NY 10012

PHOTOBUG SHOP INC *(212) 695-6706* 845 Sixth Ave NY, NY 10001

PHOTRON MARKETING *(212) 221-1011* 256 W 38th St NY, NY 10018

PRAGAN CAMERA STORE *(212) 929-3910* 215 W 14th St NY, NY 10011

PRO-FOTO *(212) 564-6171* 128 W 31st St NY, NY 10001

PROF PHOTO SUPPLY *(212) 924-1200* 141 W 20th St NY, NY 10011

PAGE 6

SMP *(212) 674-2701* 38 Gramercy Park E NY, NY 10010

SPIRATONE *(212) 594-5269* 130 W 31st St NY, NY 10016

TRI-STATE CAMERAS *(212) 349-2555* 160 Broadway NY, NY 10038

WALL STREET CAMERA *(212) 344-0011* 82 Wall St NY, NY 10005

WEST SIDE CAMERA *(212) 877-8760* 2400 Broadway NY, NY 10024

WILLOUGHBY CAMERA STORE *(212) 564-1600* 110 W 32nd St NY, NY 10001

ART SUPPLY

a - h

AMBER ART & DRAFTING *(212) 371-4430* 436 Madison Ave NY, NY 10022

ARTMANS ART SUPPLY CO *(212) 838-4350* 235 E 57th St NY, NY 10022

BEC-KO COMPANY INC *(212) 682-4224* 150 E 43rd St NY, NY 10016

BERLIN, IRVING INC *(212) 532-3600* 14 E 37th St NY, NY 10016

BROWN. ARTHUR & BROTHERS
(212) 575-5555 2 W 46th St NY, NY 10036

CHARETTE CORPORATION *(212) 683-8822* 215 Lexington Ave NY, NY 10016

CLODER CORP *(212) 962-1600* 49 Ann St NY, NY 10038

COMMERCIAL & MATERIALS CO
(212) 685-6858 165 Lexington Ave NY, NY 10016

DELSEMMES ARTISTS MATERIALS
(212) 675-2742 27 W 14th St NY, NY 10011

EASTERN ARTISTS *(212) 645-5555* 5 W 22nd St NY, NY 10010

EMPIRE ARTISTS MATERIALS

(212) 737-5002 851 Lexington Ave NY, NY 10021

FINE ART MATERIALS INC *(212) 982-7100* 346 Lafayette NY, NY 10012

FLAX, SAM *(212) 620-3040* 25 E 28th St NY, NY 10016

PAGE 8

FLAX, SAM *(212) 620-3050* 747 Third Ave NY, NY 10022

PAGE 8

FLAX, SAM *(212) 620-3030* 15 Park Row NY, NY 10047

PAGE 8

FLAX, SAM *(212) 620-3038* 12 W 20th St NY, NY 10011

PAGE 8

FLAX, SAM *(212) 620-3060* 55 E 55th St NY, NY 10022

PAGE 8

FRIEDMAN, A I INC *(212) 243-9000* 44 W 18th St NY, NY 10011

FRIEDMAN, A I INC *(212) 243-9000* 25 W 45th St NY, NY 10036

GELLER ARTIST MATERIALS *(212) 673-5500* 37 E 18th Street NY, NY 10003

GLASNER ART SUPPLY *(212) 684-2477* 17 E 37th St NY, NY 10016

GOLDEN ARTIST MATERIALS *(212) 749-3100* 2512 Broadway NY, NY 10025

GRAND CENTRAL ARTISTS' MATR *(212) 679-0023* 18 E 40th St NY, NY 10016

GREENWICH ARTISTS' SUPPLY CO *(212) 677-6038* 32 Third Ave NY, NY 10003

k - z

KARL ART SUPPLY INC *(212) 752-3591* 230 E 54th St NY, NY 10022

KLASS ARTIST MATERIAL *(212) 737-4500* 970 Lexington Ave NY, NY 10021

LEE'S ART SHOP *(212) 247-0110* 220 W 57th St NY, NY 10019

MICHAELS, M M INC *(212) 695-2200* 13 W 30th St NY, NY 10001

NATIONAL ARTIST MATERIALS *(212) 675-0100* 4 W 20th St NY, NY 10011

NEW YORK CENTRAL ART SUPPLY

(212) 477-0400 130 E 12th St NY, NY 10003

NEW YORK CENTRAL SUPPLY CO

(212) 473-7705 62 Third Ave NY, NY 10003

PALETTE ART CO *(212) 753-7338* 436 Madison Ave NY, NY 10016

PARSONS ART SUPPLY *(212) 675-6406* 70 Fifth Ave NY, NY 10003

PEARL PAINT CO *(212) 431-7932* 308 Canal St NY, NY 10002

PLAZA ARTIST MATERIALS *(212) 689-2870* 173 Madison Ave NY, NY 10016

SCHNEIDER & CO INC *(212) 877-8554* 306 Columbus Ave NY, NY 10023

SET SHOP *(212) 929-4845* 3 W 20th St NY, NY 10011

TAY ART SUPPLIES *(212) 475-7365* 212 E 9th St NY, NY 10003

TORCH ART SUPPLY *(212) 243-3534* 36 W 13th St NY, NY 10011

TRIBECA ARTISTS SUPPLIES *(212) 349-2223* 142 Chambers St NY, NY 10007

UTRECHT ART & DRAFTING *(212) 777-5353* 111 Fourth Ave NY, NY 10003

BACKDROPS

a - z

BIMA BACKDROPS *(718) 392-4747* 25-19 Borden Ave LIC, NY 11101

BRAND, ROSE *(212) 594-7424* 517 W 35th St NY, NY 10001

BRODERSON INC *(212) 925-9392* 873 Broadway NY, NY 10003

DROP EVERYTHING BACKDROPS *(212) 620-0685* 72 Bedford St NY, NY 10014

EASTERN SCENIC BACKDROPS *(212) 244-2700* 560 W 34th St NY, NY 10001

HARVEY, JULIE PAINTED BACKDROPS

(212) 242-0480 38 W 21st St NY, NY 10011

LAFERLA, SANDRO *(212) 620-0693* 108 W 25th St NY, NY 10001

LECLERC BACKDROPS *(212) 869-6970* 233 W 42nd St NY, NY 10036

MERIT STUDIO *(212) 736-5674* 110 W 32nd St NY, NY 10001

NELSON, JANE STUDIO *(212) 431-4642* 21 Howard St NY, NY 10013

OLIPHANT BACKDROPS *(212) 741-1233* 38 Cooper Sq NY, NY 10003

ROGERS, WILLIAM BACKDROPS *(212) 206-0016* NY, NY

SET SHOP *(212) 929-4845* 3 W 20th St NY, NY 10011

SET TWO *(212) 924-1191* 20 W 20th St NY, NY 10011

TAMIN PRODUCTIONS *(212) 807-6691* 440 West End Ave NY, NY 10024

THOMAS & O'BRIEN STUDIOS *(212) 629-5930* 450 W 31st St NY, NY 10001

WEITMAN, RUTH *(718) 636-5185* 150 St Marks Ave Brooklyn, NY 11238

SET CONSTRUCTION

a - z

BILL THE SET BUILDER *(718) 935-9560* 153 Sullivan St Brooklyn, NY 11231

BROOKLYN MODEL WORKS
(718) 834-1944 60 Washington Ave Brooklyn, NY 11205

BRUCE & BRUCE SCENERY *(212) 460-5050* 155 Attorney St NY, NY 10002

CBS TELEVISION PLASTIC DESIGNS
(212) 975-2751 524 W 57th St NY, NY 10019

CONSTRUCTIVE DISPLAY *(212) 675-7320* 142 W 26th St NY, NY 10010

CREATIVE DESIGNS *(718) 386-3869* 5601 Arnold Ave Maspeth, NY 11378

DESIGNERS WORKSHOP *(718) 330-0921* 25 Jay St Brooklyn, NY 11201

DONAHUE, JAMES F *(718) 388-9175* 143 Roebling St Brooklyn, NY 11211
PAGE 9

FIELD STUDIOS INC *(718) 855-4431* 232 Sixth St Brooklyn, NY 11215

FOREPLAY STUDIOS *(212) 226-0188* 33 Greene St NY, NY 10013

GLASS, JAMES *(212) 870-1515* 2109 Broadway NY, NY 10023

GRATSON, JIM PROPS *(718) 855-4379* 280 Nevins St Brooklyn, NY 11217

GREENWICH STUDIOS *(212) 966-3225* 472 Greenwich St NY, NY 10013

HUDSON SCENIC STUDIO *(212) 585-6704* 125 Bruckner Blvd Bronx, NY 10454

KUNZ, PETER *(914) 687-0400* RD 1 Box 223 High Falls, NY 12440

LANZER ASSOCIATES INC *(718) 625-0095* 79 Bridge St Brooklyn, NY 11201

LINCOLN SCENIC STUDIOS *(212) 244-2700* 560 W 34th St NY, NY 10001

MALLIE & CO *(718) 706-1233* 35-30 38th St Astoria, NY 11101

MANHATTAN MODEL SHOP *(212) 473-6312* 40 Great Jones St NY, NY 10012

MCHUGH ROLLINS ASSOCIATES
(718) 643-0990 79 Bridge St Brooklyn, NY 11201

MCKINNEY, PETER *(212) 353-8840* 12 E 22nd St NY, NY 10010

MCL DESIGN *(212) 206-7500* 31-33 W 21st St NY, NY 10010

MESSMORE & DAMON *(212) 594-8070* 530 W 28th St NY, NY 10001

METRO SCENIC STUDIOS INC
(718) 464-6329 215-31 99th Ave Queens Village, NY 11429

NOLAN SCENERY STUDIO *(718) 783-6910* 1163 Atlantic Ave Brooklyn, NY 11216

PATTERSON, J SCENIC STUDIOS
(201) 866-0316 4312 Liberty Ave No Bergen, NJ 07047

Romeo Scenic Workshop *(914) 965-3994* 44 Wells Ave Yonkers, NY 10701

Set Control Inc *(718) 729-8719* 43-56 10th St LIC, NY 11101

Set Shop *(212) 929-4845* 3 W 20th St NY, NY 10011

Set Two *(212) 924-1191* 20 W 20th St NY, NY 10011

Showtech *(203) 854-9336* 15 Chapel St Norwalk, CT 06850

Stiegelbauer Associates

(718) 624-0835 Brooklyn Navy Yard Bldg #20 Brooklyn, NY 11205

PAGE 9

Variety Scenic Studios *(718) 392-4747* 25-19 Borden Ave LIC, NY 11101

Warshaw Scenic Design *(212) 677-4225* 205 E 10th St NY, NY 10003

Weiss Designs *(212) 477-2659* 32 Union Sq East NY, NY 10003

MODEL MAKING SPFX

a - z

Actors Make-up Studio *(212) 719-3772* 165 W 47th St NY, NY 10036

AOKI Studio *(212) 564-4285* 424 W 33rd St NY, NY 10001

Bargsten *(212) 827-5332* 247 Barrow St Jersey City, NJ 07302

Borow, Mark *(212) 254-1486* 5 East 19th St NY, NY 10003

Brooklyn Model Works

(718) 834-1944 60 Washington Ave Brooklyn, NY 11205

Cimmelli *(914) 356-2232* 120 No Pascack Rd Spring Valley, NY 10977

Cleland Studio *(212) 431-9185* 122 Spring St NY, NY 10012

Dale Mallie & Co *(718) 706-1233* 35-30 38th St Astoria, NY 11101

DeFilippo, Dom Studio Inc *(212) 986-5444* 215 E 37th St NY, NY 10016

DePaolo, William *(212) 677-4550* 529 E 6th St NY, NY 10009

Donahue, James (718) 388-9175 143 Roebling St Brooklyn, NY 11211

PAGE 9

EFEX Specialists *(718) 937-2417* 35-39 37th St LIC, NY 11101

Eoin Sprott Studio *(718) 784-1407* 37-11 35th Ave Astoria, NY 11101

Fabulous Fakes *(212) 941-0728* 270 Lafayette St NY, NY 10012

Finer Works *(201) 798-3567* 1317-19 Willow Ave Hoboken, NJ 07030

Gluck, Lewis *(212) 242-6754* 152 W 25th St NY, NY 10001

Graphics for Industry *(212) 889-6202* 8 W 30th St NY, NY 10001

Gratson, Jim Props *(718) 855-4379* 280 Nevins St Brooklyn, NY 11217

Hera Model Makers *(212) 695-5378* 307 W 38th St NY, NY 10018

Jauchem & Meeh Inc *(718) 875-0140* 79 Bridge St NY, NY 11201

Jeffers, Kathy *(212) 475-1756* 106 E 19th St NY, NY 10003

Kirshoff, Steve *(914) 937-9345* 251 N Ridge Rd Portchester, NY 10573

Kruger Associates Inc *(212) 571-0617* 9 Murray St NY, NY 10007

Kunz, Peter *(914) 687-0400* RD 1 Box 223 High Falls, NY 12440

Lance Studios *(212) 382-0290* 151 W 46th St NY, NY 10036

Manhattan Model Shop *(212) 473-6312* 40 Great Jones St NY, NY 10012

Maniatis, Michael *(212) 620-0398* 48 W 22nd St NY, NY 10010

Maxilla & Mandible Ltd *(212) 724-6173* 78 W 82nd St NY, NY 10024

MCL Design *(212) 206-7500* 31-33 W 21st St NY, NY 10010

Mendez, Raymond *(212) 864-4689* 220 W 98th St NY, NY 10025

Michael Miller Model Making *(718) 875-0381* , NY

MS 25 Modelmaking *(212) 989-2100* 516 W 25th St NY, NY 10001

Mulder/Goodwin Studios *(212) 213-5558* 220 E 23rd St NY, NY 10010

Puppet Projects *(718) 383-6110* 97 Eagle St Brooklyn, NY 11222

Special Creations Inc *(212) 966-9038* 181 Hudson St NY, NY 10013

Special Make-up Effects

(914) 693-2752 68 Colonial Ave Dobbs Ferry, NY 10522

Stiegelbauer Associates Inc

(718) 624-0835 Brooklyn Navy Yard Bldg #20 Brooklyn, NY 11205

PAGE 9

Variety Scenic Studios *(718) 392-4747* 25-19 Borden Ave LIC, NY 11101

Weiss Designs *(212) 477-2659* 32 Union Sq East NY, NY 10003

Whole Art *(212) 868-0478* 259 W 30th St NY, NY 10001

Wizardworks *(718) 786-8383* 39-40 W 21st St LIC, NY 11101

Yurikiw Studio *(212) 226-6338* 568 Broadway NY, NY 10012

Zakarian Prop Shop *(718) 522-4606* 26 College Pl Brooklyn Hghts, NY 11201

Zeller International *(212) 627-7676* Main St POB Z Downsville, NY 13755

PROPS

a - z

Abet Rent-A-Fur (212) 989-5757 307 Seventh Ave NY, NY 10001

PAGE 11

Antique Supermarket *(212) 226-2880* 84 Wooster St NY, NY 10012

Arenson's Office Furnishings

(212) 838-8880 315 E 62nd St NY, NY 10021

PAGE 2

Artistic Neon by Gasper *(718) 821-1550* 75-49 61st St Glendale, NY 11385

Arts & Crafters Inc *(718) 875-8151* 175 Johnson St Brooklyn, NY 11201

Baker, JL *(203) 265-9231* 478 N Main St Wallingford, CT 06492

Bizarre Bazaar *(212) 688-1830* 1050 Second Ave NY, NY 10022

COBWEB *(212) 505-1558* 116 W Houston NY, NY 10012

COOPER CLASSICS *(212) 929-3909* 132 Perry St NY, NY 10014

EARLY HALLOWEEN *(212) 691-2933* 130 W 25th St NY, NY 10001

ECLECTIC ENCORE INC *(212) 645-8880* 620 W 26th St NY, NY 10001

EOIN SPROTT STUDIO LTD *(718) 784-1407* 37-11 35th Ave Astoria, NY 11106

FONE BOOTH, THE *(212) 751-8310* 12 E 53rd St NY, NY 10022

IRREPLACEABLE ARTIFACTS *(212) 982-5000* 14 Second Ave NY, NY 10003

KENMORE/NY *(212) 683-1888* 352 Park Ave So NY, NY 10010

LAZAR COSTUME DESIGN & SOFT PROPS
(212) 473-0363 155 E 23rd St NY, NY 10010

MAYHEW PROP RENTALS *(212) 759-8120* 507 Park Ave NY, NY 10022

NICCOLINI ANTIQUES *(212) 254-2900* 114 E 25th St NY, NY 10010

NOSTALGIA ALLEY *(212) 695-6578* 425-459 W 15th St NY, NY 10011
PAGE 11

ONE-STOP PROPPING *(212) 465-8654* 531 W 26th St NY, NY 10001

PLACE FOR ANTIQUES, THE *(212) 308-4066* 993 Second Ave NY, NY 10022

PLACE FOR PROPS *(212) 308-4066* 993 Second Ave NY, NY 10022

PROP HOUSE INC *(212) 713-0760* 653 Eleventh Ave NY, NY 10036

PROPART *(212) 947-0900* 5 W 36th St NY, NY 10018

PROPS DISPLAYS & INTERIORS INC
(212) 620-3840 132 W 18th St NY, NY 10011

PROPS FOR TODAY *(212) 206-0330* 15 W 20th St NY, NY 10011

RENT-A-THING *(914) 628-9298* POB 337 Baldwin Pl, NY 10505

SCHOEPFER INC *(212) 736-6939* 138 W 31st St NY, NY 10001

SECOND HAND ROSE *(212) 243-9522* 573 Hudson St NY, NY 10014

SET SHOP *(212) 929-4845* 3 W 20th St NY, NY 10011

SHOWROOM OUTLET *(212) 581-0470* 625-35 W 55th St NY, NY 10019

STATE SUPPLY EQUIP & PROPS

(212) 645-1430 **210 Eleventh Ave NY, NY 10001**

PAGE 12

UNIQUE SURFACES *(212) 696-9229* 28 W 27th St NY, NY 10001

WHOLE ART *(212) 868-0478* 259 W 30th St NY, NY 10001

ZELLER INTERNATIONAL *(212) 627-7676* Box 2 Main St Downsville, NY 13755

ANTIQUE & FURNITURE

a - b

AARON'S BARGAIN SPOT *(212) 674-1188* 64 Third Ave NY, NY 10003

ABE'S ANTIQUES INC *(212) 260-6424* 815 Broadway NY, NY 10003

AC DC APPLIANCE RENTAL *(212) 686-8884* 40 W 29th St NY, NY 10001

ACE GALLERIES *(212) 260-2720* 91 University Pl NY, NY 10003

AGOSTINO ANTIQUES *(212) 533-3355* 808 Broadway NY, NY 10003

ALBINO ANTIQUES *(212) 677-8820* 55 E 11th St NY, NY 10003

ALLAN, DAVID ANTIQUES *(212) 598-9030* 812 Broadway NY, NY 10003

AMERICA HURRAH ANTIQUES

(212) 535-1930 766 Madison Ave NY, NY 10021

ANN-MORRIS ANTIQUES *(212) 755-3308* 239 E 60th St NY, NY 10022

ANTIQUE SUPERMARKET *(212) 226-2880* 84 Wooster NY, NY 10012

ANTIQUE TEXTILE CUSHIONS

(212) 472-1446 146 E 84th St NY, NY 10028

ARENSON'S OFFICE FURN ***(212) 838-8880*** **315 E 62nd St NY, NY 10021**

PAGE 2

ART FOR INDUSTRY *(212) 757-3638* 521 Fifth Ave NY, NY 10024

BACK PAGE ANTIQUES *(212) 460-5998* 125 Greene St NY, NY 10012

BEIGE *(212) 691-5488* 119 Greenwich Ave NY, NY 10014

BEN'S BABYLAND *(212) 674-1353* 87 Ave A NY, NY 10009

BETTER TIMES ANTIQUES

(212) 496-9001 500 Amsterdam Ave NY, NY 10024

BIJAN ROYAL INC *(212) 228-3757* 60 E 11th St NY, NY 10003

BOLERO ANTIQUES INC *(212) 219-8900* 134 Spring St NY, NY 10012

BUK ANTIQUES *(212) 226-6891* 151 Spring St NY, NY 10012

c - g

Capo Antiques *(212) 982-3356* 831 Broadway NY, NY 10003

Churchill/Winchester Furniture Rental

(212) 686-0444 44 E 32nd St NY, NY 10016

Cinema Galleries *(212) 627-1222* 517 W 35th St NY, NY 10001

Circa 1890 *(212) 734-7388* 265 E 78th St NY, NY 10021

Cobweb *(212) 505-1558* 116 W Houston St NY, NY 10012

Darrow's Fun Antiques *(212) 838-0730* 309 E 61st St NY, NY 10021

Decorator's Warehouse *(212) 489-7573* 665 Eleventh Ave NY, NY 10019

East Side Antiques *(212) 677-8820* 55 E 11th St NY, NY 10003

Echo Antiques *(212) 689-4241* 415 Third Ave NY, NY 10016

Eclectic Encore Inc *(212) 645-8880* 620 W 26th St NY, NY 10001

Evergreen Antiques *(212) 966-6458* 120 Spring St NY, NY 10012

Evergreen Antiques *(212) 744-5664* 1249 Third Ave NY, NY 10021

Fifty-50 *(212) 777-3208* 793 Broadway NY, NY 10003

First 1/2 of the 20th Century

(212) 533-2519 131 Thompson St NY, NY 10012

Gali Kitchen Rental Equipment

(212) 289-5405 404 E 88th St NY, NY 10028

Global Fine Reproductions *(212) 533-5810* 801 Broadway NY, NY 10003

Golden Office Interiors *(212) 719-5150* 574 Fifth Ave NY, NY 10036

Gotham Galleries *(212) 677-3303* 80 Fourth Ave NY, NY 10003

Great American Salvage *(212) 505-0070* 34 Cooper Sq NY, NY 10003

h - m

Horseman Antiques *(718) 596-1048* 351 Atlantic Ave Brooklyn, NY 11217

Interior Associates *(212) 206-1321* 11 W 20th St NY, NY 10010

Irreplaceable Artifacts *(212) 982-5000* 14 Second Ave NY, NY 10003

IS Furniture Prop Rentals *(212) 947-1731* 290 Fifth Ave NY, NY 10011

Joia Interiors Inc *(212) 759-1224* 149 E 60th St NY, NY 10022

Kaplan French Country Store

(212) 674-1000 827 Broadway NY, NY 10003

Kempler Co *(212) 989-1180* 160 Fifth Ave NY, NY 10010

Kenmore Furniture Co *(212) 683-1888* 352 Park Ave So NY, NY 10010

Kentshire Galleries *(212) 673-6644* 37 E 12th St NY, NY 10003

Kuttner Antiques *(212) 242-7969* 56 W 22nd St NY, NY 10011

Laufer, Fran The Collection Ltd

(212) 686-7373 200 Lexington AVe NY, NY 10016

Leiderman's *(212) 254-9646* 200 Orchard St NY, NY 10002

Lewis of London *(212) 688-3669* 215 E 52st St NY, NY 10022

Little Antique Shop *(212) 673-5173* 44 E 11th St NY, NY 10003

Madison Galleries *(212) 529-5020* 840 Broadway NY, NY 10003

Manhattan Doll Hospital *(212) 989-5220* 176 Ninth Ave NY, NY 10011

Mark's Antiques *(718) 284-4591* 595 Coney Island Ave Brooklyn, NY 11218

Martell Antiques *(212) 777-4360* 53 E 10th St NY, NY 10003

Midtown Antiques Inc *(212) 529-1880* 814 Broadway NY, NY 10003

Modernage *(212) 674-5603* 795 Broadway NY, NY 10003

Moss, Alan *(212) 219-1663* 88 Wooster St NY, NY 10012

n - z

Niccolini Antiques *(212) 254-2900* 19 W 21st St NY, NY 10010

Nostalgia Alley *(212) 695-6578* 425-459 W 15th St NY/ NY 10011

Page 11

Oaksmith Antiques *(212) 535-1451* 1321 Second Ave NY, NY 10021

Oldies, Goldies & Moldies Ltd

(212) 737-3935 1609 Second Ave NY, NY 10028

Pierre Deux *(212) 243-7740* 369 Bleecker St NY, NY 10014

Pine Country Antiques *(212) 529-3480* 42 E 12th St NY, NY 10003

Place for Antiques *(212) 308-4066* 993 Second Ave NY, NY 10022

Pony Circus Antiques Ltd *(212) 679-9637* 381 Second Ave NY, NY 10010

Prophecies Antiques *(718) 855-4285* 483 Atlantic Ave Brooklyn, NY 11217

Props For Today *(212) 206-0330* 15 W 20th St NY, NY 10011

Putting Antiques *(212) 838-3850* 226 E 51st St NY, NY 10022

Reed, Claude Lace Collages

(212) 689-1268 88 Lexington Ave NY, NY 10016

Salvage Barn Antiques *(212) 929-5787* 525 Hudson St NY, NY 10014

Schneider's *(212) 228-3540* 20 Ave A NY, NY 10009

Scottie's Gallery & Antiques

(718) 851-8325 624 Coney Island Ave Brooklyn, NY 11218

Second Comming, The *(212) 431-4424* 72 Greene St NY, NY 10001

Second Hand Rose *(212) 243-9522* 573 Hudson St NY, NY 10014

Showroom Outlet *(212) 581-0470* 625 W 55th St NY, NY 10019

Simply Stated *(203) 629-2525* 106 Mason St Greenwich, CT 06830

Smith & Watson Inc *(212) 355-5615* 305 E 63rd St NY, NY 10021

State Supply Equipmemt & Props Co

***(212) 645-1430* 210 Eleventh Ave NY, NY 10001**

Page 12

Things Antique *(212) 873-4655* 470 Amsterdam Ave NY, NY 10024

U S Art *(212) 226-6117* 100 Wooster St NY, NY 10012

Urban Archeology Ltd *(212) 431-6969* 285 Lafayette St NY, NY 10012

Waves Antiques *(212) 989-9284* 32 E 13th St NY, NY 10003

Welcome Home Antiques *(212) 362-4293* 556 Columbus Ave NY, NY 10024

FLORISTS

a - z

Atlas FLowers *(212) 753-3260* 2 Central Park So NY, NY 10019

Bill's Flower Market *(212) 889-8154* 816 Ave of Americas NY, NY 10022

Bonsai Dynasty Co *(212) 695-2973* 851 Sixth Ave NY, NY 10001

Chelsea Garden Center *(212) 929-2477* 501 W 23rd St NY, NY 10011

Cultured Design Ltd *(212) 594-8690* 548 W 28th St NY, NY 10001

PAGE 14

Duval Inc *(212) 751-2126* 833 Lexington Ave NY, NY 10021

Evan-Hughes *(212) 489-0350* 62 W 56th St NY, NY 10019

Farm & Garden *(212) 431-3577* 2 Ave of Americas NY, NY 10013

Florenco Foliage Systems World

(212) 402-0500 920 E 149th St NY, NY 10455

Flowers by Reuven *(212) 874-4560* 2020 Broadway NY, NY 10023

Fuss, William *(212) 688-0350* 218 E 53rd St NY, NY 10022

Gastle Pierpont *(212) 570-1284* 1441 York Ave NY, NY 10021

Greenhouse Garden Center

(718) 636-0020 115 Flatbush Ave Brooklyn, NY 11217

Karp, Robert Flowers *(212) 472-1574* 78 York Ave NY, NY 10011

Kayla, Sura Design *(212) 714-2216* 115 W 28th St NY, NY 10001

Modern Artificial Flowers

(212) 265-0414 517 W 46th St NY, NY 10036

New York Gardener Ltd

(212) 929-2477 501 W 23rd St NY, NY 10011

Noble Plants *(212) 206-1164* 106 W 28th St NY, NY 10001

Paper White Florists *(212) 477-3361* 80 Second Ave NY, NY 10003

Paradise Design *(212) 684-3397* 800 Sixth Ave NY, NY 10001

Paradise Palms *(212) 689-4968* 810 Sixth Ave NY, NY 10001

People's Flowers Corp *(212) 686-6291* 786 Sixth Ave NY, NY 10001

Plaza Hotel Florist *(212) 753-3260* 2 Central Park S NY, NY 10019

Rialto Florist *(212) 688-3234* 707 Lexington Ave NY, NY 10022

Saul Assoc *(212) 243-8555* 777 Sixth Ave NY, NY 10001

Shields-Warendorff Florists

(212) 489-0350 62 W 56th St NY, NY 10019

Terrestris *(212) 758-8181* 409 E 60th St NY, NY 10019

Twigs Inc *(212) 620-8188* 399 Bleecker St NY, NY 10014

York Floral *(212) 627-1840* 104 W 27th St NY, NY 10001

ANIMALS

a - z

Actorpets *(914) 235-3172* 110 Broadview Ave New Rochelle, NY 10804

All Tame Animals *(212) 245-6740* 250 W 57th St NY, NY 10019

Animal Actors *(201) 689-7539* Box 221 River Rd Washington, NJ 7882

Animals for Advertising *(212) 245-2590* 310 W 55th St NY, NY 10019

Captain Haggerty Theatrical Dogs Zzz

(212) 220-7771 1748 First Ave NY, NY 10021

Chateau Theatrical Animals

(212) 246-0520 608 W 48th St NY, NY 10019

Claremont Riding Academy *(212) 724-5101* 175 W 89th St NY, NY 10024

Dawn Animal Agency *(212) 575-9396* 750 Eighth Ave NY, NY 10036

Horses for Courses *(516) 533-7557* 349 Plainfield St Westbury, NY 11590

Indian Field Ranch *(516) 668-2744* Ranch Road Box 835 Montauk, NY 11954

Mendez, Raymond A *(212) 864-4689* 220 W 98th St NY, NY 10025

Parrots of the World

(516) 764-0717 239 Sunrise Highway Rockville Ctr, NY 11570

COSTUMERS

a - z

Abet Rent-A-Fur *(212) 989-5757* 307 Seventh Ave NY, NY 10001

PAGE 11

Animal Outfitters/Doherty Studios

(212) 840-6219 POB 790 Planetarium Stn NY, NY 10024

Bobin, Chris *(212) 475-7268* 5 E 17th St NY, NY 10003

Brumberger, Carla *(212) 242-8226* 295 W 11th St NY, NY 10014

Carelli Costumes *(212) 765-6166* 594 Ninth Ave NY, NY 10036

Chenko Studios *(212) 944-0215* 167 W 46th St NY, NY 10036

Costume Collection *(212) 989-5855* 601 W 26th St NY, NY 10001

Costume Shop Inc *(212) 255-2345* 114 W 26th St NY, NY 10001

Creative Costumes *(212) 564-5552* 330 W 38th St NY, NY 10018

Eaves-Brooks Costume Co *(718) 729-1010* 21-07 41st Ave LIC, NY 11101

Eccentricities *(212) 924-9411* 41 Union Sq W NY, NY 10003

Grace Costumes *(212) 586-0260* 250 W 54th St NY, NY 10019

Happel, Marc Ltd *(212) 675-6019* 39 W 14th St NY, NY 10011

Harper & Nihda Studio (212) 645-0469 142 W 14th St NY, NY 10011

Huey, Camilla (212) 459-9716` 145 W 58th St NY, NY 10019

In Costume Inc (212) 255-5502 37 W 20th St NY, NY 10011

Izquierdo Studio (212) 807-9757 118 W 22nd St NY, NY 10011

Johns-Cronk Inc (212) 741-8161 39 W 19th St NY, NY 10011

Klein, Mary Ellen (212) 683-6351 NY, NY

Lazar, Cathy Costume Design

(212) 473-0363 155 E 23rd St NY, NY 10010

Lymelite Group (212) 787-6586 118 W 79th St NY, NY 10024

MCL Designs Inc (212) 206-7500 31 W 21st St NY, NY 10010

Michael-Jon Costumes Inc (212) 741-3440 39 W 19th St NY, NY 10011

Mulder/Goodwin Inc (212) 689-9037 1200 Broadway NY, NY 10001

Odds Costume Rentals (212) 575-5927 233 W 42nd St NY, NY 10036

Parsons-Meares Ltd (212) 242-3378 142 W 14th St NY, NY 10011

Reid, John Costumes Inc (212) 242-6059 49 W 24th St NY, NY 10010

Rubie's Costume Co Inc

(718) 846-1008 120-08 Jamaica Ave Richmond Hill, NY 11418

Second Coming (212) 431-4424 72 Greene St NY, NY 10012

Slice of Life Clothing Rental

(212) 242-2850 39 W 38th St NY, NY 10036

Source III (212) 243-2164 49 W 24th St NY, NY 10010

Starr, Jana/Hoffman, Jean Antiques

(212) 861-8256 236 E 80th St NY, NY 10021

Studio (212) 967-4736 322 Seventh Ave NY, NY 10001

Taylor Costume & Soft Sculptre

(212) 580-1725 6 W 90th St NY, NY 10024

Tint, Francine (212) 475-3366 1 University Pl NY, NY 10003

Universal Costume (212) 239-3222 535 Eighth Ave NY, NY 10018

Vincent Costume (212) 741-3423 136 W 21st St NY, NY 10011

ACRYLICS

a - z

Abacus Acrylic Outlet (212) 807-7966 135 W 26th St NY, NY 10001

Canal Plastics (212) 925-1032 345 Canal St NY, NY 10013

CBS Television Plastic Design

(212) 975-2751 524 W 57th St NY, NY 10019

Industrial Plastic Supply (212) 226-2010 309 Canal St NY, NY 10013

Plactic Works (212) 535-6486 1407 Third Ave NY, NY 10021

Plastic Works (212) 362-1000 2107 Broadway NY, NY 10023

Plastic Works (212) 627-4010 496 Sixth Ave NY, NY 10011

Plexi Craft Quality Prod (212) 924-3244 514 W 24th St NY, NY 10011

Plexibility Ltd (212) 679-7826 200 Lexington Ave NY, NY 10016

Starbuck Studio (212) 807-7299 162 W 21st St NY, NY 10011

PAGE 16

Trengove Studio (212) 255-2857 60 W 22nd St NY, NY 10010